15th International Conference on Parsing Technologies 2017 (IWPT 2017)

Pisa, Italy
20 – 22 September 2017

ISBN: 978-1-5108-4861-0

IWPT 2017

**15th International Conference on
Parsing Technologies**

Proceedings of the Conference

September 20–22, 2017
Pisa, Italy

Sponsored by:

Associazione Italiana di
Linguistica Computazionale

Preface

Welcome to the 15th International Conference on Parsing Technologies (IWPT 2017) in Pisa, Italy. IWPT 2017 continues the tradition of biennial conferences organized by SIGPARSE, the Special Interest Group on Natural Language Parsing of the Association for Computational Linguistics (ACL), serving as the primary specialized forum for research on natural language parsing.

This year, for the first time, IWPT is co-located with the International Conference on Dependency Linguistics (DepLing), and will feature joint sessions meant to foster communication and collaboration between the two closely related communities. As part of their joint programs, DepLing and IWPT will host the First Shared Task on Extrinsic Parser Evaluation (EPE 2017), which has separate organizers, program committee and proceedings.

IWPT 2016 received 26 valid submissions (11 long and 15 short papers). Each submission was reviewed by three members of the program committee, and finally 5 long and 13 short papers were accepted for presentation. The conference will feature two invited speakers, Vera Demberg (Saarland University) and David Hall (Semantic Machines), and a conference dinner on September 21.

We are indebted to a number of people whose work made the conference possible. First and foremost, we thank the members of the local organization committee, whose outstanding contributions involved every aspect of hosting both DepLing and IWPT: Giuseppe Attardi (University of Pisa), Felice Dell'Orletta (ILC-CNR, Pisa), Alessandro Lenci (University of Pisa), Simonetta Montemagni (ILC-CNR, Pisa), and Maria Simi (University of Pisa). We thank the members of the program committee for their in-depth and constructive reviews, and the program chairs of DepLing (Simonetta Montemagni and Joakim Nivre) and EPE (Stephan Oepen) for their help and support with various aspects of the conference, including design of the joint portion of our programs. Finally, we thank the Associazione Italiana di Linguistica Computazionale (AILC) for its generous financial support.

Enjoy the conference!

Kenji Sagae (General Chair) and Yusuke Miyao (Program Chair)

Organizers:

Kenji Sagae, UC Davis, United States (General Chair)
Yusuke Miyao, National Institute of Informatics, Japan (Programme Chair)
Giuseppe Attardi, University of Pisa, Italy (Local Organizer)
Felice Dell'Orletta, ILC-CNR, Pisa, Italy (Local Organizer)
Alessandro Lenci, University of Pisa, Italy (Local Organizer)
Simonetta Montemagni, ILC-CNR, Pisa, Italy (Local Organizer)
Maria Simi, University of Pisa, Italy (Local Organizer)

Programme Committee:

Željko Agić, IT University of Copenhagen
Miguel Ballesteros, IBM Research
Anders Björkelund, IMS, Stuttgart
Philippe Blache, LPL CNRS
Harry Bunt, Tilburg University
Xavier Carreras, Naver Labs
John Carroll, University of Sussex
Wanxiang Che, Harbin Institute of Technology
David Chiang, University of Notre Dame
Stephen Clark, University of Cambridge
Berthold Crysmann, CNRS, Laboratoire de linguistique formelle
Michael Elhadad, Ben Gurion University
Federico Fancellu, University of Edinburgh
Carlos Gómez-Rodríguez, Universidade da Coruña
Sadao Kurohashi, Kyoto University
Yuji Matsumoto, Nara Institute of Science and Technology
Yusuke Miyao, National Instutite of Informatics
Mark-Jan Nederhof, University of St Andrews
Giorgio Satta, University of Padova
Natalie Schluter, IT University of Copenhagen
Djamé Seddah, Université Paris Sorbonne (Paris IV)
Hiroyuki Shindo, Nara Institute of Science and Technology
Weiwei Sun, Peking University
Christoph Teichmann, Saarland University
Ivan Titov, University of Edinburgh / University of Amsterdam
Daniel Zeman, Charles University
Yi Zhang, Nuance Communications GmbH
Yue Zhang, Singapore University of Technology and Design
Hai Zhao, Shanghai Jiao Tong University

Keynote 1: Syntactic processing in humans: time course, shallow processing and processing failure

Vera Demberg
Saarland University, Germany

Abstract

Human syntactic processing is generally remarkably robust and accurate. In this talk, I will go through some recent psycholinguistic research on sentence processing which can give us a glimpse into how human parsing works. This talk will focus on some crucial properties (such as incrementality and prediction), but will also highlight some informative cases of where humans struggle to analyse a sentence correctly. I will also briefly describe current psycholinguistic frameworks for modelling human processing, which try to account for these cases.

Biography

Vera Demberg is professor for Computer Science and Computational Linguistics at Saarland University, Saarbrcken, Germany. From 2010 till 2016, she held a position as an independent research group leader at the Cluster of Excellence "Multimodal Computing and Interaction", Saarland University. She received her PhD in 2010 from the University of Edinburgh, for which she was awarded the Glushko Dissertation Prize by the Cognitive Science Society and the runner-up prize of the CPHC / BCS Distinguished Dissertations Competition. Her research interests include psycholinguistic experimental research and computational modelling on human sentence processing at the levels of syntax, thematic role assignment, event cognition and coherence relations in discourse.

Keynote 2: What good is a grammar anyway?

David Hall
Semantic Machines, United States

Abstract

Until recently, a large fraction of constituency parsing research consisted of finding clever ways of "augmenting" a base treebank grammar with extra information to work around the limitations of dynamic programming-based parsing algorithms. Nowadays, the art of grammar engineering for statistical parsing is slipping away, as neural network models are now able to easily obtain state of the art performance with basically no grammar engineering. What's going on? In this talk, I'll explore this trend and reflect on the importance of grammar in the modern era. Along the way, I'll also touch on some related issues affecting parsing (both syntactic and semantic) that I've encountered in my time in industry and discuss a few lessons learned.

Biography

David Hall is a senior research scientist working on conversational computing at Semantic Machines. He received his PhD in Computer Science from UC Berkeley advised by Dan Klein. He is the recipient of the 2012 Google PhD Fellowship in Natural Language Processing, an NSF graduate research fellowship, the 2011 EECS Outstanding Graduate Student Instructor award, the journal Language's 2016 best paper award, and a distinguished paper at EMNLP 2012. He has authored fifteen publications at top conferences and has built and released numerous software systems, including a fast GPU-based constituency parser, state-of-the-art parsers for ten languages, the Breeze scientific computing library, and the award-winning Overmind StarCraft agent. He has a B.S. and M.S. from Stanford University, both in Symbolic Systems.

Table of Contents

Automatically Acquired Lexical Knowledge Improves Japanese Joint Morphological and Dependency Analysis
Daisuke Kawahara, Yuta Hayashibe, Hajime Morita and Sadao Kurohashi 1

Dependency Language Models for Transition-based Dependency Parsing
Juntao Yu and Bernd Bohnet 11

Lexicalized vs. Delexicalized Parsing in Low-Resource Scenarios
Agnieszka Falenska and Özlem Çetinoğlu 18

Improving neural tagging with lexical information
Benoît Sagot and Héctor Martínez Alonso 25

Prepositional Phrase Attachment over Word Embedding Products
Pranava Swaroop Madhyastha, Xavier Carreras and Ariadna Quattoni 32

L1-L2 Parallel Dependency Treebank as Learner Corpus
John Lee, Keying Li and Herman Leung 44

Splitting Complex English Sentences
John Lee and J. Buddhika K. Pathirage Don 50

Hierarchical Word Structure-based Parsing: A Feasibility Study on UD-style Dependency Parsing in Japanese
Takaaki Tanaka, Katsuhiko Hayashi and Masaaki Nagata 56

Leveraging Newswire Treebanks for Parsing Conversational Data with Argument Scrambling
Riyaz A. Bhat, Irshad Bhat and Dipti Sharma 61

Using hyperlinks to improve multilingual partial parsers
Anders Søgaard 67

Correcting prepositional phrase attachments using multimodal corpora
Sebastien Delecraz, Alexis Nasr, Frederic Bechet and Benoit Favre 72

Exploiting Structure in Parsing to 1-Endpoint-Crossing Graphs
Robin Kurtz and Marco Kuhlmann 78

Effective Online Reordering with Arc-Eager Transitions
Ryosuke Kohita, Hiroshi Noji and Yuji Matsumoto 88

Arc-Hybrid Non-Projective Dependency Parsing with a Static-Dynamic Oracle
Miryam de Lhoneux, Sara Stymne and Joakim Nivre 99

Encoder-Decoder Shift-Reduce Syntactic Parsing
Jiangming Liu and Yue Zhang 105

Arc-Standard Spinal Parsing with Stack-LSTMs
Miguel Ballesteros and Xavier Carreras 115

Coarse-To-Fine Parsing for Expressive Grammar Formalisms
Christoph Teichmann, Alexander Koller and Jonas Groschwitz 122

Evaluating LSTM models for grammatical function labelling
Bich-Ngoc Do and Ines Rehbein 128

xii

Conference Programme

Wednesday, September 20, 2017

08:30–09:30	*Registration*
09:30–11:00	**Depling Long Talk Session**
11:00–11:30	*Break*
11:30–12:00	**Report on the CoNLL 2017 Shared Task on "Multilingual Parsing from Raw Text to Universal Dependencies"**
12:00–13:00	**First Shared Task on Extrinsic Parser Evaluation (EPE 2017)**
13:00–14:30	*Lunch*
14:30–16:00	**First Shared Task on Extrinsic Parser Evaluation (EPE 2017)**
16:00–16:30	*Break*
16:30–18:00	**Joint Depling & IWPT Panel Discussion**

Thursday, September 21, 2017

08:30–09:30   *Registration*

09:30–10:00   *Opening*

10:00–11:00   **Keynote 1**

10:00–11:00   *Syntactic processing in humans: time course, shallow processing and processing failure*
Vera Demberg

11:00–11:30   *Break*

11:30–13:00   **Long and short talks**

11:30–12:00   *Automatically Acquired Lexical Knowledge Improves Japanese Joint Morphological and Dependency Analysis*
Daisuke Kawahara, Yuta Hayashibe, Hajime Morita and Sadao Kurohashi

12:00–12:20   *Dependency Language Models for Transition-based Dependency Parsing*
Juntao Yu and Bernd Bohnet

12:20–12:40   *Lexicalized vs. Delexicalized Parsing in Low-Resource Scenarios*
Agnieszka Falenska and Özlem Çetinoğlu

12:40–13:00   *Improving neural tagging with lexical information*
Benoît Sagot and Héctor Martínez Alonso

13:00–14:30   *Lunch*

Thursday, September 21, 2017 (continued)

14:30–16:00   Long and short talks

14:30–15:00   *Prepositional Phrase Attachment over Word Embedding Products*
Pranava Swaroop Madhyastha, Xavier Carreras and Ariadna Quattoni

15:00–15:20   *L1-L2 Parallel Dependency Treebank as Learner Corpus*
John Lee, Keying Li and Herman Leung

15:20–15:40   *Splitting Complex English Sentences*
John Lee and J. Buddhika K. Pathirage Don

15:40–16:00   *Hierarchical Word Structure-based Parsing: A Feasibility Study on UD-style Dependency Parsing in Japanese*
Takaaki Tanaka, Katsuhiko Hayashi and Masaaki Nagata

16:00–16:30   *Break*

16:30–17:30   Short talks

16:30–16:50   *Leveraging Newswire Treebanks for Parsing Conversational Data with Argument Scrambling*
Riyaz A. Bhat, Irshad Bhat and Dipti Sharma

16:50–17:10   *Using hyperlinks to improve multilingual partial parsers*
Anders Søgaard

17:10–17:30   *Correcting prepositional phrase attachments using multimodal corpora*
Sebastien Delecraz, Alexis Nasr, Frederic Bechet and Benoit Favre

Friday, September 22, 2017

08:30–09:30   *Registration*

09:30–10:00   *IWPT Business Meeting*

10:00–11:00   **Keynote 2**

10:00–11:00   *What good is a grammar anyway?*
David Hall

11:00–11:30   *Break*

11:30–13:00   **Long and short talks**

11:30–12:00   *Exploiting Structure in Parsing to 1-Endpoint-Crossing Graphs*
Robin Kurtz and Marco Kuhlmann

12:00–12:30   *Effective Online Reordering with Arc-Eager Transitions*
Ryosuke Kohita, Hiroshi Noji and Yuji Matsumoto

12:30–12:50   *Arc-Hybrid Non-Projective Dependency Parsing with a Static-Dynamic Oracle*
Miryam de Lhoneux, Sara Stymne and Joakim Nivre

13:00–14:30   *Lunch*

Friday, September 22, 2017 (continued)

14:30–16:00   Long and short talks

14:30–15:00   *Encoder-Decoder Shift-Reduce Syntactic Parsing*
Jiangming Liu and Yue Zhang

15:00–15:20   *Arc-Standard Spinal Parsing with Stack-LSTMs*
Miguel Ballesteros and Xavier Carreras

15:20–15:40   *Coarse-To-Fine Parsing for Expressive Grammar Formalisms*
Christoph Teichmann, Alexander Koller and Jonas Groschwitz

15:40–16:00   *Evaluating LSTM models for grammatical function labelling*
Bich-Ngoc Do and Ines Rehbein

16:00–16:30   *Closing*

Automatically Acquired Lexical Knowledge Improves
Japanese Joint Morphological and Dependency Analysis

Daisuke Kawahara and **Yuta Hayashibe**[1] and **Hajime Morita**[2] and **Sadao Kurohashi**

Graduate School of Informatics, Kyoto University

{dk, kuro}@i.kyoto-u.ac.jp
hayashibe@fairydevices.jp, hmorita@jp.fujitsu.com

Abstract

This paper presents a joint model for morphological and dependency analysis based on automatically acquired lexical knowledge. This model takes advantage of rich lexical knowledge to simultaneously resolve word segmentation, POS, and dependency ambiguities. In our experiments on Japanese, we show the effectiveness of our joint model over conventional pipeline models.

1 Introduction

Morphological analysis, i.e., word segmentation, POS tagging and lemmatization, is the first step for processing unsegmented languages such as Chinese and Japanese. Words segmented by a morphological analyzer are usually fed into subsequent analyzers, such as dependency parsers and predicate-argument structure (PAS) analyzers, in a pipeline manner. One problem with this pipeline process is that errors in morphological analysis are propagated to the subsequent steps. In morphological analysis, it is also difficult in some cases to determine word segmentations without syntactic and structural knowledge, which could be available at the step of dependency or PAS analysis.

For instance, the Japanese phrase "あるかない" in Sentence (1) can be segmented into (2a) or (2b).[3]

(1)　　可能性　　が　　あるかない か 分から ない
　　　　possibility NOM　　　　　　　 or know　 not

(2)　a.　ある / か / ない
　　　　exist / or / not
　　b.　あるか / ない
　　　　walk　 / not

In this case, (2a) is the correct segmentation, which means "whether a possibility exists," while the incorrect segmentation (2b) is meaningless: "a possibility does not walk." It might be possible to select the correct segmentation if a morphological analyzer could look up selectional preference knowledge of the predicates "exist" and "walk."

Thus far, several models have been proposed for joint morphological and dependency analysis, but the performance improvement is not stable among target languages. For Chinese joint analysis, where the parsing accuracy of a baseline pipeline model is around 80%, an F1 improvement of around 2% was reported (Hatori et al., 2012; Zhang et al., 2014). For Japanese joint analysis, where the parsing accuracy of a pipeline model is around 90%, there have been no studies that report a significant improvement (Tawara et al., 2015). One of the reasons for such instability is that most of these joint models are trained only on a small-scale treebank, which consists of several tens of thousands of sentences. These models do not make use of large-scale external lexical knowledge. Since it is necessary to use lexical knowledge of selectional preferences to address the abovementioned ambiguities, these joint models cannot solve such ambiguities in many cases.

This paper proposes a joint model for morphological and dependency analysis based on automatically acquired lexical knowledge. The lexical knowledge includes case frames acquired from a large-scale raw corpus, which provide useful clues to resolve morphological and syntactic ambiguities. In our experiments on Japanese corpora, we show a significant improvement over conventional

---

[1]The second author is now affiliated with Fairy Devices Inc.

[2]The third author is now affiliated with Fujitsu Laboratories Ltd.

[3]In this paper, we use the following abbreviations: NOM (nominative), ACC (accusative), DAT (dative), LOC (locative), ABL (ablative), and TOP (topic marker).

Proceedings of the 15th International Conference on Parsing Technologies, pages 1–10,
Pisa, Italy; September 20–22, 2017. ©2017 Association for Computational Linguistics

pipeline models.

The remainder of this paper is organized as follows. Section 2 summarizes previous joint models for morphological and dependency analysis. Section 3 describes our method for constructing lexical knowledge. Section 4 illustrates our idea and describes our joint analysis model in detail. Section 5 is devoted to our experiments. Finally, section 6 gives the conclusions.

2 Related Work

Some variants of transition-based parsing methods have been proposed for joint POS tagging and parsing (Bohnet and Nivre, 2012; Bohnet et al., 2013; Wang and Xue, 2014) and joint Chinese word segmentation, POS tagging, and dependency parsing (Hatori et al., 2012; Zhang et al., 2014). As an external knowledge source, Hatori et al. (2012) used a word dictionary extracted mainly from Wikipedia, but it did not provide lexical knowledge for resolving syntactic ambiguities.

Lattice parsing methods have been proposed for Hebrew and Arabic (Goldberg and Tsarfaty, 2008; Goldberg et al., 2009; Green and Manning, 2010; Goldberg and Elhadad, 2011). These methods first generate a word lattice and then apply PCFG parsing to the word lattice. Starting with a word lattice, the methods of Wang et al. (2013) and Zhang et al. (2015) select the best parse using dual decomposition and the randomized greedy algorithm, respectively. Of these methods, Goldberg et al. (2009) incorporated an external morphological lexicon, which does not provide selectional preferences.

As a different method from lattice parsing, Qian and Liu (2012) trained separate models for Chinese word segmentation, POS tagging, and constituency parsing. They proposed a unified decoding algorithm that combines the scores from these three models. This is a purely supervised method that does not use lexical knowledge.

As dependency parsing models using lexical knowledge, there have been semi-supervised approaches that use knowledge of word classes, lexical preferences or selectional preferences acquired from raw corpora (e.g., (van Noord, 2007; Koo et al., 2008; Chen et al., 2009; Zhou et al., 2011; Bansal and Klein, 2011)). However, these dependency parsing models cannot be applied to joint morphological and dependency analysis.

For Japanese, Morita et al. (2015) proposed a morphological analyzer that jointly performs segmentation and POS tagging using recurrent neural network language models, but does not perform dependency parsing. We employ this morphological analyzer, JUMAN++[4], as a pre-processor to generate word lattice (described in Section 4.1). Kawahara and Kurohashi (2006) proposed a probabilistic model for Japanese dependency parsing and PAS analysis based on case frames automatically compiled from a large raw corpus, which are also used as a source of selectional preferences in our model (described in Section 3.1). Kudo and Matsumoto (2002), Sassano (2004), Iwatate (2012) and Yoshinaga and Kitsuregawa (2014) proposed supervised models for Japanese dependency parsing without using external knowledge sources. These models need a 1-best output of segmentation and POS tagging as an input, and are not a joint model of morphological analysis and dependency parsing. We adopt KNP[5] and CaboCha[6] as baseline dependency parsers, which are implementations of Kawahara and Kurohashi (2006) and Sassano (2004), respectively.[7]

Tawara et al. (2015) proposed a joint model for Japanese morphological analysis and dependency parsing without lexical knowledge. However, they failed to achieve significant improvements over conventional pipeline methods.

To the best of our knowledge, there have been no joint models of morphological and dependency analysis that use large-scale lexical knowledge which includes selectional preferences.

3 Lexical Knowledge Acquisition

In our joint analysis model, we use the following three types of lexical knowledge automatically acquired from a large raw corpus: case frames, cooccurrence probabilities of noun-noun / predicate-predicate dependencies, and word embeddings. We deeply utilize case frames in our joint model

---

[4] http://nlp.ist.i.kyoto-u.ac.jp/EN/?JUMAN++

[5] http://nlp.ist.i.kyoto-u.ac.jp/?KNP

[6] https://taku910.github.io/cabocha/

[7] As baseline parsers, we did not use J.DepP (http://www.tkl.iis.u-tokyo.ac.jp/~ynaga/jdepp/) and the tournament model proposed by Iwatate (2012). J.DepP is an implementation of Yoshinaga and Kitsuregawa (2014), which uses the same shift-reduce model as CaboCha with a similar feature set. It was also empirically proved by the author of CaboCha that the tournament model of Iwatate (2012) did not significantly outperform the shift-reduce model. Iwatate (2012) further improved the performance of a single parser using parser stacking. This kind of parser combination technique is complementary to our model and can be incorporated into our model in the future.

and also consider these resources as features in our scoring function described in Section 4.2. Below, we describe the methods for constructing each of the resources, which are basically based on previous work.

3.1 Case Frames

We use case frames to evaluate the plausibility of PASs. Case frames are predicate-specific semantic frames like PropBank (Palmer et al., 2005), which are distinguished for each predicate sense or usage. Although PropBank was elaborated by hand and does not have frequency information, we automatically compile large-scale case frames that reflect real predicate uses.

Each predicate has several case frames that are semantically distinguished. Each case frame consists of case slots, each of which consists of word instances that can be filled. Examples of Japanese case frames are shown in Table 1. Case frames are the source of selectional preferences, which are compiled by aggregating PASs for each predicate usage.

We adapted the method of Kawahara et al. (2014) to Japanese case frame compilation. They proposed an unsupervised method for compiling English case frames from a large raw corpus. The procedure for inducing case frames is as follows:

1. apply dependency parsing to a raw corpus and extract PASs for each predicate from the automatic parses,

2. merge the PASs that have presumably the same meaning based on the assumption of one sense per collocation to get a set of initial frames, and

3. apply clustering to the initial frames based on the Chinese Restaurant Process (Aldous, 1985) to produce predicate-specific case frames.

While the original method used Stanford dependency labels as the representations of case slots, we use case-marking postpositions in Japanese, such as "が" (NOM), "を" (ACC), and "に" (DAT). At Step 1, we apply the morphological and dependency analyzers, JUMAN++ and KNP, to the raw corpus. To alleviate the influence of errors in segmentations, POS tags and dependencies, we extract only reliable PASs that have no syntactic ambiguities. At Step 2, the PASs that have presumably the same meaning are identified by cou-

	CS	instances
ある:1 (exist:1)	が に *time*	necessity:297865, case:190109, ⋯ thing:40, me:29, trend:29, ⋯ <time>:398
ある:2 (exist:2)	が に で	interest:34236, confidence:21326, ⋯ point:702, way:490, me:442, ⋯ feeling:70, aspect:58, ⋯
ある:3 (exist:3)	が に で	possibility:121867 price:23, myself:20, you:18, ⋯ step:4, influence:4, ⋯
⋮	⋮	⋮
あるく:1 (walk:1)	が を から	person:57, I:13, ⋯ road:24236, trail:4066, ⋯ parking:175, station:88, ⋯
あるく:2 (walk:2)	が を で	I:35, parade:27, ⋯ city:13548, town:5336, park:3264, ⋯ alone:464, feeling:74, ⋯
あるく:3 (walk:3)	が を で	person:60, cat:24, ⋯ inside:18858, top:9969, bottom:1769, ⋯ alone:216, barefoot:198, ⋯
⋮	⋮	⋮

Table 1: Acquired case frames for the Japanese verbs "ある" (exist) and "あるく" (walk). CS denotes case slots, such as "が" (NOM), "を" (ACC), "に" (DAT), "で" (LOC), and "から" (ABL). Instances in each CS are originally Japanese words but expressed only in English due to space limitation. The number following each word denotes its frequency.

pling a predicate and the closest argument. That is, PASs are distinguished by predicate-argument pairs, such as "道を あるく" (walk road) and "町 を あるく" (walk city).

We crawled the Web to obtain a large-scale Japanese Web corpus. As a result, we extracted 10 billion Japanese sentences without duplicates from three billion Web pages. We automatically compiled case frames from these sentences and acquired case frames for approximately 100,000 predicates. Examples of acquired case frames are shown in Table 1.

3.2 Cooccurrence Probabilities of Noun-noun / Predicate-predicate Dependencies

To evaluate dependencies that cannot be captured by PASs, cooccurrence statistics of these dependencies are collected from a large raw corpus. For such dependencies, we consider noun-noun and predicate-predicate dependencies. Noun-noun dependencies cover the dependency relations between nouns including compound nouns and predicate-predicate dependencies are the dependency relations between predicates.

We collect noun-noun and predicate-predicate dependencies from automatic parses and calculate cooccurrence probabilities of these dependencies. We acquired these probabilities from automatic parses of 1.6 billion Japanese Web sentences, which are a part of the Japanese Web corpus constructed for case frame compilation.

3.3 Word Embeddings

To detect coordinate structures, which cover a large proportion of dependency relations in a sentence, it is important to capture similarities between words and word sequences. In this paper, we employ word embeddings to calculate similarities between words and word sequences.

We trained word embeddings using 100 million Japanese Web sentences by word2vec[8] (Mikolov et al., 2013) using skip-gram and negative sampling. The dimension of word embeddings was set to 500. To calculate the similarity between two words, we compute the cosine measure between the embeddings of these words.

4 Joint Morphological and Dependency Analysis based on Automatically Acquired Lexical Knowledge

4.1 Joint Analysis Model

We deal with dependencies between base phrases, which are the dependency unit defined in the annotation guidelines of the Japanese treebanks described in Section 5.1. A base phrase consists of a content word and zero or more function words. Although the traditional dependency unit for Japanese is *bunsetsu*, which can contain more than one content word,[9] we adopt base phrase dependencies instead of *bunsetsu* dependencies. This is because base phrase dependencies are basically based on *bunsetsu* dependencies but extended to consider the dependencies inside compound nouns. Hereafter, we call base phrases simply *phrases*.

We adopt the widely used CKY algorithm for our joint analysis model. In our model, a cell in the CKY table corresponds to a span of characters in the input sentence. This model outputs the best parse tree, which contains all the disambiguated results of words, phrases, and dependencies. The

procedure of our joint analysis model is described below.

1. Projection of candidate words onto the CKY table

First, a word lattice is generated using a morphological analyzer. All the words included in the word lattice are projected onto the CKY table.

For instance, in Figure 1, the input sentence is "可能性があるかないか." The possible words for this sentence are projected as described in Figure 1(a). For example, the span "あるか" has the following three possible word cells: "ある" (exist), "か" (or), and "あるか" (walk).

2. Generation of phrases

Possible phrases are generated on the CKY table using POS-based phrase chunking rules. These rules are extracted from the Japanese dependency parser KNP. Because there are ambiguities in words and POS tags, there are also ambiguities in phrases. Each of the generated phrases is regarded as the smallest sub-tree consisting of only one phrase.

In Figure 1, by concatenating words in Figure 1(a) using the phrase chunking rules, the light blue cells in Figure 1(b) are generated as candidate phrases. For example, the span "あるか" has the following two possible phrases: "あるか" (walk) and "ある / か" (exist or).

3. Merging neighboring sub-tree pairs

Neighboring sub-tree pairs are merged to generate a new possible sub-tree. This process is iterated in a bottom-up manner, and finally possible trees for the whole input sentence are generated.

In general, there can be multiple sub-trees that correspond to the same span. When merging two spans with multiple sub-trees, it is necessary to consider all the possible combinations of these sub-trees. New sub-trees generated by merging are ranked by the scoring function described in Section 4.2 and only top-b sub-trees are kept for the subsequent process, where b is the beam width.

Different from the usual CKY algorithm for dependency parsing, we perform PAS analysis for each cell whose head is a predicate. This analysis is done using the method of Kawahara and Kurohashi (2006), which is the process of matching between the arguments in the span and each of the case frames of the predicate. The best-matching

---

[8] https://code.google.com/p/word2vec/
[9] A *bunsetsu* consists of one or more content words and zero or more function words. A compound noun containing multiple content words constitutes a *bunsetsu*.

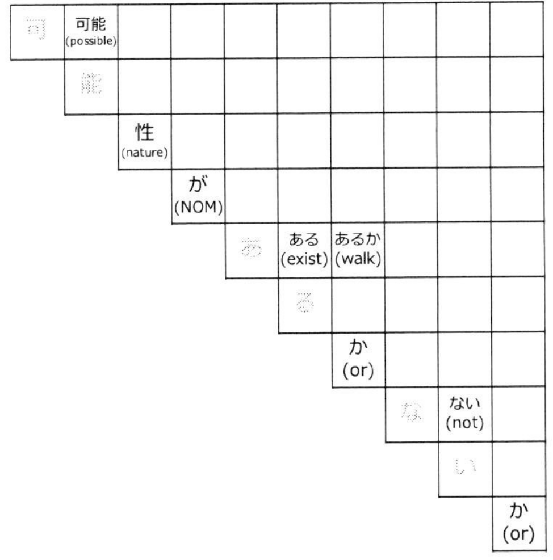

(a) Projection of candidate words onto the CKY table

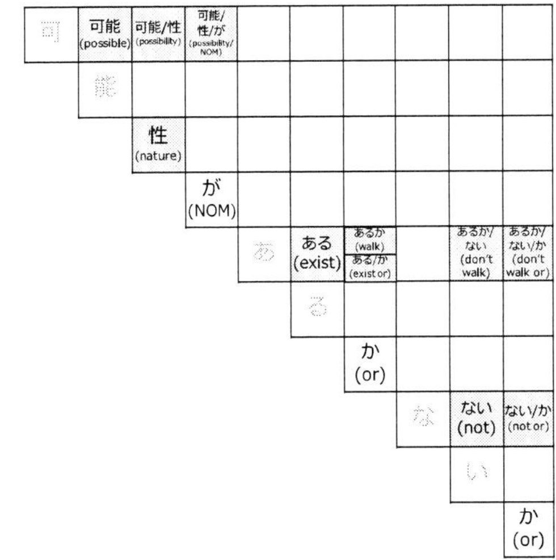

(b) Generation of phrases

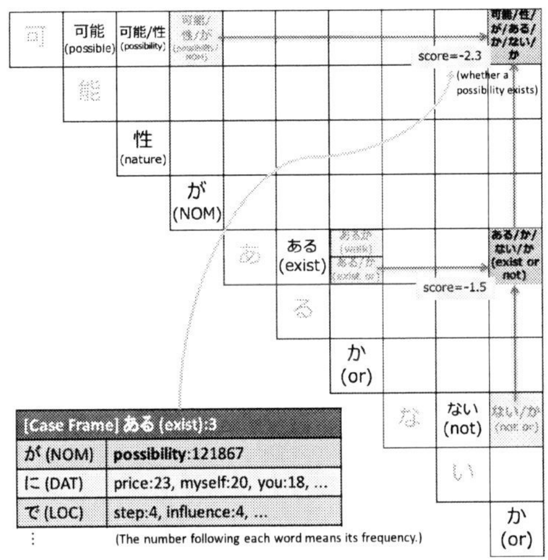

(c) Generation process of the tree for "可能/性/が/ある/か/ない/か" (correct analysis)

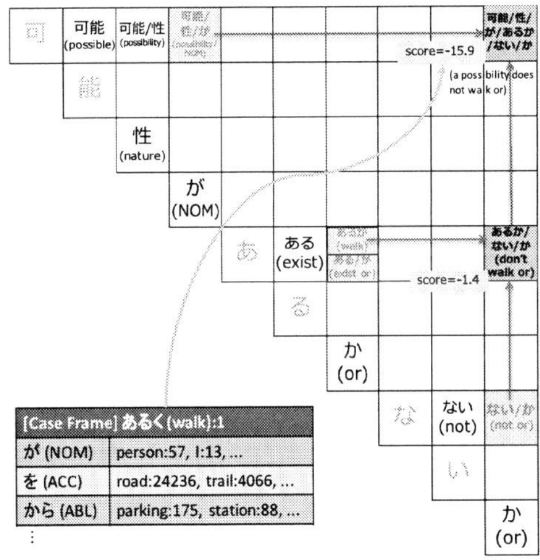

(d) Generation process of the tree for "可能/性/が/あるか/ない/か" (incorrect analysis)

Figure 1: Illustration of our joint analysis model.

case frame with the highest score is selected according to the scoring function.

For example, Figure 1(c) shows the merging process for the interpretation "可能/性/が/ある/か/ない/か" (whether a possibility exists), and Figure 1(d) shows the merging process for "可能/性/が/あるか/ない/か" (possibility does not walk). The best-matching case frame "ある:3" (exist:3) was selected for the interpretation in Figure 1(c), and the case frame "あるく:1" (walk:1) was selected in Figure 1(d), respectively.

4. Selection of the tree with the highest score

The tree with the highest score is selected as an output from the candidate trees for the whole input sentence using the following equation:

$$\hat{y} = \underset{y \in Y}{\operatorname{argmax}} \, score(y), \tag{1}$$

where $\hat{y}$ is the output tree, and Y is the candidate trees for the input sentence. The scoring function $score(y)$ is defined in Section 4.2.

Word feature
· Marginal score of morphological analysis
Phrase features
· Word 2,3-grams in a phrase
· # of phrases in a sentence
· Words at a phrase boundary
· # of predicates
· A predicate representation
Dependency features
· A dependency label
· Content/function words and punctuations of a modifier
· Content/function words and punctuations of a head
· Distance between a modifier and its head
Features derived from lexical knowledge
· # of predicates that do not have case frames
· Probabilities calculated based on case frames
(case frame/slot generating probability, etc.)
· A cooccurrence probability between nouns
· A cooccurrence probability between predicates
· Content word similarity between a modifier and its head
· Similarity of word sequences for coordination

Table 2: Features.

In Figure 1, the upper-right corner cell of the CKY table, which keeps the interpretations of the whole input sentence, contains two possible trees illustrated in Figures 1(c) and 1(d). Our algorithm selects the tree of 1(c), which has the highest score. Here, selectional preferences from case frames tell that "ある" (exist) is more likely to take the nominative filler "可能性" (possibility) than "あるく" (walk).

4.2 Scoring Function and Training

The score of a tree for the input sentence x is defined as the weighted sum of features. This score is calculated using the following scoring function:

$$score(y) = \sum_i (w_i \cdot \phi_i(x, y)), \qquad (2)$$

where ϕ_i is a feature function corresponding to feature i, and w_i is a weight of feature i. This scoring function is also used for calculating the score of a sub-tree, which is constructed at an intermediate step of parsing, i.e., an intermediate cell built at Step 3.

Table 2 lists the features used, which include words constituting a phrase, dependencies between phrases, and the plausibility of a PAS measured by case frames. The basic features that are not derived from lexical knowledge (the upper part of Table 2) are based on the features used in the CaboCha parser.[10]

<hr>

[10]Although the features for dependency parsing in CaboCha were designed for *bunsetsu* dependency parsing, we found out that these features are also compatible with base-phrase dependency parsing.

Corpus	Training	Test
NEWS	2,727 articles	200 articles
	(36,623 sentences)	(1,783 sentences)
WEB	4,427 articles	700 articles
	(13,853 sentences)	(2,195 sentences)

Table 3: Statistics of the treebanks.

We use the following learning procedure. First, the feature weights are initialized, and the word lattice for each sentence in a training corpus is input. A sentence is analyzed using the method described in Section 4.1 with a beam width of b, and candidate trees for this sentence are obtained. The tree with the highest dependency score (UAS) against the gold tree is regarded as a positive instance, and the remaining candidate trees are regarded as negative instances. The feature weights are optimized using the training instances generated from all the sentences in the training corpus. We adopt candidate selection learning and optimize the feature weights using L-BFGS. The above procedure is iterated several times to obtain the final feature weights.

5 Experiments

5.1 Experimental Settings

In our experiments, we used the Kyoto University Text Corpus[11] (Kawahara et al., 2002) (NEWS) and the Kyoto University Web Document Leads Corpus[12] (Hangyo et al., 2012) (WEB) as Japanese treebanks. NEWS consists of news articles and WEB consists of web pages in various domains. We split these into training and test sets as shown in Table 3. We merged the training sets of NEWS and WEB to generate a training set in our experiment and conducted evaluations on each test set of NEWS and WEB.

For the parser input, we used the Japanese morphological analyzer JUMAN++ (Morita et al., 2015) to generate a word lattice. We did not use all possible words in the lexicon of JUMAN++, but converted the N-best output of JUMAN++ to a word lattice to speed up parsing. This is reasonable because the segmentation accuracy of JUMAN++ is between 98%–99% and its N-best output contains only plausible words. N-best outputs were obtained using the option –autoN of JU-

<hr>

[11]http://nlp.ist.i.kyoto-u.ac.jp/EN/
?KyotoUniversity\%20Text\%20Corpus
[12]http://nlp.ist.i.kyoto-u.ac.jp/EN/?KWDLC

| Input | | Model | Word | | | Phrase | Dependency | |
Data	Morph output		Seg	POS	All	pSeg	UAS	LAS
NEWS	1-best	KNP	99.38	98.97	97.50	98.35	89.68	87.98
		CaboCha	99.38	98.97	97.50	96.17	89.06	-
		KNP+CaboCha	99.38	98.97	97.50	98.35	91.00	-
	1-best	Our model wo/LK	99.38	98.97	97.50	98.38	89.89	88.20
	N-best		99.37	98.98	97.51	98.39	90.40	88.73
	1-best	Our model	99.38	98.97	97.50	98.39	91.26	89.54
	N-best		99.38	**99.00**	**97.54**	**98.44**	**91.61**	**89.91**
WEB	1-best	KNP	98.45	97.91	96.34	96.30	87.87	85.61
		CaboCha	98.45	97.91	96.34	92.65	86.14	-
		KNP+CaboCha	98.45	97.91	96.34	96.30	89.05	-
	1-best	Our model wo/LK	98.45	97.91	96.34	96.13	88.36	86.12
	N-best		98.48	97.93	96.39	96.26	88.79	86.52
	1-best	Our model	98.45	97.91	96.34	96.11	89.54	87.27
	N-best		**98.53**	**97.99**	**96.45**	96.31	**89.82**	**87.53**

Table 4: Evaluation results. "wo/LK" means "without lexical knowledge."

MAN++, which increases N proportionally to the length of the input sentence. We applied 10-way jackknifing to the training set and analyzed the test set using a model trained on the whole training set.

To train our joint model, we used Classias[13] with L1 regularization. We set the beam width b of our model to 10 for both training and testing.

For comparison, we adopted the latest versions of KNP and CaboCha, both of which are widely used Japanese dependency parsers. KNP is an implementation of Kawahara and Kurohashi (2006), which accepts the 1-best output of morphological analysis, applies rule-based phrase chunking and performs probabilistic labeled dependency parsing based on case frames. In KNP, we used the same case frames compiled in this paper. CaboCha is an implementation of Sassano (2004), which accepts the 1-best output of morphological analysis, applies CRF-based phrase chunking and performs transition-based unlabeled dependency parsing using SVM. The training of CRF and SVM was conducted using the training data in this paper. Because phrase chunking in CaboCha was designed to identify *bunsetsu*, we also tested KNP+CaboCha for fair comparison, which identifies phrases using KNP and parses using CaboCha. Since KNP and CaboCha are not a joint model and accept only the 1-best output of morphological analysis, we fed the 1-best morphological analysis into KNP and CaboCha. We fed both 1-best and N-best morphological analysis outputs into

our model for comparison. We also tested our model without the automatically acquired lexical knowledge.

We measured the performance of each system using the F1-scores of the following aspects: word segmentation (Seg), "segmentation + POS" (POS), "segmentation+ POS + fine-grained POS + base form" (All), phrase segmentation (pSeg), and unlabeled/labeled dependency attachment score (UAS/LAS). For the dependency labels, the following four labels are defined in the treebanks: D (dependency), P (parallel), I (incomplete parallel), and A (apposition).

5.2 Results and Discussion

Table 4 lists the evaluation results. In this table, the accuracies in bold of "our model with N-best input" are significantly higher than the other models. Statistical testing was conducted using the bootstrap method (Efron and Tibshirani, 1986, 1993) at $p < 0.01$.

The following is typical examples improved by our joint model.

(3)   a.   あの 店　は　で　もの×　が　　よく
that　shop TOP LOC thing　NOM often
見つかる
found

      b.   あの 店　は　でもの○　が　　よく
that　shop TOP bargain　NOM often
見つかる
found

In this example, (3a) is the incorrect output of the

---

[13] http://www.chokkan.org/software/classias/

	Seg	POS	All	pSeg	UAS	LAS
1-best	97.01	95.26	94.51	94.21	86.87	85.52
N-best	**97.38**	**95.63**	**95.13**	**94.44**	**87.84**	**86.49**

Table 5: Results on a corpus with ambiguities.

baseline systems, and (3b) is the correct output of our joint model. Here, case frames tell that the verb "見つかる" (be found) is likely to take "でもの" (bargain) as its nominative.

(4) a. お　　いや_× めい と　わかれる
     (prefix) nasty　niece ABL part

   b. おい　や_○ めい と　わかれる
     nephew and　niece ABL part

In this example, (4a) is the incorrect output of the baseline systems, and (4b) is the correct output of our joint model. In this case, "わかれる" (part) is likely to take people including "おい" (nephew) and "めい" (niece) as the ablative fillers. Also, because "おい" (nephew) and "めい" (niece) are judged to be similar by the word embeddings, these are recognized as a coordinate structure.

In Table 4, while the dependency accuracies were improved well, the improvements in morphological analysis (Seg, POS, and All) and phrase segmentation (pSeg) were moderate, even though most of them were significant. In Japanese, the same word segments can have multiple possible words with the same POS and base form, which do not influence the segmentation and POS accuracy. For example, consider the following sentence.

(5) 皮 を むく
    rind ACC peel/turn

The verb "むく" is represented as two possible words with different meanings "peel" and "turn," both of which appear in the N-best output of morphological analysis. Although "peel" is correct, this kind of meaning difference is not distinguished in the evaluation of segmentation and POS tagging.[14] However, such ambiguities are resolved based on lexical knowledge in our joint analysis model, and this disambiguation leads to the improvement of case frame selection and dependency parsing.

To further verify the improvements in morpho-

logical analysis, we manually annotated 50 sentences with various morphological ambiguities using the same annotation criteria as NEWS and WEB. We tested our model given 1-best and N-best morphological analysis with lexical knowledge. Table 5 shows the results. The joint model (N-best) outperformed the pipeline model (1-best) in terms of all the measures by a large margin.

6 Conclusion

This paper proposed a joint model for morphological and dependency analysis based on automatically acquired lexical knowledge. This model takes advantage of rich lexical knowledge to jointly resolve word segmentation, POS, and dependency ambiguities. In our Japanese experiments, we succeeded in showing the effectiveness of our joint model over conventional pipeline models.

In the future, we will try to incorporate lexical knowledge into a neural network-based model for joint morphological and dependency analysis. By doing this, we can automatically consider feature combinations as the polynomial kernel used in CaboCha. We also plan to integrate PAS analysis including zero anaphora resolution into our joint model.

References

David Aldous. 1985. Exchangeability and related topics. *École d'Été de Probabilités de Saint-Flour XIII —1983* pages 1–198.

Mohit Bansal and Dan Klein. 2011. Web-scale features for full-scale parsing. In *Proceedings of the 49th Annual Meeting of the Association for Computational Linguistics: Human Language Technologies*. Association for Computational Linguistics, Portland, Oregon, USA, pages 693–702. http://www.aclweb.org/anthology/P11-1070.

Bernd Bohnet and Joakim Nivre. 2012. A transition-based system for joint part-of-speech tagging and labeled non-projective dependency parsing. In *Proceedings of the 2012 Joint Conference on Empirical Methods in Natural Language Processing and Computational Natural Lan-*

---

[14] If this verb "むく" is written using a Chinese character, such as "向く" (turn) and "剥く" (peel), this kind of ambiguity does not occur. However, there are many uses of words without using Chinese characters, especially on Web texts.

guage Learning. Association for Computational Linguistics, Jeju Island, Korea, pages 1455–1465. http://www.aclweb.org/anthology/D12-1133.

Bernd Bohnet, Joakim Nivre, Igor Boguslavsky, Richárd Farkas, Filip Ginter, and Jan Hajič. 2013. Joint morphological and syntactic analysis for richly inflected languages. *Transactions of the Association for Computational Linguistics* 1:415–428. http://www.aclweb.org/anthology/Q13-1034.

Wenliang Chen, Jun'ichi Kazama, Kiyotaka Uchimoto, and Kentaro Torisawa. 2009. Improving dependency parsing with subtrees from auto-parsed data. In *Proceedings of the 2009 Conference on Empirical Methods in Natural Language Processing*. Association for Computational Linguistics, Singapore, pages 570–579. http://www.aclweb.org/anthology/D/D09/D09-1060.

Bradley Efron and Robert Tibshirani. 1986. Bootstrap methods for standard errors, confidence intervals, and other measures of statistical accuracy. *Statistical science* 1(1):54–75.

Bradley Efron and Robert J. Tibshirani. 1993. *An Introduction to the Bootstrap*. Chapman and Hall/CRC.

Yoav Goldberg and Michael Elhadad. 2011. Joint Hebrew segmentation and parsing using a PCFGLA lattice parser. In *Proceedings of the 49th Annual Meeting of the Association for Computational Linguistics: Human Language Technologies*. Association for Computational Linguistics, Portland, Oregon, USA, pages 704–709. http://www.aclweb.org/anthology/P11-2124.

Yoav Goldberg and Reut Tsarfaty. 2008. A single generative model for joint morphological segmentation and syntactic parsing. In *Proceedings of ACL-08: HLT*. Association for Computational Linguistics, Columbus, Ohio, pages 371–379. http://www.aclweb.org/anthology/P/P08/P08-1043.

Yoav Goldberg, Reut Tsarfaty, Meni Adler, and Michael Elhadad. 2009. Enhancing unlexicalized parsing performance using a wide coverage lexicon, fuzzy tag-set mapping, and EM-HMM-based lexical probabilities. In *Proceedings of the 12th Conference of the European Chapter of the ACL (EACL 2009)*. Association for Computational Linguistics, Athens, Greece, pages 327–335. http://www.aclweb.org/anthology/E09-1038.

Spence Green and Christopher D. Manning. 2010. Better Arabic parsing: Baselines, evaluations, and analysis. In *Proceedings of the 23rd International Conference on Computational Linguistics (Coling 2010)*. Coling 2010 Organizing Committee, Beijing, China, pages 394–402. http://www.aclweb.org/anthology/C10-1045.

Masatsugu Hangyo, Daisuke Kawahara, and Sadao Kurohashi. 2012. Building a diverse document leads corpus annotated with semantic relations. In *Proceedings of the 26th Pacific Asia Conference on Language, Information, and Computation*. Faculty of Computer Science, Universitas Indonesia, Bali,Indonesia, pages 535–544. http://www.aclweb.org/anthology/Y12-1058.

Jun Hatori, Takuya Matsuzaki, Yusuke Miyao, and Jun'ichi Tsujii. 2012. Incremental joint approach to word segmentation, POS tagging, and dependency parsing in Chinese. In *Proceedings of the 50th Annual Meeting of the Association for Computational Linguistics (Volume 1: Long Papers)*. Association for Computational Linguistics, Jeju Island, Korea, pages 1045–1053. http://www.aclweb.org/anthology/P12-1110.

Masakazu Iwatate. 2012. Development of pairwise comparison-based Japanese dependency parsers and application to corpus annotation. Ph.D dissertation at Nara Institute of Science and Technology.

Daisuke Kawahara and Sadao Kurohashi. 2006. A fully-lexicalized probabilistic model for Japanese syntactic and case structure analysis. In *Proceedings of the Human Language Technology Conference of the NAACL, Main Conference*. Association for Computational Linguistics, New York City, USA, pages 176–183. http://www.aclweb.org/anthology/N/N06/N06-1023.

Daisuke Kawahara, Sadao Kurohashi, and Koiti Hasida. 2002. Construction of a Japanese relevance-tagged corpus. In *Proceedings of the 3rd International Conference on Language Resources and Evaluation*. pages 2008–2013. http://www.lrec-conf.org/proceedings/lrec2002/pdf/302.pdf.

Daisuke Kawahara, Daniel Peterson, Octavian Popescu, and Martha Palmer. 2014. Inducing example-based semantic frames from a massive amount of verb uses. In *Proceedings of the 14th Conference of the European Chapter of the Association for Computational Linguistics*. Association for Computational Linguistics, Gothenburg, Sweden, pages 58–67. http://www.aclweb.org/anthology/E14-1007.

Terry Koo, Xavier Carreras, and Michael Collins. 2008. Simple semi-supervised dependency parsing. In *Proceedings of ACL-08: HLT*. Association for Computational Linguistics, Columbus, Ohio, pages 595–603. http://www.aclweb.org/anthology/P/P08/P08-1068.

Taku Kudo and Yuji Matsumoto. 2002. Japanese dependency analysis using cascaded chunking. In *Proceedings of the 6th Conference on Natural Language Learning*. pages 63–69. http://www.aclweb.org/anthology/W/W02/W02-2016.pdf.

Tomas Mikolov, Chen Kai, Greg Corrado, and Jeffrey Dean. 2013. Efficient Estimation of Word Representations in Vector Space. In *Proceedings of Workshop at International Conference on Learning Representations*.

Hajime Morita, Daisuke Kawahara, and Sadao Kurohashi. 2015. Morphological analysis for unsegmented languages using recurrent neural network language model. In *Proceedings of the 2015 Conference on Empirical Methods in Natural Language Processing*. Association for Computational Linguistics, Lisbon, Portugal, pages 2292–2297. http://aclweb.org/anthology/D15-1276.

Martha Palmer, Daniel Gildea, and Paul Kingsbury. 2005. The Proposition Bank: An Annotated Corpus of Semantic Roles. *Computational Linguistics* 31(1):71–106.

Xian Qian and Yang Liu. 2012. Joint Chinese word segmentation, POS tagging and parsing. In *Proceedings of the 2012 Joint Conference on Empirical Methods in Natural Language Processing and Computational Natural Language Learning*. Association for Computational Linguistics, Jeju Island, Korea, pages 501–511. http://www.aclweb.org/anthology/D12-1046.

Manabu Sassano. 2004. Linear-time dependency analysis for Japanese. In *Proceedings of Coling 2004*. COLING, Geneva, Switzerland, pages 8–14. http://www.aclweb.org/anthology/C04-1002.

Yuki Tawara, Ai Azuma, and Yuji Matsumoto. 2015. Japanese morphological analysis using dependency information (*in Japanese*). In *IPSJ 2015-NL-220*. pages 1–7.

Gertjan van Noord. 2007. Using self-trained bilexical preferences to improve disambiguation accuracy. In *Proceedings of the Tenth International Conference on Parsing Technologies*. Association for Computational Linguistics, Prague, Czech Republic, pages 1–10. http://www.aclweb.org/anthology/W/W07/W07-2201.

Zhiguo Wang and Nianwen Xue. 2014. Joint POS tagging and transition-based constituent parsing in Chinese with non-local features. In *Proceedings of the 52nd Annual Meeting of the Association for Computational Linguistics (Volume 1: Long Papers)*. Association for Computational Linguistics, Baltimore, Maryland, pages 733–742. http://www.aclweb.org/anthology/P14-1069.

Zhiguo Wang, Chengqing Zong, and Nianwen Xue. 2013. A lattice-based framework for joint Chinese word segmentation, POS tagging and parsing. In *Proceedings of the 51st Annual Meeting of the Association for Computational Linguistics (Volume 2: Short Papers)*. Association for Computational Linguistics, Sofia, Bulgaria, pages 623–627. http://www.aclweb.org/anthology/P13-2110.

Naoki Yoshinaga and Masaru Kitsuregawa. 2014. A self-adaptive classifier for efficient text-stream processing. In *Proceedings of COLING 2014, the 25th International Conference on Computational Linguistics: Technical Papers*. Dublin City University and Association for Computational Linguistics, Dublin, Ireland, pages 1091–1102. http://www.aclweb.org/anthology/C14-1103.

Meishan Zhang, Yue Zhang, Wanxiang Che, and Ting Liu. 2014. Character-level Chinese dependency parsing. In *Proceedings of the 52nd Annual Meeting of the Association for Computational Linguistics (Volume 1: Long Papers)*. Association for Computational Linguistics, Baltimore, Maryland, pages 1326–1336. http://www.aclweb.org/anthology/P14-1125.

Yuan Zhang, Chengtao Li, Regina Barzilay, and Kareem Darwish. 2015. Randomized greedy inference for joint segmentation, POS tagging and dependency parsing. In *Proceedings of the 2015 Conference of the North American Chapter of the Association for Computational Linguistics: Human Language Technologies*. Association for Computational Linguistics, Denver, Colorado, pages 42–52. http://www.aclweb.org/anthology/N15-1005.

Guangyou Zhou, Jun Zhao, Kang Liu, and Li Cai. 2011. Exploiting web-derived selectional preference to improve statistical dependency parsing. In *Proceedings of the 49th Annual Meeting of the Association for Computational Linguistics: Human Language Technologies*. Association for Computational Linguistics, Portland, Oregon, USA, pages 1556–1565. http://www.aclweb.org/anthology/P11-1156.

Dependency Language Models for Transition-based Dependency Parsing

Juntao Yu
University of Birmingham
Birmingham, UK
j.yu.1@cs.bham.ac.uk

Bernd Bohnet
Google
London, UK
bohnetbd@google.com

Abstract

In this paper, we present an approach to improve the accuracy of a strong transition-based dependency parser by exploiting dependency language models that are extracted from a large parsed corpus. We integrated a small number of features based on the dependency language models into the parser. To demonstrate the effectiveness of the proposed approach, we evaluate our parser on standard English and Chinese data where the base parser could achieve competitive accuracy scores. Our enhanced parser achieved state-of-the-art accuracy on Chinese data and competitive results on English data. We gained a large absolute improvement of one point (UAS) on Chinese and 0.5 points for English.

1 Introduction

In recent years, using unlabeled data to improve natural language parsing has seen a surge of interest as the data can easy and inexpensively be obtained, cf. (Sarkar, 2001; Steedman et al., 2003; McClosky et al., 2006; Koo et al., 2008; Søgaard and Rishøj, 2010; Petrov and McDonald, 2012; Chen et al., 2013; Weiss et al., 2015). This is in stark contrast to the high costs of manually labeling new data. Some of the techniques such as self-training (McClosky et al., 2006) and co-training (Sarkar, 2001) use auto-parsed data as additional training data. This enables the parser to learn from its own or other parser's annotations. Other techniques include word clustering (Koo et al., 2008) and word embedding (Bengio et al., 2003) which are generated from a large amount of unannotated data. The outputs can be used as features or inputs for parsers. Both groups

of techniques have been shown effective on syntactic parsing tasks (Zhou and Li, 2005; Reichart and Rappoport, 2007; Sagae, 2010; Søgaard and Rishøj, 2010; Yu et al., 2015; Weiss et al., 2015). However, most word clustering and the word embedding approaches do not consider the syntactic structures and most self-/co-training approaches can use only a relatively small additional training data as training parsers on a large corpus might be time-consuming or even intractable on a corpus of millions of sentences.

Dependency language models (DLM) (Shen et al., 2008) are variants of language models based on dependency structures. An N-gram DLM is able to predict the next child when given N-1 immediate previous children and their head. Chen et al. (2012) integrated first a high-order DLM into a second-order graph-based parser. The DLM allows the parser to explore high-order features but not increasing the time complexity. Following Chen et al. (2012), we adapted the DLM to transition-based dependency parsing. Our approach is different from Chen et al. (2012)'s in a number of important aspects:

1. We applied the DLM to a strong parser that on its own has a competitive performance.

2. We revised their feature templates to integrate the DLMs with a transition-based system and labeled parsing.

3. We used DLMs in joint tagging and parsing, and gained up to 0.4% on tagging accuracy.

4. Our approach could use not only single DLM but also multiple DLMs during parsing.

5. We evaluated additionally with DLMs extracted from higher quality parsed data which two parsers assigned the same annotations.

Proceedings of the 15th International Conference on Parsing Technologies, pages 11–17,
Pisa, Italy; September 20–22, 2017. ©2017 Association for Computational Linguistics

Overall, our approach improved upon a competitive baseline by 0.51% for English and achieved state-of-the-art accuracy for Chinese.

2 Related work

Previous studies using unlabeled text could be classified into two groups by how unlabeled data is used for training.

The first group uses unlabeled data (usually parsed data) directly in the training process as additional training data. The most common approaches in this group are self-/co-training. McClosky et al. (2006) applied first self-training to a constituency parser. This was later adapted to dependency parsing by Kawahara and Uchimoto (2008) and Yu et al. (2015). Compared to the self-training approach used by McClosky et al. (2006), both self-training approaches for dependency parsing need an additional selection step to predict high-quality parsed sentences for retraining. The basic idea behind this is similar to Sagae and Tsujii (2007)'s co-training approach. Instead of using a separately trained classifier (Kawahara and Uchimoto, 2008) or confidence-based methods (Yu et al., 2015), Sagae and Tsujii (2007) used two different parsers to obtain the additional training data. Sagae and Tsujii (2007) shows that when two parsers assign the same syntactic analysis to sentences then the parse trees have usually a higher parsing accuracy. Tri-training (Zhou and Li, 2005; Søgaard and Rishøj, 2010) is a variant of co-training which involves a third parser. The base parser is retrained on additional parse trees that the other two parsers agreed on.

The second group uses the unlabeled data indirectly. Koo et al. (2008) used word clusters built from unlabeled data to train a parser. Chen et al. (2008) used features extracted from short distance relations of a parsed corpus to improve a dependency parsing model. Suzuki et al. (2009) used features of generative models estimated from large unlabelled data to improve a second order dependency parser. Their enhanced models improved upon the second order baseline models by 0.65% and 0.15% for English and Czech respectively. Mirroshandel et al. (2012) used the relative frequencies of nine manually selected head-dependent patterns calculated from parsed French corpora to rescore the n-best parses. Their approach gained a labeled improvement of 0.8% over the baseline. Chen et al. (2013) combined meta features based on frequencies with the basic first-/second-order features. The meta features are extracted from parsed annotations by counting the frequencies of basic feature representations in a large corpus. With the help of meta features, the parser achieved the state-of-the-art accuracy on Chinese. Kiperwasser and Goldberg (2015) added features based on the statistics learned from unlabeled data to a weak first-order parser and they achieved 0.7% improvement on the English data. Word embeddings that represent words as high dimensional vectors are mostly used in neural network parsers (Chen and Manning, 2014; Weiss et al., 2015) and play an important role in those parsers. The approach most close to ours is reported by Chen et al. (2012) who applied a high-order DLM to a second-order graph-based parser for unlabeled parsing. Their DLMs are extracted from an English corpus that contains 43 million words (Charniak, 2000) and a 311 million word corpus of Chinese (Huang et al., 2009) parsed by a parser. From a relatively weak baseline, additional DLM-based features gained 0.6% UAS for English and an impressive 2.9% for Chinese.

3 Our Approach

Dependency language models were introduced by Shen et al. (2008) to capture long distance relations in syntactic structures. An N-gram DLM predicts the next child based on N-1 immediate previous children and their head. We integrate DLMs extracted from a large parsed corpus into the Mate parser (Bohnet et al., 2013). We first extract DLMs from a corpus parsed by the base model. We then retrain the parser with additional DLM-based features.

Further, we experimented with techniques to improve the quality of the syntactic annotations which we use to build the DLMs. We parse the sentences with two different parsers and then select the annotations which both parsers agree on. The method is similar to co-training except that we do not train the parser directly on these sentences.

We build the DLMs with the method of Chen et al. (2012). For each child x_{ch}, we gain the probability distribution $P_u(x_{ch}|H)$, where H refers $N-1$ immediate previous children and their head x_h. The previous children for x_{ch} are those who share the same head with x_{ch} but closer to the head word according to the word sequence in the sentence. Let's consider the left side child x_{Lk} in the

$< NO_{DLM}, \phi(P_u(s_0)), \phi(P_u(s_1)), label >$
$< NO_{DLM}, \phi(P_u(s_0)), \phi(P_u(s_1)), label, s_0\_pos >$
$< NO_{DLM}, \phi(P_u(s_0)), \phi(P_u(s_1)), label, s_0\_word >$
$< NO_{DLM}, \phi(P_u(s_0)), \phi(P_u(s_1)), label, s_1\_pos >$
$< NO_{DLM}, \phi(P_u(s_0)), \phi(P_u(s_1)), label, s_1\_word >$
$< NO_{DLM}, \phi(P_u(s_0)), \phi(P_u(s_1)), label, s_0\_pos, s_1\_pos >$
$< NO_{DLM}, \phi(P_u(s_0)), \phi(P_u(s_1)), label, s_0\_word, s_1\_word >$

Table 1: Feature templates which we use in the parser.

	train	dev	test
PTB	2-21	22	23
CTB5	001-815, 1001-1136	886-931, 1148-1151	816-885, 1137-1147

Table 2: Our data splits for English and Chinese

dependency relations $(x_{Lk}...x_{L1}, x_h, x_{R1}...x_{Rm})$ as an example, the N-1 immediate previous children for x_{Lk} are $x_{Lk-1}..x_{Lk-N+1}$. In our approach, we estimate $P_u(x_{ch}|H)$ by the relative frequency:

$$P_u(x_{ch}|H) = \frac{count(x_{ch}, H)}{\sum_{x'_{ch}} count(x'_{ch}, H)} \quad (1)$$

By their probabilities, the N-grams are sorted in a descending order. We then used the thresholds of Chen et al. (2012) to replace the probabilities with one of the three classes (PH, PM, PL) according to their position in the sorted list, i.e. the N-grams whose probability has a rank in the first 10% receives the tag PH, PM refers probabilities ranked between 10% and 30%, probabilities that ranked below 30% are replaced with PL. During parsing, we use an additional class PO for relations not presented in the DLM. In the preliminary experiments, the PH class is mainly filled by unusual relations that only appeared a few times in the parsed text. To avoid this, we configured the DLMs to only use elements which have a minimum frequency of three, i.e. $count(x_{ch}, H) \geq 3$. Table 1 shows our feature templates, where NO_{DLM} is an index which allows DLMs distinguish from each other, s_0, s_1 are the top and the second top of the stack, $\phi(P_u(s_0/s_1))$ refers the coarse label of probabilities $P_u(x_{s_0/s_1}|H)$ (one of the PH, PM, PL, PO), s_0/s_1_pos, s_0/s_1_word refer to the part-of-speech tag, word form of s_0/s_1, and $label$ is the dependency label between the s_0 and the s_1.

4 Experimental Set-up

For our experiments, we used the Penn English Treebank (PTB) (Marcus et al., 1993) and Chinese Treebank 5 (CTB5) (Xue et al., 2005). For English, we follow the standard splits and used Stanford parser [1] v3.3.0 to convert the constituency trees into Stanford style dependencies (de Marneffe et al., 2006). For Chinese, we follow the splits of Zhang and Nivre (2011), the constituency trees are converted to dependency relations by Penn2Malt[2] tool using head rules of Zhang and Clark (2008). Table 2 shows the splits of our data. We used gold segmentation for Chinese tests to make our work comparable with previous work. We used predicted part-of-speech tags for both languages in all evaluations. Tags are assigned by base parser's internal joint tagger trained on the training set. We report labeled (LAS) and unlabeled (UAS) attachment scores, punctuation marks are excluded from the evaluation.

For the English unlabeled data, we used the data of Chelba et al. (2013) which contains around 30 million sentences (800 million words) from the news domain. For Chinese, we used Xinhua portion of Chinese Gigaword [3] Version 5.0 (LDC2011T13). The Chinese unlabeled data we used consists of 20 million sentences which is roughly 450 million words after being segmented by ZPar[4] v0.7.5. The word segmentor is trained on the CTB5 training set. In most of our experiments, the DLMs are extracted from data annotated by our base parser. For the evaluation on higher quality DLMs, the unlabeled data is additionally tagged and parsed by Berkeley parser (Petrov and Klein, 2007) and is converted to dependency trees with the same tools as for gold data.

We used Mate transition-based parser with its default setting and a beam of 40 as our baseline.

5 Results and Discussion

Combining different N-gram DLMs. We first evaluated the effects of adding different number of DLMs. Let m be the DLMs we used in the experiments, e.g. m=1-3 refers all three (unigram, bigram and trigram) DLMs are used. We evaluate

[1]http://nlp.stanford.edu/software/lex-parser.shtml
[2]http://stp.lingfil.uu.se/ nivre/research/Penn2Malt.html
[3]We excluded the sentences of CTB5 from Chinese Gigaword corpus.
[4]https://github.com/frcchang/zpar

with both single and multiple DLMs that extracted from 5 million sentences for both languages. We started from only using unigram DLM (m=1) and then increasing the m until the accuracy drops. Table 3 shows the results with different DLM settings. The unigram DLM is most effective for English, which improves above the baseline by 0.38%. For Chinese, our approach gained a large improvement of 1.16% with an m of 1-3. Thus, we use m=1 for English and m=1-3 for Chinese in the rest of our experiments.

Exploring DLMs built from corpora of different size and quality. To evaluate the influence of the size and quality of the input corpus for building the DLMs, we experiment with corpora of different size and quality.

We first evaluate with DLMs extracted from the different number of single-parsed sentences. We extracted DLMs start from a 5 million sentences corpus and increase the size of the corpus in step until all of the auto-parsed sentences are used. Table 4 shows our results on English and Chinese development sets. For English, the highest accuracy is still achieved by DLM extracted from 5 million sentences. While for Chinese, we gain the largest improvement of 1.2% with DLMs extracted from 10 million sentences.

We further evaluate the influence of DLMs extracted from higher quality data. The higher quality corpora are prepared by parsing unlabeled sentences with the Mate parser and the Berkeley parser and adding the sentences to the corpus where both parsers agree. For Chinese, only 1 million sentences that consist of 5 tokens in average had the same syntactic structures assigned by the two parsers. Unfortunately, this amount is not sufficient for the experiments as their average sentence length is in stark contrast with the training data (27.1 tokens). For English, we obtained 7 million sentences with an average sentence length of 16.9 tokens.

To get a first impression of the quality, we parsed the development set with the two parsers. When the parsers agree, the parse trees have an accuracy of 97% LAS, while the labeled scores of both parsers are around 91%. This indicates that parse trees where both parsers return the same tree have a higher accuracy. The DLM extracted from 7 million higher quality English sentences achieved a higher accuracy of 91.56% which outperform the baseline by 0.51%.

m	0	1	2	3	1-2	1-3	1-4
English	91.05	**91.43**	91.14	91.22	91.27	91.26	N/A
Chinese	78.95	79.85	79.42	79.06	79.97	**80.11**	79.73

Table 3: Effects (LAS) of different number of DLMs for English and Chinese. $m = 0$ refers the baseline.

Size	0	5	10	20	30
English	91.05	**91.43**	91.38	91.13	91.28
Chinese	78.95	80.11	**80.15**	79.72	N/A

Table 4: Effects (LAS) of DLMs extracted from different size (in million sentences) of corpus. Size = 0 refers the baseline.

Main Results on Test Sets. We applied the best settings tuned on the development sets to the test sets. The best setting for English is the unigram DLM derived from the double parsed sentences. Table 5 presents our results and top performing dependency parsers which were evaluated on the same English data set. Our approach with 40 beams surpasses our baseline by 0.46/0.51% (LAS/UAS) [5] and is only lower than the few best neural network systems. When we enlarge the beam, our enhanced models achieved similar improvements. Our semi-supervised result with 150 beams are more competitive when compared with the state-of-the-art. We cannot directly compare our results with that of Chen et al. (2012) as they evaluated on an old Yamada and Matsumoto (2003) format. In order to have an idea of the accuracy difference between our baseline and the second-order graph-based parser they used, we include our baseline on Yamada and Matsumoto (2003) conversion. As shown in table 5 our baseline is 0.62% higher than their semi-supervised result and this is 1.28% higher than their baseline. This confirms our claim that our baseline is much stronger.

For Chinese, we extracting the DLMs from 10 million sentences parsed by the Mate parser and using the unigram, bigram and the trigram DLMs together. Table 6 shows the results of our approach and a number of best Chinese parsers. Our system gained a large improvement of 0.93/0.98% [6] for labeled and unlabeled attachment scores when using a beam of 40. When larger beams are used our approach achieved even larger improvement of more than one percentage point for both labeled and un-

---

[5]Significant in Dan Bikel's test ($p < 10^{-3}$).
[6]Significant in Dan Bikel's test ($p < 10^{-5}$).

System	Beam	POS	LAS	UAS
Zhang and Nivre (2011)	32	97.44	90.95	93.00
Bohnet and Kuhn (2012)	80	97.44	91.19	93.27
Martins et al. (2013)	N/A	97.44	90.55	92.89
Zhang and McDonald (2014)	N/A	97.44	91.02	93.22
Chen and Manning (2014)†	1	N/A	89.60	91.80
Dyer et al. (2015)†	1	97.30	90.90	93.10
Weiss et al. (2015)†	8	97.44	92.05	93.99
Andor et al. (2016)†	32	97.44	92.79	94.61
Dozat and Manning (2017)†	N/A	N/A	94.08	95.74
Liu and Zhang (2017)†	N/A	N/A	**95.20**	**96.20**
Chen et al. (2012) Baseline *	8	N/A	N/A	92.10
Chen et al. (2012) DLM *	8	N/A	N/A	92.76
Our Baseline *	40	97.33	92.44	93.38
Our Baseline	40	97.36	90.95	93.08
	80	97.34	91.05	93.28
	150	97.34	91.05	93.29
Our DLM	40	97.38	91.41	93.59
	80	97.39	91.47	93.65
	150	97.42	91.56	93.74

Table 5: Comparing with top performing parsers on English. (* means results that are evaluated on Yamada and Matsumoto (2003) conversion. † means neural network-based parsers)

System	Beam	POS	LAS	UAS
Hatori et al. (2011)	64	93.94	N/A	81.33
Li et al. (2012)	N/A	94.60	79.01	81.67
Chen et al. (2013)	N/A	N/A	N/A	83.08
Chen et al. (2015)	N/A	93.61	N/A	82.94
Our Baseline	40	93.99	78.49	81.52
	80	94.02	78.48	81.58
	150	93.98	78.96	82.11
Our DLM	40	94.27	79.42	82.51
	80	94.39	79.79	82.79
	150	94.40	**80.21**	**83.28**

Table 6: Comparing with top performing parsers on Chinese.

labeled accuracy when compared to the respective baselines. Our scores with the default beam size (40) are competitive and are 0.2% higher than the best reported result (Chen et al., 2013) when increasing the beam size to 150. Moreover, we gained improvements up to 0.42% for part-of-speech tagging on Chinese tests.

6   Conclusion

In this paper, we applied dependency language models (DLM) extracted from a large parsed corpus to a strong transition-based parser. We integrated a small number of DLM-based features into the parser. We demonstrate the effectiveness of our DLM-based approach by applying our approach to English and Chinese. We achieved statistically significant improvements on labeled and unlabeled scores of both languages. Our parsing system improved by DLMs outperforms most of the systems on English and is competitive. For Chinese, we gained a large improvement of one point and our accuracy is 0.2% higher than the best reported result. In addition to that, our approach gained an improvement of 0.4% on Chinese part-of-speech tagging.

References

Daniel Andor, Chris Alberti, David Weiss, Aliaksei Severyn, Alessandro Presta, Kuzman Ganchev, Slav Petrov, and Michael Collins. 2016. Globally normalized transition-based neural networks. In *Proceedings of the 54th Annual Meeting of the Association for Computational Linguistics*. pages 2442–2452.

Yoshua Bengio, Réjean Ducharme, Pascal Vincent, and Christian Janvin. 2003. A neural probabilistic language model. *J. Mach. Learn. Res.* 3:1137–1155. http://dl.acm.org/citation.cfm?id=944919.944966.

Bernd Bohnet and Jonas Kuhn. 2012. The best of both worlds – a graph-based completion model for transition-based parsers. In *Proceedings of the 13th Conference of the European Chpater of the Association for Computational Linguistics (EACL)*. pages 77–87.

Bernd Bohnet, Joakim Nivre, Igor Boguslavsky, Richárd Farkas Filip Ginter, and Jan Hajic. 2013. Joint morphological and syntactic analysis for richly inflected languages. *Transactions of the Association for Computational Linguistics* 1.

Eugene Charniak. 2000. A maximum-entropy-inspired parser. In *Proceedings of the First Meeting of the North American Chapter of the Association for Computational Linguistics (NAACL)*. pages 132–139.

Ciprian Chelba, Tomas Mikolov, Mike Schuster, Qi Ge, Thorsten Brants, and Philipp Koehn. 2013. One billion word benchmark for measuring progress in statistical language modeling. *Computing Research Repository (CoRR)* abs/1312.3005:1–6.

Danqi Chen and Christopher D Manning. 2014. A fast and accurate dependency parser using neural networks. In *Empirical Methods in Natural Language Processing (EMNLP)*.

Wenliang Chen, Youzheng Wu, and Hitoshi Isahara. 2008. Learning reliable information for dependency parsing adaptation. In *Proceedings of the 22nd International Conference on Computational Linguistics-Volume 1*. Association for Computational Linguistics, pages 113–120.

Wenliang Chen, Min Zhang, and Haizhou Li. 2012. Utilizing dependency language models for graph-based dependency parsing models. In *Proceedings of the 50th Annual Meeting of the Association for*

Computational Linguistics: Long Papers-Volume 1. Association for Computational Linguistics, pages 213–222.

Wenliang Chen, Min Zhang, and Yue Zhang. 2013. Semi-supervised feature transformation for dependency parsing. In *Proceedings of the 2013 Conference on Empirical Methods in Natural Language Processing.* Association for Computational Linguistics, pages 1303–1313. http://aclweb.org/anthology/D13-1129.

Wenliang Chen, Min Zhang, and Yue Zhang. 2015. Distributed feature representations for dependency parsing. *IEEE/ACM Trans. Audio, Speech and Lang. Proc.* 23(3):451–460. https://doi.org/10.1109/TASLP.2014.2365359.

Marie-Catherine de Marneffe, Bill MacCartney, and Christopher D. Manning. 2006. Generating typed dependency parses from phrase structure parses. In *Proceedings of the 5th International Conference on Language Resources and Evaluation (LREC).*

Timothy Dozat and Christopher Manning. 2017. Deep biaffine attention for neural dependency parsing. In *Proceedings of the 5th International Conference on Learning Representations.* https://openreview.net/pdf?id=Hk95PK9le.

Chris Dyer, Miguel Ballesteros, Wang Ling, Austin Matthews, and Noah A. Smith. 2015. Transition-based dependency parsing with stack long short-term memory. In *Proceedings of the 53rd Annual Meeting of the Association for Computational Linguistics and the 7th International Joint Conference on Natural Language Processing (Volume 1: Long Papers).* Association for Computational Linguistics, Beijing, China, pages 334–343. http://www.aclweb.org/anthology/P15-1033.

Jun Hatori, Takuya Matsuzaki, Yusuke Miyao, and Jun'ichi Tsujii. 2011. Incremental joint pos tagging and dependency parsing in chinese. In *Proceedings of 5th International Joint Conference on Natural Language Processing.* Asian Federation of Natural Language Processing, Chiang Mai, Thailand, pages 1216–1224. http://www.aclweb.org/anthology/I11-1136.

Liang Huang, Wenbin Jiang, and Qun Liu. 2009. Bilingually-constrained (monolingual) shift-reduce parsing. In *Proceedings of the Conference on Empirical Methods in Natural Language Processing (EMNLP).* pages 1222–1231.

Daisuke Kawahara and Kiyotaka Uchimoto. 2008. Learning reliability of parses for domain adaptation of dependency parsing. In *IJCNLP.* volume 8.

Eliyahu Kiperwasser and Yoav Goldberg. 2015. Semi-supervised dependency parsing using bilexical contextual features from auto-parsed data. In *Proceedings of the 2015 Conference on Empirical Methods in Natural Language Processing.* Association for

Computational Linguistics, Lisbon, Portugal, pages 1348–1353. http://aclweb.org/anthology/D15-1158.

Terry Koo, Xavier Carreras, and Michael Collins. 2008. Simple semi-supervised dependency parsing. In *Proceedings of the 46th Annual Meeting of the Association for Computational Linguistics (ACL).* pages 595–603.

Zhenghua Li, Min Zhang, Wanxiang Che, and Ting Liu. 2012. A separately passive-aggressive training algorithm for joint POS tagging and dependency parsing. In *Proceedings of COLING 2012.* The COLING 2012 Organizing Committee, Mumbai, India, pages 1681–1698. http://www.aclweb.org/anthology/C12-1103.

J. Liu and Y. Zhang. 2017. In-Order Transition-based Constituent Parsing. *ArXiv e-prints* .

Mitchell P. Marcus, Beatrice Santorini, and Mary Ann Marcinkiewicz. 1993. Building a large annotated corpus of English: The Penn Treebank. *Computational Linguistics* 19:313–330.

A. Martins, M. Almeida, and N. A. Smith. 2013. "turning on the turbo: Fast third-order non-projective turbo parsers". In *Annual Meeting of the Association for Computational Linguistics - ACL.* volume -, pages 617 – 622.

David McClosky, Eugene Charniak, and Mark Johnson. 2006. Effective self-training for parsing. In *Proceedings of the Human Language Technology Conference of the NAACL, Main Conference.* pages 152–159.

Seyed Abolghasem Mirroshandel, Alexis Nasr, and Joseph Le Roux. 2012. Semi-supervised dependency parsing using lexical affinities. In *Proceedings of the 50th Annual Meeting of the Association for Computational Linguistics: Long Papers - Volume 1.* Association for Computational Linguistics, Stroudsburg, PA, USA, ACL '12, pages 777–785. http://dl.acm.org/citation.cfm?id=2390524.2390634.

Slav Petrov and Dan Klein. 2007. Improved inference for unlexicalized parsing. In *Proceedings of Human Language Technologies: The Annual Conference of the North American Chapter of the Association for Computational Linguistics (NAACL HLT).* pages 404–411.

Slav Petrov and Ryan McDonald. 2012. Overview of the 2012 shared task on parsing the web. In *Notes of the First Workshop on Syntactic Analysis of Non-Canonical Language (SANCL).*

Roi Reichart and Ari Rappoport. 2007. Self-training for enhancement and domain adaptation of statistical parsers trained on small datasets. In *ACL.* volume 7, pages 616–623.

Kenji Sagae. 2010. Self-training without reranking for parser domain adaptation and its impact on semantic role labeling. In *Proceedings of the 2010 Workshop on Domain Adaptation for Natural Language Processing*. Association for Computational Linguistics, pages 37–44.

Kenji Sagae and Jun'ichi Tsujii. 2007. Dependency parsing and domain adaptation with LR models and parser ensembles. In *Proceedings of the CoNLL Shared Task of EMNLP-CoNLL 2007*. pages 1044–1050.

Anoop Sarkar. 2001. Applying co-training methods to statistical parsing. In *Proceedings of the Second Meeting of the North American Chapter of the Association for Computational Linguistics (NAACL)*. pages 175–182.

Libin Shen, Jinxi Xu, and Ralph Weischedel. 2008. A new string-to-dependency machine translation algorithm with a target dependency language model. *ACL-08: HLT* page 577.

Anders Søgaard and Christian Rishøj. 2010. Semi-supervised dependency parsing using generalized tri-training. In *Proceedings of the 23rd International Conference on Computational Linguistics*. Association for Computational Linguistics, Stroudsburg, PA, USA, COLING '10, pages 1065–1073. http://dl.acm.org/citation.cfm?id=1873781.1873901.

Mark Steedman, Rebecca Hwa, Miles Osborne, and Anoop Sarkar. 2003. Corrected co-training for statistical parsers. In *Proceedings of the International Conference on Machine Learning (ICML)*. pages 95–102.

Jun Suzuki, Hideki Isozaki, Xavier Carreras, and Michael Collins. 2009. An empirical study of semi-supervised structured conditional models for dependency parsing. In *Proceedings of the 2009 Conference on Empirical Methods in Natural Language Processing*. Association for Computational Linguistics, Singapore, pages 551–560. http://www.aclweb.org/anthology/D/D09/D09-1058.

David Weiss, Chris Alberti, Michael Collins, and Slav Petrov. 2015. Structured training for neural network transition-based parsing. In *Proceedings of ACL 2015*. pages 323–333.

Naiwen Xue, Fei Xia, Fu-Dong Chiou, and Martha Palmer. 2005. The Penn Chinese Treebank: Phase structure annotation of a large corpus. *Journal of Natural Language Engineering* 11:207–238.

Hiroyasu Yamada and Yuji Matsumoto. 2003. Statistical dependency analysis with support vector machines. In *Proceedings of the 8th International Workshop on Parsing Technologies (IWPT)*. pages 195–206.

Juntao Yu, Mohab Elkaref, and Bernd Bohnet. 2015. Domain adaptation for dependency parsing via self-training. In *Proceedings of the 14th International Conference on Parsing Technologies*. Association for Computational Linguistics, Bilbao, Spain, pages 1–10. http://www.aclweb.org/anthology/W15-2201.

Hao Zhang and Ryan McDonald. 2014. Enforcing structural diversity in cube-pruned dependency parsing. In *Proceedings of the 52nd Annual Meeting of the Association for Computational Linguistics (Volume 2: Short Papers)*. Association for Computational Linguistics, Baltimore, Maryland, pages 656–661. http://www.aclweb.org/anthology/P/P14/P14-2107.

Yue Zhang and Stephen Clark. 2008. A tale of two parsers: Investigating and combining graph-based and transition-based dependency parsing. In *Proceedings of the Conference on Empirical Methods in Natural Language Processing (EMNLP)*. pages 562–571.

Yue Zhang and Joakim Nivre. 2011. Transition-based parsing with rich non-local features. In *Proceedings of the 49th Annual Meeting of the Association for Computational Linguistics (ACL)*.

Zhi-Hua Zhou and Ming Li. 2005. Tri-training: Exploiting unlabeled data using three classifiers. *Knowledge and Data Engineering, IEEE Transactions on* 17(11):1529–1541.

Lexicalized vs. Delexicalized Parsing in Low-Resource Scenarios

Agnieszka Falenska and **Özlem Çetinoğlu**
Institute for Natural Language Processing
University of Stuttgart
`{falenska,ozlem}@ims.uni-stuttgart.de`

Abstract

We present a systematic analysis of lexicalized vs. delexicalized parsing in low-resource scenarios, and propose a methodology to choose one method over another under certain conditions. We create a set of simulation experiments on 41 languages and apply our findings to 9 low-resource languages. Experimental results show that our methodology chooses the best approach in 8 out of 9 cases.

1 Introduction

The recent CoNLL Shared Task on Parsing Universal Dependencies (CoNLL-ST) (Zeman et al., 2017) gave researchers the opportunity to study dependency parsing on a wide selection of treebanks. While the ultimate goal remained the same, i.e., achieving the best accuracy in predicting the head and dependency label of a token, the starting point changed from one group of languages to another, depending on the available resources.

In the *surprise languages* scenario, participants were given a very small training treebank, no development set, relatively accurate POS tags for the test set, and little or no parallel data.[1] When parallel data is not available, many of the standard cross-lingual parsing techniques (e.g. annotation projection (Hwa et al., 2005; McDonald et al., 2011); treebank translation (Tiedemann and Agić, 2016); utilizing cross-lingual word clusters (Täckström et al., 2012) or word embeddings

(Duong et al., 2015; Guo et al., 2015)) become impossible to apply.

Delexicalized parsing (Zeman and Resnik, 2008) provides a suitable alternative, while it does not require parallel data. The central idea is to train a source-side parser without any lexical features, i.e., typically using only POS tags, and then use this trained parser to parse a target, low-resource language that shares the same POS tag set. No gold trees are required on the target side, and only POS tags have to be predicted prior to parsing. Given the simplicity of this method, several CoNLL-ST participants have chosen delexicalized approaches, not only for surprise languages but also for the other CoNLL-ST scenario – *small languages*[2]. In this scenario, as opposed to the surprise languages, the small training treebanks were the only source of gold POS tags.

When the data for training POS taggers is small – as for the small languages scenario as well as for many upcoming UD treebanks[3] – the delexicalized methods might be affected by poor POS accuracy. On the other hand, there are *some* gold trees for those scenarios and it is *possible* to train lexicalized parsers on them. Could there be cases in which such a low-resource lexicalized parser is preferred over a delexicalized one?

The central question we examine is whether we can find cases where a low-resource lexicalized parser achieves better accuracy than a delexicalized one. As a related problem, we investigate the following case: when there is a new language to parse, with no treebank but with the chance to predict POS tags, should one pursue a delexicalized parsing or invest in some tree annotation?

Our goal is to investigate those questions sys-

---

[1]This is due to the CoNLL-ST rules that restricted the use of parallel resources to OPUS (Tiedemann, 2012). But actually no or little parallel data is not an unrealistic assumption. Among four surprise languages, three of them have only Linux distro translations in OPUS, none are part of the 135-language Watchtower Corpus (Agić et al., 2016) (but two have a few documents on the Watchtower website), and none are part of the 100-language Edinburgh Bible Corpus (Christodouloupoulos and Steedman, 2015).

[2]The set of small treebanks with no development sets.

[3]For instance, currently there are 17 upcoming treebank projects within Universal Dependencies http://universaldependencies.org/#upcoming-ud-treebanks.

Proceedings of the 15th International Conference on Parsing Technologies, pages 18–24,
Pisa, Italy; September 20–22, 2017. ©2017 Association for Computational Linguistics

tematically in low-resource settings and to find the conditions under which one strategy leads to better results than the other. While our scenarios originate from the CoNLL-ST, our approach should be applicable to other settings. For example, our conclusions might prove helpful in developing early parsing models of a new treebank or in deciding how to proceed when there is a large gold POS tagged corpus but no trees (e.g. Echelmeyer et al. (2017) present a Middle High German corpus with 20,000 tokens of gold POS, no trees, and no apparent parallel data). They can also help plan resource creation. While POS annotation can be relatively fast (Garrette and Baldridge, 2013), creating treebanks is costly (Zeman and Resnik, 2008; Souček et al., 2013). The decision of building a large POS annotated corpus vs. a small treebank in a limited time, could depend on whether delexicalized models would work well for a target language.

2 Methodology

We compare low-resource lexicalized vs. delexicalized parsing in two settings used for surprise and small languages scenarios of the CoNLL-ST. In the first scenario, we assume the existence of a small treebank, and an external POS-annotated corpus – larger than the treebank – to train a POS tagger (**ExtPos**). In the second scenario, only the treebank exists, thus the gold POS tags necessary to train a tagger must be extracted from the treebank (**TBPos**). In both cases, we change the treebank sizes to observe the difference in accuracy between lexicalized and delexicalized parsing. While the POS accuracy is not affected from the treebank size in ExtPos, it changes with the size of the treebank in TBPos.

We employ multi-source delexicalized parsing (McDonald et al., 2011) in both scenarios. We follow Rosa and Žabokrtský (2015) and Agić (2017) in combining sources by blending (also known as reparsing) (Sagae and Lavie, 2006). Unlike in their original study, we apply blending on labeled arcs. We also employ weighted blending by assigning weights to sources based on language/treebank similarity measures.

2.1 Similarity Measures

We employ two measures of similarity between languages used in previous work:

KL_{pos}: Rosa and Žabokrtský's (2015) KL divergence metric (Kullback and Leibler, 1951) between POS trigrams. Instead of their smoothing, we use Laplace smoothing with $\alpha = 0.01$.

WALS: Agić's (2017) Hamming distance between each language's feature vectors from The World Atlas of Language Structures (WALS) (Dryer and Haspelmath, 2013). For languages with no WALS entry, or for languages with less than 10 features in common, WALS is not defined.

2.2 Weights

We use three methods employing aforementioned similarity measures for weighting source languages while blending:

R&Z15: Rosa and Žabokrtský's (2015) KL_{pos} calculation between the gold POS tags of the source and target training data, and their KL^{-4} weighting.

A17: Agić's (2017) combined weighting that calculates KL_{pos} between the gold POS tags of the source training data and the predicted POS tags of the target development data, and then combines it with WALS.

LAS$_{tgt}$: We utilize gold trees as a source of weights for the blender. We parse the target training trees with the source delexicalized parsers and use their LAS as weights. Moreover, we rank the sources and take the n-best giving the best blended accuracy. n is tuned for every treebank and every training size separately on the training data.

3 Experimental Setup

Data We use the Universal Dependencies v2.0 treebanks (Nivre et al., 2016) released for the CoNLL-ST (Nivre et al., 2017). We use all the treebanks except *domain-specific*[4] ones as sources (46 languages). As targets we take two groups of languages from the CoNLL-ST that correspond to the two settings we experiment with:

Surprise languages: Kurmanji (kmr), Upper Sorbian (hsb), North Sami (sme), Buryat (bxr). Each language contains a small sample of gold training data (see Table 1) and its test set is provided with POS tags predicted by a system trained on a data set much larger than the training data. Those languages represent the ExtPos setting.

Small languages: Latin (la), Irish (ga), Ukrainian (uk), Kazakh (kk), Uyghur (ug). They have small treebanks (especially Kazakh and

---

[4]Some languages have multiple UD treebanks, often from different domains. In such cases we chose the canonical treebank for a language.

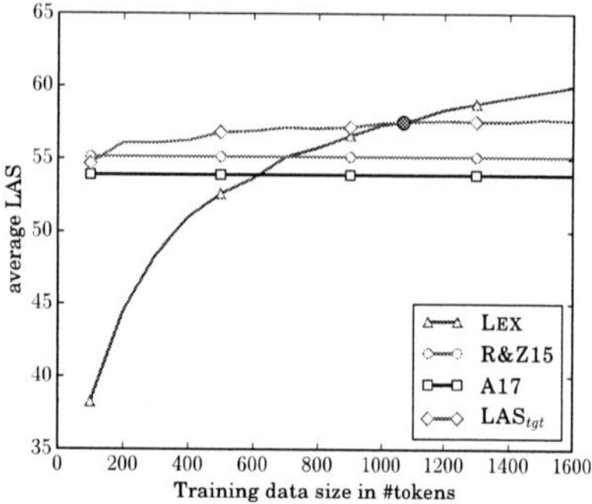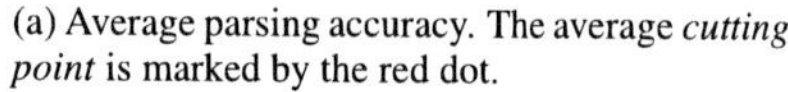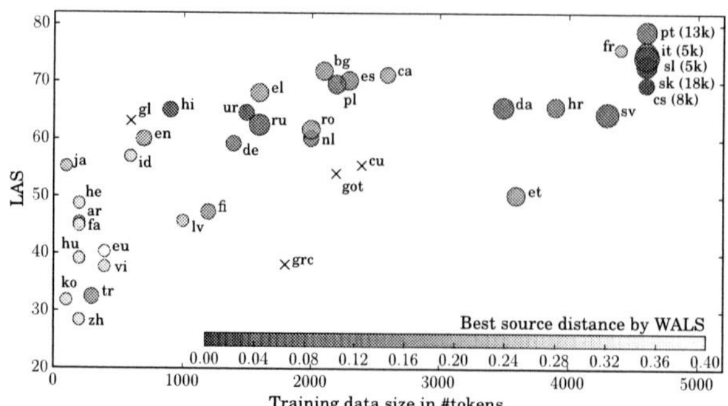

(a) Average parsing accuracy. The average *cutting point* is marked by the red dot.

(b) Cutting points for all targets. Points which fall far right are moved left and their corresponding training sizes are given in brackets. cross (X): no WALS entry. circle size ~ number of most similar sources (WALS < 0.2).

Figure 1: Parsing accuracies for EXTPOS scenario.

Uyghur), with no additional POS data. They correspond to the TBPOS setting.

The 9 target treebanks do not contain development sets, so as to not compromise our test sets, we set those languages aside as test cases. We perform analysis on simulated low-resource languages instead. For this purpose we use the subset of source treebanks that has a development set (41 languages). For each of them we sample small training treebanks starting with only 100 tokens.

Tools To train POS taggers, we employ Mar-MoT (Müller et al., 2013). In EXTPOS, POS taggers are trained on the whole treebanks, where in TBPOS, training is done only on small samples. We use Universal Part of Speech tags (UPOS) in all experiments.

For parsing, we use a beam-search transition-based parser (Björkelund and Nivre, 2015).[5] Delexicalized parsers (**DELEX**), and lexicalized parsers (**LEX**) for TBPOS are trained on gold POS tags. For EXTPOS lexicalized parsers are trained on 5-fold jackknifed POS tags for better performance (we sample the small treebanks after performing jackknifing). We blend delexicalized models' outputs via methods described in Section 2.2. In presenting the experimental results, we refer to these DELEX models with their weighting scheme, namely **R&Z15**, **A17**, and **LAS**$_{tgt}$.

Evaluation We use labeled attachment score (LAS) as the evaluation metric and evaluate using the script provided by the CoNLL-ST organizers.

---

[5]We also experimented with the graph-based parser Mate (Bohnet, 2010) to test our hypotheses on a different parsing architecture. We achieved results parallel to the transition-based parser, thus we only present one set of results.

4 Results and Analysis

We apply LEX and DELEX to our artificially created low-resource languages and analyze the results for EXTPOS and TBPOS scenarios.

4.1 The EXTPOS Scenario

Figure 1(a) shows average results for EXTPOS. We observe that DELEX methods using POS tags as weight source (A17 and R&Z15) achieve on average 55% LAS. Both of them are surpassed by LEX when gold trees are available for only 750 tokens (which corresponds to 40 sentences for the used treebanks). Creating weights from gold trees (LAS$_{tgt}$) instead of POS tags improves the performance but the improvement is modest and LEX trained on only 1,100 tokens (avg. 55 sentences) outperforms it. We find this small number surprising, and investigate it further.

Instead of looking at averages we analyze target languages separately. We call the point in which LEX surpasses LAS$_{tgt}$ (the red dot in Figure 1(a)) a *cutting point* and plot the cutting points for all the target languages separately (Figure 1(b)). We note that most of the languages do not fall around the average cutting point of 1,100 tokens. Instead they can be grouped into three clusters: 10 languages on the far left for which LEX trained on even less than 500 tokens (avg. 25 sentences) is better than DELEX; 9 languages on the far right for which even 3,400 tokens (avg. 176 sentences) is not enough to surpass DELEX; and the middle part. In order to explain this distribution we take a look at the target languages characteristics.

We use WALS to measure the distance between languages (we normalize WALS by the number of

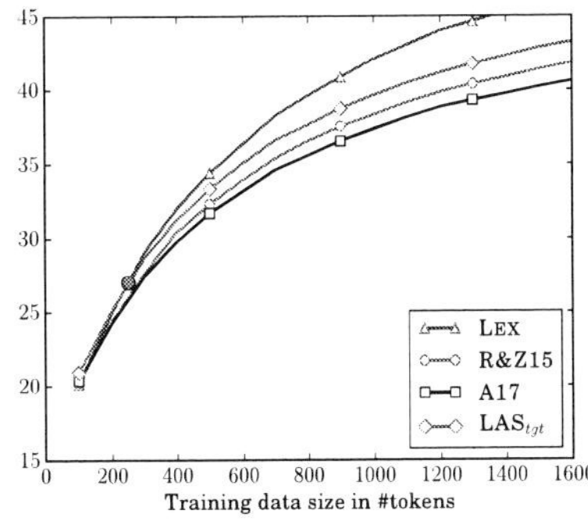
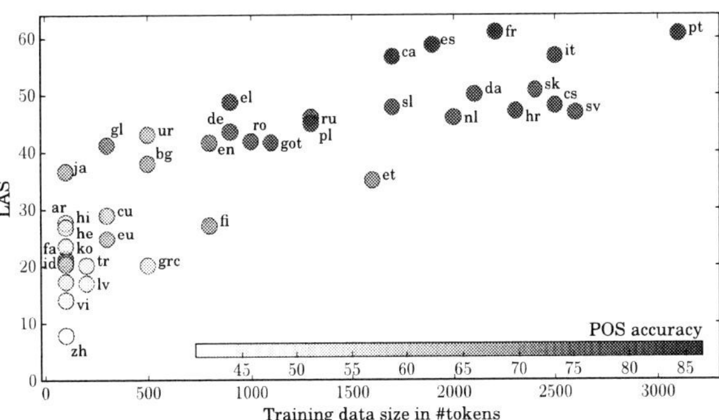

(a) Average parsing accuracy. The average *cutting point* is marked by the red dot.

(b) Cutting points for all target languages.

Figure 2: Parsing accuracies for TBPOS scenario.

common features). For every target we select the best source according to WALS and represent its distance by color (the darker the circle the more similar the best source is). The number of good sources (WALS < 0.2) is represented by size (the bigger the circle the more good sources exist). For example, Korean's (ko) best source according to WALS is Urdu with a distance of 0.27 and its circle is light and small. In contrast, Slovenian (sl) for which five good sources exist (among which Ukrainian has the smallest distance of 0.03) is represented by a dark and big circle.

In Figure 1(b) we can observe a pattern among the two border groups. The left group tends to have small and light circles which means that there is no good source for them. When we look at the languages which fall into this group (like Arabic (ar) and Vietnamese (vi)) we see that they come from language families less represented among the source languages. The far right circles in comparison are bigger and darker which means that they fit well into the set of existing source languages. Indeed many Slavic languages fall here.

4.2 The TBPOS Scenario

Figure 2(a) shows average results for TBPOS. As expected the accuracy of parsers drops due to lower POS accuracy. Other than the LAS scores, there are two major differences between those two plots. In this setting, POS taggers are trained on tags coming from the treebanks and POS accuracy changes with the data size. That is why the A17 and R&Z15 lines are not flat any more. The difference between them is once again very slight and LAS_{tgt} outperforms both of them for all data sizes.

As the second major difference to EXTPOS,

LEX quickly outperforms DELEX methods at around 250 tokens. We show the breakdown of this cutting point by target language in Figure 2(b). The shades of the circles denote the POS accuracy (the darker the more accurate). In this case, the circles are placed in a smaller area with an upper limit of 3,100 tokens. Note that the source language similarity is not shown in this plot, yet it still affects the underlying distribution of targets. Comparing to Figure 1(b), the relative placement of the languages is almost the same. The dense distribution also causes a more homogeneous scatter making the groupings less visible.

4.3 Overall Picture

Delexicalized models use only POS tags as features and therefore are more influenced by low POS tagging accuracy than lexicalized parsers. That is why the choice which method to apply depends strongly on the existing resources.

In EXTPOS in order for DELEX to work better than LEX good sources must exist. If the target belongs to an underrepresented language family, even a very small sample of gold trees is enough for LEX to achieve better results. In contrast, if the target is similar to many sources DELEX can help even if the target gold data exists. In that case, the gold trees can be exploited for example as a source for weights for blending. For all our targets regardless of existing sources, having a treebank bigger than 18,000 tokens is enough for LEX to give higher accuracies than any DELEX model.

In TBPOS on average LEX outperforms DELEX even when trained on only few gold sentences. The only situation when using other sources might help is when there are many similar sources and

21

gold trees for more than 1,000 tokens (avg. 50 sentences). In that case, the POS tagging accuracy is able to reach a reasonable 70% and DELEX achieves comparable performance to LEX. But already having a treebank bigger than only 3,100 tokens (avg. 160 sentences) is enough for LEX to work better for all our targets.

5 Application to Test Languages

We use findings from Section 4 to decide which test languages should employ DELEX methods.

In EXTPOS all the treebanks have less than 500 tokens and according to Figure 1(a) DELEX methods might be a good choice. We compare the test languages with the breakdown in Figure 1(b). Buryat is a Mongolic language and does not have any close relatives among the source languages. For Kurmanji there is only one similar language – Persian. Therefore for both of those languages the cutting point would likely occur quickly and DELEX would give no or very little improvement over LEX. On the contrary, North Sami is Finno-Ugric and Finnish and Estonian should be good sources for it. Upper Sorbian is Slavic and its family is well represented (e.g. by Czech or Polish). Therefore DELEX should work very well for them.

In TBPOS, most of the languages are much bigger than 3,100 tokens and for none of them DELEX should help. Kazakh is smaller than the threshold of 1,000 tokens. Most probably POS tagging accuracy for it would be poor and LEX should be a better choice to overcome that. The only language for which DELEX methods might help is Uyghur. But it is a language for which not many good sources exist, the closest being Turkish. Most probably LEX is also a better choice in this case.

To test our hypotheses, we apply all the methods to the test languages and present results in Table 1. For languages not present in WALS (Kazakh, Uyghur) A17 uses only KL_{pos}. We do not apply R&Z15 to the surprise languages since their POS tagging training data is not available[6]. We see that our intuition was right in 8 out of 9 cases. For all the small languages LEX performs better. For the surprise languages as expected Upper Sorbian and North Sami gain from DELEX the most – 9.22 and 6 points LAS respectively when compared to LAS_{tgt}. For Kurmanji LEX trained on only 242 tokens (20 sentences) gives 2.12 points

---

[6]Their test sets were annotated via jackknifing by the CoNLL-ST organizers to mimic EXTPOS scenario.

		size	POS	LEX	R&Z15	A17	LAS_{tgt}
Small	la	18184	84.41	**41.02**	33.62	35.06	35.06
	ga	13826	89.99	**64.66**	41.75	42.17	44.54
	uk	12846	88.58	**64.81**	62.20	58.46	63.67
	ug	1662	74.96	**34.81**	21.04	20.72	30.11
	kk	529	58.48	**26.55**	21.49	24.49	26.17
Surprise	hsb	460	90.30	49.59	–	57.09	**58.81**
	kmr	242	90.04	**40.94**	–	38.82	38.17
	bxr	153	84.12	28.06	–	29.07	**32.01**
	sme	147	86.81	29.8	–	33.44	**35.80**

Table 1: Results on the test languages.

LAS more than the best DELEX. Surprisingly, for Buryat both DELEX methods outperform LEX.

6 Conclusion

In this paper we looked into lexicalized vs. delexicalized parsing in cases where there are few trees for targets, POS tagging accuracies for the test set vary, and no reasonable amount of parallel data between source and target languages is available. To systematically compare these two approaches and to observe under what circumstances one is more favorable than the other, we created a simulation scenario of 41 low-resource languages and applied our findings to a set of 9 real low-resource targets.

We found out that lexicalized parsing can surpass delexicalized methods even when trained on very few sentences, so one should not be deceived by the small size of a target treebank. By analyzing the typological relations between the source and target languages, and the accuracy of POS tagging it is possible to develop intuition about which of two methods to apply to a new language. For 8 out of 9 test languages our findings hold true.

In our experiments we assumed specific constraints on existing resources, e.g., no parallel data between source and target languages. If some parallel data is available, other transfer parsing approaches should be taken into comparison. For instance, Agić et al. (2016) analyze a related scenario where parallel data is available but no gold trees. They show that projecting POS and dependency annotations from multiple source languages outperforms single-best delexicalized parsing as well as blending. Whether such a method would be a preferable choice when a small amount of gold trees is available is a venue to explore.

Acknowledgments

This project is funded by the Deutsche Forschungsgemeinschaft (DFG) via the SFB 732, projects D2 and D8 (PI: Jonas Kuhn).

References

Željko Agić. 2017. Cross-lingual parser selection for low-resource languages. In *Proceedings of the NoDaLiDa 2017 Workshop on Universal Dependencies*. Gothenburg Sweden, pages 1–10.

Željko Agić, Anders Johannsen, Barbara Plank, Hctor Martnez Alonso, Natalie Schluter, and Anders Søgaard. 2016. Multilingual projection for parsing truly low-resource languages. *Transactions of the Association for Computational Linguistics* 4:301–312.

Anders Björkelund and Joakim Nivre. 2015. Non-deterministic oracles for unrestricted non-projective transition-based dependency parsing. In *Proceedings of the 14th International Conference on Parsing Technologies*. Association for Computational Linguistics, Bilbao, Spain, pages 76–86.

Bernd Bohnet. 2010. Very high accuracy and fast dependency parsing is not a contradiction. In *Proc. of COLING*.

Christos Christodouloupoulos and Mark Steedman. 2015. A massively parallel corpus: the bible in 100 languages. *Language resources and evaluation* 49(2):375.

Matthew S. Dryer and Martin Haspelmath, editors. 2013. *WALS Online*. Max Planck Institute for Evolutionary Anthropology, Leipzig. http://wals.info/.

Long Duong, Trevor Cohn, Steven Bird, and Paul Cook. 2015. A neural network model for low-resource universal dependency parsing. In *Proceedings of the 2015 Conference on Empirical Methods in Natural Language Processing*. Association for Computational Linguistics, Lisbon, Portugal, pages 339–348.

Nora Echelmeyer, Nils Reiter, and Sarah Schulz. 2017. Ein PoS-Tagger fur das Mittelhochdeutsche . In *Book of Abstracts of DHd 2017* . Bern, Switzerland. https://doi.org/10.18419/opus-9023.

Dan Garrette and Jason Baldridge. 2013. Learning a part-of-speech tagger from two hours of annotation. In *Proceedings of the 2013 Conference of the North American Chapter of the Association for Computational Linguistics: Human Language Technologies*. Association for Computational Linguistics, Atlanta, Georgia, pages 138–147.

Jiang Guo, Wanxiang Che, David Yarowsky, Haifeng Wang, and Ting Liu. 2015. Cross-lingual dependency parsing based on distributed representations. In *Proceedings of ACL-IJCNLP*. Beijing, China, pages 1234–1244.

Rebecca Hwa, Philip Resnik, Amy Weinberg, Clara Cabezas, and Okan Kolak. 2005. Bootstrapping parsers via syntactic projection across parallel texts. *Natural language engineering* 11(3):311–325.

Solomon Kullback and Richard A Leibler. 1951. On information and sufficiency. *The Annals of Mathematical Statistics* pages 79–86.

Ryan McDonald, Slav Petrov, and Keith Hall. 2011. Multi-source transfer of delexicalized dependency parsers. In *Proceedings of the conference on empirical methods in natural language processing*. Association for Computational Linguistics, pages 62–72.

Thomas Müller, Helmut Schmid, and Hinrich Schütze. 2013. Efficient higher-order CRFs for morphological tagging. In *Proceedings of EMNLP*. Seattle, Washington, USA, pages 322–332.

Joakim Nivre, Željko Agić, Lars Ahrenberg, Maria Jesus Aranzabe, Masayuki Asahara, Aitziber Atutxa, Miguel Ballesteros, John Bauer, Kepa Bengoetxea, Riyaz Ahmad Bhat, Eckhard Bick, Cristina Bosco, Gosse Bouma, Sam Bowman, Marie Candito, Gülşen Cebirolu Eryiit, Giuseppe G. A. Celano, Fabricio Chalub, Jinho Choi, Çar Çöltekin, Miriam Connor, Elizabeth Davidson, Marie-Catherine de Marneffe, Valeria de Paiva, Arantza Diaz de Ilarraza, Kaja Dobrovoljc, Timothy Dozat, Kira Droganova, Puneet Dwivedi, Marhaba Eli, Tomaž Erjavec, Richárd Farkas, Jennifer Foster, Cláudia Freitas, Katarína Gajdošová, Daniel Galbraith, Marcos Garcia, Filip Ginter, Iakes Goenaga, Koldo Gojenola, Memduh Gökrmak, Yoav Goldberg, Xavier Gómez Guinovart, Berta Gonzáles Saavedra, Matias Grioni, Normunds Grūzītis, Bruno Guillaume, Nizar Habash, Jan Hajič, Linh Hà M, Dag Haug, Barbora Hladká, Petter Hohle, Radu Ion, Elena Irimia, Anders Johannsen, Fredrik Jørgensen, Hüner Kaşkara, Hiroshi Kanayama, Jenna Kanerva, Natalia Kotsyba, Simon Krek, Veronika Laippala, Phng Lê Hng, Alessandro Lenci, Nikola Ljubešić, Olga Lyashevskaya, Teresa Lynn, Aibek Makazhanov, Christopher Manning, Cătălina Mărănduc, David Mareček, Héctor Martínez Alonso, André Martins, Jan Mašek, Yuji Matsumoto, Ryan McDonald, Anna Missilä, Verginica Mititelu, Yusuke Miyao, Simonetta Montemagni, Amir More, Shunsuke Mori, Bohdan Moskalevskyi, Kadri Muischnek, Nina Mustafina, Kaili Müürisep, Lng Nguyn Th, Huyn Nguyn Th Minh, Vitaly Nikolaev, Hanna Nurmi, Stina Ojala, Petya Osenova, Lilja Øvrelid, Elena Pascual, Marco Passarotti, Cenel-Augusto Perez, Guy Perrier, Slav Petrov, Jussi Piitulainen, Barbara Plank, Martin Popel, Lauma Pretkalnia, Prokopis Prokopidis, Tiina Puolakainen, Sampo Pyysalo, Alexandre Rademaker, Loganathan Ramasamy, Livy Real, Laura Rituma, Rudolf Rosa, Shadi Saleh, Manuela Sanguinetti, Baiba Saulīte, Sebastian Schuster, Djamé Seddah, Wolfgang Seeker, Mojgan Seraji, Lena Shakurova, Mo Shen, Dmitry Sichinava, Natalia Silveira, Maria Simi, Radu Simionescu, Katalin Simkó, Mária Šimková, Kiril Simov, Aaron Smith, Alane Suhr, Umut Sulubacak, Zsolt Szántó, Dima Taji, Takaaki Tanaka, Reut Tsarfaty, Francis Tyers, Sumire Uematsu, Larraitz Uria, Gertjan van Noord, Viktor Varga, Veronika Vincze, Jonathan North

Washington, Zdeněk Žabokrtský, Amir Zeldes, Daniel Zeman, and Hanzhi Zhu. 2017. Universal dependencies 2.0. LINDAT/CLARIN digital library at the Institute of Formal and Applied Linguistics, Charles University. http://hdl.handle.net/11234/1-1983.

Joakim Nivre, Marie-Catherine de Marneffe, Filip Ginter, Yoav Goldberg, Jan Hajic, Christopher D. Manning, Ryan McDonald, Slav Petrov, Sampo Pyysalo, Natalia Silveira, Reut Tsarfaty, and Daniel Zeman. 2016. Universal dependencies v1: A multilingual treebank collection. In *Proceedings of the Tenth International Conference on Language Resources and Evaluation (LREC 2016)*.

Rudolf Rosa and Zdeněk Žabokrtský. 2015. Klcpos3 - a language similarity measure for delexicalized parser transfer. In *Proceedings of ACL-IJCNLP*.

Kenji Sagae and Alon Lavie. 2006. Parser combination by reparsing. In *Proceedings of NAACL*. pages 129–132.

Milan Souček, Timo Järvinen, and Adam LaMontagne. 2013. Managing a multilingual treebank project. In *Proceedings of the Second International Conference on Dependency Linguistics (DepLing 2013)*. Charles University in Prague, Matfyzpress, Prague, Czech Republic, Prague, Czech Republic, pages 292–297. http://www.aclweb.org/anthology/W13-3732.

Oscar Täckström, Ryan McDonald, and Jakob Uszkoreit. 2012. Cross-lingual word clusters for direct transfer of linguistic structure. In *Proceedings of the 2012 Conference of the North American Chapter of the Association for Computational Linguistics: Human Language Technologies*. Montreal, Canada, NAACL HLT '12, pages 477–487.

Jörg Tiedemann. 2012. Parallel data, tools and interfaces in opus. In Nicoletta Calzolari (Conference Chair), Khalid Choukri, Thierry Declerck, Mehmet Ugur Dogan, Bente Maegaard, Joseph Mariani, Jan Odijk, and Stelios Piperidis, editors, *Proceedings of the Eight International Conference on Language Resources and Evaluation (LREC'12)*. Istanbul, Turkey.

Jörg Tiedemann and Željko Agić. 2016. Synthetic treebanking for cross-lingual dependency parsing. *Journal of AI Research* 55(1):209–248.

Daniel Zeman, Martin Popel, Milan Straka, Jan Hajic, Joakim Nivre, Filip Ginter, Juhani Luotolahti, Sampo Pyysalo, Slav Petrov, Martin Potthast, Francis Tyers, Elena Badmaeva, Memduh Gokirmak, Anna Nedoluzhko, Silvie Cinkova, Jan Hajic jr., Jaroslava Hlavacova, Václava Kettnerová, Zdenka Uresova, Jenna Kanerva, Stina Ojala, Anna Missilä, Christopher D. Manning, Sebastian Schuster, Siva Reddy, Dima Taji, Nizar Habash, Herman Leung, Marie-Catherine de Marneffe, Manuela Sanguinetti, Maria Simi, Hiroshi Kanayama, Valeria de-Paiva, Kira Droganova, Héctor Martínez Alonso, Çağr Çöltekin, Umut Sulubacak, Hans Uszkoreit, Vivien Macketanz, Aljoscha Burchardt, Kim Harris, Katrin Marheinecke, Georg Rehm, Tolga Kayadelen, Mohammed Attia, Ali Elkahky, Zhuoran Yu, Emily Pitler, Saran Lertpradit, Michael Mandl, Jesse Kirchner, Hector Fernandez Alcalde, Jana Strnadová, Esha Banerjee, Ruli Manurung, Antonio Stella, Atsuko Shimada, Sookyoung Kwak, Gustavo Mendonca, Tatiana Lando, Rattima Nitisaroj, and Josie Li. 2017. Conll 2017 shared task: Multilingual parsing from raw text to universal dependencies. In *Proceedings of the CoNLL 2017 Shared Task: Multilingual Parsing from Raw Text to Universal Dependencies*. Association for Computational Linguistics, Vancouver, Canada, pages 1–19.

Daniel Zeman and Philip Resnik. 2008. Cross-language parser adaptation between related languages. In *Proceedings of the IJCNLP-08 Workshop on NLP for Less Privileged Languages*. Hyderabad, India.

Improving neural tagging with lexical information

Benoît Sagot and **Héctor Martínez Alonso**
Inria
Paris, France
{benoit.sagot,hector.martinez-alonso}@inria.fr

Abstract

Neural part-of-speech tagging has achieved competitive results with the incorporation of character-based and pre-trained word embeddings. In this paper, we show that a state-of-the-art bi-LSTM tagger can benefit from using information from morphosyntactic lexicons as additional input. The tagger, trained on several dozen languages, shows a consistent, average improvement when using lexical information, even when also using character-based embeddings, thus showing the complementarity of the different sources of lexical information. The improvements are particularly important for the smaller datasets.

1 Introduction

Part-of-speech tagging is now a classic task in natural language processing. Its aim is to associate each "word" with a morphosyntactic tag, whose granularity can range from a simple morphosyntactic category, or part-of-speech (hereafter PoS), to finer categories enriched with morphological features (gender, number, case, tense, mood, person, etc.).

The use of machine learning algorithms trained on manually annotated corpora has long become the standard way to develop PoS taggers. A large variety of algorithms have been used, such as (in approximative chronological order) bigram and trigram hidden Markov models (Merialdo, 1994; Brants, 1996, 2000), decision trees (Schmid, 1994; Magerman, 1995), maximum entropy Markov models (MEMMs) (Ratnaparkhi, 1996) and Conditional Random Fields (CRFs) (Lafferty et al., 2001; Constant and Tellier, 2012). Recently, neural approaches have reached very competitive ac-

curacy levels, improving over the state of the art in a number of settings (Plank et al., 2016).

As a complement to annotated training corpora, external lexicons can be a valuable source of information. First, morphosyntactic lexicons provide a large inventory of (word, PoS) pairs. Such lexical information can be used in the form of constraints at tagging time (Kim et al., 1999; Hajič, 2000) or during the training process as additional features combined with standard features extracted from the training corpus (Chrupała et al., 2008; Goldberg et al., 2009; Denis and Sagot, 2012).

Second, lexical information encoded in vector representations, known as word embeddings, have emerged more recently (Bengio et al., 2003; Collobert and Weston, 2008; Chrupała, 2013; Ling et al., 2015; Ballesteros et al., 2015; Müller and Schütze, 2015). Such representations, often extracted from large amounts of raw text, have proved very useful for numerous tasks including PoS tagging, in particular when used in recurrent neural networks (RNNs) and more specifically in mono- or bi-directional, word-level or character-level long short-term memory networks (LSTMs) (Hochreiter and Schmidhuber, 1997; Ling et al., 2015; Ballesteros et al., 2015; Plank et al., 2016).

Character-level embeddings are of particular interest for PoS tagging as they generate vector representations that result from the internal character-level make-up of each word. It can generalise over relevant sub-parts such as prefixes or suffixes, thus directly addressing the problem of unknown words. However, unknown words do not always follow such generalisations. In such cases, character-level models cannot bring any advantage. This is a difference with external lexicons, which provides information about any word it contains, yet without any quantitative distinction between relevant and less relevant information.

Therefore, a comparative assessment of the ad-

Proceedings of the 15th International Conference on Parsing Technologies, pages 25–31,
Pisa, Italy; September 20–22, 2017. ©2017 Association for Computational Linguistics

vantages of using character-level embeddings and external lexical information is an interesting idea to follow. However, the inclusion of morphosyntactic information from lexicons into neural PoS tagging architecture, as a replacement or complement to character-based or pre-computed word embeddings, remains to be investigated. In this paper, we describe how such an inclusion can be achieved and show, based on experiments using the Universal Dependencies corpora (version 1.3), that it leads to significant improvements over Plank et al.'s (2016) state-of-the-art results.

2 Baseline bi-LSTM tagger

As shown by Plank et al. (2016), state-of-the-art performance can be achieved using a bi-LSTM architecture fed with word representations. Optimal performance is achieved representing words using the concatenation of (i) a word vector $\vec{w}$ built using a word embedding layer, called its *word embedding*, and (ii) a representation $\vec{c}$ of the word's characters, called its *character-based embedding* built using a character-level bi-LSTM, which is trained jointly with the word-level layers. Further improvements can be obtained on most but not all languages by initialising the word embedding layer with pre-computed word embeddings. We refer to Plank et al. (2016) for further details.

3 Integrating lexical information

We extend this bi-LSTM architecture with an additional input layer that contains token-wise features obtained from a lexicon. The input vector $\vec{l}$ for a given word is an n hot vector where each active value corresponds to one of the possible labels in the lexicon. For instance, the English word *house*, which is both a singular noun and a verb in its base form, will be associated to a 2-hot input vector. Words that are not in the lexicon are represented in the form of a zero vector. Note there is no need for the morphosyntactic features to be harmonized with the tagset to predict.

Figure 1 shows how the output of this input layer is concatenated to that of the two baseline input layers, i.e. the word embedding $\vec{w}$ and (if enabled) the character-based embedding $\vec{c}$. The result of this concatenation feeds the bi-LSTM layer.

4 Data

We use the Universal Dependencies (UD) datasets for our experiments. In order to facilitate compar-

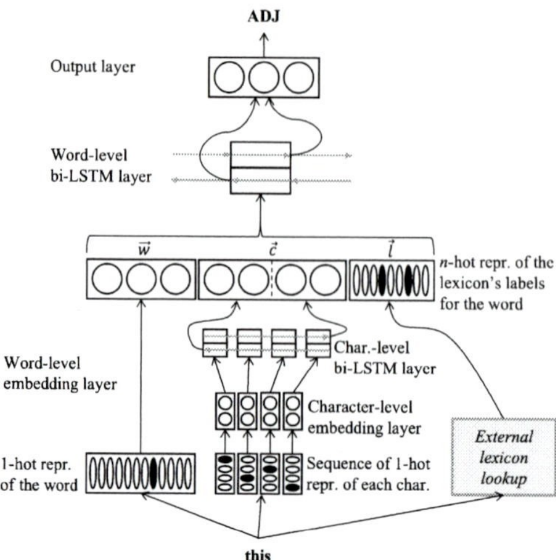

Figure 1: Schema of our extension of Plank et al.'s (2016) bi-LSTM tagging architecture for integrating external morphosyntactic lexical information. This schema concerns a single word, here "this." Connections of the word-level LSTM cell to its counterparts for the preceeding and following word are represented with grey arrows.

ison with Plank et al.'s (2016), we performed our experiments on the version 1.3 of UD (Nivre et al., 2016).

Lexicons Our sources of lexical information we used are twofold. The first one is the Apertium[2] and the Giellatekno[3] projects. We used Apertium morphological lexicons whenever available. For other languages, we downloaded the corresponding monolingual part of OPUS's OpenSubtitles2016 corpus, tokenised it, extracted the 1 million most frequent tokens, and retrieved all their morphological analyses by the corresponding morphological analyser provided by Apertium (or, failing that, Giellatekno). All these analyses were then gathered in the form of a lexicon. In a second step, we converted all lexicons obtained using manually crafted rules, so that each lexical entry contains a (inflected) wordform, a lemma, a Universal PoS,[4] and morphological features from the Universal Features.[5] We then created two variants of the lexicons obtained: a *coarse* variant in which labels are Universal PoS, and a *full* variant

---

[2]https://svn.code.sf.net/p/apertium/svn/languages
[3]https://victorio.uit.no/langtech/trunk/langs
[4]http://universaldependencies.org/u/pos/all.html
[5]http://universaldependencies.org/u/feat/all.html

	Name	#entries ($\times 10^3$)	#tags	TTR	PG
ar	Apertium	651	15		yes
bg	Multext-East	53	12	0.18	yes
ca	Apertium	379	13	0.06	yes
cs	Apertium	1,875	15	0.10	yes
da	Apertium	683	15	0.19	yes
de	DeLex	465	52	0.18	yes
el	Apertium	47	12	0.20	yes
en	Apertium	127	12	0.09	yes
es	Le*ff*e	756	34	0.12	yes
et	GiellateknoMA	44	12	0.23	yes
eu	Apertium$_{full}$	53	14	0.22	yes
fa	PerLex	512	37	0.10	yes
fi	GiellateknoMA	228	13	0.29	yes
fr	Le*fff*	539	25	0.11	yes
ga	inmdb	114	32	0.26	yes
gl	Apertium	241	12	0.12	no
grc	Diogenes	1,314	18	0.20	no
he	Apertium	268	16	0.12	yes
hi	Apertium	159	14	0.05	yes
hr	HML	1,361	22	0.21	yes
id	Apertium$_{full}$	12	38	0.18	no
it	Apertium	278	14	0.10	yes
kk	ApertiumMA	434	16	0.48	no
la	Diogenes	562	16	0.31	no
lv	Apertium	314	14	0.33	no
nl	Alpino lexicon	81	65	0.14	yes
no	Apertium	2,470	13	0.11	yes
pl	Apertium	1,316	15	0.31	yes
pt	Apertium	159	155	0.13	yes
ro	Multext-East	378	14	0.18	no
ru	Apertium	4,401	16	0.32	no
sl	Apertium	654	14	0.24	yes
sv	Saldo	1,215	214	0.17	yes
tr	ApertiumMA	417	14	0.32	no
zh	Apertium	8	13	0.16	no

Table 1: Dataset information. Best per-language lexicon along with its size and number of tags over the UD1.3 corpora. "MA" stands for morphological-analyser-based lexicon. Lexicons based on Apertium and Giellatekno data are in their *coarse* version unless *full* is indicated. Other lexicons have been adapted from available resources.[1] We also provide the type-token ratio of the corpus (TTR) and whether there were available Polyglot embeddings (PG) to initialize $\vec{w}$.

Lang	Coverage (%)		
	OOTC	OOTC, in Lex.	OOLex
ar	8,0	1,0	55,0
bg	12,3	4,6	32,6
ca	4,9	2,5	20,5
cs	7,0	2,9	31,7
da	15,6	7,3	29,0
de	11,9	5,3	15,1
el	13,4	2,0	52,7
en	9,1	2,6	26,1
es	7,3	3,5	11,3
et	16,9	1,4	48,9
eu	17,8	2,3	57,7
fa	8,2	2,9	31,0
fi	24,4	4,0	46,0
fr	5,7	3,0	9,9
ga	22,8	7,2	66,5
gl	9,9	5,9	14,9
grc	17,9	13,6	57,6
he	10,9	5,1	28,4
hi	4,6	1,6	17,4
hr	20,9	15,1	16,5
id	13,8	2,4	38,3
it	5,7	3,4	21,4
kk	40,5	30,7	23,0
la	26,4	23,4	3,5
lv	36,3	16,9	42,6
nl	18,8	4,4	27,6
no	11,2	4,0	33,0
pl	23,1	9,1	38,9
pt	8,6	3,0	29,2
ro	12,1	6,8	33,1
ru	26,0	15,5	38,7
sl	19,9	11,1	28,7
sv	14,9	10,4	10,4
tr	24,8	13,3	25,6
zh	12,5	0,5	66,5

Table 2: Coverage of the training set and of the best lexicon on the test set for each dataset of the UD 1.3 corpora. "OOTC" stands for "out of training corpus" and OOLex for "out of (external) lexicon". The "OOTC, in Lex." column displays the percentage of words that are not in the training corpus but are covered by the lexicon. Best improvements are expected for these words.

in which labels are the concatenation of the Universal PoS and Universal Features.

We also took advantage of other existing lexicons. For space reasons, we are not able to describe here the language-specific transformations we applied to some of these lexicons. See Table 1 and its caption for more information. We determine the best performing lexicon for each language based on tagging accuracy on the development set. In the remainder of this paper, all information about the lexicons (Table 1) and accuracy results are restricted to these best performing lexicons.

Coverage information on the test sets for both the training data and the best external lexicon for each dataset is provided in Table 2.

Pre-computed embeddings Whenever available and following Plank et al. (2016), we performed experiments using Polyglot pre-computed embeddings (Al-Rfou et al., 2013). Languages for which Polyglot embeddings are available are indicated in Table 1.

We trained our tagger with and without character-based embeddings, and with or without Polyglot-based initialisation (when available), both without lexical information and with lexicon information from all available lexicons, resulting in 4 to 12 training configurations.

Language	Baseline (no lexicon)			With best lexicon (selected on dev, cf. Tab. 1)			Gain when using best lexicon		
	$\vec{w}$	$\vec{w}+\vec{c}$	$\vec{w}_P+\vec{c}$	$\vec{w}+\vec{l}$	$\vec{w}+\vec{c}+\vec{l}$	$\vec{w}_P+\vec{c}+\vec{l}$	$\vec{w}(+\vec{l})$	$\vec{w}+\vec{c}(+\vec{l})$	$\vec{w}_P+\vec{c}(+\vec{l})$
Arabic (ar)	93.90	95.99	96.20	94.58	96.05	96.22	+0.68	+0.06	+0.02
Bulgarian (bg)	94.50	98.11	97.62	96.29	98.30	97.86	+1.79	+0.18	+0.24
Catalan (ca)	96.14	98.03	98.17	97.58	98.21	98.26	+1.44	+0.18	+0.09
Czech (cs)	95.93	98.03	98.10	96.74	98.46	98.41	+0.81	+0.43	+0.31
Danish (da)	90.16	95.41	95.62	94.20	96.24	96.14	+4.04	+0.83	+0.53
German (de)	87.94	92.64	92.96	91.52	93.08	93.18	+3.58	+0.44	+0.23
Greek (el)	95.62	97.76	98.22	96.03	97.67	98.17	+0.41	−0.09	−0.05
English (en)	91.12	94.38	94.56	92.97	94.63	94.70	+1.85	+0.25	+0.14
Spanish (es)	93.10	94.96	95.27	94.62	94.84	95.07	+1.52	−0.11	−0.20
Estonian (et)	90.73	96.10	96.40	90.07	96.14	96.66	−0.65	+0.04	+0.26
Basque (eu)	88.54	94.34	95.07	88.52	94.78	95.03	−0.02	+0.44	−0.04
Persian (fa)	95.57	96.39	97.35	96.22	97.09	97.35	+0.65	+0.71	+0.00
Finnish (fi)	87.26	94.84	95.12	88.67	94.87	95.13	+1.40	+0.03	+0.01
French (fr)	94.30	95.97	96.32	95.92	96.71	96.28	+1.62	+0.74	−0.04
Irish (ga)	86.94	89.87	91.91	88.88	91.18	91.76	+1.94	+1.31	−0.16
Galician (gl)	94.78	96.94	—	95.72	97.18	—	+0.94	+0.24	—
Ancient Greek (grc)	88.69	94.40	—	89.76	93.75	—	+1.07	-0.65	—
Hebrew (he)	92.82	95.05	96.57	94.11	95.53	96.76	+1.29	+0.48	+0.19
Hindi (hi)	95.55	96.22	95.93	96.22	96.50	96.95	+0.67	+0.28	+1.02
Croatian (hr)	86.62	95.01	95.93	93.53	96.29	96.34	+6.91	+1.28	+0.41
Indonesian (id)	89.07	92.78	93.27	91.17	92.79	92.89	+2.11	+0.02	−0.38
Italian (it)	95.29	97.48	97.77	97.54	97.81	97.88	+2.26	+0.33	+0.11
Kazakh (kk)	72.74	76.32	—	82.28	82.79	—	+9.54	+6.47	—
Latin (la)	85.18	92.18	—	90.63	93.29	—	+5.44	+1.12	—
Latvian (lv)	78.22	89.39	—	83.56	91.07	—	+5.35	+1.68	—
Dutch (nl)	84.91	89.97	87.80	85.20	90.69	89.85	+0.29	+0.72	+2.05
Norwegian (no)	93.65	97.50	97.90	95.80	97.72	97.96	+2.15	+0.22	+0.07
Polish (pl)	87.99	96.21	96.90	90.81	96.40	97.02	+2.83	+0.18	+0.13
Portuguese (pt)	93.61	97.00	97.27	94.76	96.79	97.11	+1.15	−0.21	−0.16
Romanian (ro)	92.63	95.76	—	94.49	96.26	—	+1.86	+0.51	—
Russian (ru)	84.72	95.73	—	93.50	96.32	—	+8.79	+0.60	—
Slovene (sl)	83.96	97.30	95.27	94.07	97.74	95.44	10.11	+0.44	+0.17
Swedish (sv)	92.06	96.26	96.56	95.61	97.03	97.00	+3.55	+0.77	+0.44
Turkish (tr)	87.02	93.98	—	90.03	93.90	—	+3.01	−0.08	—
Chinese (zh)	89.17	92.99	—	89.29	93.04	—	+0.12	+0.05	—
Macro-avg.	90.01	94.61	—	92.60	95.18	—	+2.59	+0.57	—
Macro-avg. w/embed	91.43	95.52	95.77	93.52	95.91	95.98	+2.09	+0.38	+0.21

Table 3: Overall results. PoS accuracy scores are given for each language in the baseline configuration (the same as Plank et al., 2016) and in the lexicon-enabled configuration. For each configuration, scores are given when using word embeddings only ($\vec{w}$), word and character-based embeddings ($\vec{w}+\vec{c}$), and word and character-based embeddings with initialisation of word embeddings with Polyglot vectors ($\vec{w}_P+\vec{c}$). The last columns show the difference between lexicon-enabled and baseline configurations.

5 Experimental setup

We use as a baseline the state-of-the-art bi-LSTM PoS tagger `bilty`, a freely available[6] and "significantly refactored version of the code originally used" by Plank et al. (2016). We use its standard configuration, with one bi-LSTM layer, character-based embeddings size of 100, word embedding size of 64 (same as Polyglot embeddings), no multitask learning,[7] and 20 iterations for training.

We extended `bilty` for enabling integration of lexical morphosyntactic information, in the way described in the previous section.

For each lexicon-related configuration, we trained three variants of the tagger: (i) a variant without using character-based embeddings and standard (zero) initialisation of word embeddings before training, (ii) a variant with character-based embeddings and standard initialisation of word embeddings, and (iii) when Polyglot embeddings are available for the language at hand, a variant with character-based embeddings and initialisation of the word embeddings with the Polyglot embeddings. This is deliberately similar to Plank et al.'s (2016) experimental setup, in order to facilitate the comparison of results.[8]

---

[5]Bouma et al., 2000; Oliver and Tadić, 2004; Heslin, 2007; Borin et al., 2008; Molinero et al., 2009; Sagot, 2010; Erjavec, 2010; Sagot and Walther, 2010; Měchura, 2014; Sagot, 2014.

[6]https://github.com/bplank/bilstm-aux

[7]Plank et al.'s (2016) secondary task—predicting the frequency class of each word—results in better OOV scores but virtually identical overall scores when averaged over all tested languages/corpora.

[8]Note that we discarded alternative UD 1.3 corpora (e.g. nl_lassysmall vs. nl), as well as corpora for languages for which we had neither a lexicon nor Polyglot embeddings (Old Church Slavonic, Hungarian, Gothic, Tamil).

lang	$w_{\vec{(P)}} + \vec{c} + \vec{l}$		Δ w.r.t. $w_{\vec{(P)}} + \vec{c}$	
	OOTC	OOTC in Lex.	OOTC	OOTC in Lex.
ar	82,09	94,78	-0,53	-0,51
bg	92,79	96,84	+4,67	+0,98
ca	94,21	98,38	+0,31	-0,11
cs	90,84	96,82	+5,21	+0,57
da	88,54	95,03	+3,17	+0,70
de	86,05	87,00	+3,32	+0,41
el	89,22	96,52	-1,97	-0,90
en	78,23	89,31	+3,89	+1,02
es	76,34	79,33	-1,21	-1,12
et	88,24	94,80	-1,62	-0,70
eu	82,02	93,26	-0,09	-0,41
fa	84,94	95,34	-1,22	-0,76
fi	85,31	92,03	-0,76	-0,95
fr	85,50	86,35	+2,25	+0,43
ga	77,43	89,09	-0,34	-1,77
gl	85,20	91,21	+21,73	+5,60
grc	83,71	94,40	+25,16	+2,00
he	81,36	92,25	-5,81	-2,61
hi	78,91	93,84	-4,22	-0,78
hr	90,74	88,66	+1,50	+0,44
id	86,07	90,72	-1,29	-0,55
it	89,15	96,46	+1,12	-0,43
kk	76,89	52,59	+23,53	-2,96
la	84,51	88,89	+28,95	+10,53
lv	80,98	83,64	+35,13	+15,83
nl	69,49	78,60	+12,75	+8,19
no	92,44	96,97	-0,24	-0,48
pl	90,48	93,95	-2,65	-2,04
pt	88,13	95,69	+0,19	-0,60
ro	88,39	95,47	+23,18	+3,71
ru	90,49	93,80	+40,87	+13,05
sl	93,31	95,77	+11,56	+4,41
sv	92,43	93,31	+3,88	-0,47
tr	85,33	87,33	+26,68	+9,13
zh	78,30	92,08	+24,97	+5,07
Macro avg.	85,37	90,87	+8,06	+1,83

Table 4: Accuracy of the best system using a lexicon for words out of the training corpus (OOTC), and for words out of the training corpus that are present in the lexicon (OOTC in Lex.), as well as difference between the best system and the baseline without lexicon for these two subsets of words.

6 Results

Our results show that using lexical information as an additional input layer to a bi-LSTM PoS tagger results in consistent improvements over 35 corpora. The improvement holds for all configurations on almost all corpora. As expected, the greatest improvements are obtained without character-based embeddings, with a macro-averaged improvement of +2.56, versus +0.57 points when also using character-based embeddings. When also using pre-computed embeddings, improvements are only slightly lower. External lexical information is useful as it covers both words with an irregular morphology and words not present in the training data.

The improvements are particularly high for the smaller datasets; in the $\vec{w} + \vec{c}$ setup, the three languages with the highest improvements when using a lexicon are those with smallest datasets.

Table 4 shows the accuracy of the best system, compared with the baseline, for words not in the training data (OOTC), and for whose that are present in the lexicon but not in the training data (OOTC in Lex).

While lexicon coverage is an important, it is not the only factor. we observe the improvements are much larger for the smaller datasets like Kazakh (kk) or Russian (ru). However, the improvement is smaller for words that are not in the training data but are nevertheless present in the lexicon, which indicates that the contribution of the lexicon features to PoS prediction is not limited to the words that are covered by the lexicon but spreads throught the contexts by means of the bi-LSTM architecture. Moreover, we argue that the presence of the lexicon features aids compensate for character embeddings fit on smaller datasets, which are not necessarily more trustworthy.

7 Conclusion

Our work shows that word embeddings and external lexical information are complementary sources of morphological information, which both improve the accuracy of a state-of-the-art neural part-of-speech tagger. It also confirms that both lexical information and character-based embeddings capture morphological information and help part-of-speech tagging, especially for unknown words.

Interestingly, we also observe improvements when using external lexical information together with character-based embeddings, and even when initialising with pre-computed word embeddings. This shows that the use of character-based embeddings is not sufficient for addressing the problem of out-of-vocabulary words.

Further work includes using lexicons to tag finer-grained tag inventories, as well as a more thorough analysis on the relation between lexicon and training data properties.

Another natural follow-up to the work presented here would be to examine the interplay between lexical features and more complex neural architectures, for instance by using more than one bi-LSTM layer, or by embedding the n-hot lexicon-based vector before concatenating it to the word- and character-based embeddings.

References

Rami Al-Rfou, Bryan Perozzi, and Steven Skiena. 2013. Polyglot: Distributed word representations for multilingual nlp. In *Proc. of the Seventeenth Conf. on Computational Natural Language Learning*. Sofia, Bulgaria, pages 183–192.

Miguel Ballesteros, Chris Dyer, and Noah A. Smith. 2015. Improved Transition-based Parsing by Modeling Characters instead of Words with LSTMs. In *Proc. of the 2015 Conf. on Empirical Methods in Natural Language Processing*. Lisbon, Portugal, pages 349–359.

Yoshua Bengio, Réjean Ducharme, Pascal Vincent, and Christian Janvin. 2003. A neural probabilistic language model. *J. Mach. Learn. Res.* 3(1):1137–1155.

Lars Borin, Markus Forsberg, and Lennart Lönngren. 2008. The hunting of the BLARK - SALDO, a freely available lexical database for swedish language technology. In *Resourceful language technology. Festschrift in honor of Anna Sågvall Hein*, Uppsala University, Uppsala, Sweden, pages 21–32.

Gosse Bouma, Gertjan van Noord, and Rob Malouf. 2000. Alpino: Wide-coverage computational analysis of dutch. In *Computational Linguistics in the Netherlands 2000, Selected Papers from the Eleventh CLIN Meeting, Tilburg, November 3, 2000*. pages 45–59.

Thorsten Brants. 1996. Estimating markov model structures. In *Proc. of the 4th Conf. on Spoken Language Processing (ICSLP-96)*. pages 893–896.

Thorsten Brants. 2000. TnT: A Statistical Part-of-speech Tagger. In *Proc. of the Sixth Conf. on Applied Natural Language Processing*. Seattle, Washington, USA, pages 224–231.

Grzegorz Chrupała. 2013. Text segmentation with character-level text embeddings. In *Proc. of the ICML Workshop on Deep Learning for Audio, Speech and Lang. Processing*. Atlanta, Georgia, USA.

Grzegorz Chrupała, Georgiana Dinu, and Josef van Genabith. 2008. Learning morphology with morfette. In *Proc. of the 6th Language Resource and Evaluation Conf.*. Marrakech, Morocco.

Ronan Collobert and Jason Weston. 2008. A unified architecture for natural language processing: Deep neural networks with multitask learning. In *Proc. of the 25th International Conf. on Machine Learning*. Helsinki, Finland, pages 160–167.

Matthieu Constant and Isabelle Tellier. 2012. Evaluating the Impact of External Lexical Resources into a CRF-based Multiword Segmenter and Part-of-Speech Tagger. In *Proc. of LREC'12*. Istanbul, Turkey, pages 646–650.

Pascal Denis and Benoît Sagot. 2012. Coupling an annotated corpus and a lexicon for state-of-the-art POS tagging. *Language Resources and Evaluation* 46(4):721–736.

Tomaž Erjavec. 2010. Multext-east version 4: Multilingual morphosyntactic specifications, lexicons and corpora. In *Proc. of LREC 2010*. Valletta, Malta.

Y. Goldberg, R. Tsarfaty, M. Adler, and M. Elhadad. 2009. Enhancing unlexicalized parsing performance using a wide coverage lexicon, fuzzy tag-set mapping, and em-hmm-based lexical probabilities. In *Proc. of the 12th Conf. of the European Chapter of the ACL*. pages 327–335.

Jan Hajič. 2000. Morphological Tagging: Data vs. Dictionaries. In *Proc. of ANLP'00*. Seattle, Washington, USA, pages 94–101.

Peter J. Heslin. 2007. Diogenes, version 3.1. `http://www.dur.ac.uk/p.j.heslin/ Software/Diogenes/`.

Sepp Hochreiter and Jürgen Schmidhuber. 1997. Long short-term memory. *Neur. Comp.* 9(8):1735–1780. https://doi.org/10.1162/neco.1997.9.8.1735.

J.-D. Kim, S.-Z. Lee, and H.-C. Rim. 1999. HMM Specialization with Selective Lexicalization. In *Proc. of the join SIGDAT Conf. on Empirical Methods in Natural Lang. Processing and Very Large Corpora*.

John D. Lafferty, Andrew McCallum, and Fernando C. N. Pereira. 2001. Conditional random fields: Probabilistic models for segmenting and labeling sequence data. In *ICML*. pages 282–289.

Wang Ling, Tiago Luís, Luís Marujo, Ramón Fernandez Astudillo, Silvio Amir, Chris Dyer, Alan W. Black, and Isabel Trancoso. 2015. Finding Function in Form: Compositional Character Models for Open Vocabulary Word Representation. In *Proc. of the 2015 Conf. on Empirical Methods in Natural Lang. Processing*. Lisbon, Portugal, pages 1520–1530.

David M. Magerman. 1995. Statistical decision-tree models for parsing. In *Proc. of the 33rd Annual Meeting on ACL*. Cambridge, Mass., USA, pages 276–283.

Bernard Merialdo. 1994. Tagging English Text with a Probabilistic Model. *Computational Linguistics* 20(2):155–171.

Miguel Ángel Molinero, Benoît Sagot, and Lionel Nicolas. 2009. A morphological and syntactic wide-coverage lexicon for Spanish: The *leffe*. In *Proc. of the 7th conference on Recent Advances in Natural Language Processing (RANLP 2009)*. Borovets, Bulgaria.

Thomas Müller and Hinrich Schütze. 2015. Robust morphological tagging with word representations. In *Proc. of the 2015 Conf. of the North American Chapter of the ACL: Human Language Technologies*. Denver, Colorado, USA.

Michal Boleslav Měchura. 2014. Irish National Morphology Database: A High-Accuracy Open-Source Dataset of Irish Words. In *Proc. of the Celtic Language Technology Workshop at CoLing*. Dublin, Ireland.

Joakim Nivre, Željko Agić, Lars Ahrenberg, Maria Jesus Aranzabe, Masayuki Asahara, Aitziber Atutxa, Miguel Ballesteros, John Bauer, Kepa Bengoetxea, Yevgeni Berzak, Riyaz Ahmad Bhat, Cristina Bosco, Gosse Bouma, Sam Bowman, Gülşen Cebirolu Eryiit, Giuseppe G. A. Celano, Çar Çöltekin, Miriam Connor, Marie-Catherine de Marneffe, Arantza Diaz de Ilarraza, Kaja Dobrovoljc, Timothy Dozat, Kira Droganova, Tomaž Erjavec, Richárd Farkas, Jennifer Foster, Daniel Galbraith, Sebastian Garza, Filip Ginter, Iakes Goenaga, Koldo Gojenola, Memduh Gokirmak, Yoav Goldberg, Xavier Gómez Guinovart, Berta Gonzáles Saavedra, Normunds Grūzītis, Bruno Guillaume, Jan Hajič, Dag Haug, Barbora Hladká, Radu Ion, Elena Irimia, Anders Johannsen, Hüner Kaşkara, Hiroshi Kanayama, Jenna Kanerva, Boris Katz, Jessica Kenney, Simon Krek, Veronika Laippala, Lucia Lam, Alessandro Lenci, Nikola Ljubešić, Olga Lyashevskaya, Teresa Lynn, Aibek Makazhanov, Christopher Manning, Cătălina Mărănduc, David Mareček, Héctor Martínez Alonso, Jan Mašek, Yuji Matsumoto, Ryan McDonald, Anna Missilä, Verginica Mititelu, Yusuke Miyao, Simonetta Montemagni, Keiko Sophie Mori, Shunsuke Mori, Kadri Muischnek, Nina Mustafina, Kaili Müürisep, Vitaly Nikolaev, Hanna Nurmi, Petya Osenova, Lilja Øvrelid, Elena Pascual, Marco Passarotti, Cenel-Augusto Perez, Slav Petrov, Jussi Piitulainen, Barbara Plank, Martin Popel, Lauma Pretkalnia, Prokopis Prokopidis, Tiina Puolakainen, Sampo Pyysalo, Loganathan Ramasamy, Laura Rituma, Rudolf Rosa, Shadi Saleh, Baiba Saulīte, Sebastian Schuster, Wolfgang Seeker, Mojgan Seraji, Lena Shakurova, Mo Shen, Natalia Silveira, Maria Simi, Radu Simionescu, Katalin Simkó, Kiril Simov, Aaron Smith, Carolyn Spadine, Alane Suhr, Umut Sulubacak, Zsolt Szántó, Takaaki Tanaka, Reut Tsarfaty, Francis Tyers, Sumire Uematsu, Larraitz Uria, Gertjan van Noord, Viktor Varga, Veronika Vincze, Jing Xian Wang, Jonathan North Washington, Zdeněk Žabokrtský, Daniel Zeman, and Hanzhi Zhu. 2016. Universal dependencies 1.3. LINDAT/CLARIN digital library at the Institute of Formal and Applied Linguistics, Charles University. http://hdl.handle.net/11234/1-1699.

Antoni Oliver and Marko Tadić. 2004. Enlarging the Croatian morphological lexicon by automatic lexical acquisition from raw corpora. In *Proc. of LREC 2004*. Lisbon, Portugal, pages 1259–1262.

Barbara Plank, Anders Søgaard, and Yoav Goldberg. 2016. Multilingual Part-of-Speech Tagging with Bidirectional Long Short-Term Memory Models and Auxiliary Loss. In *Proc. of the 54th Annual Meeting of the ACL*. Berlin, Germany.

Adwait Ratnaparkhi. 1996. A maximum entropy model for part-of-speech tagging. In *Proc. of International Conf. on Empirical Methods in Natural Language Processing*. pages 133–142.

Benoît Sagot. 2010. The le*fff*, a freely available, accurate and large-coverage lexicon for french. In *Proc. of LREC 2010*. Valletta, Malta.

Benoît Sagot. 2014. DeLex, a freely-avaible, large-scale and linguistically grounded morphological lexicon for German. In *Language Resources and Evaluation Conf.*. Reykjavik, Iceland.

Benoît Sagot and Géraldine Walther. 2010. A morphological lexicon for the Persian language. In *Proc. of LREC 2010*. Valletta, Malta.

Helmut Schmid. 1994. Probabilistic part-of-speech tagging using decision trees. In *Proc. of International Conf. on New Methods in Language Processing*. Manchester, UK.

Prepositional Phrase Attachment over Word Embedding Products

Pranava Swaroop Madhyastha[†*] **Xavier Carreras**[‡] **Ariadna Quattoni**[‡]

[†]University of Sheffield

p.madhyastha@sheffield.ac.uk

[‡]Naver Labs Europe

{xavier.carreras,ariadna.quattoni}@naverlabs.com

Abstract

We present a low-rank multi-linear model for the task of solving prepositional phrase attachment ambiguity (PP task). Our model exploits tensor products of word embeddings, capturing all possible conjunctions of latent embeddings. Our results on a wide range of datasets and task settings show that tensor products are the best compositional operation and that a relatively simple multi-linear model that uses only word embeddings of lexical features can outperform more complex non-linear architectures that exploit the same information. Our proposed model gives the current best reported performance on an out-of-domain evaluation and performs competively on out-of-domain dependency parsing datasets.

1 Introduction

The Prepositional Phrase (PP) attachment problem (Ratnaparkhi et al., 1994) is a classic ambiguity problem and is one of the main sources of errors for syntactic parsers (Kummerfeld et al., 2012).

Consider the examples in Figure 1. For the first case, the correct attachment is the prepositional phrase attaching to the *restaurant*, the noun. Whereas, in the second case the attachment site is the verb *went*. While the attachments are ambiguous, the ambiguity is more severe when unseen or infrequent words like *Hudson* are encountered.

Classical approaches for the task exploit a wide range of lexical, syntactic, and semantic features and make use of knowledge resources like Word-Net and VerbNet (Stetina and Nagao, 1997; Agirre et al., 2008; Zhao and Lin, 2004).

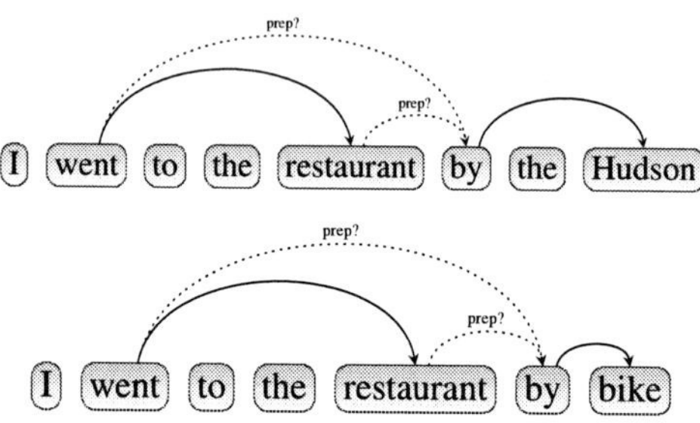

Figure 1: PP Attachment Ambiguity

In recent years, word embeddings have become a very popular representation for lexical items (Mikolov et al., 2013; Pennington et al., 2014). The idea is that the dimensions of a word embedding capture lexical, syntactic, and semantic features of words –in essence, the type of information that is exploited in PP attachment systems. Recent work in dependency parsing (Chen and Manning, 2014; Lei et al., 2014) suggests that these embeddings can also be useful to resolve **PP attachment** ambiguities. We follow this last line of research and investigate the use of word embeddings for PP attachment. Different from previous works, we consider several types of compositions for the vector embeddings corresponding to the words involved in a PP attachment decision. In particular, our model will define parameters over the tensor product of these embeddings. We control the capacity of the model by imposing low-rank constraints on the corresponding tensor which we formulate as a convex loss minimization.

We conduct experiments on several datasets and settings and show that this relatively simple multi-linear model can give performances comparable (and in some cases, even superior) than more complex neural network models that use the same information. Our results suggest that for the

---

* This work was carried out when the author was a PhD student at the Universitat Politècnica de Catalunya

Proceedings of the 15th International Conference on Parsing Technologies, pages 32–43,
Pisa, Italy; September 20–22, 2017. ©2017 Association for Computational Linguistics

PP attachment problem, exploring product spaces of dense word representations produces improvements in performance comparable to those obtained by incorporating non-linearities via a neural network.

Our main contributions are: a) we present a simple multi-linear model that makes use of tensor products of word embeddings, capturing all possible conjunctions of latent embeddings; b) we conduct comprehensive experiments of different embeddings and composition operations for PP attachment and observe that syntax infused embeddings perform significantly better; c) our proposed simple multi-linear model that uses only word embeddings can outperform complex non-linear architectures that exploit similar information; d) for out-of-domain evaluation sets, we observe significant improvements by using word embeddings trained from the source and target domains. With these imrpovements, our tensor products outperform state-of-the art dependency parsers on PP attachment decisions.

2 PP Attachment

Ratnaparkhi et al. (1994) first proposed a formulation of PP attachment as a binary prediction problem. The task is as follows: we are given a four-way tuple $\langle v, o, p, m \rangle$ where v is a verb, o is a noun object, p is a preposition, and m is a modifier noun; the goal is to decide whether the prepositional phrase $\langle p, m \rangle$ attaches to the verb v or to the noun object o.

More recently, Belinkov et al. (2014) proposed a generalization of PP attachment that considers multiple attachment candidates. Formally, we are given a tuple $\langle H, p, m \rangle$, where H is a set of candidate attachment tokens, and the goal is to decide what is the correct attachment for the $\langle p, m \rangle$ prepositional phrase. The binary case corresponds to $H = \{v, o\}$.

In this paper we use the generalized definition. Given a tuple $\langle H, p, m \rangle$, the models we present in this paper compute the following prediction:

$$\operatorname*{argmax}_{h \in H} f(h, p, m) \qquad , \qquad (1)$$

where f is a function that scores a candidate attachment h for the $\langle p, m \rangle$ phrase. Next section discusses several definitions of f based on tensor products of word embeddings.

3 Tensor Products for PP Attachment

For any word x in the vocabulary, we denote as $\boldsymbol{v}_x \in \mathcal{R}^n$ the n-dimensional vector for w, known as the word embedding of w. We will assume access to existing word embeddings for all words in our data.

Let $\boldsymbol{a} \in \mathcal{R}^{n_1}$ and $\boldsymbol{b} \in \mathcal{R}^{n_2}$ be two vectors. We denote as $\boldsymbol{a} \otimes \boldsymbol{b} \in \mathcal{R}^{n_1 * n_2}$ the Kronecker product of the two vectors, which results in a vector that has one dimension for any two dimensions of the argument vectors: the product of the i-th coordinate of $\boldsymbol{a}$ times the j-th coordinate of $\boldsymbol{b}$ results in the $(i - 1) * n_1 + j$ coordinate of $\boldsymbol{a} \otimes \boldsymbol{b}$.

The tensor product model for PP attachment is as follows (see also Figure 2):

$$f(h, p, m) = \boldsymbol{v}_h^\top \, \boldsymbol{W} \, [\boldsymbol{v}_p \otimes \boldsymbol{v}_m] \qquad , \qquad (2)$$

where $\boldsymbol{W} \in \mathcal{R}^{n \times n^2}$ is a matrix of parameters, taking the embedding of the attachment candidate h on the left, and the product of embeddings of the $\langle p, m \rangle$ phrase on the right.

This is a multi-linear function: it is a function that is non-linear on each of the three argument vectors, but is linear in their product. Thus, our model is exploiting all conjunctions of *latent features* present in the word embeddings, resulting in a cubic number of parameters with respect to n. We note that if we pre-process the word embeddings to have a special dimension fixed to 1, then our model has parameters for each of the word embeddings alone, all binary conjunctions between any two vectors, and all ternary conjunctions.

Equation (2) is a multi-linear tensor written as a bilinear form. That is, we unfold the tensor into a matrix $\boldsymbol{W}$ that groups vectors based on the nature of the attachment problem: the vector for the head candidate is on the left side, while the vectors for the prepositional phrase are on the right side. Without any constraints on the parameters $\boldsymbol{W}$, this grouping is irrelevant. [1] However, our learning algorithm imposes low-rank constraints on $\boldsymbol{W}$ (see Section 3.2 below), for which the unfolding of the tensor becomes relevant.

3.1 Variations of the Tensor

We now discuss variations to the above model. In all cases we will write our models as bilinear func-

---

[1] In fact, we could choose to write a standard linear model between a weight vector and the Kronecker product of the three vectors: $\boldsymbol{w} \cdot [\boldsymbol{v}_h \otimes \boldsymbol{v}_p \otimes \boldsymbol{v}_m]$.

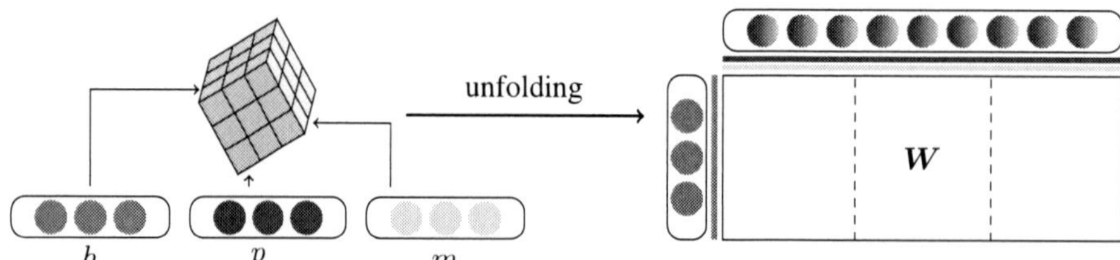

Figure 2: The tensor product of word embeddings. Here, h, p, and m are the head, preposition and modifier of the PP attachment structure, represented by their word embeddings. The tensor product forms a cube, which we unfold with respect to the head and the prepositional phrase. The resulting matrix $W \in \mathcal{R}^{n \times n^2}$ has a row for each head dimension, and a column for each pair of preposition and modifier dimensions.

tions of the following form:

$$f(h, p, m) = \alpha(h)^\top W \beta(p, m) \qquad (3)$$

where α is a representation vector of the attachment, and β is a representation vector of the prepositional phrase. Setting $\alpha(h) = v_h$ and $\beta(p, m) = v_p \otimes v_m$ gives our basic tensor. These are the variations:

- **Sum and Concatenation:** Let us first consider variations of the prepositional phrase representation. Instead of using the product of embeddings, we can consider the sum $\beta(p, m) = v_p + v_m$, or the concatenation $\beta(p, m) = [v_p; v_m]$. These cases drastically reduce the expressivity and dimension of the β vector, from n^2 for the product to n for the sum, or $2n$ for the concatenation. Both sum, averaging and concatenation are common ways to compose word embeddings, while it is more rare to find compositions based on the product.

- **Preposition Identities:** Our basic model is defined essentially over word embeddings, and ignores the actual identity of the words in either sides. However, for PP attachment, it is common to have parameters for each preposition, and we can easily model this. Let $\mathcal{P}$ be the set of prepositions, and let $i_p \in \mathcal{R}^{|\mathcal{P}|}$ be an indicator vector for preposition p. We can then set $\beta(p, m) = i_p \otimes v_m$. Our model is now equivalent to writing:

$$f(h, p, m) = v_h^\top W_p v_m \qquad (4)$$

where we have one separate parameter matrix $W_p \in \mathcal{R}^{n \times n}$ per preposition p. This is the model proposed by Madhyastha et al. (2014).

- **Positional Information:** Positional information often improves syntactic models in general, and PP attachment is no exception as shown by Belinkov et al. (2014). Following that work, we consider H to be *ordered* with respect to the distance of each candidate to the preposition, and we let δ_h be the position of element h (thus δ_h is 1 if h is the closest candidate to p, 2 if it's the 2nd closest, ...). In vector form, let $\delta_h \in \mathcal{R}^{|H|}$ be a positional indicator vector for h (i.e. the coordinate δ_h is 1). We can now compose the word embedding of h with positional information as $\alpha(h) = \delta_h \otimes v_h$, which is equivalent to writing:

$$f(h, p, m) = v_h^\top W_{\delta_h} [v_p \otimes v_m] \qquad . \quad (5)$$

A neural network with a weight matrix for each position was proposed by Belinkov et al. (2014).

In the experimental section we present an empirical comparison of these variations, essentially showing that making tensor products of vector representations effectively results in more accurate attachment models.

3.2 Low-rank Matrix Learning

To learn the parameters we optimize the logistic loss with *nuclear norm regularization* (ℓ_*), an objective that favors matrices W that have low-rank (Srebro et al., 2004). This regularized objective has been used in previous work to learn low-rank matrices (Madhyastha et al., 2014), and has been shown to be very effective for feature spaces that are highly conjunctive (Primadhanty et al., 2015), such as those that result from tensor products of word embeddings.

In our basic model, the number of parameters is n^3 (where n is the size of the individual embeddings). If W has rank k, then we can rewrite $W = UV^\top$ where $U \in \mathcal{R}^{n \times k}$ and $V \in \mathcal{R}^{n^2 \times k}$. Thus the score function can we rewritten as a k-dimensional inner product between the left and right vectors projected down to k dimensions. If k is low, then the score is defined in terms of a few projected features, which can benefit generalization.

Specifically, let $\mathcal{T}$ be the training set. We optimize this convex objective:

$$\underset{W}{\mathrm{argmin}}\ \mathrm{logistic}(\mathcal{T}, W) + \lambda \|W\|_\star \qquad (6)$$

which combines the logistic loss with the nuclear norm regularizer ($\|W\|_\star$), weighted by the constant λ. To find the optimum, we follow previous work and use a simple optimization scheme based on Forward-Backward Splitting (FOBOS) (Duchi and Singer, 2009).

We describe FOBOS briefly in Algorithm 1. Essentially the algorithm works by first computing the gradient of the negative log likelihood function as can be observed in line 4: η_t is the step size, and $g(W_t)$ is the gradient at time t (we choose $\eta_t = c/\sqrt{t}$). Now, for the proximal step. For ℓ_2 regularization, the weights are regularized by using geometric shrinkage (line 6). For nuclear norm regularization (ℓ_*), first Singular Value Decomposition (SVD) of the weight matrix is performed followed by iterative shrinkage and thresholding of the singular values (lines 8 and 9).

This algorithm has fast convergence rates, sufficient for our application. Many other optimization approaches are possible, for example one could express the regularizer as a convex constraint and utilize a projected gradient method which has a similar convergence rate. Proximal methods are slightly more simple to implement and we chose the proximal approach.

For nuclear norm based regularization, we are required to compute the Singular Value Decomposition of W at each iteration. In practice, for our experiments, the dimensions of W were relatively small, allowing fast SVD computations.

4 Experiments

This section presents experiments using tensor models for PP attachment. Our interest is to evaluate the accuracy of our models with respect to the type and size of word embeddings, and with respect to how these embeddings are composed. We start describing the data and word embeddings, and then present results on two settings, binary and multiple attachments, comparing to the state-of-the-art in each case.

Algorithm 1: FOBOS Algorithm

Input: Gradient function g
Constants : λ (regularization factor), T (max iterations) and c (step size)
Output: W_{t+1}

1   $W_1 = 0$
2   **while** $t < T$ **do**
3      $\eta_t = \frac{c}{\sqrt{t}}$
4      $W_{t+0.5} = W_t - \eta_t g(W_t)$
5   **if** ℓ_2 *regularizer* **then**
6        $W_{t+1} = \frac{1}{1+\eta_t \lambda} W_{t+0.5}$
7   **else if** ℓ_* *regularizer* **then**
8        $U\Sigma V^\top = \mathrm{SVD}(W_{t+0.5})$
9        $\bar{\Sigma}_{i,i} = \max(\Sigma_{i,i} - \eta_t \lambda, 0)$
10       $W_{t+1} = U\bar{\Sigma}V^\top$
11   **end**

4.1 Data and Evaluation

We use standard datasets for PP attachment for two settings: binary and multiple attachments. In both cases, the evaluation metric is the attachment accuracy. The details are as follows.

RRR Dataset. This is the classic English dataset for PP attachment proposed by Ratnaparkhi et al. (1994) (referred to as RRR dataset), which is extracted from the Penn TreeBank (PTB). The dataset contains 20,801 training samples of PP attachment tuples $\langle v, o, p, m \rangle$. We preprocess the data as in previous work (Collins and Brooks, 1999): we lowercase all tokens, map numbers to a special token NUM and symbols to SYM. We use the development set from PTB, with 4,039 samples, to compare various configurations of our model. For testing, we consider several test sets proposed in the literature: a) The test set from the RRR dataset, with 3,097 samples from the PTB. b) The New York Times test set (NYT) released by (Nakashole and Mitchell, 2015). It contains 293 test samples. c) Wikipedia test set (WIKI) by (Nakashole and Mitchell, 2015). It contains 381 test samples from Wikipedia. Because the texts are not news articles, this is an out-of-domain test.

Belinkov et al. (2014) Datasets. We use the datasets released by Belinkov et al. (2014) for

English and Arabic.[2] These datasets follow the generalized version of PP attachment, and each sample consists of a preposition p, the noun below the preposition m, and a list of possible attachment heads H (which contain candidate nouns and verbs in the same sentence of the prepositional phrase). The English dataset is extracted from PTB, and has 35,359 training samples and 1,951 test samples. The Arabic dataset is extracted from the SPMRL shared task data (Seddah et al., 2014), and consists of 40,121 training samples and 3,647 test samples.

4.2 Word Embeddings

As our models exploit pre-trained word embeddings, we perform experiments with a variety of types of word embeddings. We use two word embedding methods and estimate vectors using different data sources. The methods are: (a) Skip-gram (Mikolov et al., 2013): We use the Skip-gram model from `word2vec`, and induce embeddings of different dimensionalities: 50, 100 and 300. In all cases we use a window of size 5 during training.[3] (b) Skip-dep (Bansal et al., 2014): This is essentially a Skip-gram model that uses dependency trees to define the context words during training, thus it captures syntactic correlations. We trained 50, 100 and 300 dimensional dependency-based embeddings, using the setting described in Bansal et al. (2014) however we made use of TurboParser (Martins et al., 2013) to obtain dependency trees from the source data [4].

For evaluations on English, we use the following data sources to train word embeddings: (a) BLLIP (Charniak et al., 2000), with ~1.8 million sentences and ~43 million tokens of Wall Street Journal text (and excludes PTB evaluation sets); (b) English Wikipedia[5], with ~13.1 million sentences and ~129 million tokens; (c) The New York Times portion of the GigaWord corpus, with ~52 million sentences and ~1,253 million tokens.

For Arabic, we used pre-trained 100-dimensional word embeddings from the arTenTen corpus that are distributed with the data.

We created a special *unknown* vector for unseen words by averaging the word vectors of least frequent words (i.e., with frequency less than 5). Further, we appended a fixed dimension set to 1 to all word vectors. As explained in Section 3, when doing tensor compositions, this special dimension has the effect of keeping all lower-order conjunctions, including each elementary coefficient of the word embeddings and a bias term.

4.3 Experiments on the Binary Attachment Setting

This section presents a series of experiments using the classic binary setting by Ratnaparkhi et al. (1994).

Comparing Word Embeddings. We start comparing word embeddings of different types (Skip-gram and Skip-dep) trained on different source data, for different dimensions. For this comparison we use the tensor product model of Eq. 2, that resolves the attachment using only a product of word embeddings, and used ℓ_* regularization. Table 1 presents the results on the RRR development set. Looking at results using Skip-gram, we observe two clear trends that are expected: results improve whenever (1) we increase the dimensionality of the embeddings (n); and (2) we increase the size of the corpus used to induce the embeddings (BLLIP is the smallest, NYT is the largest).[6] When looking at the performance of models using Skip-dep vectors, which are induced using parse trees, then the results are better than when using Skip-gram. This is a signal that syntactic-based word embeddings favor PP attachment, which after all is a syntactic disambiguation task. We note that this was also found by Belinkov et al. (2014). The peak performance is for Skip-dep using 100 dimensional vectors trained on BLLIP.[7] For this test, we do not see a benefit from training on larger data.

Comparing Compositions. Our model composes word embeddings using tensor products. Section 3.1 presents variations that compose the prepositional phrase (i.e. the preposition and modifier vectors) in different ways. We now compare

---

[2] http://groups.csail.mit.edu/rbg/code/pp.

[3] In preliminary experiments we tried a window of 2, which performed worse in our setting. According to Bansal et al. (2014) with larger context window, words that are topically-related tend to get closer.

[4] http://www.cs.cmu.edu/~ark/ TurboParser

[5] The corpus and preprocessing script were sourced from http://mattmahoney.net/dc/textdata.

[6] For this experimental comparison, we also tried Glove (Pennington et al., 2014), another popular word embedding method, but the results were generally inferior.

[7] Under the sign test, the difference between the best Skip-dep and Skip-gram models was significant with $p < 0.05$, but other differences between Skip-dep models were not.

Word Embedding		Accuracy wrt. dimension (n)		
Type	Source Data	$n = 50$	$n = 100$	$n = 300$
Skip-gram	BLLIP	83.23	83.77	83.84
Skip-gram	Wikipedia	83.74	84.25	84.22
Skip-gram	NYT	84.76	85.06	85.15
Skip-dep	BLLIP	85.52	**86.33**	85.97
Skip-dep	Wikipedia	84.23	84.39	84.32
Skip-dep	NYT	85.27	85.48	–
Skip-gram & Skip-dep	BLLIP	–	83.44	–

Table 1: Attachment accuracy on the RRR development set for tensor product models using different word embeddings. We vary the type of word embedding (Skip-gram, Skip-dep), the source data used to induce vectors (BLLIP, Wikipedia, NYT) and the dimensionality of the vectors (50, 100, 300). The last row "Skip-gram & Skip-dep" corresponds to the concatenation of two 50-dimensional word embeddings, for a total of 100 dimensions.

Composition of p and m		Tensor Size	Acc.
Sum	$[\boldsymbol{v}_p + \boldsymbol{v}_m]$	$n \times n$	84.42
Concatenation	$[\boldsymbol{v}_p; \boldsymbol{v}_m]$	$n \times 2n$	84.94
p Indicator	$[\boldsymbol{i}_p \otimes \boldsymbol{v}_m]$	$n \times |\mathcal{P}| * n$	84.36
Product	$[\boldsymbol{v}_p \otimes \boldsymbol{v}_m]$	$n \times n * n$	**85.52**

Table 2: Development accuracy for several ways of composing the word embeddings of the prepositional phrase. $\boldsymbol{i}_p \in \mathcal{R}^{|\mathcal{P}|}$ denotes an indicator vector for preposition p, where $\mathcal{P}$ is the set of prepositions.

these variants empirically, using Skip-dep vectors with $n = 50$ as word embeddings. Table 2 summarizes the accuracy results on the development set, where we compare: summing the two vectors; concatenating them; making the product of embeddings; or using indicator vectors for the preposition, which replicates the model by Madhyastha et al. (2014). The table also shows the size of the resulting tensor (we note that $|\mathcal{P}|$ is 66 for the RRR data, thus using a 50-dimensional embedding for p results in a more compact tensor than using p's identity). The results show that the product model is the best of all[8], despite the fact that the number of parameters is cubic in the dimension of the word embeddings. We observed the same trend for larger vectors.

Comparison to the State of the Art. We now present results on the test sets for the binary setting, and compare to the state-of-the-art. The results are in Table 3, which lists representative and top-performing methods of the literature, as well

as our tensor product model running with three different word embeddings. Two of the representative systems we list are the back-off model by Collins and Brooks (1999), and the neural model by Belinkov et al. (2014), which composes word embeddings in a neural fashion. These two systems use no other information that the lexical items (i.e., explicit words or word embeddings). The other two systems, by Stetina and Nagao (1997) and Nakashole and Mitchell (2015), use additional features, and most notably semantic information from WordNet or other ontologies, which has been shown to be beneficial for PP attachment. In general, the results that our models obtain are remarkably good, despite the fact that we only combine word embeddings in a straightforward way. On the RRR test, with the exception of the classic result by Stetina and Nagao (1997), our method using Skip-dep embeddings clearly outperforms any other recent system. On the WIKI test our method is clearly the best, while on the NYT test, our system is behind that of Nakashole and Mitchell (2015) but it is still competitive. In terms of the embeddings we use, the table shows that for the RRR test, embeddings induced from BLLIP perform clearly better, while for the out-of-domain tests, the embeddings induced from NYT are slightly better for the Wikipedia test, and clearly better for the NYT test.

4.4 Experiments on the Multiple Attachment Setting

We now examine the performance of our models on the setting and data by Belinkov et al. (2014), which deals with multiple head candidates. We

---

[8]The differences, though, were not significant under the sign test.

		Test Accuracy		
Method	Word Embedding	RRR	WIKI	NYT
Tensor product	Skip-gram, Wikipedia, $n=100$	84.96	83.48	82.13
"	Skip-gram, NYT, $n=100$	85.11	83.52	82.65
"	Skip-dep, BLLIP, $n=100$	*86.13*	83.60	82.30
"	Skip-dep, Wikipedia, $n=100$	85.01	83.53	82.10
"	Skip-dep, NYT, $n=100$	85.49	**83.64**	*83.47*
Stetina and Nagao (1997) (*)		**88.1**	-	-
Collins and Brooks (1999)		84.1	72.7	80.9
Belinkov et al. (2014)		85.6	-	-
Nakashole and Mitchell (2015) (*)		84.3	79.3	**84.3**

Table 3: Accuracy results over the RRR, NYT and WIKI test sets. (*) indicates that the system uses additional semantic features.

perform experiments on both English and Arabic datasets. For this setting, following Belinkov et al. (2014), we found necessary to use positional information of the head candidate, as described by Eq. 5. Without it the performance was much worse (possibly because in this data, a large number of samples attach to the first or second candidate in the list —about 93% of cases on the English data).

Table 4 presents our results. For English, we present results for models trained with nuclear-norm (ℓ_*) and ℓ_2 regularization, using 50-dimensional embeddings. Imposing low-rank on the product tensor yields some gains with respect to ℓ_2, however the improvements are not drastic. This is probably because embeddings are already compressed representations, and even products of them do not result in overfitting to training. We obtain a slight gain by using 100-dimensional embeddings, which results in an accuracy of 88.4 for English and 81.1 for Arabic. In any case, one characteristic of low-rank regularization is the inherent compression of the tensor. Figure 3 plots accuracy versus rank for the tensor working with 50-dimensional embeddings composed with positional information[9]: with rank 50 the model obtains 88% of accuracy while reducing the number of parameters by a factor of 6. For PP attachment, this has a computational advantage: the prepositional phrase needs to be projected only once (from 2,601 dimensions to k, where k is the rank) for all the head candidates in the sentence.

We compare our method to a series of results by Belinkov et al. (2014). Their "basic" model

	Test Accuracy	
	Arabic	English
Tensor product ($n=50$, ℓ_2)	-	87.8
Tensor product ($n=50$, ℓ_*)	-	88.3
Tensor product ($n=100$, ℓ_*)	*81.1*	*88.4*
Belinkov et al. (2014) (basic)	77.1	85.4
Belinkov et al. (2014) (syn)	79.1	87.1
Belinkov et al. (2014) (feat)	80.4	87.7
Belinkov et al. (2014) (full)	**82.6**	88.7
Yu et al. (2016)	-	**90.3**

Table 4: Test accuracy for PP attachment with multiple head candidates.

uses Skip-gram, and like us, by moving to syntactic vectors (noted "syn") they observed a gain in accuracy. However, in this comparable setting, our model outperforms theirs by 1.3% in English and 2% in Arabic. They also explored adding standard features (from WordNet and VerbNet, noted "feat"), and combining everything (noted "full"), which then surpasses our results. Very recently, Yu et al. (2016) has used a tensor model that combines standard feature templates (again using WordNet) with word embeddings, with significant improvements; however they do not report results on combining word embeddings only, which is our focus.

Comparison to Dependency Parsers. We now compare our tensor models to state-of-the-art dependency parsers, specifically looking at PP attachment decisions. For this comparison, we took the English Web Treebank (WTB) (Petrov and McDonald, 2012), which has annotated evaluation sets for five domains, and extracted PP-attachment tuples using the procedure described by Belinkov

---

[9]We consider 7 head positions, and word vectors are 51 dimensions in practicei (with the dummy dimention). Thus, the unfolded matrix W has 357 rows and 2,601 columns.

	PTB	Web Treebank Development						Web Treebank Test					
	Test	A	E	N	R	W	Avg	A	E	N	R	W	Avg
	(2523)	(814)	(1025)	(969)	(783)	(1064)	(4655)	(868)	(936)	(839)	(902)	(788)	(4333)
Tensor BLLIP	**89.0**	83.7	80.2	81.9	83.2	85.3	82.8	82.7	82.6	87.4	82.5	86.3	84.2
Tensor BLLIP+WTB	88.9	**86.2**	**81.8**	84.1	**83.7**	**86.7**	**84.5**	83.3	**85.2**	**90.1**	**85.9**	86.6	**86.1**
Stanford	87.3	80.3	79.7	**84.5**	81.5	84.9	82.3	79.3	79.7	85.7	82.2	83.8	82.0
Turbo 2nd	88.8	84.5	80.1	82.8	83.1	85.1	83.1	83.6	83.7	87.6	84.2	**87.8**	85.3
Turbo 3rd	88.9	85.1	80.4	83.3	83.3	84.8	83.3	**84.2**	84.5	87.6	84.4	87.6	85.6

Table 5: Comparison between tensor products and dependency parsers, on PP attachment tuples in the Penn Treebank test (PTB) and in the English Web Treebank (WTB) evaluation sets – with separate results for each domain: answers (A), emails (E), newsgroups (N), reviews (R), and weblogs (W). The number of evaluation instances in each set appears in parenthesis. The tensor products use embeddings trained on BLLIP and BLLIP+WTB, and for both $n = 100$.

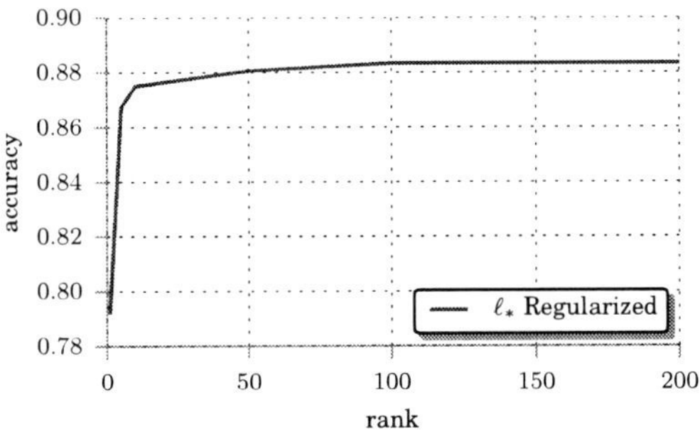

Figure 3: Accuracy versus rank of the tensor model on the English data by Belinkov et al. (2014). The tensor model uses 50-dimensional vectors composed with head position, and has size $357 \times 2,601$.

et al. (2014), resulting in 4,655 tuples on the development set and 4,333 tuples on the test set. We also applied the same procedure to the Penn Treebank test set, with 2.523 instances.[10] We selected two state-of-the-art dependency parsers which are publicly available. The first is the Stanford transition-based neural parser (Chen and Manning, 2014), which uses word embeddings but not as products.[11] The other is TurboParser (Martins et al., 2013)[12] which offers 2nd and 3rd order arc-factored models, with grandchildren features that capture the conjunction of the three words in a PP-attachment decision, even though those models do not use word embeddings. We ran the parsers on the evaluation sentences, and extracted the PP-attachment decision from the parse tree.[13] We also evaluated two 100-dimensional Skip-dep tensor products, one using embeddings trained on BLLIP, and a second one using embeddings trained on BLLIP and the unlabeled data from the Web Treebank.[14]

Table 5 presents the results. Comparing the tensor products, using PTB+WTB embeddings gives an improvement of 1.7% in accuracy on the WTB development test, for a slight decrease of 0.1% on the PTB test. This confirms that tensor products of word embeddings are a valid and simple approach to domain adaptation.

Comparing to parsers, our best tensor product performs better in almost all domains, and on average it performs significantly better in the WTB evaluation sets.[15] First, this confirms that PP attachment decisions are still an important source of errors of state-of-the-art parsers. And we see that a specialized model for PP attachment, despite its simplicity, can improve on these decisions.

Error Analysis. To further understand the performance of the tensor products and parsers on WTB development set, we consider PP attachment instances where the words are observed less than five times in the training data (1,565 cases out of

---

[10]The evaluation test by (Belinkov et al., 2014) has 1,951 instances. Hence, the results of our models are slightly different in this evaluation. We will release our extraction script.

[11]We used Stanford CoreNLP 3.7.0. We could not determine the characteristics of the embeddings in the model.

[12]We used version 2.3, available from `http://www.cs.cmu.edu/~ark/TurboParser`

[13]We ran all parsing models on correct PoS tags. Thus, these are optimistic performances. This choice rules out cases where the parsers fail because of tagging errors, which would be unfair because our models work on pre-selected head candidate lists which depend on correct PoS tags.

[14]We mixed the unlabeled data from all domains, for a total of $\sim$4.7 million sentences and $\sim$75.5 million tokens.

[15]Under the sign test, the differences on WTB evaluation sets between the tensor product on BLLIP+WTB and other models were significant: TurboParser with $p < 0.05$, the Stanford parser with $p < 0.01$, and the tensor product on BLLIP with $p < 0.01$.

4,655). The best tensor product obtains an accuracy of 84.3% (vs. 84.5%), while the 3rd order TurboParser gets 83.0% (vs. 83.3%) and the Stanford parser gets 81.3% (vs. 82.3%). The parsers suffer a drop, while the tensor model does not, suggesting that the tensor model is able to generalize better to less frequent words. Figure 4 shows two sample sentences from the Web Treebank that illustrate two cases of ambiguities. Sentence (a) is an example of lexical paucity, because the words of the attached phrase, *disintegration with LSD*, are absent in the training set. The tensor model correctly predicts the attachment, while the parsers do not. Sentence (b) is an example of sense ambiguity: the tensor model incorrectly predicts *address* as head of *to Senators*, which is plausible, but in this case the sentence is about the *return address* of the *letter to Senators*, which the parsers correctly predict. There are clear complementary benefits between parsers and products of embeddings, and these examples suggest combinations of both.

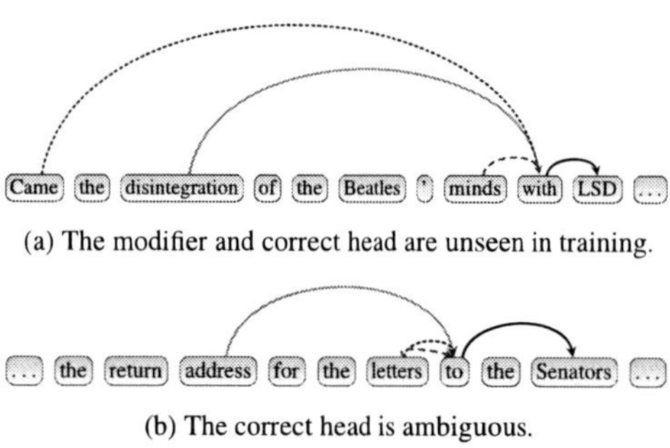

(a) The modifier and correct head are unseen in training.

(b) The correct head is ambiguous.

Figure 4: Examples from the Web Treebank development set, with the attachments predicted by the tensor product (solid green arc), the Stanford neural parser (dashed red arc) and the 3rd order TurboParser (dotted blue arc).

5   Related Work

5.1   Resolving PP Attachment Ambiguity

Several approaches have been proposed for solving the PP attachment problem, including maximum likelihood with back-off (Hindle and Rooth, 1993; Collins and Brooks, 1999), and discriminative training (Ratnaparkhi et al., 1994; Olteanu and Moldovan, 2005), among others. A key part of such systems is the representation they use, in the form of lexical, syntactic and semantic features of the main words involved in an attachment decision. Crucially, the best performing models are obtained when exploring conjunctions of such features. Some works have also explored using external knowledge resources in the form of ontologies and syntactic information (Stetina and Nagao, 1997; Zhao and Lin, 2004; Nakashole and Mitchell, 2015).

In our paper, we use word embeddings as the only source of lexical information. Previous work has explored word representations as extra features (Zhao and Lin, 2004). In our case, we define a model that exploits all conjunctions of the word vectors in an attachment decision. Our model is in fact a generalization of that of Madhyastha et al. (2014), as described in section 3.1. From that work, our application to PP attachment differs in using compact word embeddings as opposed to sparse distributional vectors. Mitchell and Lapata (2008) compared a variety of composition operations, including the tensor product, in the context of distributional lexical semantics.

Closely related to our work is the approach by Belinkov et al. (2014), who use neural networks that compose the embeddings of the words in the PP attachment structure. Their model composes word embeddings by first concatenating vectors and then projecting to a low-dimensional vector using a non-linear hidden layer. This basic composition block is used to define several compositional models for PP attachment. One difference is that we represent tensor products of embeddings, which result in projected hidden conjunctions when the tensor has low rank. In contrast, projecting concatenated embeddings results in hidden disjunctions of the input coefficients.

More recently, Yu et al. (2016) have also explored tensor models for PP attachment. Their focus is on representing standard feature templates (which are conjunctions of features of a variety of sources) as tensors, and on using low-rank constraints to favor parameter sharing among templates. One of their templates is the conjunction of the head, preposition and modifier (and word embeddings of these), which is the focus case of our paper. While there are differences in the way we learn a low-rank tensor (see below), they show superior performance, probably due to the combination of different features. Our experiments, in contrast, offer a controlled study over different aspects of word embeddings and their product.

Beyond applications to PP attachment, word embeddings have been used for a number of prediction tasks. In most cases, embeddings of two or more words are composed by concatenation – see (Turian et al., 2010; Chen and Manning, 2014; Dyer et al., 2015) to name a few, or averaging (Socher et al., 2011; Huang et al., 2012). Compositions based on product of embeddings have been explored in tensor models, which we discuss next.

5.2 Low Rank Tensors in NLP

Using tensors to represent products of elementary vectors has been a recent trend in NLP. Because most tasks in NLP benefit from exploiting conjunctions of elementary features, tensor models offer the appropriate framework for defining conjunctive feature spaces. A main benefit of the tensor representation is that it allows to control the model capacity using low-rank constraints. There are several ways to define the rank of a tensor, while for a matrix there is a unique definition. A natural and simple way to impose low-rank constraints on a tensor is by first unfolding the tensor into a matrix, and let the rank of the tensor be the rank the unfolded matrix. With this one can apply low-rank constraints by regularization, using the nuclear norm (which is a convex relaxation for low-rank regularization). In practice, this leads to a simple convex optimization that uses an SVD routine to solve the core part of the problem. This technique has been used recently for several problems (Balle and Mohri, 2012; Quattoni et al., 2014; Madhyastha et al., 2014, 2015; Primadhanty et al., 2015). There are 2^d ways to unfold a tensor of d modes. In our case, we have made the choice based on the application: we have grouped the preposition and modifier together. This choice has a clear computational advantage for the task: at prediction time, we can first project the prepositional phrase (which is fixed) to its low-dimensional representation, and then do the inner product with the projection of each head candidate. In general, one could try different unfoldings, or use multiple of them in a combination.

Another popular approach to low-rank tensor learning is directly optimizing over a low-rank decomposition of the tensor, such as the canonical polyadic or the Tucker forms (Lei et al., 2014; Fried et al., 2015; Yu et al., 2016). In the Tucker form, a tensor d modes has one projection matrix for each of the modes, where each projection matrix is a mapping from the original input vector space to a low-dimensional one, i.e. an embedding of the feature of the corresponding mode. One advantage of this approach is that there is no need to choose an unfolding. However, the optimization is non-convex.

6 Conclusion

We have described a simple PP attachment model based on tensor products of the word vectors in a PP attachment decision. We have established that the product of vectors improves over more simple compositions (based on sum or concatenation), while it remains computationally manageable due to the compact nature of word embeddings. In experiments on standard PP attachment datasets, our tensor models perform better than other methods using lexical information only, and are close in performance to methods using richer feature spaces. In out-of-domain tests we obtain improvements over state-of-the-art parsers. As our models only depend on word embeddings, this is a clear signal that word embeddings are appropriate representations to generalize to unseen structures.

By using low-rank constraints during learning we have observed small improvements over ℓ_2 regularization, but not drastic ones (compared to, for example, tensor compositions of sparse vectors, in which case low-rank constraints are generally much more beneficial). All in all, low-rank constraints are essential tools to control the capacity of tensor models. This framework is arguably more simple than neural compositions, because it avoids non-linearities and can be optimized with global routines like SVD. In our PP attachment experiments, we have obtained some gains in accuracy over the neural models by Belinkov et al. (2014) that use comparable representations. We have also obtain improvements over state-of-the-art dependency parsers.

In NLP, and in syntax in particular, there exist other paradigmatic lexical attachment ambiguities that, like PP attachment, can be framed within a particular scope of the dependency tree: adjectives, conjunctions, raising and control verbs, etc.. The tensor product we have presented can serve as a building block to define dependency parsing methods that make a central use of products of word embeddings.

References

Eneko Agirre, Timothy Baldwin, and David Martinez. 2008. Improving parsing and pp attachment performance with sense information. In *ACL*. pages 317–325.

Borja Balle and Mehryar Mohri. 2012. Spectral learning of general weighted automata via constrained matrix completion. *In Proceedings of Advances in Neural Information Processing Systems (NIPS)* .

Mohit Bansal, Kevin Gimpel, and Karen Livescu. 2014. Tailoring continuous word representations for dependency parsing. In *Proceedings of Association of Computational Linguistics(ACL) Short Papers*.

Yonatan Belinkov, Tao Lei, Regina Barzilay, and Amir Globerson. 2014. Exploring compositional architectures and word vector representations for prepositional phrase attachment. *Transactions of the Association for Computational Linguistics* 2:561–572.

Eugene Charniak, Don Blaheta, Niyu Ge, Keith Hall, John Hale, and Mark Johnson. 2000. BLLIP 1987-89 WSJ Corpus Release 1, LDC No. LDC2000T43. Linguistic Data Consortium.

Danqi Chen and Christopher Manning. 2014. A fast and accurate dependency parser using neural networks. In *Proceedings of the 2014 Conference on Empirical Methods in Natural Language Processing (EMNLP)*. Association for Computational Linguistics, Doha, Qatar, pages 740–750. http://www.aclweb.org/anthology/D14-1082.

Michael Collins and James Brooks. 1999. Prepositional phrase attachment through a backed-off model. In *Natural Language Processing Using Very Large Corpora*, Springer, pages 177–189.

John Duchi and Yoram Singer. 2009. Efficient online and batch learning using forward backward splitting. *Journal of Machine Learning Research* 10:2899–2934.

Chris Dyer, Miguel Ballesteros, Wang Ling, Austin Matthews, and Noah A. Smith. 2015. Transition-based dependency parsing with stack long short-term memory. In *Proceedings of the 53rd Annual Meeting of the Association for Computational Linguistics and the 7th International Joint Conference on Natural Language Processing (Volume 1: Long Papers)*. Association for Computational Linguistics, Beijing, China, pages 334–343. http://www.aclweb.org/anthology/P15-1033.

Daniel Fried, Tamara Polajnar, and Stephen Clark. 2015. Low-rank tensors for verbs in compositional distributional semantics. In *Short Papers of the 53rd Annual Meeting of the Association for Computational Linguistics (ACL 2015)*. pages 731–736.

Donald Hindle and Mats Rooth. 1993. Structural ambiguity and lexical relations. *Computational linguistics* 19(1):103–120.

Eric H Huang, Richard Socher, Christopher D Manning, and Andrew Y Ng. 2012. Improving word representations via global context and multiple word prototypes. In *Proceedings of the 50th Annual Meeting of the Association for Computational Linguistics: Long Papers-Volume 1*. Association for Computational Linguistics, pages 873–882.

Jonathan K Kummerfeld, David Hall, James R Curran, and Dan Klein. 2012. Parser showdown at the wall street corral: An empirical investigation of error types in parser output. In *Proceedings of the 2012 Joint Conference on Empirical Methods in Natural Language Processing and Computational Natural Language Learning*. Association for Computational Linguistics, pages 1048–1059.

Tao Lei, Yu Xin, Yuan Zhang, Regina Barzilay, and Tommi Jaakkola. 2014. Low-rank tensors for scoring dependency structures. In *Proceedings of the 52nd Annual Meeting of the Association for Computational Linguistics (Volume 1: Long Papers)*. Association for Computational Linguistics, Baltimore, Maryland, pages 1381–1391. http://www.aclweb.org/anthology/P14-1130.

Pranava Swaroop Madhyastha, Xavier Carreras, and Ariadna Quattoni. 2014. Learning task-specific bilexical embeddings. In *Proceedings of COLING 2014, the 25th International Conference on Computational Linguistics: Technical Papers*. Dublin City University and Association for Computational Linguistics, pages 161–171. http://aclweb.org/anthology/C14-1017.

Pranava Swaroop Madhyastha, Xavier Carreras, and Ariadna Quattoni. 2015. Tailoring word embeddings for bilexical predictions: An experimental comparison. *In International Conference on Learning Representations (Workshop Contribution)* .

Andre Martins, Miguel Almeida, and A. Noah Smith. 2013. Turning on the turbo: Fast third-order non-projective turbo parsers. In *Proceedings of the 51st Annual Meeting of the Association for Computational Linguistics (Volume 2: Short Papers)*. Association for Computational Linguistics, pages 617–622. http://aclweb.org/anthology/P13-2109.

Tomas Mikolov, Kai Chen, Greg Corrado, and Jeffrey Dean. 2013. Efficient estimation of word representations in vector space. *In Proceedings of International Conference on Learning Representations* .

Jeff Mitchell and Mirella Lapata. 2008. Vector-based models of semantic composition. In *Proceedings of the Annual Meeting of the Association for Computational Linguistics (Volume 2: Short Papers)*. pages 236–244.

Ndapandula Nakashole and Tom M Mitchell. 2015. A knowledge-intensive model for prepositional phrase attachment. In *Proceedings of the 53rd Annual Meeting of the Association for Computational Linguistics,(ACL)*. pages 365–375.

Marian Olteanu and Dan Moldovan. 2005. Pp-attachment disambiguation using large context. In *Proceedings of the Conference on Human Language Technology and Empirical Methods in Natural Language Processing*. Association for Computational Linguistics, pages 273–280.

Jeffrey Pennington, Richard Socher, and Christopher D. Manning. 2014. Glove: Global vectors for word representation. In *Empirical Methods in Natural Language Processing (EMNLP)*. pages 1532–1543. http://www.aclweb.org/anthology/D14-1162.

Slav Petrov and Ryan McDonald. 2012. Overview of the 2012 shared task on parsing the web. Notes of the First Workshop on Syntactic Analysis of Non-Canonical Language (SANCL).

Audi Primadhanty, Xavier Carreras, and Ariadna Quattoni. 2015. Low-rank regularization for sparse conjunctive feature spaces: An application to named entity classification. In *Proceedings of the 53rd Annual Meeting of the Association for Computational Linguistics and the 7th International Joint Conference on Natural Language Processing (Volume 1: Long Papers)*. Association for Computational Linguistics, Beijing, China, pages 126–135. http://www.aclweb.org/anthology/P15-1013.

Ariadna Quattoni, Borja Balle, Xavier Carreras, and Amir Globerson. 2014. Spectral regularization for max-margin sequence tagging. In Tony Jebara and Eric P. Xing, editors, *Proceedings of the 31st International Conference on Machine Learning (ICML-14)*. JMLR Workshop and Conference Proceedings, pages 1710–1718. http://jmlr.org/proceedings/papers/v32/quattoni14.pdf.

Adwait Ratnaparkhi, Jeff Reynar, and Salim Roukos. 1994. A maximum entropy model for prepositional phrase attachment. In *Proceedings of the workshop on Human Language Technology*. Association for Computational Linguistics, pages 250–255.

Djamé Seddah, Sandra Kübler, and Reut Tsarfaty. 2014. Introducing the spmrl 2014 shared task on parsing morphologically-rich languages. In *Proceedings of the First Joint Workshop on Statistical Parsing of Morphologically Rich Languages and Syntactic Analysis of Non-Canonical Languages*. Dublin City University, Dublin, Ireland, pages 103–109. http://www.aclweb.org/anthology/W14-6111.

Richard Socher, Eric H Huang, Jeffrey Pennin, Christopher D Manning, and Andrew Y Ng. 2011. Dynamic pooling and unfolding recursive autoencoders for paraphrase detection. In *In Proceedings of Advances in Neural Information Processing Systems*. pages 801–809.

Nathan Srebro, Jason Rennie, and Tommi S Jaakkola. 2004. Maximum-margin matrix factorization. In *In proceedings of Advances in Neural Information Processing Systems (NIPS)*. pages 1329–1336.

Jiri Stetina and Makoto Nagao. 1997. Corpus based pp attachment ambiguity resolution with a semantic dictionary. In *Proceedings of the fifth workshop on very large corpora*.

Joseph Turian, Lev Ratinov, and Yoshua Bengio. 2010. Word representations: A simple and general method for semi-supervised learning. In *Proceedings of the 48th Annual Meeting of the Association for Computational Linguistics*. Association for Computational Linguistics, Stroudsburg, PA, USA, ACL '10, pages 384–394. http://dl.acm.org/citation.cfm?id=1858681.1858721.

Mo Yu, Mark Dredze, Raman Arora, and Matthew R. Gormley. 2016. Embedding lexical features via low-rank tensors. In *Proceedings of the 2016 Conference of the North American Chapter of the Association for Computational Linguistics: Human Language Technologies*. Association for Computational Linguistics, San Diego, California, pages 1019–1029. http://www.aclweb.org/anthology/N16-1117.

Shaojun Zhao and Dekang Lin. 2004. A nearest-neighbor method for resolving pp-attachment ambiguity. In *Natural Language Processing–IJCNLP 2004*, Springer, pages 545–554.

L1-L2 Parallel Dependency Treebank as Learner Corpus

John Lee, Keying Li, Herman Leung
Department of Linguistics and Translation
City University of Hong Kong
jsylee@cityu.edu.hk, keyingli3-c@my.cityu.edu.hk, leung.hm@gmail.com

Abstract

This opinion paper proposes the use of parallel treebank as learner corpus. We show how an L1-L2 parallel treebank — i.e., parse trees of non-native sentences, aligned to the parse trees of their target hypotheses — can facilitate retrieval of sentences with specific learner errors. We argue for its benefits, in terms of corpus reuse and interoperability, over a conventional learner corpus annotated with error tags. As a proof of concept, we conduct a case study on word-order errors made by learners of Chinese as a foreign language. We report precision and recall in retrieving a range of word-order error categories from L1-L2 tree pairs annotated in the Universal Dependency framework.

1 Introduction

A parallel treebank consists of multiple treebanks with alignments at the sentence level, and often also at the phrase and word levels. Growing interest in parallel treebanks have yielded treebanks of many language combinations (Čmejrek et al., 2004; Megyesi et al., 2010; Sulger et al., 2013; Volk et al., 2017).

So far, there has been no reported attempt to build an L1-L2 parallel treebank — i.e., parse trees of sentences written by non-native speakers (henceforth, "L2 sentences"), aligned to parse trees of their target hypotheses (henceforth, "L1 sentences"). Figure 1 shows an example parse tree pair in such a treebank. The pair consists of the parse tree of a Chinese sentence written by a learner, and the parse tree of its corrected version, or "target hypothesis". Although a number of L2 treebanks have been built, they either do not provide explicit target hypotheses (Ragheb and Dick-

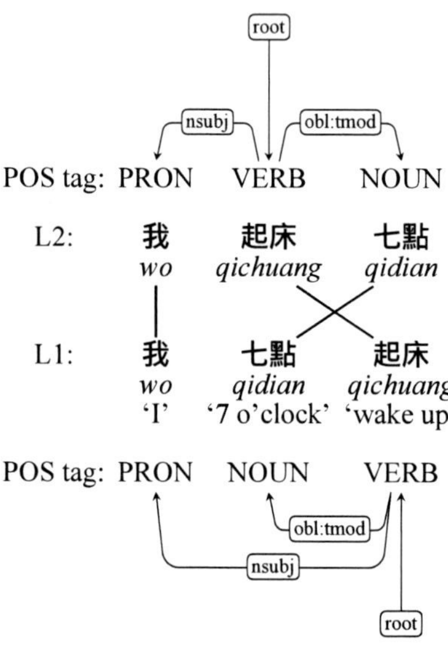

Figure 1: An example L1-L2 tree pair, including word alignments between the learner sentence ("L2") and its target hypothesis ("L1"), and the parse trees of the two sentences, annotated in Universal Dependencies for Chinese (Leung et al., 2016; Lee et al., 2017).

inson, 2014; Nagata and Sakaguchi, 2016), or have not yet provided parse trees for the target hypotheses (Berzak et al., 2016).

Parallel L1-L2 treebanks can be expected to serve a number of research agendas. First, they would support quantitative studies in Contrastive Interlanguage Analysis (CIA) (Granger, 2015) and Error Analysis (EA). For CIA, they would enable comparisons between native and interlanguages not only on the lexical level but also on the syntactic level. For EA, parallel parse trees would give more fine-grained characterization of the syntactic environment in which learner errors occur, which can inform the design of language teaching peda-

Proceedings of the 15th International Conference on Parsing Technologies, pages 44–49,
Pisa, Italy; September 20–22, 2017. ©2017 Association for Computational Linguistics

gogy. Further, just as parallel treebanks can help train machine translation (MT) systems (Čmejrek et al., 2004; Sennrich, 2015), L1-L2 treebanks can supply sentence pairs to train systems for automatic grammatical error correction (GEC). Indeed, some GEC systems obtained state-of-the-art results by casting the task as an MT problem (Rozovskaya and Roth, 2016; Junczys-Dowmunt and Grundkiewicz, 2014).

In this opinion paper, we focus on demonstrating how L1-L2 parallel treebanks can benefit learner language analysis. In the next section, we argue that these treebanks can better facilitate re-use and interoperability among learner corpora, because they provide a more precise and flexible encoding of learner errors. As a proof of concept, Section 3 presents a case study on identifying different word-order errors in Chinese L1-L2 parallel trees. Finally, Section 4 concludes.

2 Learner corpora and L1-L2 parallel treebanks

A major function of a learner corpus is to facilitate retrieval of sentences with specific errors. We first discuss the limitations of the use of error tags (Section 2.1), and then propose tree search in an L1-L2 parallel treebank as an alternative approach (Section 2.2).

2.1 Error tags

Errors in a learner sentence are commonly marked with error tags. Each tag labels a problematic text span with an error category, and often also provides a corrected version of the text span (Izumi et al., 2005; Zhang, 2009; Yannakoudakis et al., 2011; Dahlmeier et al., 2013). For example, the Cambridge Learner Corpus uses XML tags to mark error categories (Nicholls, 2003), and supplements the original text with a vertical bar and the target hypothesis:

He <MV> | is </MV> happy.

The annotation above indicates that the learner sentence "He happy" lacks the verb "is", and categorizes this error as "missing verb" (MV). Despite their widespread usage, however, error tags alone do not optimize corpus re-use and interoperability.

2.1.1 Corpus re-use

A major limitation of the error tagging approach is that learner errors must be pre-categorized. It is difficult, or perhaps impossible, to develop a robust and general-purpose error typology that covers "all" possible types at a suitable level of granularity. Unless one can foresee research questions in the future, any tagset is by definition limited in error coverage and may not be easily reused.

As a concrete example, consider the "incomplete sentence" error in English. A typical definition of this error is a sentence without subject or finite verb, or a stand-alone subordinate clause (Bram, 1995). The Cambridge Learner Corpus does not enable automatic search for sentences with this error, however; its closest error category, MV ("missing verb"), also covers sentences that are not incomplete, for instance those that are missing modal verbs.

As another example, consider word-order errors in Chinese, which Jiang (2009) classified into a number of categories. It is impossible to directly search for sentences with these error categories in current Chinese learner corpora. The widely used HSK Dynamic Composition Corpus (Zhang, 2009) puts all word-order errors in a single category, CJX. The Test of Chinese as a Foreign Language Learner Corpus (Lee et al., 2016a), which was used in the most recent shared task on Chinese Grammatical Error Diagnosis (Lee et al., 2016b), annotates the POS involved in word-order errors but does not provide more fine-grained distinctions as in Jiang (2009).

2.1.2 Corpus interoperability

Since existing error tagsets vary widely in granularity, it is difficult to combine information from multiple learner corpora. To cite but a few examples, NUCLE (Dahlmeier et al., 2013) uses a tagset with 27 error categories; the NICT Japanese Learner English Corpus has 46 tags (Izumi et al., 2005); while different combinations in the Cambridge Learner Corpus tagset can recognize up to 80 types of different errors (Nicholls, 2003).

In general, there is no clear mapping between these error tagsets. Returning to the incomplete sentence error as example, the closest category in NUCLE is "sentence fragment" (SFrag). However, it applies not only to the kinds of incomplete sentences described by Bram (1995), but also more broadly to complete sentences that suffer from stylistic issues, or those that should be merged with their neighbors. As such, SFrag only partially overlaps with the MV category in the Cambridge Learner Corpus.

2.2 Tree query for learner error retrieval

In view of the limitations of error tags described above, we propose the use of L1-L2 parallel treebank for learner error retrieval. A search query on such a treebank, consisting of a pair of parse tree patterns with alignments (Table 1), can be viewed as a dynamically defined error category.

The idea of leveraging linguistic annotations to search for learner errors is not new. As noted by Reznicek et al. (2013), when both learner sentences and target hypotheses are POS-tagged and word-aligned, a search query with constraints on POS and word positions can effectively express an error category. This approach is becoming more widely applicable, as more learner corpora are enriched with POS annotation (Lüdeling et al., 2008; Díaz-Negrillo et al., 2010) and enhanced alignments (Felice et al., 2016).

Many learner errors, however, cannot be adequately specified with POS alone. Take subject-verb agreement as an example. It does not suffice to search for two aligned verbs with different tags (e.g., VB and VBZ), since the change in conjugation may be a result of other errors (e.g., noun number). The tree query in Table 1(a) provides a more precise and transparent definition of the error. It requires the aligned verbs in both the L1 and L2 sentences to have a singular noun (NN) as subject. Hence, it specifically targets the subject-verb agreement error where the learner mistakes the root form of the verb for the third-person singular present tense. Similarly, to search for Chinese word-order errors involving time expressions, the tree query in Table 1(b) requires a specific dependency relation between the aligned verbs and nouns. This requirement helps exclude other errors that exhibit similar POS patterns, for example violations of the SVO word order.

This proposed approach promotes both corpus re-use and interoperability. Free from a fixed error typology, the user may interrogate the corpus with any suitable tree query, at an arbitrary level of granularity; the learner corpus is thus re-usable to the extent that the desired error type can be defined with POS tags and dependency relations. In terms of interoperability, mappings between error tagsets are no longer necessary; instead, this approach requires mappings between POS tagsets and dependency relations. This is admittedly still a considerable problem, but one that is arguably easier to solve, especially with the emergence of

(a) Subject-verb agreement error	(b) Time expression word-order error
L2: NN ... VB L1: NN ... VBZ (nsubj)	L2: VERB ... NOUN L1: NOUN ... VERB (obl:tmod)

Table 1: Tree queries for (a) subject-verb agreement in English (in Stanford Dependencies); and (b) time expression word-order errors in Chinese (in Universal Dependencies).

Error type	Freq	P	R
Time Expressions	21.1%	0.92	0.92
Modifiers + V	15.8%	0.50	0.50
Action Series	11.4%	0.65	0.85
Locative Expressions	11.4%	0.91	0.77
Subsidiary Relations	8.8%	1.00	0.80
Beneficiary	7.9%	1.00	0.56
Modifiers + N	7.0%	0.89	1.0
DE position	7.0%	1.00	0.38
Topic-comment	6.1%	0.83	0.71
Question	3.5%	1.00	0.50

Table 2: Precision (P) and recall (R) of the manually crafted tree queries in retrieving various error types in the test set. See Jiang (2009) for a description of the error types.

international standards such as Universal Dependencies (Nivre et al., 2016).

3 Case study

As a proof of concept, we conducted a case study on word-order errors, a frequent error in learner Chinese (Lee et al., 2016a), and measured the extent to which the proposed approach succeeded in retrieving sentences with specific error categories.

3.1 Set-up

At least three taxonomies have been proposed for Chinese word-order errors, by Yu (1986), Ko (1997), and Jiang (2009), respectively. We selected the one by Jiang, the most fine-grained of the three, with 27 categories grouped under 9 principles. This taxonomy has been applied on a dataset of 408 sentences, written by students at various proficiency levels, labelled as levels 1 (least proficient) through 3 (most proficient). We

(a) Modifiers + V (Adverb + V)	
L2: 我去第一次中國… *wo qu*/VERB *diyici*/NOUN *zhongguo* 'I' 'go' 'first time' 'China' L1: 我第一次去中國… *wo diyici*/NOUN *qu*/VERB *zhongguo* 'I' 'first time' 'go' 'China' "I go for the first time to China …"	
(b) Action Series (LE position)	
L2: 我們去了參觀故宮 *women qu*/VERB *le canguan*/VERB *gugong* 'we' 'go' LE 'visit' 'Forbidden City' L1: 我們去參觀了故宮 *women qu*/VERB *canguan*/VERB *le gugong* 'we' 'go' 'visit' LE 'Forbidden City' "We went to visit the Forbidden City"	
(c) Locative Expressions (Location + V)	
L2: 你做什麼在這裡 *ni zuo*/VERB *shenme zai*/ADP *zheli*/NOUN 'you' 'do' 'what' 'at' 'here' L1: 你在這裡做什麼 *ni zai*/ADP *zheli*/NOUN *zuo*/VERB *shenme* 'you' 'at' 'here' 'do' 'what' "What are you doing here?"	

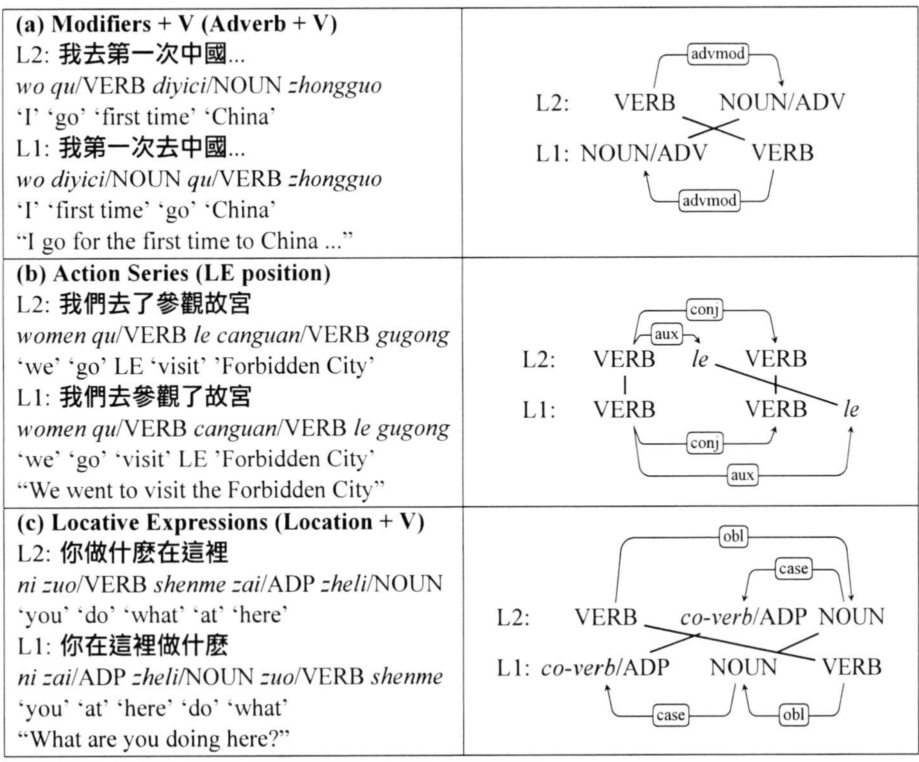

Table 3: Examples of L1-L2 tree queries used in the case study (Section 3.1).

focused on the first three principles, namely the "Greenberg Pattern Principle", which prescribes the canonical word order in Chinese; the "Principle of Modifier Before Head"; and "Temporal Sequence".[1] These are the largest and more syntax-oriented principles, covering a majority of the errors attested in the dataset.

As development set, we used 58 sentence pairs from Level 1. We manually annotated the learner sentences with the Universal Dependencies (UD) scheme for Learner Chinese (Lee et al., 2017), and the target hypotheses with the UD scheme for standard Chinese (Leung et al., 2016); we then performed word alignment between each sentence pair. Based on the development set and on error definitions in Jiang (2009), we manually crafted 30 parse tree patterns for 10 error categories under the three principles mentioned above. Table 3 shows some example patterns.

As test set, we drew 114 sentences from Levels 2 and 3, and manually performed similar dependency annotation and word alignment. Compared with those in the development set, these sentences are linguistically more complex and likely contain more diverse errors, thus ensuring that the accuracy of the proposed approach is not overestimated.

3.2 Results

We applied the manually crafted tree queries on the test set, and measured their accuracy in retrieving and distinguishing between sentences with different kinds of word-order errors. As shown in Table 2, the highest precision was achieved for the categories "Question", "DE position", "Beneficiary" and "Subsidiary Relations" (all at 100%), since their parse structures are most distinct and predictable. Precision was lowest for "Modifiers + V" (50%). Because of unclear meaning in the L2 sentences, their parse trees are often prone to matching similar patterns from other error categories, such as "Time Expressions". In certain cases, the L2 sentence contains multiple errors but the gold annotation marks only one.

Recall was highest for "Modifiers + N" (100%) and "Time Expressions" (92%), and lowest for

---

[1] The interested reader is referred to Jiang (2009) for details about these principles.

"DE position" (38%). Error analysis revealed that while the L1 parse patterns were mostly adequate, the L2 parse patterns were sometimes not sufficiently general to cover the variety of learner usage that could produce unexpected parse tree structures.

4 Conclusion

This opinion paper advocates the use of L1-L2 parallel treebank as learner corpus. We have argued that such a treebank can better facilitate corpus re-use and interoperability than a fixed error tagset. We have shown the feasibility of the proposed approach in a case study, by measuring the accuracy of tree queries in distinguishing between fine-grained categories of word-order errors in learner Chinese sentences. It is hoped that this paper will spur development of L1-L2 parallel treebanks. They in turn should lead to more accurate parsers for learner text, eventually enabling the proposed approach to be fully automated.

Acknowledgments

This work was partially supported by a Strategic Research Grant (Project no. 7004494) from City University of Hong Kong.

References

Yevgeni Berzak, Jessica Kenney, Carolyn Spadine, Jing Xian Wang, Lucia Lam, Keiko Sophie Mori, Sebastian Garza, and Boris Katz. 2016. Universal Dependencies for Learner English. In *Proc. ACL*.

Barli Bram. 1995. *Write Well, Improving Writing Skills*. Kanisius.

Daniel Dahlmeier, Hwee Tou Ng, and Siew Mei Wu. 2013. Building a Large Annotated Corpus of Learner English: The NUS Corpus of Learner English. In *Proc. 8th Workshop on Innovative Use of NLP for Building Educational Applications*.

Ana Díaz-Negrillo, Detmar Meurers, Salvador Valera, and Holger Wunsch. 2010. Towards Interlanguage POS Annotation for Effective Learner Corpora in SLA and FLT. *Language Forum* 36(1-2):139–154.

Mariano Felice, Christopher Bryant, and Ted Briscoe. 2016. Automatic Extraction of Learner Errors in ESL Sentences Using Linguistically Enhanced Alignments. In *Proc. COLING*.

Sylviane Granger. 2015. Contrastive Interlanguage Analysis: A Reappraisal. *International Journal of Learner Corpus Research* 1(1):7–24.

Emi Izumi, Kiyotaka Uchimoto, and Hitoshi Isahara. 2005. Error Annotation for Corpus of Japanese Learner English. In *Proc. 6th International Workshop on Linguistically Interpreted Corpora*.

Wenying Jiang. 2009. Acquisition of Word Order in Chinese as a Foreign Language. In Peter Jordens, editor, *Studies on Language Acqusition 38*. De Gruyter Mouton.

M. Junczys-Dowmunt and R. Grundkiewicz. 2014. The AMU system in the CoNLL-2014 shared task: grammatical error correction by data-intensive and feature-rich statistical machine translation. In *Proc. 18th Conference on Computational Natural Language Learning: Shared Task*.

T. J. Ko. 1997. *Acquisition of Word Order in Chinese as a Foreign Language*. PhD Dissertation, Rutgers University.

John Lee, Herman Leung, and Keying Li. 2017. Towards Universal Dependencies for Learner Chinese. In *Proc. Workshop on Universal Dependencies*.

Lung-Hao Lee, Li-Ping Chang, and Yuen-Hsien Tseng. 2016a. Developing Learner Corpus Annotation for Chinese Grammatical Errors. In *Proc. International Conference on Asian Language Processing (IALP)*.

Lung-Hao Lee, Gaoqi Rao, Liang-Chih Yu, Endong Xun, Baolin Zhang, and Li-Ping Chang. 2016b. Overview of NLP-TEA 2016 Shared Task for Chinese Grammatical Error Diagnosis. In *Proc. 3rd Workshop on Natural Language Processing Techniques for Educational Applications*.

Herman Leung, Rafaël Poiret, Tak sum Wong, Xinying Chen, Kim Gerdes, and John Lee. 2016. Developing Universal Dependencies for Mandarin Chinese. In *Proc. Workshop on Asian Language Resources*.

Anke Lüdeling, Seanna Doolittle, Hagen Hirschmann, Karin Schmidt, and Maik Walter. 2008. Das lernerkorpus falko. *Deutsch als Fremdsprache* 2:67–73.

Beáta Megyesi, Bengt Dahlqvist, Éva Á. Csató, and Joakim Nivre. 2010. The English-Swedish-Turkish Parallel Treebank. In *Proc. Seventh International Conference on Language Resources and Evaluation (LREC)*. pages 55–60.

Ryo Nagata and Keisuke Sakaguchi. 2016. Phrase Structure Annotation and Parsing for Learner English. In *Proc. ACL*.

Diane Nicholls. 2003. The Cambridge Learner Corpus - error coding and analysis for lexicography and ELT. In *Proc. Computational Linguistics Conference*.

Joakim Nivre, Marie-Catherine de Marneffe, Filip Ginter, Yoav Goldberg, Jan Hajic, Christopher D. Manning, Ryan McDonald, Slav Petrov, Sampo Pyysalo, Natalia Silveira, Reut Tsarfaty, and Daniel Zeman. 2016. Universal Dependencies v1: A Multilingual Treebank Collection. In *Proc. LREC*.

Marwa Ragheb and Markus Dickinson. 2014. Developing a Corpus of Syntactically-Annotated Learner Language for English. In *Proc. 13th International Workshop on Treebanks and Linguistic Theories (TLT)*.

Marc Reznicek, Anke Lüdeling, and Hagen Hirschmann. 2013. Competing Target Hypotheses in the Falko Corpus: A Flexible Multi-Layer Corpus Architecture. In Ana Díaz-Negrillo, editor, *Automatic Treatment and Analysis of Learner Corpus Data*. John Benjamins, Amsterdam, pages 101–123.

Alla Rozovskaya and Dan Roth. 2016. Grammatical Error Correction: Machine Translation and Classifiers. In *Proc. ACL*.

Rico Sennrich. 2015. Modelling and Optimizing on Syntactic N-Grams for Statistical Machine Translation. *Transactions of the Association for Computational Linguistics* 3:169–182.

Sebastian Sulger, Miriam Butt, Tracy Holloway King, Paul Meurer, Tibor Laczkó, György Rákosi, Cheikh Bamba Dione, Helge Dyvik, Victoria Rosén, Koenraad De Smedt, Agnieszka Patejuk, Özlem Cetinoğlu, I Wayan Arka, and Meladel Mistica. 2013. ParGramBank: The ParGram Parallel Treebank. In *Proc. ACL*.

Martin Čmejrek, Jan Cuřín, Jiří Havelka, Jan Hajič, and Vladislav Kuboň. 2004. Prague Czech-English Dependency Treebank Syntactically Annotated Resources for Machine Translation. In *Proc. EAMT*.

Martin Volk, Torsten Marek, and Yvonne Samuelsson. 2017. Building and Querying Parallel Treebanks. In Silvia Hansen-Schirra, Stella Neumann, and Oliver Čulo, editors, *Annotation, Exploitation and Evaluation of Parallel Corpora*. Language Science Press, Berlin, pages 7–30.

Helen Yannakoudakis, Ted Briscoe, and Ben Medlock. 2011. A New Dataset and Method for Automatically Grading ESOL Texts. In *Proc. ACL*.

Shuhuai Yu. 1986. Word Order and Topic Prominence in the Interlanguage of an Australian Learner of Chinese. *Australian Review of Applied Linguistics* 9:83–91.

Baolin Zhang. 2009. The Characteristics and Functions of the HSK Dynamic Composition Corpus. *International Chinese Language Education* 4(11).

Splitting Complex English Sentences

John Lee
Department of Linguistics and Translation
City University of Hong Kong
jsylee@cityu.edu.hk

J. Buddhika K. Pathirage Don[*]
Hong Kong Applied Science
and Technology Research Institute
bpathiragedon@astri.org

Abstract

This paper applies parsing technology to the task of syntactic simplification of English sentences, focusing on the identification of text spans that can be removed from a complex sentence. We report the most comprehensive evaluation to-date on this task, using a dataset of sentences that exhibit simplification based on coordination, subordination, punctuation/parataxis, adjectival clauses, participial phrases, and appositive phrases. We train a decision tree with features derived from text span length, POS tags and dependency relations, and show that it significantly outperforms a parser-only baseline.

1 Introduction

The task of text simplification aims to rewrite a sentence so as to reduce its complexity, while preserving its meaning and grammaticality. The rewriting may involve various aspects, including lexical simplification, syntactic simplification, content deletion, and content insertion for clarification. This paper focuses on syntactic simplification and, specifically, on splitting a complex sentence into two simpler sentences.[1] Consider the input sentence S in Table 1, a complex sentence containing a participial phrase, "carrying numerous books". After removing this phrase from S, the system generates S_2 from the phrase by turning the participle "carrying" into the finite form "was carrying", and by generating the pronoun "he" as the subject.

A number of systems can already perform this task (Chandrasekar et al., 1996; Siddharthan,

S	The man, carrying numerous books, entered the room.
S_1	The man entered the room.
S_2	He was carrying numerous books.

Table 1: Example input (S) and output sentences (S_1, S_2) for the task of syntactic simplification.

2002a; Inui et al., 2003; Belder and Moens, 2010; Bott et al., 2012; Siddharthan and Angrosh, 2014; Saggion et al., 2015). While some systems have undergone task-based evaluations, such as reading comprehension (Angrosh et al., 2014), most have adopted holistic assessment, which commonly includes human ratings on the grammaticality, fluency, meaning preservation, and simplicity of the system output (Štajner et al., 2016). These ratings are indeed helpful in indicating the overall quality of a system; however, the need for human intervention restricts the scale of the evaluations, and makes direct comparisons difficult. Other systems have been evaluated with automatic metrics, such as BLEU and readability metrics (Aluisio et al., 2010; Narayan and Gardent, 2014), which overcome the limitations of human ratings, but do not reveal what aspects of the simplification process caused the most difficulties.

The contribution of this paper is two-fold. First, it presents the first publicly available dataset that facilitates detailed, automatic evaluation on syntactic simplification. Second, we report the results of a decision tree approach that incorporates parse features, giving a detailed analysis on its performance for various constructs.

2 Previous Work

The phrase-based and syntax-based machine translation approaches have been used in many text simplification systems (Vickrey and Koller,

---

[*]The second author completed this work as a Postdoctoral Fellow at City University of Hong Kong.

[1]The simplified sentences can in turn be split iteratively.

Proceedings of the 15th International Conference on Parsing Technologies, pages 50–55,
Pisa, Italy; September 20–22, 2017. ©2017 Association for Computational Linguistics

Construct	Complex sentence example	Freq.
Coordination	I ate fish *and he drank wine.*	463
	Peter came *and saw.*	
Adjectival clause	Peter ate an apple, *which was green.*	119
Participial phrase	Peter, *running fast,* arrived.	90
Appositive phrase	Peter, *my friend,* ate the apple.	69
Subordination	*After Peter came,* I left.	158
	After calling Peter, I left.	
Punctuation/Parataxis	I ate fish; *he drank wine.*	155
	Peter *(twenty years old)* is a linguistics major.	
Prepositional phrase	The final was played at Manchester *on 14 May 2008.*	16

Table 2: Distribution of syntactic constructs in the test set (Section 3). The complex sentence can be split into two simpler sentences by (i) removing the text span (italicized); and (ii) transforming the text span into a new sentence with the referent (underlined). This paper focuses on step (i).

2008; Zhu et al., 2010; Coster and Kauchak, 2011; Wubben et al., 2012). While these approaches are effective for lexical substitution and deletion, they are less so for sentence splitting, sentence reordering, and morphological changes (Bott et al., 2012; Siddharthan, 2014).

Most syntactic simplification systems start by analyzing the input sentence via a parse tree, or a deep semantic representation (Narayan and Gardent, 2014). For identifying the referent NP (clause attachment), accuracy can reach 95%; for identifying clause boundary, accuracy is at 97% when there is punctuation, and 80% in general (Siddharthan, 2002b). Noun post-modifiers can be extracted at an F-measure of 92% (Dornescu et al., 2014; Stanovsky and Dagan, 2016).

Given a syntactic analysis of the input sentence, the system then applies manually written transformation rules (Siddharthan, 2002a; Belder and Moens, 2010; Bott et al., 2012; Siddharthan and Angrosh, 2014; Saggion et al., 2015). These rules identify specific constructs in a parse tree, such as the participial phrase in S in Table 1; they then determine whether the construct should be split, and if so, generate an independent sentence from it. For example, Aluísio et al. (2008) used a set of transformation rules to treat 22 syntactic constructs. Siddharthan (2011) used 63 rules, which handle coordination of both verb phrases and full clauses, subordination, apposition and relative clauses, as well as conversion of passive voice to active voice. Siddharthan and Angorsh (2014) used 26 hand-crafted rules for apposition, relative clauses and combinations of the two; as well as 85 rules handle subordination and coordination.

3   Data

Many evaluation datasets are available for lexical simplification (Paetzold and Specia, 2016), but there is not yet any that enables automatic evaluation on syntactic simplification systems. We created an annotated dataset for this purpose, based on the 167,689 pairs of "normal" and simplified sentences from Wikipedia and Simple Wikipedia aligned by Kauchak (2013). While a majority of these pairs are one-to-one alignments, 23,715 of them are one-to-two alignments.[2] These aligned sentences, in their raw form, can serve as triplets of S, S_1 and S_2 (Table 1).

However, as pointed out by Xu et al. (2015), Wikipedia and Simple Wikipedia contain rather noisy data; indeed, upon manual inspection, not all triplets are good examples for syntactic simplification. These fall into two cases. In the first case, significant content from S is deleted and appear neither in S_1 nor S_2; these triplets provide examples of content deletion rather than splitting. In the second case, S_2 (or S_1) consists mostly of new content. In some instances, S_1 (or S_2) is so similar to S that no real splitting occurs. In others, the new content put into doubt whether the splitting of S was motivated by syntactic complexity alone, or were influenced by the new content. To reduce the noise, we employed human annotation to create the test set, and an automatic procedure to clean up the training set.

---

[2]There is no one-to-n alignments for $n > 2$.

```
<S><ref>The man</ref> <split type="participial">, carrying numerous
books,</split> entered the room.</S>
<S1><ref1>The man</ref1> entered the room.</S1>
<S2><ref2>He</ref2> was carrying numerous books.</S2>
```

Table 3: Each triplet in our corpus contains a complex sentence (S) and the two shorter sentences (S_1, S_2) into which it was re-written.

3.1 Test set

An annotator marked up 1,070 triplets of (S, S_1, S_2) in the format shown in Table 3, with the following items:[3]

Removed text span The <split> element encloses the text span that is removed from S. This text span usually, though not necessarily, appears in S_1 or S_2.

Construct Type The `type` attribute inside the <split> element indicates the construct type of the removed text span. Table 2 gives a list of the construct types and their distribution.

Re-ordering If the removed text span forms the basis of S_1 (S_2), the `dest` attribute inside the <split> element takes the value `S1` (`S2`). This attribute indicates whether sentence re-ordering has occurred.

Referent There are often referring expressions in S_1 and S_2 for an entity in S. For example, in Table 1, the words "the man" and "he" in S_1 and S_2 refer to "the man" in S. These referring expressions are marked as <ref1> and <ref2>, and the entity in S is marked as <ref>.

3.2 Training set

The rest of the triplets form our training instances. To filter out instances that are not genuine splits (see above) and to determine the value of `dest`, we require at least 75% of the words in either S_1 or S_2 to appear in S. To determine the value of `type`, we ran the baseline system (Section 4), which is unsupervised and has relatively high recall, on S. Thus, the training set has all the annotations in Table 3, except for <ref>, <ref1> and <ref2>.

---

[3]The annotations on re-ordering and referent were not used in this study, but will be useful for evaluation on sentence re-generation.

4 Approach

Baseline system. We manually developed tree patterns, in the form of dependency relations and POS tags, to identify text spans that should be removed from a complex sentence (Table 4). These patterns are designed to yield high recall but lower precision. The system parses the input sentence with the Stanford parser (Manning et al., 2014), and then performs breadth-first search on the dependency tree for these patterns, returning the first match it finds. This algorithm removes at most one text span from each complex sentence; this assumption is consistent with the material in our dataset, which was derived from one-to-two sentence alignments.

Proposed system. Even if one of the constructs in Table 2 is present in a complex sentence, it may not be appropriate or worthwhile to remove it. To refine the tree patterns developed for the baseline system, we trained a decision tree with the scikit-learn package. For each word in the sentence, the decision tree considers the features listed in Table 5. If the decision tree predicts a split, the text span headed by the word is removed from the sentence.

5 Evaluation

We evaluate our system's performance at identifying a text span, if any, in a complex sentence that should be removed to form an independent sentence.

As expected, the baseline system achieved relatively high recall (0.88) but low precision (0.34), since it always tries to split a text span that matches any of the tree patterns in Table 4. The decision tree was able to substantially increase precision (0.63) by learning some useful rules, at the expense of lower recall (0.72).

Some rules that substantially contributed to the performance gain are as follows. Consider the rule that a comma should separate the word from its parent when the dependency relation is `xcomp`. It was able to block the system from mistakenly tak-

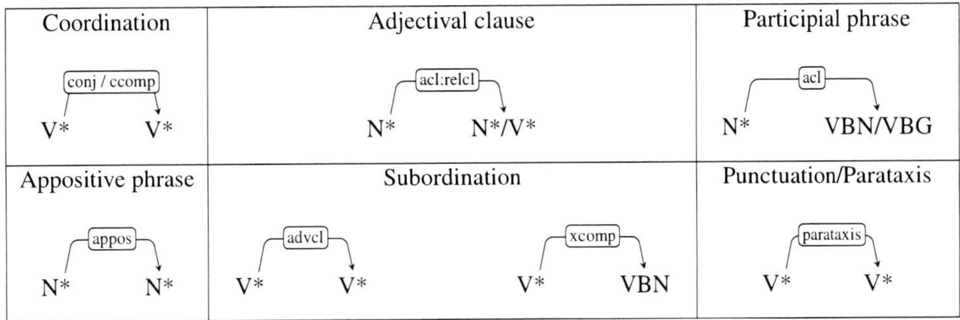

Table 4: Manually crafted tree patterns, written in Stanford dependencies (Manning et al., 2014), that are used in the baseline system. If the pattern exists in S, the text span headed by the child word (e.g., VBN/VBG for participial phrases) is to be removed from S.

Feature	Description
POS	Tag is JJ, N*, VBN, VBG, or V*?
Parent POS	Tag of parent word is JJ, N*, VBN, VBG, or V*?
Root	Parent word is root?
Sibling POS	Tag of a sibling word is IN, TO, WP, WRB, WP$, or WDT?
Child POS	Tag of child word is IN, TO, WP, WRB, WP$, or WDT?
Comma	There is a comma between the word and its parent word?
Det	Subject of S is tagged DT?
Length	Number of words in text span

Table 5: Features used by the decision tree.

System →	Baseline	Proposed
↓ Construct	P/R/F	P/R/F
Coordination	0.31/0.84/0.45	0.61/0.80/0.69
Adjectival clause	0.29/0.97/0.45	0.59/0.79/0.68
Participial phrase	0.33/0.90/0.48	0.56/0.58/0.57
Appositive phrase	0.21/0.91/0.34	0.36/0.56/0.44
Subordination	0.39/0.84/0.53	0.70/0.74/0.72
Punctuation/ Parataxis	0.78/0.99/0.87	0.92/0.95/0.93
Overall	0.34/0.88/0.49	**0.63/0.72/0.67**

Table 6: Precision, recall and F-measure for identifying the text span to be removed from S.

ing the phrase "conducting at Montreux ..." out of the sentence "He began conducting at Montreux ...". Another useful rule was that the parent word in the `conj` relation must be root; otherwise, the structure is likely coordinated NPs rather than coordinated clauses. Further, when the modifier is tagged as TO (i.e., an infinitive), or when the subject of the sentence is a determiner (e.g., "this", "that"), no splitting should be done. Finally, shorter text spans are less likely to be split up.

Among the different constructs, the proposed system performed best for punctuation/parataxis, with precision at 0.92 and recall at 0.95. This construct is not only clearly marked, but also more consistently split up. The most challenging construct turned out to be appositive phrases, with precision at 0.36 and recall at 0.56. Many of the errors trickled down from inaccurate analysis by the automatic parser, especially mistakes in relative clause attachment and clause boundary identification (Siddharthan and Angrosh, 2014).

The precision figures can be viewed as lower bounds. In post-hoc analysis, we found that many of the proposed text spans by our system can be acceptable, but they were not deemed necessary to be split up by the editors of Simple Wikipedia. Ultimately, the decision to split a complex sentence should be made in consideration of the reader's proficiency, but our current dataset does not support the modelling of this factor.

6 Conclusions and Future Work

We have presented a study on syntactic simplification, focusing on the identification of text spans that should be removed from a complex sentence.

We trained a decision tree to learn to recognize these text spans, using dependencies, POS tags and text span length as features. Experimental results showed that it outperformed a parser-only baseline.

We have reported the most detailed evaluation to-date on this task. This evaluation was made possible with a new dataset, derived from Wikipedia and Simple Wikipedia, that covers co-ordinated clauses, subordinated clauses, punctuation/parataxis, adjectival clauses, participial clauses, appositive phrases, and prepositional phrases.

In future work, we plan to investigate the next steps in syntactic simplification, i.e., sentence re-ordering and the generation of referring expressions. Our dataset, which traces sentence order and annotates referring expressions, is well suited for automatic evaluation for these tasks.

Acknowledgments

This work was partially supported by the Innovation and Technology Fund (Ref: ITS/132/15) of the Innovation and Technology Commission, the Government of the Hong Kong Special Administrative Region.

References

Sandra Aluisio, Lucia Specia, Caroline Gasperin, and Carolina Scarton. 2010. Readability Assessment for Text Simplification. In *Proc. 5th Workshop on Innovative Use of NLP for Building Educational Applications*. pages 1–9.

Sandra Aluisio, Lucia Specia, T. A. Pardo, E. G. Maziero, and R. P. Fortes. 2008. Towards Brazilian Portuguese Automatic Text Simplification Systems. In *Proc. 8th ACM Symposium on Document Engineering*.

M. A. Angrosh, Tadashi Nomoto, and Advaith Siddharthan. 2014. Lexico-syntactic text simplification and compression with typed dependencies. In *Proc. COLING*.

J. De Belder and M. F. Moens. 2010. Text Simplification for Children. In *Proc. SIGIR Workshop on Accessible Search Systems*.

Stefan Bott, Horacio Saggion, and David Figueroa. 2012. A Hybrid System for Spanish Text Simplification. In *Proc. Workshop on Speech and Language Processing for Assistive Technologies*.

R. Chandrasekar, Christine Doran, and B. Srinivas. 1996. Motivations and Methods for Text Simplification. In *Proc. COLING*.

William Coster and David Kauchak. 2011. Learning to Simplify Sentences using Wikipedia. In *Proc. Workshop on Monolingual Text-to-Text Generation*.

Iustin Dornescu, Richard Evans, and Constantin Orăsan. 2014. Relative Clause Extraction for Syntactic Simplification. In *Proc. Workshop on Automatic Text Simplification: Methods and Applications in the Multilingual Society*. Dublin, Ireland.

Kentaro Inui, Atsushi Fujita, Tetsuro Takahashi, Ryu Iida, and Tomoya Iwakura. 2003. Text Simplification for Reading Assistance: A Project Note. In *Proc. 2nd International Workshop on Paraphrasing*.

David Kauchak. 2013. Improving Text Simplification Language Modeling using Unsimplified Text Data. In *Proc. ACL*.

Christopher D. Manning, Mihai Surdeanu, John Bauer, Jenny Finkel, Steven J. Bethard, and David Mc-Closky. 2014. The Stanford CoreNLP Natural Language Processing Toolkit. In *Proc. ACL System Demonstrations*. pages 55–60.

Shashi Narayan and Claire Gardent. 2014. Hybrid Simplification using Deep Semantics and Machine Translation. In *Proc. ACL*.

Gustavo H. Paetzold and Lucia Specia. 2016. Benchmarking Lexical Simplification Systems. In *Proc. LREC*.

Horacio Saggion, Sanja Štajner, Stefan Bott, Simon Mille, Luz Rello, and Biljana Drndarevic. 2015. Making It Simplext: Implementation and Evaluation of a Text Simplification System for Spanish. *ACM Transactions on Accessible Computing (TACCESS)* 6(4).

Advaith Siddharthan. 2002a. An Architecture for a Text Simplification System. In *Proc. Language Engineering Conference (LEC)*.

Advaith Siddharthan. 2002b. Resolving attachment and clause boundary ambiguities for simplifying relative clause constructs. In *Proc. Student Workshop, ACL*.

Advaith Siddharthan. 2011. Text Simplification using Typed Dependencies: A Comparison of the Robustness of Different Generation Strategies. In *Proc. 13th European Workshop on Natural Language Generation*.

Advaith Siddharthan. 2014. A Survey of Research on Text Simplification. *International Journal of Applied Linguistics* 165(2):259–298.

Advaith Siddharthan and M. A. Angrosh. 2014. Hybrid Text Simplification using Synchronous Dependency Grammars with Hand-written and Automatically Harvested Rules. In *Proc. EACL*.

Gabriel Stanovsky and Ido Dagan. 2016. Annotating and Predicting Non-Restrictive Noun Phrase Modifications. In *Proc. ACL*.

David Vickrey and Daphne Koller. 2008. Sentence Simplification for Semantic Role Labeling. In *Proc. ACL*.

Sanja Štajner, Maja Popović, Horacio Saggion, Lucia Specia, and Mark Fishel. 2016. Shared task on quality assessment for text simplification. In *Proc. LREC*.

Sander Wubben, Antal van den Bosch, and Emiel Krahmer. 2012. Sentence Simplification by Monolingual Machine Translation. In *Proc. ACL*.

Wei Xu, Chris Callison-Burch, and Courtney Napoles. 2015. Problems in current text simplification research: New data can help. *Transactions of the Association for Computational Linguistics* 3:283–297.

Zhemin Zhu, Delphine Bernhard, and Iryna Gurevych. 2010. A Monolingual Tree-based Translation Model for Sentence Simplification. In *Proc. ACL*.

Hierarchical Word Structure-based Parsing: A Feasibility Study on UD-style Dependency Parsing in Japanese

Takaaki Tanaka and **Katsuhiko Hayashi** and **Masaaki Nagata**
NTT Comminication Science Laboratories
2-4, Hikaridai, Seika-cho, Soraku-gun, Kyoto, 619-0237, Japan
{tanaka.takaaki,hayashi.katsuhiko,nagata.masaaki}@lab.ntt.co.jp

Abstract

In applying word-based dependency parsing such as Universal Dependencies (UD) to Japanese, the uncertainty of word segmentation emerges for defining a word unit of the dependencies. We introduce the following hierarchical word structures to dependency parsing in Japanese: morphological units (a short unit word, SUW) and syntactic units (a long unit word, LUW). This paper describes the results of a feasibility study on the ability and the effectiveness of parsing methods based on hierarchical word structure (LUW chunking+parsing) by comparing them with methods using single layer word structure (SUW parsing). We also show joint analysis of LUW-chunking and dependency parsing improves the performance of identifying predicate-argument structures, while there is not much difference between overall results of them.

1 Introduction

Some research has recently been introducing word-based dependency schemes into Japanese syntactic parsing from a cross-lingual standpoint such as Universal Dependencies (UD) (Nivre et al., 2016; Kanayama et al., 2015; Tanaka et al., 2016), although syntactic structures are traditionally represented as dependencies between chunks called *bunsetsus*.

However, for languages like Japanese where words are not segmented by white spaces in orthography, word-based dependency parsing is problematic due to difficulties in defining a word unit. Actually, in Japanese several word unit standards exists that can be found in corpus annotation schemes or in the outputs of morpho-logical analyzers. The word unit must be more consistently defined in word-based dependencies than bunsetsu-based dependencies, since the inconsistency of word units directly affects the discordance of the syntactic structure. UD for Japanese adopted a "short unit word" (SUW) defined for building the Balanced Corpus of Contemporary Written Japanese (BCCWJ) (Maekawa et al., 2014), since the word unit is designed to maintain internal consistency in the corpus.

An SUW is the smallest token that conveys mor-phological information, and generally corresponds to the head word of a morphological analysis dictionary called UniDic, which is compiled based on linguistic analysis and is used for morphological analyzers. Even though SUWs are well-organized as morphological units, they are sometimes too short to represent syntactic construction. There-fore, we also introduce another unit named "long unit word" (LUW), which consists of one or more SUWs with a single syntactic function, and is also defined for BCCWJ. For constructing an LUW-based syntactic structure, we need two types of analyses: LUW chunking and LUW-based dependency parsing. Note that LUWs include two kinds of multiwords: lexicalized phrases and institution-alized phrases (Sag et al., 2001), and for syntactic parsing, it is essential to discriminate functional multiwords that are classified into the latter in par-ticular. Even though a pipeline process is a sim-ple way of combining these two analyses, it may cause inconsistency between dependency parsing and chunking. Therefore, we introduce a joint analysis method of parsing and chunking to unify these two analyses by deciding dependency struc-tures and chunks in the same process.

We describe two methods of hierarchical word-based parsing in Section 3: a pipeline analysis us-ing a current LUW-chunking method and a joint analysis method. We present our evaluation of the

Proceedings of the 15th International Conference on Parsing Technologies, pages 56–60,
Pisa, Italy; September 20–22, 2017. ©2017 Association for Computational Linguistics

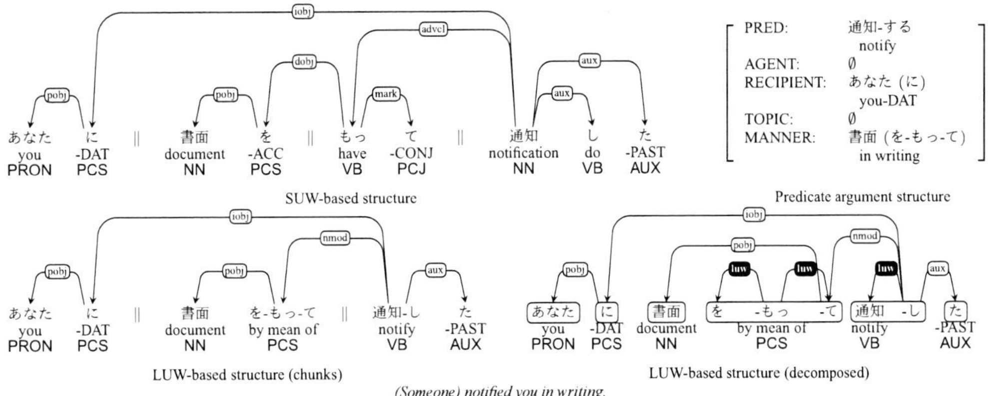

Figure 1: Examples of word-based dependencies. "luw" is a special dependency type that denotes intra-dependencies in an LUW. The symbols '‖' denote the borders of bunsetsu chunks.

JP Dep		#Sent	#SUW	#LUW
	test	2,000	53,193	41,192
	train	17,953	497,309	383,797

Table 1: Corpus statistics.

results of hierarchical word-based parsing (LUW-based) and single layer word-based (SUW-based) parsing in Section 4.

2 Hierarchical Word Dependencies

We employed two levels of word unit definitions as described in Section 1. A sentence is consistently segmented into morphological units of SUWs, while a syntactic structure is constructed based on syntactic units of LUWs since compound nouns and functional multiwords have a single syntactic function and are usually treated as single LUWs. The relationship between SUW and LUW almost correspond to the one between single word and multiword in other language. Note that an LUW that consists of just an SUW exists, and about 20% of LUWs belongs to a multiword.

Figure 1 shows the differences between SUW- and LUW-based dependency structures. Note that the scheme (described in Section 4.1) in the figure is similar to UD, but they differ in the manners of head selection. For instance, the scheme selects the case particle に -DAT as the head of the noun あなた *you*, while UD treats the noun as the head of the particle. In SUW-based dependencies (top left), SUW verb もつ *have*, a component of functional multiword を-もっ-て [1] *by mean of*, is treated as a main verb, creating a spurious complex structure between a verb and an argument.

The pseudo predicates hinder the extraction of *true* predicate argument structures as shown in the top right of the figure. In an LUW-based dependency structure (bottom left), multiword を-もっ-て is considered an LUW with a flat structure, which clearly indicates the relation between main verb 通知-する *notify* and argument あなた に *you*-DAT. The conversion from SUW sequences into LUWs contains ambiguity. For example, sequence を も っ て in the sentence, "彼 は その 本 をもって いる", *lit. He has the book.*, is not just a single LUW but three LUWs with a main verb.

The amount of research on Japanese word-based dependency parsing is much less than bunsetsu-based parsing. Tanaka and Nagata (2015) proposed LUW based analysis using a scheme that resembles Stanford typed dependencies (SD) (de Marneffe and Manning, 2008), however, they do not treat LUW-chunking problems. Kato et al. (2017) explored English dependency parsing models that predict multiword expression (MWE)-aware structure. We treat broader categories of multiword in this paper, e.g. LUWs contain ordinary compound nouns as well as named entities. The test set has 8,291 multiwords (LUWs) in 2,000 sentences, while their corpus has 27,949 MWE instances in 37,015 sentences.

3 Analysis Methods

3.1 Pipeline analysis

The pipeline method sequentially runs two analyses; multiword analysis chunks an input SUW sequence into an LUW sequence, and parsing analysis constructs LUW-based dependency structures,

---

[1]The SUW boundaries in an LUW are denoted by "'-'", a symbol that is not actually used in orthography.

LUW transition			Cond.
ShLUW(p)	$(\sigma_S, \sigma_L, \beta\|x_k, A, L)$	$\Rightarrow (\sigma_S\|p\langle x_k\rangle, \sigma_L, \beta, A, L)$	$\|\sigma_S\| = 0$
ReLUW$_L$(r)	$(\sigma_S, \sigma_L\|p\langle x_k\rangle\|q\langle x_m\rangle, \beta, A, L)$	$\Rightarrow (\sigma_S, \sigma_L\|p\langle x_k\rangle, \beta, A\cup\{r(p\langle x_k\rangle, q\langle x_m\rangle)\}, L)$	$\|\sigma_L\| \geq 2$
ReLUW$_R$(r)	$(\sigma_S, \sigma_L\|p\langle x_k\rangle\|q\langle x_m\rangle, \beta, A, L)$	$\Rightarrow (\sigma_S, \sigma_L\|q\langle x_m\rangle, \beta, A\cup\{r(q\langle x_m\rangle, p\langle x_k\rangle)\}, L)$	$\|\sigma_L\| \geq 2$
PopLUW	$(\sigma_S\|p\langle x_k\rangle, \sigma_L, \beta, A, L)$	$\Rightarrow \{\sigma_S, \sigma_L\|p\langle x_k\rangle, \beta, A, L\cup\{p\langle x\rangle\}\}$	$\|\sigma_S\| = 1$

SUW transition			Cond.
ShSUW	$(\sigma_S\|p\langle x_k\rangle, \sigma_L, \beta\|x_m, A, L)$	$\Rightarrow (\sigma_S\|p\langle x_k\rangle\|x_m, \sigma_L, \beta, A, L)$	
ReSUW$_L$	$(\sigma_S\|p\langle x_k\rangle\|x_m, \sigma_L, \beta, A, L)$	$\Rightarrow (\sigma_S\|p\langle x_k\rangle, \sigma_L, \beta, A, L\cup\{\ell(x_k, x_m)\})$	$\|\sigma_S\| \geq 2$
ReSUW$_R$	$(\sigma_S\|p\langle x_k\rangle\|x_m, \sigma_L, \beta, A, L)$	$\Rightarrow (\sigma_S\|p\langle x_m\rangle, \sigma_L, \beta, A, L\cup\{\ell(x_m, x_k)\}$	$\|\sigma_S\| \geq 2$

x_k — SUW
$p\langle x\rangle$ — POS of an LUW (head: x)
$r(x, y)$ — syntactic dep. (head: x, rel: r)
$\ell(x, y)$ — internal dep. in an LUW
Initial state $([], [], [x_0, ..., x_n], \emptyset, \emptyset)$
Final state $([], [], [], A_f, L_f)$

Figure 2: Transitions in our joint parsing algorithm.

as shown in the bottom left of Figure 1.

Kozawa et al. (2014) proposed a method that creates an LUW sequence from an SUW sequence in two steps: chunking an SUW sequence using an LUW-chunking model and assigning an LUW POS to each LUW with an LUW POS estimation model. LUW chunking is done by assigning each SUW in a given sequence either a "B" tag or an "I" tag by a sequence labeling method using CRF.

3.2 Joint analysis

The joint method simultaneously processes an SUW sequence with LUW chunking and syntactic parsing so that the LUW chunking is consistent with the syntactic analysis. The method directly constructs a dependency structure from an SUW sequence, as shown at the bottom right of Figure 1. LUWs consisting of multiple SUWs such as を-もっ-て and 通知-する are represented as a flat structure with a special dependency type *luw*.

We employed an algorithm based on shift-reduce parsing and defined two types of transitions: LUW chunking and dependency parsing. This algorithm is devised by applying a joint analysis method of word segmentation and dependency parsing in Chinese (Zhang et al., 2014; Hatori et al., 2012), or a method which combines lexical and syntactic analysis (Constant and Nivre, 2016). One of features of our algorithm is that a shift transition (ShLUW) assigns a leftmost SUW of an LUW with a POS. We found this obtains better scores than a pop transition (PopLUW) does.

Two stacks, σ_S and σ_L, are provided for SUWs to be processed and chunked LUWs respectively. The algorithm outputs an LUW sequence and an LUW-based parsed tree to a set of internal dependencies in LUW chunks L, and a set of dependencies A. A parsing status is represented as quintuple $(\sigma_S, \sigma_L, \beta, A, L)$, where β is a buffer that initially contains all SUWs in an input sentence, $(x_0, ..., x_n)$. Figure 2 shows transitions used in our algorithm. The necessary condition for each action is shown in the rightmost column. The notion $|\sigma|$ denotes depth of stack σ. For example, $|\sigma_S| = 0$ represents the condition that stack $|\sigma_S|$ is empty.

JP Dep		all deps		w/o luw deps	
Method		UAS	LAS	UAS	LAS
LUW-based	SR joint	95.0	91.4	93.7	89.3
	Coma + SR single	94.9	91.3	93.5	88.9
	Coma + Malt	94.7	91.4	93.3	89.0
	Coma + MST	94.9	91.3	93.5	88.9
SUW-based	SR single	93.6	89.6	92.3	87.5
	Malt	92.9	89.2	90.9	86.7
	MST	93.5	89.4	91.8	86.9

Table 2: Parsing results.

JP Dep	Pred Args	Adnom	Adverb	Coord
Method				
LUW-based				
SR joint	76.6	68.5	65.4	66.5
Coma + SR single	75.9	65.9	65.3	65.9
Coma + Malt	75.3	68.2	64.6	65.7
Coma + MST	75.5	65.8	63.4	65.8
SUW-based				
SR single	74.2	63.8	60.9	63.5
Malt	73.2	63.5	58.4	59.7
MST	73.2	62.2	58.6	63.9

Table 3: F$_1$ scores of individual categories of dependency types.

4 Evaluation

We compared two LUW-based parsing methods and an SUW-based parsing method. A simple SUW-based parsing method directly constructs a dependency structure without considering LUWs. The SUW-based method regards "luw" as an ordinary dependency type.

4.1 Setting

Since the current UD Japanese corpora are SUW-based and do not have complete LUW information[2], we used another typed word dependency treebank in Japanese described in (Tanaka and Nagata, 2015)(JP Dep). JP Dep is annotated with LUW-based dependencies in accordance with

---

[2] They have partly compound word information by annotating dependencies with relation types "mwe"(UD1.2), "fixed"(UD 2.0) and so on.

a scheme that resembles SD, and consists of 20,000 sentences (Table 1) from a newspaper corpus, Kyoto Corpus (Kurohashi and Nagao, 2003).

SR joint employs a shift-reduce parser based on dynamic programming (Huang and Sagae, 2010; Hayashi et al., 2013) that is expanded with LUW-chunking transitions. We used the features related to LUW and the function compound words, in addition to the original features. Moreover, we employ features with flag where SUW may form an LUW of a function compound word. The flag becomes 1 only if a function compound word that begins with a target SUW exists in dictionaries, and otherwise is 0. The features are similar to the additional features used for the joint model (Joint+dict) proposed in (Kato et al., 2017) in terms of utilizing lexical knowledge in dictionaries. We chose 12 for the beam width based on trial results.

For the pipeline methods, we used Comainu (Coma) (Kozawa et al., 2014) as an LUW chunker that is independent of a syntactic parser. We compared the following three parsers by combining them with Comainu: MST Parser (McDonald et al., 2006), MaltParser (Nivre et al., 2007), and SR joint without LUW-chunking transition (SR single). The LUW-chunking model and the LUW-based dependency parsing models were built with the training division of **JP Dep**.

The SUW-based dependency parsing models were also trained to directly test the parsing of the SUW sequence. The model was trained with LUW-based structures decomposed into SUWs as a structure shown at the bottom right of Figure 1.

4.2 Results

The parsing results are shown in Table 2 [3]. UAS and LAS are calculated on two conditions: the scores of all the dependencies (all deps) and only the scores of the dependencies between LUWs (w/o luw deps), i.e., ignoring the internal dependencies in LUWs. Since the internal dependencies in LUWs are right-to-left and monotonous structures, as shown in Figure 1, and easier to be estimated than the inter-LUW dependencies, the scores of all the dependencies tend to be higher than those of inter-LUW dependencies.

Overall, the results of LUW-based dependency parsing outperformed the SUW-based ones as shown in Table 2. Regarding the LUW-based pars-

---

[3] We converted LUW-based dependencies into SUW-based dependencies by decomposing each LUW into SUWs with a flat structure to compare the results.

Multiword	Freq	SR joint		SR single	
		UAS	LAS	UAS	LAS
case particle					
に-つい-て *about*	19	89	58	84	47
と-いう *(a bird,) called (swallow)*	138	94	58	88	88
conjunctive particle					
と-し-て *by way of (explanation)*	83	84	74	81	74
に-よる-と *according to*	21	91	71	81	67
に-よっ-て *by*	12	92	83	75	67

Table 4: Attachment scores of dependencies including functional multiwords.

ing results, we found few differences between SR joint and the pipeline methods. Nevertheless, the differences between the scores of the inter-LUW dependencies (w/o luw deps) is larger than those between the scores of all the dependencies. This indicates SR joint preferentially obtained better results of syntactic parsing instead of the results of LUW chunking. The differences between the results in the major dependent types are clearer as shown in Table 3. We can see the F_1 scores of the individual categories of the dependency types in the table, where predicate-argument categories (Pred Args) include "nsubj," "dobj," and "iobj." The SR joint improved more than 0.7 points over the pipeline methods in such major categories as Pred Args and adverbial modification, while we found few differences between overall results of the SR joint methods and the pipeline methods.

Treatment with the functional multiwords of a parsing method affected the scores of the dependency types in such categories as Pred Args and adverbial, where they tend to be long-distance dependencies. Table 4 shows the scores of the dependencies including major functional multiwords, and we found that SR joint obtained better scores than SR single as a whole. This suggests the advantages of identifying functional multiwords contribute the higher scores of the specific types.

5 Conclusion

We presented methods for processing word dependency parsing by treating hierarchical word structures by combining LUW chunking and LUW-based dependency parsing for Japanese syntactic parsing. LUW-based parsing outperformed the SUW-based method, and the joint analysis method is superior to the pipeline methods in identifying the major syntactic relations.

We are planning to apply our joint analysis method on an UD corpus for Japanese and other languages to handle multiword units in syntactic parsing based on UD schemes.

References

Matthieu Constant and Joakim Nivre. 2016. A transition-based system for joint lexical and syntactic analysis. In *Proceedings of the 54th Annual Meeting of the Association for Computational Linguistics*. volume 1 of *ACL 2016*, pages 161–171.

Marie-Catherine de Marneffe and Christopher D. Manning. 2008. The stanford typed dependencies representation. In *Proceedings of COLING 2008 Workshop on Cross-framework and Cross-domain Parser Evaluation*. pages 1–8.

Jun Hatori, Takuya Matsuzaki, Yusuke Miyao, and Jun'ichi Tsujii. 2012. Incremental joint approach to word segmentation, pos tagging, and dependency parsing in chinese. In *Proceedings of the 50th Annual Meeting of the Association for Computational Linguistics*. volume 1 of *ACL 2012*, pages 1045–1053.

Katsuhiko Hayashi, Shuhei Kondo, and Yuji Matsumoto. 2013. Efficient stacked dependency parsing by forest reranking. *Transactions of the Association for Computational Linguistics* 1:139–150.

Liang Huang and Kenji Sagae. 2010. Dynamic programming for linear-time incremental parsing. In *Proceedings of the 48th Annual Meeting of the Association for Computational Linguistics*. ACL 2010, pages 1077–1086.

Hiroshi Kanayama, Yusuke Miyao, Takaaki Tanaka, Shinsuke Mori, Masayuki Asahara, and Sumire Uematsu. 2015. A draft of universal dependencies for japanese (in japanese). In *the 21st annual meeting of the Association for Natural Language Processing*. pages 505–508.

Akihiko Kato, Hiroyuki Shindo, and Yuji Matsumoto. 2017. English multiword expression-aware dependency parsing including named entities. In *Proceedings of the 55th Annual Meeting of the Association for Computational Linguistics*. volume 2 of *ACL 2017*, pages 427–432.

Shunsuke Kozawa, Kiyotaka Uchimoto, and Yoshiharu Den. 2014. Adaptation of long-unit-word analysis system to different part-of-speech target (in japanese). In *Journal of Natural Language Processing*. volume 21, pages 379–401.

Sadao Kurohashi and Makoto Nagao. 2003. *Building a Japanese Parsed Corpus – while Improving the Parsing System*, Kluwer Academic Publishers, chapter 14, pages 249–260.

Kikuo Maekawa, Makoto Yamazaki, Toshinobu Ogiso, Takehiko Maruyama, Hideki Ogura, Wakako Kashino, Hanae Koiso, Masaya Yamaguchi, Makiro Tanaka, and Yasuharu Den. 2014. Balanced corpus of contemporary written Japanese. *Language Resources and Evaluation* 48(2):345–371.

Ryan McDonald, Kevin Lerman, and Fernando Pereira. 2006. Multilingual dependency analysis with a two-stage discriminative parser. In *Proceedings of the Tenth Conference on Computational Natural Language Learning*. CoNLL 2006, pages 216–220.

Joakim Nivre, Marie-Catherine de Marneffe, Filip Ginter, Yoav Goldberg, Jan Haji , Christopher Manning, Ryan McDonald, Slav Petrov, Sampo Pyysalo, Natalia Silveira, Reut Tsarfaty, and Daniel Zeman. 2016. Universal Dependencies v1: A multilingual treebank collection. In *Proceedings of the 10th International Conference on Language Resources and Evaluation*. LREC 2016, pages 1659–1666.

Joakim Nivre, Johan Hall, Jens Nilsson, Atanas Chanev, Gülşen Eryiğit, Sandra Kübler, Svetoslav Marinov, and Erwin Marsi. 2007. Maltparser: A language-independent system for data-driven dependency parsing. *Journal of Natural Language Engineering* 13(2):95–135.

Ivan A. Sag, Timothy Baldwin, Francis Bond, Ann Copestake, and Dan Flickinger. 2001. Multiword expressions: A pain in the neck for nlp. In *Proceedings of the 3rd International Conference on Intelligent Text Processing and Computational Linguistics*. CICLing-2002, pages 1–15.

Takaaki Tanaka, Yusuke Miyao, Masayuki Asahara, Sumire Uematsu, Hiroshi Kanayama, Mori Shinsuke, and Yuji Matsumoto. 2016. Universal dependencies for Japanese. In *Proceedings of 10th edition of the Language Resources and Evaluation Conference*. LREC 2016.

Takaaki Tanaka and Masaaki Nagata. 2015. Word-based Japanese typed dependency parsing with grammatical function analysis. In *Proceedings of the 53rd Annual Meeting of the Association for Computational Linguistics and the 7th International Joint Conference on Natural Language Processing*. volume 2 of *ACL 2015*, pages 237–242.

Meishan Zhang, Yue Zhang, Wanxiang Che, and Ting Liu. 2014. Character-level Chinese dependency parsing. In *Proceedings of the 52nd Annual Meeting of the Association for Computational Linguistics*. volume 1 of *ACL 2014*, pages 1326–1336.

Leveraging Newswire Treebanks for Parsing Conversational Data with Argument Scrambling

Riyaz Ahmad Bhat
Department of Computer Science
University of Colorado Boulder
riyaz.bhat@colorado.edu

Irshad Ahmad Bhat
LTRC, IIIT-H, Hyderabad
Telangana, India
irshad.bhat@research.iiit.ac.in

Dipti Misra Sharma
LTRC, IIIT-H, Hyderabad
Telangana, India
dipti@iiit.ac.in

Abstract

We investigate the problem of parsing conversational data of morphologically-rich languages such as Hindi where argument scrambling occurs frequently. We evaluate a state-of-the-art non-linear transition-based parsing system on a new dataset containing 506 dependency trees for sentences from Bollywood (Hindi) movie scripts and Twitter posts of Hindi monolingual speakers. We show that a dependency parser trained on a newswire treebank is strongly biased towards the canonical structures and degrades when applied to conversational data. Inspired by Transformational Generative Grammar (Chomsky, 1965), we mitigate the sampling bias by generating all theoretically possible alternative word orders of a clause from the existing (kernel) structures in the treebank. Training our parser on canonical and transformed structures improves performance on conversational data by around 9% LAS over the baseline newswire parser.

1 Introduction

In linguistics, every language in assumed to have a basic constituent order in a clause (Comrie, 1981). In some languages, constituent order is fixed to define the grammatical structure of a clause and the grammatical relations therein, while in others, that convey grammatical information through inflection or word morphology, constituent order assumes discourse function and defines the information structure of a sentence (Kiss, 1995). Despite word order freedom, most of the morphologically-rich languages exhibit a preferred word order in formal registers such as newswire. Word order alternations are more commonplace in informal language use such as day-to-day conversations and social media content. For statistical parsing, word order alternations (argument scrambling) are a major bottleneck. Given appropriate pragmatic conditions a transitive sentence in a morphologically-rich language allows n factorial ($n!$) permutations, where n is the number of verb arguments and/or adjuncts. Argument scrambling often leads to structural discontinuities. Moreover, these scramblings worsen the data sparsity problem since data-driven parsers are usually trained on a limited size treebank where most of the valid structures may never show up. More importantly, most of the available treebanks are built on newswire text which is more formal (Plank, 2016). The chances of any deviation from the canonical word order are smaller, thereby creating sampling bias.

A common solution to address the sampling bias is to alter the distribution of classes in the training data by using sampling techniques (Van Hulse et al., 2007). However, simple sampling techniques such as minority oversampling may not be a feasible solution for parsing argument scramblings which are almost non-existent in the newswire treebanks (see Table 1). Newswire data usually represent only a sample of possible syntactic structures and, therefore, suffer from non-representation of certain classes that encode valid arc directionalities. In the Hindi dependency treebank (HTB) (Bhat et al., 2015), for example, dependency relations such as source, time and place are never extraposed. Therefore, we instead generate training examples for varied arc directionalities by transforming the gold syntactic trees in the training data. We experiment with the Hindi dependency treebank and show that such transformations are indeed helpful when we deal with data with diverse word-orders such as movie dialogues. Our work is in conformity with earlier attempts where modifying source syntactic trees to match

Proceedings of the 15th International Conference on Parsing Technologies, pages 61–66,
Pisa, Italy; September 20–22, 2017. ©2017 Association for Computational Linguistics

target distributions benefited parsing of noisy, conversational data (Van der Plas et al., 2009; Foster, 2010).

S.No.	Order	Percentage
1	S O V	91.83
2	O S V	7.80
3	O V S	0.19
4	S V O	0.19
5	V O S	0.0
6	V S O	0.0

Table 1: The table shows theoretically possible orders of Subject (S), Object (O) and Verb (V) in transitive sentences in the HTB training data with their percentages of occurrence.

2 Sampling Argument Scrambling via Syntactic Transformations

In (Chomsky, 1965), Noam Chomsky famously described syntactic transformations which abstract away from divergent surface realizations of related sentences by manipulating the underlying grammatical structure of simple sentences called kernels. For example, a typical transformation is the operation of subject-auxiliary inversion which generates yes-no questions from the corresponding declarative sentences by swapping the subject and auxiliary positions. These transformations are essentially a tool to explain word-order variations (Mahajan, 1990; Taylan, 1984; King, 1995).

We apply this idea of transformations to canonical structures in newswire treebanks for generating trees that represent all of the theoretically viable word-orders in a morphologically-rich language. For example, we create a dependency tree where an indirect object is extraposed by inverting its position with the head verb, as shown in Figure 1.

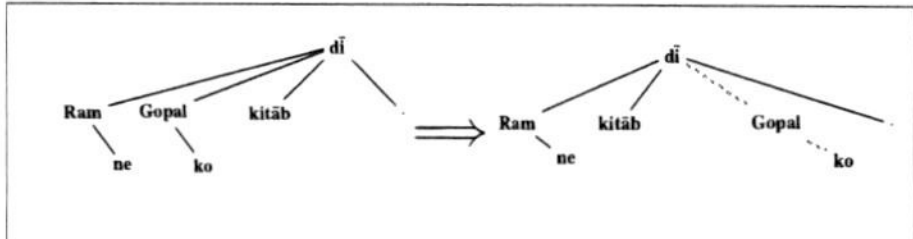

Figure 1: The figure depicts one possible permutation for the sentence *Ram ne Gopal ko kitāb dī*. 'Ram ERG Gopal DAT book give.' (Ram gave Gopal a book.). The indirect object *Gopal ko* (red, dashed arcs) is postposed by swapping its position with the ditransitive verb *dī* 'give'.

Recently, a related approach was proposed by Wang and Eisner (2016), who employed the concept of creolization to synthesize artificial treebanks from Universal Dependency (UD) treebanks. They transform nominal and verbal projections in each tree of a UD language as per the word-order parameters of other UD language(s) by using their supervised word-order models. In single-source transfer parsing, the authors showed

that a parser trained on a target language chosen from a large pool of synthetic treebanks can significantly outperform the same parser when it is limited to selecting from a smaller pool of natural language treebanks.

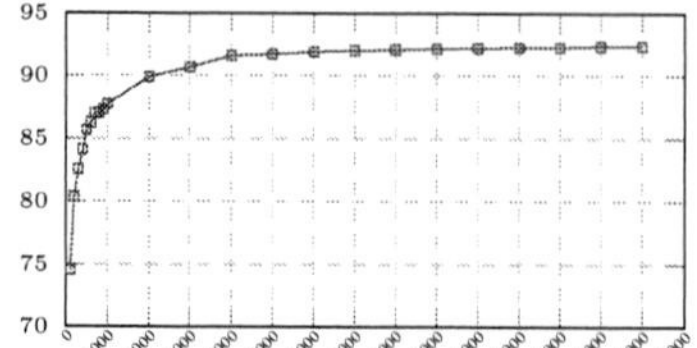

Figure 2: Learning curves plotted against data size on the X axis and LAS score on the Y axis.

Unlike Wang and Eisner (2016), we do not choose one word-order for a verbal projection based on a target distribution, but instead generate all of its theoretically possible orders. For each dependency tree, we alter the linear precedence relations between arguments of a verbal projection in '$n!$' ways, while keeping their dominance relations intact. However, simply permuting all the nodes of verbal projections can lead to an overwhelming number of trees. For example, a data set of 't' syntactic trees each containing an average of 10 nodes would allow around $t \times 10!$ i.e., 3 million possible permutations for our training data size, making training infeasible. Moreover, we may only need a subset of the permutations to have a uniform distribution over the possible word orders. We therefore apply a number of filters to restrict the permutations. First, we only permute a subset of the training data which is representative of the newswire domain. It is often the case that domain specific constructions are covered by a limited number of sentences. This can be seen from the learning curves in Figure 2; the learning curves flatten out after 4,000 training instances. Second, for each sentence, we only take the k permutations with the lowest perplexity assigned by a language model where k is set to the number of nodes permuted for each verbal projection. The language model is trained on a large and diverse data set (newswire, entertainment, social media, stories, etc.) Finally, we make sure that the distribution of the possible word-orders is roughly uniform or at least less skewed in the augmented training data.

3 Evaluation Data

For an intrinsic evaluation of the parsing models on conversational data, we manually annotated dependency trees for sentences that represent natural conversation with at least one structural variation from the canonical structures of Hindi.[1] We used Bollywood movie scripts as our primary source of conversational data. Although, dialogues in a movie are technically artificial, they mimic an actual conversation. We also mined Twitter posts of Hindi monolingual speakers. Tweets can often be categorized as conversational. The data set was sampled from old and new Bollywood movies and a large set of tweets of Indian language users that we crawled from Twitter using Tweepy[2]. For Twitter data, we used an off-the-shelf language identification system[3] to select Hindi only tweets. From this data, we only want those dialogues/tweets that contain a minimum of one argument scrambling. For this purpose we trained an off-the-shelf convolutional neural network classifier for identifying sentences with argument scrambling (Kim, 2014).[4] We trained the model using the canonical and transformed treebank data and achieved around ~97% accuracy on canonical and transformed versions of HTB test data.[5] After automatic identification, we manually selected 506 sentences from the true positives for annotation. For POS tagging and dependency annotation, we used the AnnCorra guidelines defined for treebanking of Indian languages (Bharati et al., 2009). The data was annotated by an expert linguist with expertise in Indian language treebanking. The annotations were automatically converted to Universal Dependencies (UD) following UD v1 guidelines for multilingual experimentation (De Marneffe et al., 2014). Table 2 shows the distribution of theoretically possible word orders in transitive sentences in the evaluation set. Unlike their distribution in the HTB training data, the word orders in the evaluation set are relatively less skewed.

S.No.	Order	Percentage
1	S O V	33.07
2	O S V	23.62
3	O V S	17.32
4	S V O	14.17
5	V O S	9.45
6	V S O	2.36

Table 2: The table shows theoretically possible orders of Subject, Object and Verb in transitive sentences in the Evaluation set with their percentages of occurrence.

[1] HTB's conversation section has around ~16,00 sentences taken from fiction which, however, strictly obey Hindi's preferred SOV word-order. Therefore, we needed a new dataset with word-order variations.

[2] http://www.tweepy.org/

[3] https://github.com/irshadbhat/litcm

[4] https://github.com/yoonkim/CNN_sentence

[5] The system often misclassified noisy sentences from movie scripts and tweets as scrambled.

Most of the movie scripts available online and the tweets are written in Roman script instead of the standard Devanagari script, requiring back-transliteration of the sentences in the evaluation set before running experiments. We also need normalization of non-standard word forms prevalent in tweets. We followed the procedure adapted by Bhat et al. (2017a) to learn a single back-transliteration and normalization system. We also performed sentence-level decoding to resolve homograph ambiguity in Romanized Hindi vocabulary.

4 Experimental Setup

The parsing experiments reported in this paper are conducted using a non-linear neural network-based transition system which is similar to (Kiperwasser and Goldberg, 2016). The monolingual models are trained on training files of HTB which uses the Pāninian Grammar framework (PG) (Bharati et al., 1995), while the multilingual models are trained on Universal Dependency Treebanks of Hindi and English released under version 1.4 of Universal Dependencies (Nivre et al., 2016).

Parsing Models Our underlying parsing method is based on the arc-eager transition system (Nivre, 2003). The arc-eager system defines a set of configurations for a sentence $w_1, \ldots, w_n$, where each configuration $C = (S, B, A)$ consists of a stack S, a buffer B, and a set of dependency arcs A. For each sentence, the parser starts with an initial configuration where $S = [ROOT]$, $B = [w_1, \ldots, w_n]$ and $A = \emptyset$ and terminates with a configuration C if the buffer is empty and the stack contains the ROOT. The parse trees derived from transition sequences are given by A. To derive the parse tree, the arc-eager system defines four types of transitions (t): Shift, Left-Arc, Right-Arc, and Reduce.

We use a non-linear neural network to predict the transitions for the parser configurations. The neural network model is the standard feedforward neural network with a single layer of hidden units. We use 128 hidden units and the ReLU activation function. The output layer uses a softmax function for probabilistic multi-class classification. The model is trained by minimizing negative log-likelihood loss with $l2$-regularization over

[6] We also experimented with minority oversampling and instance weighting, however improvments over newswire were minimal (see §1 for possible reasons).

Data-set	Newswire$^{PG/UD}$				Newswire$^{PG/UD}$+Transformed Newswire$^{PG/UD}$				Newswire^{UD}+English^{UD}			
	Gold POS		Auto POS		Gold POS		Auto POS		Gold POS		Auto POS	
	UAS	LAS	UAS	LAS	UAS	LAS	UAS	LAS	UAS	LAS	UAS	LAS
Newswire^{PG}	96.41	92.08	94.55	89.51	96.07$^{-0.34}$	91.75$^{-0.33}$	94.29$^{-0.26}$	89.28$^{-0.23}$	-	-	-	-
Conversation^{PG}	74.03	64.30	69.52	58.91	84.68$^{+10.65}$	73.94$^{+9.64}$	79.07$^{+9.55}$	67.41$^{+8.5}$	-	-	-	-
Newswire^{UD}	95.04	92.65	93.85	90.59	94.59$^{-0.45}$	92.03$^{-0.62}$	93.32$^{-0.53}$	89.98$^{-0.61}$	94.56$^{-0.48}$	91.87$^{-0.78}$	93.22$^{-0.63}$	89.72$^{-0.87}$
Conversation^{UD}	73.23	64.77	68.81	59.43	83.97$^{+10.74}$	74.61$^{+9.84}$	78.38$^{+9.57}$	67.98$^{+8.55}$	77.73$^{+4.5}$	68.12$^{+3.35}$	71.29$^{+2.48}$	62.46$^{+3.03}$

Table 3: Accuracy of our different parsing models on conversational data as well as newswire evaluation sets. Improvements in superscript are over the newswire baseline. [6]

the entire training data. We use Momentum SGD for optimization (Duchi et al., 2011) and apply dropout (Hinton et al., 2012).

From each parser configuration, we extract features related to the top three nodes in the stack, the top node in the buffer and the leftmost and rightmost children of the top three nodes in the stack and the leftmost child of the top node in the buffer. Similarly to Kiperwasser and Goldberg (2016), we use two stacked Bidirectional LSTMs with 128 hidden nodes for learning the feature representations over conjoined word-tag sequences for each training sentence. We use an additional Bidirectional LSTM (64 nodes) for learning separate representations of words over their character sequences for capturing out-of-vocabulary (OOV) words at testing time. We use word dropout with a dropout probability of 0.1 which enables character embeddings to drive the learning process around 10% of the time instead of full word representations. This is important for evaluation on noisy data where OOV words are quite frequent. The monolingual models are initialized using pre-trained 64 dimensional word embeddings of Hindi, while multilingual models use Hindi-English bilingual embeddings from Bhat et al. (2017a)[7], while POS embeddings are randomly initialized within a range of -0.25 to +0.25 with 32 dimensions.

Moreover, we use pseudo-projective transformations of Nivre and Nilsson (2005) to handle a higher percentage of non-projective arcs in the evaluation data (6% as opposed to 2% in the training data). We use the most informative scheme of head+path to store the transformation information. Inverse transformations based on breadth-first search are applied to recover the non-projective arcs in a post-processing step.

5   Experiments and Results

We ran two experiments to evaluate the effectiveness of the tree transformations on the parsing of conversational data. In the first, we leverage the monolingual annotations by applying syntactic transformations; in the second we use a cross-lingual treebank with diverse word-orders. For each experiment type, we report results using both predicted and gold POS tags. The POS taggers are trained using an architecture similar to the parser's with a single layer MLP which takes its input from Bi-LSTM representation of the focus word (see Appendix for the results). We used the newswire parsing models as the baseline for evaluating the impact of tree transformations and multilingual annotations. The augmented models are trained on the union of the original newswire training data and the transformed trees. We generated 9K trees from 4K representative sentences (Figure 2) which were projectivized before applying syntactic transformations to preserve non-projective arcs. Our results are reported in Table 3.

As the table shows, our newswire models suffer heavily when applied to conversational data. The parser indeed seems biased towards canonical structures of Hindi. It could not correctly parse extraposed arguments, and could not even identify direct objects if they were not adjacent to the verb. However, in both gold and predicted settings, our augmented parsing models produce results that are approximately 9% LAS points better than the state-of-the-art baseline newswire parsers (Bhat et al., 2017b). Our augmented models even provided better results with UD dependencies. Probably due to the increased structural ambiguity, augmenting transformed trees with the original training data led to a slight decrease in the results on the original Hindi test sets in both UD and PG dependencies. Interestingly, our cross-lingual model also captured certain levels of scrambling which could be because the English treebank would at least provide training instances for SVO word order.

6   Conclusion

In this paper, we showed that leveraging formal newswire treebanks can effectively handle

[7]https://bitbucket.org/irshadbhat/indic-word2vec-embeddings

argument scrambling in informal registers of morphologically-rich languages such as Hindi. Inspired by Chomskyan syntactic tradition, we demonstrated that sampling bias can be mitigated by using syntactic transformations to generate non-canonical structures as additional training instances from canonical structures in newswire. We also showed that multilingual resources can be helpful in mitigating sampling bias.

The code of the parsing models is available at the GitHub repository `https://github.com/riyazbhat/conversation-parser`, while the data can be found under the Universal Dependencies of Hindi at `https://github.com/UniversalDependencies/UD_Hindi`.

References

Akshar Bharati, Vineet Chaitanya, Rajeev Sangal, and KV Ramakrishnamacharyulu. 1995. *Natural Language Processing: A Paninian Perspective*. Prentice-Hall of India New Delhi.

Akshar Bharati, DM Sharma S Husain, L Bai, R Begam, and R Sangal. 2009. Anncorra: Treebanks for indian languages, guidelines for annotating hindi treebank (version–2.0).

Irshad Bhat, Riyaz A. Bhat, Manish Shrivastava, and Dipti Sharma. 2017a. Joining hands: Exploiting monolingual treebanks for parsing of codemixing data. In *Proceedings of the 15th Conference of the European Chapter of the Association for Computational Linguistics: Volume 2, Short Papers*. Association for Computational Linguistics, Valencia, Spain, pages 324–330. http://www.aclweb.org/anthology/E17-2052.

Riyaz Ahmad Bhat, Irshad Ahmad Bhat, and Dipti Misra Sharma. 2017b. Improving transition-based dependency parsing of hindi and urdu by modeling syntactically relevant phenomena. *ACM Transactions on Asian and Low-Resource Language Information Processing (TALLIP)* 16(3):17.

Riyaz Ahmad Bhat, Rajesh Bhatt, Annahita Farudi, Prescott Klassen, Bhuvana Narasimhan, Martha Palmer, Owen Rambow, Dipti Misra Sharma, Ashwini Vaidya, Sri Ramagurumurthy Vishnu, et al. 2015. The Hindi/Urdu treebank project. In *Handbook of Linguistic Annotation*, Springer Press.

Noam Chomsky. 1965. *Aspects of the Theory of Syntax*, volume 11. MIT press.

Bernard Comrie. 1981. Language universals and language typology. *Syntax and Morphology* .

Marie-Catherine De Marneffe, Timothy Dozat, Natalia Silveira, Katri Haverinen, Filip Ginter, Joakim Nivre, and Christopher D Manning. 2014. Universal stanford dependencies: A cross-linguistic typology. In *Proceedings of the Ninth International Conference on Language Resources and Evaluation*. volume 14, pages 4585–92.

John Duchi, Elad Hazan, and Yoram Singer. 2011. Adaptive subgradient methods for online learning and stochastic optimization. *Journal of Machine Learning Research* 12(Jul).

Jennifer Foster. 2010. cba to check the spelling investigating parser performance on discussion forum posts. In *Human Language Technologies: The 2010 Annual Conference of the North American Chapter of the Association for Computational Linguistics*. Association for Computational Linguistics, pages 381–384.

Geoffrey E Hinton, Nitish Srivastava, Alex Krizhevsky, Ilya Sutskever, and Ruslan R Salakhutdinov. 2012. Improving neural networks by preventing co-adaptation of feature detectors. *arXiv preprint arXiv:1207.0580* .

Yoon Kim. 2014. Convolutional neural networks for sentence classification. In *Proceedings of the 2014 Conference on Empirical Methods in Natural Language Processing (EMNLP)*. Association for Computational Linguistics, Doha, Qatar, pages 1746–1751. http://www.aclweb.org/anthology/D14-1181.

Tracy Holloway King. 1995. *Configuring Topic and Focus in Russian*. Ph.D. thesis, Stanford University.

Eliyahu Kiperwasser and Yoav Goldberg. 2016. Simple and accurate dependency parsing using bidirectional lstm feature representations. *Transactions of the Association for Computational Linguistics* 4:313–327.

Katalin É Kiss. 1995. *Discourse Configurational Languages*. Oxford University Press.

Anoop Kumar Mahajan. 1990. *The A/A-bar Distinction and Movement Theory*. Ph.D. thesis, Massachusetts Institute of Technology.

Joakim Nivre. 2003. An efficient algorithm for projective dependency parsing. In *Proceedings of the 8th International Workshop on Parsing Technologies (IWPT)*.

Joakim Nivre, Željko Agić, Lars Ahrenberg, Maria Jesus Aranzabe, Masayuki Asahara, Aitziber Atutxa, Miguel Ballesteros, John Bauer, Kepa Bengoetxea, Yevgeni Berzak, Riyaz Ahmad Bhat, Eckhard Bick, Carl Börstell, Cristina Bosco, Gosse Bouma, Sam Bowman, Gülşen Cebirolu Eryiit, Giuseppe G. A. Celano, Fabricio Chalub, Çar Çöltekin, Miriam Connor, Elizabeth Davidson, Marie-Catherine de Marneffe, Arantza Diaz de Ilarraza, Kaja Dobrovoljc, Timothy Dozat, Kira Droganova, Puneet Dwivedi, Marhaba Eli, Tomaž Erjavec, Richárd Farkas, Jennifer Foster, Claudia

Freitas, Katarína Gajdošová, Daniel Galbraith, Marcos Garcia, Moa Gärdenfors, Sebastian Garza, Filip Ginter, Iakes Goenaga, Koldo Gojenola, Memduh Gökrmak, Yoav Goldberg, Xavier Gómez Guinovart, Berta Gonzáles Saavedra, Matias Grioni, Normunds Grūzītis, Bruno Guillaume, Jan Hajič, Linh Hà M, Dag Haug, Barbora Hladká, Radu Ion, Elena Irimia, Anders Johannsen, Fredrik Jørgensen, Hüner Kaşkara, Hiroshi Kanayama, Jenna Kanerva, Boris Katz, Jessica Kenney, Natalia Kotsyba, Simon Krek, Veronika Laippala, Lucia Lam, Phng Lê Hng, Alessandro Lenci, Nikola Ljubešić, Olga Lyashevskaya, Teresa Lynn, Aibek Makazhanov, Christopher Manning, Cătălina Mărănduc, David Mareček, Héctor Martínez Alonso, André Martins, Jan Mašek, Yuji Matsumoto, Ryan McDonald, Anna Missilä, Verginica Mititelu, Yusuke Miyao, Simonetta Montemagni, Keiko Sophie Mori, Shunsuke Mori, Bohdan Moskalevskyi, Kadri Muischnek, Nina Mustafina, Kaili Müürisep, Lng Nguyn Th, Huyn Nguyn Th Minh, Vitaly Nikolaev, Hanna Nurmi, Petya Osenova, Robert Östling, Lilja Øvrelid, Valeria Paiva, Elena Pascual, Marco Passarotti, Cenel-Augusto Perez, Slav Petrov, Jussi Piitulainen, Barbara Plank, Martin Popel, Lauma Pretkalnia, Prokopis Prokopidis, Tiina Puolakainen, Sampo Pyysalo, Alexandre Rademaker, Loganathan Ramasamy, Livy Real, Laura Rituma, Rudolf Rosa, Shadi Saleh, Baiba Saulīte, Sebastian Schuster, Wolfgang Seeker, Mojgan Seraji, Lena Shakurova, Mo Shen, Natalia Silveira, Maria Simi, Radu Simionescu, Katalin Simkó, Mária Šimková, Kiril Simov, Aaron Smith, Carolyn Spadine, Alane Suhr, Umut Sulubacak, Zsolt Szántó, Takaaki Tanaka, Reut Tsarfaty, Francis Tyers, Sumire Uematsu, Larraitz Uria, Gertjan van Noord, Viktor Varga, Veronika Vincze, Lars Wallin, Jing Xian Wang, Jonathan North Washington, Mats Wirén, Zdeněk Žabokrtský, Amir Zeldes, Daniel Zeman, and Hanzhi Zhu. 2016. Universal dependencies 1.4. LINDAT/CLARIN digital library at the Institute of Formal and Applied Linguistics, Charles University in Prague. http://hdl.handle.net/11234/1-1827.

Joakim Nivre and Jens Nilsson. 2005. Pseudo-projective dependency parsing. In *Proceedings of the 43rd Annual Meeting on Association for Computational Linguistics*.

Barbara Plank. 2016. What to do about non-standard (or non-canonical) language in nlp. *arXiv preprint arXiv:1608.07836*.

Eser Erguvanlı Taylan. 1984. *The Function of Word Order in Turkish Grammar*, volume 106. Univ of California Press.

Lonneke Van der Plas, James Henderson, and Paola Merlo. 2009. Domain adaptation with artificial data for semantic parsing of speech. In *Proceedings of Human Language Technologies: The 2009 Annual Conference of the North American Chapter of the Association for Computational Linguistics, Companion Volume: Short Papers*. Association for Computational Linguistics, pages 125–128.

Jason Van Hulse, Taghi M Khoshgoftaar, and Amri Napolitano. 2007. Experimental perspectives on learning from imbalanced data. In *Proceedings of the 24th international conference on Machine learning*. ACM.

Dingquan Wang and Jason Eisner. 2016. The galactic dependencies treebanks: Getting more data by synthesizing new languages. *Transactions of the Association for Computational Linguistics* 4:491–505. https://transacl.org/ojs/index.php/tacl/article/view/917.

A Supplementary Material

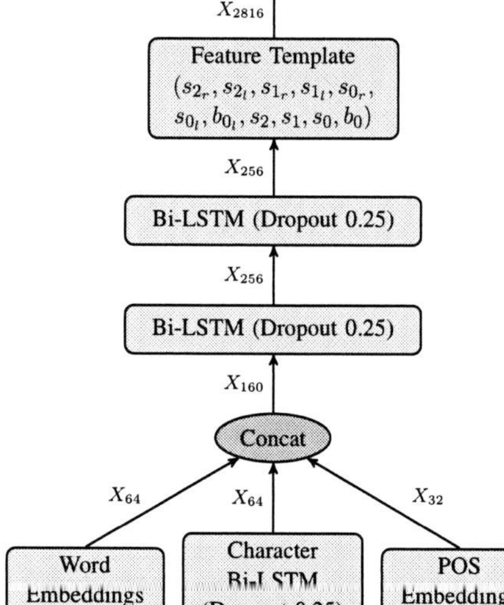

Figure 3: Parsing Architecture

S.No.	Data-set	Recall
1.	Newswire^{PG}	96.98
2.	Conversation^{PG}	91.33
3.	Newswire^{UD}	97.59
4.	Conversation^{UD}	89.40

Table 4: POS tagging accuracies on PG and UD evaluation (newswire and converstaion) data.

Using hyperlinks to improve multilingual partial parsers

Anders Søgaard

Dpt. of Computer Science, University of Copenhagen

http://cst.dk/anders/

soegaard@di.ku.dk

Abstract

Syntactic annotation is costly and not available for the vast majority of the world's languages. We show that sometimes we can do away with less labeled data by exploiting more readily available forms of mark-up. Specifically, we revisit an idea from Valentin Spitkovsky's work (2010), namely that hyperlinks typically bracket syntactic constituents or chunks. We strengthen his results by showing that not only can hyperlinks help in low resource scenarios, exemplified here by Quechua, but learning from hyperlinks can also improve state-of-the-art NLP models for English newswire. We also present out-of-domain evaluation on English Ontonotes 4.0.

1 Introduction

Syntactic analysis can be used to improve knowledge extraction, speech synthesis, machine translation, and error correction, for example, but the quality of syntactic parsers relies heavily on the quality and amount of available annotated data. This holds in particular for full syntactic parsing, but even for more robust *partial* parsers, good models require large and representative, annotated corpora.

Such annotated corpora are costly to produce and generally not available for the vast majority of the world's languages. Even for English, resources are limited, and state-of-the-art parsers for English newswire are trained on 30 years old newswire from a single newspaper. When evaluated on more recent newswire or other newspapers, we observe significant performance drops.

This is a combination of overfitting and data scarcity. While more annotated resources can im-prove this situation, annotation does not seem to scale with our needs for automated syntactic analysis, or with the rapid development of modern languages like English. Hence, we have to consider other types of data to adapt our models to other varieties of newswire, or of language, more generally.

Using (more representative) raw text in combination with (less representative) annotated data to do semi-supervised learning is challenging, but occasionally successful. In this paper, we consider an equally readily available, potential source of weak supervision, namely hypertext. Consider the following hypertext:

```
The violence, which has already been called some
evocative names -- <href>intifada<\ href>,
<href>jihad<\href>, <href>jihad<guerilla
war<\href>, <href>insurrection<\href>,
<href>rebellion<\href>, and <href>civil
war<\href> -- prompts several reflections.
```

This sentence is a random sentence taken from the Internet. The mark-up is hyperlinks, referring the reader to related websites. The hyperlinks mark passsages of the text highlighting the topics of the linked websites.

The marked passages are *intifada, jihad, guerilla war, insurrection, rebellion* and *civil war.* Note that these are not just words, but also phrases. In this example, they are all noun phrases.

Spitkovsky et al. (2010) also looked at hyperlinks and observed that the vast majority of marked passages were syntactic constituents such as noun and verb phrases. He then went on to show that this data is potentially useful for unsupervised induction of dependency parsers.

We build directly on this work, but go on to show that hyperlinks are not just useful for unsupervised induction of NLP models. It is also possible to improve state-of-the-art supervised NLP models, by jointly learning to predict hyperlinks from raw HTML files. Specifically, we show that

Proceedings of the 15th International Conference on Parsing Technologies, pages 67–71,
Pisa, Italy; September 20–22, 2017. ©2017 Association for Computational Linguistics

hard parameter sharing of hidden layers with a deep bi-LSTM model for predicting hyperlinks is an efficient regularizer for several state-of-the-art NLP models.

Contributions Our contributions are as follows: (a) We revisit the idea of using raw HTML data for weak supervision of NLP models. (b) We show that multi-task learning with hyperlink prediction as an auxiliary task improves performance across three tasks: syntactic chunking, semantic supersense tagging, and CCG supertagging. We also see improvements on out-of-domain English data, as well as in experiments with syntactic chunking with hyperlinks for Quechua.

Related work Hard parameter sharing of hidden layers has become a popular approach to multi-task learning. It was originally introduced in Caruana (1993), but first applied in NLP in Collobert et al. (2011), and it was shown, empirically, to be an effective regularizer across two different NLP tasks in Søgaard and Goldberg (2016). Using more readily available data resources that are not annotated by linguists, but still carry linguistic signals, was previously explored by Klerke et al. (2016) and Plank (2016).

Baxter (2000) shows, in the context of linear models, that if two problems, P and R, share optimal hypothesis classes, then the induction of a model from a sample of P can efficiently regularize the induction of a model from a sample of R. This is too strong an assumption for our purposes, obviously, since even our label sets are different, but we also have more wiggle room than heavily mean-constrained linear models, for example. In fact, hidden layer sharing relaxes the above assumption quite a bit. We do not need the optimal hypothesis classes to overlap. Hidden layer sharing can work even with the optimal hypothesis classes of P and R distinct, if there is a joint representation such that P and R both become linearly separable. Whether this is the case, is an empirical question.

2 Experiments

Model Our model merges two deep recurrent neural networks through hard parameter sharing. We use three-layered, bi-directional long short-term memory networks (LSTMs) (Hochreiter and Schmidhuber, 1997), in a way similar to Søgaard and Goldberg (2016). We op-

timize hyper-parameters on development data for chunking in a single-task architecture, training for 10 epochs, and using a hidden layer size that is equal to the embedding layer size. For English, we use the SENNA word embedding for English and 50-dimensional hidden layers.[1] For Quechua, we use Polyglot embeddings and 64-dimensional hidden layers.

In a multi-task learning (MTL) setting, we have several prediction tasks over the same input space. In our case, the input is the words in a sentence, and the different tasks are syntactic chunking, semantic supersense tagging and CCG supertagging. And hyperlink prediction. Each task has its own output vocabulary (a task specific tagset), but all of them map any length n input sequence into a length n output sequence.

The most common approach to multi-task learning in NLP these days is to share parameters across most of the hidden layers of two or more single task networks. In the k-layers deep bi-LSTM tagger described above this is naturally achieved by sharing the bi-LSTM part of the network across tasks, but training a specialized classification tagger $f_t(v_i^k)$ for each task t.

Note that this particular kind of multi-task learning can also be cast as a kind of mean-constrained matrix regularization. While in some sense, hard parameter sharing is more heavily regularized than more traditional approaches to multi-task learning, such as mean-constrained L2 regularization, we obtain more wiggle room by only sharing the embedding and LSTM parameters.

Our model is implemented in pyCNN and made available at:

    bitbucket.org/soegaard/hyperlink-iwpt17

English data In our English in-domain experiments, we use three datasets for our target tasks, namely the Penn Treebank for syntactic chunking (Marcus et al., 1993), the SemCor corpus for semantic supersense tagging (Miller et al., 1994; Ciaramita and Altun, 2006), and the CCGBank[2] for CCG super-tagging. See Figure 1 for an example of all three layers of annotation. The training section of the chunking dataset consists of 8936 sentences. SemCor contains 15465 sentences, and the CCGBank contains 39604 sentences. For our auxiliary task, for replicability (and as a tribute

---

[1] http://ronan.collobert.com/senna/
[2] LDC2005T13

Words:	Are	prairie	dogs	conscious
Chunking:	B-VP	B-NP	I-NP	B-ADJP
Semcor:	O	O	Animal.N	Cognition.ADJ
CCG:	(S[adj]\NP))/NP	NP	NP\NP	S[adj]\NP)
Href	O		B-HREF	I-HREF	O

Figure 1: Examples of linguistic annotation

to Valentin's seminal work), we use the hypertext dump used in Spitkovsky et al. (2010), made publicly available,[3] which contains 2000 sentences. To evaluate the robustness of our syntactic chunker, we also evaluate it across multiple domains using data from Ontonotes 4.0.[4]

Quechua data We use constituent annotations of Quechua sentences, from Rios (2015), and convert them into partial annotations. The sentences are from an autobiography. The training data consists of 1500 sentences, and the test data is 837 sentences. The annotations only provide NP and VP bracketing, leaving us with five labels. For our auxiliary task, we use 350 sentences from Quechua Wikipedia that contain hyperlinks. The data is made publicly available.[5]

Balance between tasks Our auxiliary datasets are relatively small, in the light of hyperlinks being readily available. In hard parameter sharing, it is important not to swamp the main task, and as our learning curve experiments indicate, it would not be beneficial to sample more auxiliary task data. Soft parameter sharing approaches may better leverage large volumes of hyperlink data. See discussion of learning curves in §3.

3 Results

In all our experiments, we report averages over three runs.

English in-sample tests In our first experiment, we train an LSTM on English newswire and apply it to English newswire, using the standard datasets from the English Penn Treebank, Semcor, and the CCGBank. Our baseline is a single-task LSTM architecture, with the hyper-parameters suggested by Søgaard and Goldberg (2016). We verify that this leads to state-of-the-art performance. In fact, our single-task baseline is slightly better than the

one used in Søgaard and Goldberg (2016). We then train the same network architecture with the hyperlink data from Spitkovsky et al. (2010) as our auxiliary data.

Using hyperlinks as auxiliary data leads to moderate improvements for syntactic chunking, and very big improvements for supersense tagging and CCG supertagging. Where for syntactic chunking, the error reduction is less than 3%, it is 17% for supersense tagging, and 13% for CCG supertagging.

English out-of-sample tests We use syntactic chunking data from OntoNotes 4.0. The data includes manually annotated data from several sources across several domains: newswire, broadcast, broadcasted news, and weblogs. We use a single file for training (WSJ), and a single file for development (CCTV), and all other files for testing. We have 23 files for testing, spanning weblogs from C2E to (English) news from Xinhua.

Performance is generally much lower, because of the divergence between training and test data. Whereas before, performance (F_1) on test data was about 95%, cross-domain performance is generally about 85%. See results in Table 2. The average gain from multi-task learning remains small, even when we consider the test domains with highest divergence (weblogs).

It is important to note that unlike other experiments using multi-task learning for domain adaptation, e.g., Søgaard and Goldberg (2016), our auxiliary task data is sampled from the domain of the training data (newswire), not of the test data. This may effect results quite a bit, and our results do therefore not contradict the results in Søgaard and Goldberg (2016) and related work.

Also, note that there are other possible explanations for the differences in performance gains across target tasks. One possible predictor for multi-task learning gains may for example be properties of single-task learning curves, variance across model parameters, etc. See Bingel and Søgaard (2017) for work exploring such predictors of when multi-task learning works

---

[3] `nlp.stanford.edu/valentin/pubs/markup-data.tar.bz2`
[4] LDC2011T03
[5] `bitbucket.org/soegaard/hyperlink-iwpt17`

| | **English** | | | **Quechua** |
	Chunking	SemCor	CCG	Chunking
LSTM	0.9543	0.6757	0.9169	0.7169
LSTM w. HREF	**0.9555**	**0.7312**	**0.9275**	**0.7283**
Err.red.	0.0263	0.1711	0.1276	0.0403
S&G16 (bl)	0.9528	-	0.9104	-
S&G16 (best)	0.9556	-	0.9326	-

Table 1: Improvements in F_1 using hyperlinks as auxiliary data across three NLP tasks. Søgaard and Goldberg (2016) for comparison (S&G16). S&G16 (best) is similar to our hyperlinks model, but uses POS-tag annotated data for co-supervising the initial LSTM layer instead of hyperlinks data for co-supervising *all* the hidden layers. Previous work on SemCor assumes gold-standard POS tags and achieves up to 80% F_1-score. We are not aware of previous work on Quechua.

	Best on	Macro-average	Macro-average on weblogs
LSTM	5/22	0.8516	0.8525
LSTM w. HREF	17/22	0.8536	0.8540

Table 2: Small, but consistent improvement for domain adaptation for English chunking

in general.

Learning curve Hard parameter sharing makes models less prone to overfitting (Søgaard and Goldberg, 2016). Since little labeled data means higher variance, this suggests that multi-task learning is more effective in scenarios where data is scarce. This, in our case, would mean that hyperlinks reduce the need for labeled data.

It is not straight-forward, however, to interpret standard learning curves that only vary the number of training data points for the target task, since the auxiliary task may easily swamp the target task. Even if we balance auxiliary and target data sets, results can still be hard to interpret: If we fix the hyper parameters, the regularization effect of the auxiliary task reduces with less data, since our network can effectively memorize the data points and thereby discriminate between the two tasks and allocate parts of the network for each task (Zhang et al., 2017).

When we balance the amount of target and auxiliary task data, and reduce the expressivity of our networks, we observe higher gains (error reductions of up to 15%) with small amounts of data ($20 \leq n \leq 100$). The optimal balance between the target and the auxiliary task seems to favor the target task. If we subsample the auxiliary data to be proportionally smaller (n a third of target data), we see greater and more robust improvements, especially for small n.

Quechua in-sample tests We train the same models on the Quechua data. We use the Wikipedia-trained, 64-dimensional Polyglot embeddings[6] and use 32-dimensional LSTM layers. We observe a 4% error reduction, which is higher than for our English in-sample test, but smaller than the improvements on the other tasks.

4   Conclusion

Readily available data (HTML mark-up) can be used to improve partial parsers for low-resource languages, as well as state-of-the-art partial parsers for English, with improvements that carry over to new, unseen domains.

Acknowledgements

Thanks to the anonymous reviewers for their comments that helped improve the paper. This research is funded by the ERC Starting Grant LOW-LANDS No. 313695.

---

[6]polyglot.readthedocs.io

References

Jonathan Baxter. 2000. A model of inductive bias learning. *Journal of Artificial Intelligence Research* 12:149–198.

Joachim Bingel and Anders Søgaard. 2017. Identifying beneficial task relations for multi-task learning in deep neural networks. In *EACL*.

Rich Caruana. 1993. Multitask learning: a knowledge-based source of inductive bias. In *ICML*.

Massimiliano Ciaramita and Yasemin Altun. 2006. Broad-coverage sense disambiguation and information extraction with a supersense sequence tagger. In *Proc. of Proceedings of EMNLP*. Sydney, Australia, pages 594–602.

Ronan Collobert, Jason Weston, Léon Bottou, Michael Karlen, Koray Kavukcuoglu, and Pavel Kuksa. 2011. Natural language processing (almost) from scratch. *The Journal of Machine Learning Research* 12:2493–2537.

Sepp Hochreiter and Jürgen Schmidhuber. 1997. Long short-term memory. *Neural computation* 9(8):1735–1780.

Sigrid Klerke, Yoav Goldberg, and Anders Søgaard. 2016. Improving sentence compression by learning to predict gaze. In *NAACL*.

Mitchell Marcus, Mary Marcinkiewicz, and Beatrice Santorini. 1993. Building a large annotated corpus of English: the Penn Treebank. *Computational Linguistics* 19(2):313–330.

George A. Miller, Martin Chodorow, Shari Landes, Claudia Leacock, and Robert G. Thomas. 1994. Using a semantic concordance for sense identification. In *Proceedings of the workshop on Human Language Technology*. Association for Computational Linguistics, pages 240–243.

Barbara Plank. 2016. Keystroke dynamics as signal for shallow syntactic parsing. In *COLING*.

Annette Rios. 2015. *A Basic Language Technology Toolkit for Quechua*. Ph.D. thesis, University of Zurich.

Anders Søgaard and Yoav Goldberg. 2016. Deep multitask learning with low level tasks superviser at lower layers. In *ACL*.

Valentin Spitkovsky, Daniel Jurafsky, and Hiyan Alshawi. 2010. Profiting from mark-up: Hyper-text annotations for guided parsing. In *ACL*.

Chiyuan Zhang, Samy Bengio, Moritz Hardt, Benjamin Recht, and Oriol Vinyals. 2017. Understanding deep learning requires rethinking generalization. In *ICLR*.

Correcting prepositional phrase attachments using multimodal corpora

Sebastien Delecraz and **Alexis Nasr** and **Frederic Bechet** and **Benoit Favre**
Aix-Marseille University, CNRS, LIF
`firstname.lastname@lif.univ-mrs.fr`

Abstract

PP-attachments are an important source of errors in parsing natural language. We propose in this article to use data coming from a multimodal corpus, combining textual, visual and conceptual information, as well as a correction strategy, to propose alternative attachments in the output of a parser.

1 Introduction

Prepositional phrase attachments (*PP-attachments*) are known to be an important source of errors in parsing natural language. The main reason being that, in many cases, correct attachments cannot be predicted accurately based on pure syntactic considerations: their prediction ask for precise lexical co-occurrences or non linguistic knowledge. Such information is usually not found in treebanks that are limited in their size and therefore do not model many bi-lexical phenomena.

In this paper, we propose to combine textual, conceptual and visual information extracted from a multimodal corpus to train a PP-attachment correction model. In order to do so, we have used a corpus made of pairs (S, P) where S is a sentence and P a picture. Some words of S have been manually linked to bounding boxes in P and tagged with coarse-grained conceptual types. The relative positions of the boxes in the pictures as well as conceptual types and the lexical nature of words involved in a PP-attachment are used as features for a classifier that classifies a PP-attachment as either correct or wrong. Given the parse tree T of S, and a target preposition, its different possible attachment sites are identified and the classifier is used to select the most promising one.

Our contributions in this study are the selection and the manual annotation of a corpus of ambiguous PP-attachments from the multimodal corpus *Flickr30k Entities* (Plummer et al., 2017); the study of the relative importance of different kinds of features for the PP-attachment resolution problem, from very specific ones (lexical features) to very generic ones (spatial features); and the combination of them in a single model for improving the accuracy of a syntactic dependency parser.

The structure of the paper is the following: section 2 presents some related work in the fields of PP-attachment and multimodal language processing. In section 3 the multimodal corpus is described as well as the manual annotation that has been performed on it. In section 4 the error prediction classifier is described and its performance evaluated. In section 5, the correction strategy is described. The experiments are described in section 6 and section 7 concludes the paper.

2 Related work

This work is related to two different areas: *multimodal language processing* through the joint analysis of image and text describing the same scene and *syntactic parsing* through the problem of prepositional phrase attachment resolution (*PP-attachments*).

The joint processing of image and natural language is not novel. It has been studied mostly in the context of natural language generation, for example for generating a textual description of a video or an image. Early work (Herzog and Wazinski, 1994) computes first spatial relations among objects detected in images with knowledge-based language generation model in order to generate short descriptions of videos in limited domains (traffic scenes, soccer matches). Recently open-domain language generation from

Proceedings of the 15th International Conference on Parsing Technologies, pages 72–77,
Pisa, Italy; September 20–22, 2017. ©2017 Association for Computational Linguistics

Figure 1: Example of the *F30kE* annotations.

images or videos received a lot of attention through the use of multimodal deep neural networks (Vinyals et al., 2015). Theses models built a unified representation for both image and language features and generate in an end-to-end process a text directly from an image, without an explicit representation (syntactic or semantic) of the text generated.

For syntactic parsing, the problem of PP-attachment has a long history in Natural Language Processing and a wealth of different methods and sources of information have been used to alleviate it. Giving a overview of this vast body of literature is well beyond the scope of this paper. Traditionally, two types of resources have been used to help resolving PP-attachment, semantic knowledge bases (Agirre et al., 2008; Dasigi et al., 2017), and corpora (Rakshit et al., 2016; Mirroshandel and Nasr, 2016; Belinkov et al., 2014; de Kok et al., 2017).

We are not aware of much work using multimodal information for PP-attachment. In the most relevant work that we have found (Christie et al., 2016), a parser is used to predict the k best parses for a sentence and this set is re-ranked using visual information. The main difference with their work is, in our case, the combined use of lexical, semantic and visual cues as well as the method used (k best parses v/s parse correction).

3   Data

The multimodal corpus used in this work is the Flickr30k Entities (*F30kE*) (Plummer et al., 2017), an extension of the original Flickr30k dataset (Young et al., 2014). This corpus is composed of almost $32K$ images and, for each image, five captions describing the image have been produced. Besides, every object in the image that corresponds to a mention in the captions has been manually identified with a bounding box. Bounding boxes and the mentions in the captions have been paired together via co-reference links. A total of $244K$ such links have been annotated. Furthermore, each mention in the captions has been categorized into eight coarse-grained conceptual types using manually constructed dictionaries. The types are: people, body parts, animals, clothing, instruments, vehicles, scene, and other. One example of the corpus has been reproduced in Figure 1.

Our goal in this study is to evaluate several set of features, at the lexical, conceptual and vision levels, for the PP-attachment task. The *F30kE* corpus contains already all these features, but no syntactic annotation was provided on the image captions. Focusing on the PP-attachment problem, we added such annotations with the following process: first the whole caption corpus of *F30kE* was processed by a Part-Of-Speech tagger (Nasr et al., 2011); a set of regular expressions on the POS labels were defined in order to select sentences that contain a preposition that might lead to an ambiguous PP-attachment; finally all these sentences were manually processed in order to attach the selected prepositions to their correct syntactic governor.

Captions containing ambiguous PP-attachment have been identified using two simple rules: a preposition is considered ambiguous if it is preceded by at least two nouns or a verb and a noun, in other word, the captions must match one of the following regular expressions: X* N X* N X* p X* or X* V X* N X* p X*, where N and V stand for the POS tags noun and verb, X stand for any POS tag and p is the target preposition.

22800 captions were selected this way. They constitute our *PP-corpus*. This corpus contains 29068 preposition occurrences that have been manually attached to their syntactic governor. The *PP-corpus* has been divided into a train set, made of 18241 captions (23254 annotated prepositions), a development set, made of 2271 captions (2907 annotated prepositions) and a test set, made of 2288 captions (2907 prepositions).

4 Error Prediction

The train part of the *PP-corpus* has been used to train a classifier that predicts whether a PP-attachment proposed by a parser is correct or not. The parser used is a standard arc-eager transition based parser (Nivre, 2003), trained on sections $0-18$ of the Penn Treebank (Marcus et al., 1993). The parser was run on the train set of the corpus and, for each occurrence of a manually attached preposition, a negative or a positive example has been produced depending on whether the parser has predicted the correct attachment or not. This data set is composed of 17643 positive and 5611 negative examples. It has been used to train a classifier that predicts whether the attachment made by the parser is correct or not.

The classifier used for this task is the *Icsiboost* classifier (Favre et al., 2007). This Adaboost classifier is a combination of weak learners that learn a threshold for continuous features, and a binary indicator for discrete ones. Training minimizes the exponential loss function by greedily selecting the best classifier and re-weighting the training set to focus on misclassified examples. This kind of classifier has two benefits: models are easier to interpret than in other families of models, and the greedy selection of classifier effectively selects relevant features and is less affected by noise.

Three sets of features have been used to train the classifier, from the most specific ones (lexical features) to the most generic ones (spatial features). The set T is composed of textual features, extracted from the captions. The set C is composed of conceptual features, based on the conceptual classes associated with boxes or words. Set V is composed of visual features representing spatial information about the objects annotated in the image (enriched with bounding boxes).

Let GpD be a PP-attachment where G is the governor of the preposition p and D its dependent. We define the functions $POS(X)$ that denote the POS of word X, $LEM(X)$ its lemma, $FCT(X)$ its syntactic function, $CON(X)$ the list of its conceptual types, $BB(X)$ its bounding box (in the case where X is associated with several boxes, $SBB(X)$ lists this set). $DIST(X,Y)$ represents the distance between words X and Y in the sen-

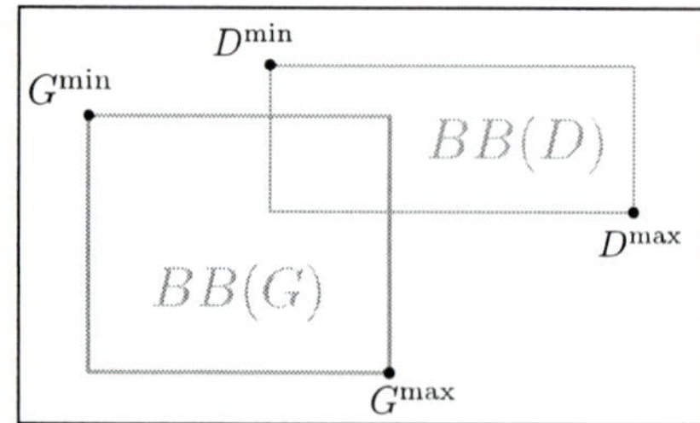

Figure 2: Points of interest from (G) and (D) boxes.

tence. Here is a detailed description of the features of the three different categories using the notations defined above[1]:

Textual features:

$$T_1 = POS(G) \qquad T_2 = LEM(G)$$
$$T_3 = POS(D) \qquad T_4 = LEM(D)$$
$$T_5 = FCT(p) \qquad T_6 = DIST(G,p)$$
$$T_7 = LEM(G) + LEM(D)$$
$$T_8 = POS(G) + POS(D)$$

Conceptual features:

$$C_1 = CON(G) \qquad C_2 = CON(D)$$
$$C_3 = CON(G) + CON(D)$$

Eight types of concept are defined: people, body parts, animals, clothing, instruments, vehicles, scene, and other. The value UNK is used if either G or D is not associated with a type.

Visual features: in Figure 2, we identify two corners for every bounding box B: $B^{\min}$ and $B^{\max}$, that are used compute the visual features:

$$V_1 = \frac{D_x^{\min} - G_x^{\min}}{G_x^{\max} - G_x^{\min}} \qquad V_2 = \frac{D_x^{\max} - G_x^{\min}}{G_x^{\max} - G_x^{\min}}$$
$$V_3 = \frac{D_y^{\min} - G_y^{\min}}{G_y^{\max} - G_y^{\min}} \qquad V_4 = \frac{D_y^{\max} - G_y^{\min}}{G_y^{\max} - G_y^{\min}}$$
$$V_5 = |SBB(D)| \qquad V_6 = |SBB(G)|$$
$$V_7 = Area(BB(D)) \ / \ Area(BB(G))$$

Features $V_1 \ldots V_4$ describe the relative position of D box with respect to G box, respectively on the x and y axis. Features V_5 and V_6 describe the number of boxes associated with D and G. V_7 is the ratio of the areas of D and G boxes. In case of multi-boxing, we compute the distance between $G^{\min}$ and $D^{\min}$ and keep the two closest boxes as $BB(G)$ and $BB(D)$. When either G or D does not have a box, the UNK value is used.

It is important to notice that the visual features in our study are limited to spatial information about bounding boxes. No image analysis of the content of the boxes is done since this level of

---

[1]All feature sets also contain the general feature $LEM(p)$: the lemma of the preposition.

Features	Train	Dev	Test
Baseline	0.76	0.76	0.75
T	0.94	0.90	0.88
C	0.83	0.84	0.83
V	0.78	0.79	0.77
T + C	0.96	0.91	0.90
T + C + V	0.98	0.91	0.89

Table 1: Classifier accuracy by model.

information is covered by the *conceptual features* which attach to each box a concept tag related to its content.

Table 1 details the classification accuracy for each model trained using different feature combinations, on train, development and test sets. The accuracy is computed on the attachments predicted by the parser. A baseline has been added to Table 1 that selects the majority class which is the *positive* class, therefore it reflects the accuracy of the parser for PP-attachment (75% accuracy on the test set).

As one can see, all four models beat the baseline. The best features are the lexical ones. This is expected as they are the most specific ones, requiring a training corpus matching closely the application domain. Conceptual features obtain very good results although they can be considered as generic since only 8 types of concepts are considered. The visual features are just slighlty better than the baseline (+2%), however we have to keep in mind that the only information considered here are spatial features of bounding boxes. Since not all prepositions in the *PP-corpus* are related to spatial positions, and considering the genericity of the features used, obtaining an accuracy of 77% without any lexical or semantic features is an interesting result.

By combining feature sets we can improve accuracy. The best combination is the textual and the conceptual features together.

5   Correction Strategy

The classifier developed in the previous section only checked if a PP-attachment proposed by the parser is correct or not. In this section we integrate this classifier in a correction strategy in order to improve the accuracy of our parser. This correction strategy is inspired from the ideas of Anguiano and Candito (2011); Attardi and Ciaramita (2007); Hall and Novák (2005): given a sentence S, a parse T for S and a target preposition p, a set

G_p of candidate governors for p is identified. The highest scoring $c \in G_p$ is then assigned as the new governor of p in T.

The set G_p is initialized with g, the actual governor of p in the parse T. The following rules are then applied to T and new potential governors are added to G_p:

$$
\begin{array}{lll}
1 & N \leftarrow V \rightarrow p & \Rightarrow G_p = G_p \cup \{N\} \\
2 & N \leftarrow P \leftarrow V \rightarrow p & \Rightarrow G_p = G_p \cup \{N\} \\
3 & N' \leftarrow N \rightarrow p & \Rightarrow G_p = G_p \cup \{N'\} \\
4 & N' \leftarrow P \leftarrow N \rightarrow p & \Rightarrow G_p = G_p \cup \{N'\} \\
5 & N' \rightarrow X \rightarrow N \rightarrow p & \Rightarrow G_p = G_p \cup \{N'\} \\
6 & N \rightarrow N \rightarrow p & \Rightarrow G_p = G_p \cup \{N\} \\
7 & V \rightarrow N \rightarrow p & \Rightarrow G_p = G_p \cup \{V\}
\end{array}
$$

Rule 1 is interpreted as follows: if target preposition p has a verbal governor which has a noun N as a direct dependent, N is added as a candidate governor. These rules have been evaluated on our development corpus. When applying the rules to the output of the parser, the correct governor of the manually annotated prepositions is in the set G_p in 92.28% of the cases. This figure is our upper bound for PP-attachments.

Given the sentence *a man throws a child into the air at a beach*, and target preposition *at* that the parser has attached to *child*, the two rules 4 and 7 apply, yielding $G_p = \{child,\ air,\ throws\}$

	man	throws	child	into	air	at
4			N	P	$N*$	p
7		$V*$	N			p

The correction strategy is the following: given an attachment GpD produced by the parser, this attachment is given as input to the error detector. If the detector predicts the CORRECT class, then the attachment is kept unchanged. Otherwise, the set G_p is computed and the element g of the set that maximizes the score $S(gpD, \text{CORRECT})$ is selected (*i.e.* the score that the classifier associates with the class CORRECT to the given input).

6   Experiments

The results of our experiments on the test set are detailed in Table 2. The table shows the attachment accuracy for the prepositions that appear at least 30 times in the corpus. For each of these prepositions, column two displays its number of occurrences, column three (BL) shows the attachment accuracy for this preposition in the output the parser. Columns four (T), five (C), six (V) and seven (TCV) show the attachment accuracy for the corrected output for four different configurations

Prep	Occ	BL	T	C	V	TCV
into	116	0.89	0.93	0.88	0.89	0.96
with	310	0.65	0.78	0.75	0.66	0.79
through	145	0.95	0.96	0.95	0.95	0.97
behind	35	0.74	0.86	0.83	0.77	0.89
under	58	0.84	0.84	0.86	0.84	0.86
down	41	0.63	0.73	0.63	0.44	0.68
in	369	0.76	0.84	0.81	0.76	0.85
in front of	51	0.90	0.88	0.90	0.90	0.90
outside	35	0.63	0.74	0.74	0.69	0.74
on	143	0.85	0.90	0.89	0.85	0.91
around	59	0.73	0.81	0.73	0.71	0.83
for	168	0.73	0.82	0.77	0.72	0.80
at	63	0.84	0.86	0.90	0.84	0.90
along	50	0.52	0.86	0.76	0.52	0.88
across	49	0.88	0.96	0.88	0.88	0.96
against	31	0.77	0.94	0.84	0.77	0.94
near	159	0.33	0.84	0.83	0.58	0.84
towards	30	0.90	0.93	0.87	0.90	0.90
next to	137	0.89	0.89	0.88	0.89	0.89
by	76	0.84	0.86	0.86	0.84	0.87
of	72	0.93	0.93	0.93	0.93	0.93
over	111	0.66	0.85	0.73	0.66	0.86
during	41	0.71	0.76	0.73	0.71	0.76
from	140	0.76	0.86	0.78	0.76	0.84
TOTAL	2907	0.75	0.85	0.82	0.77	0.86

Table 2: PP-attachment accuracy on the test set per preposition (only those with at least 30 occurrences).

Features	Accuracy
Baseline	0.75
T	0.85
C	0.82
V	0.77
T + C	0.86
T + V	0.86
C + V	0.82
T + C + V	0.86

Table 3: PP-attachment accuracy on the test set.

of the error detector: using only one type of features (Textual, Conceptual and Visual) and all features. The last line gives the attachment accuracy on all preposition.

As one can see on Table 2, the global accuracy of the parser on all PP-attachment is equal to 75%. This figure is lower than the 86% correct PP-attachment reported by Anguiano and Candito (2011) on the Penn Treebank using the same kind of parser, which does not come as a surprise, given the different nature of these two corpora. Table 3 presents the accuracy of PP-attachment after correction with different feature set combinations. Adding conceptual features to textual features improve accuracy, however spatial features have no impact when used in conjunction with other feature sets.

Several conclusions can be drawn from these results: different prepositions have very different accuracy with the parser, ranging from 95% for preposition *through*, to 33% for preposition *near*. The correction strategy implemented has a positive impact on accuracy: changing some attachments proposed by the parser using an error corrector based on limited but specific data is useful. Similarly as the results obtained on the classification accuracy, textual features are the most useful ones. Used alone, they increase accuracy by 10 points. Although improving accuracy by 2% when used alone, visual features have no impact when combined with other feature sets. The positive impact of visual features is concentrated on three prepositions in table 2: (*near*, *behind* and *outside*). It is interesting to note that these prepositions are mostly locative. It does therefore make sense that visual features only focusing on spatial information have some impact on these prepositions. On the other extreme, preposition like *during* that are mostly temporal are logically not impacted by the correction.

7 Conclusion

We have proposed in this paper an error correction strategy for PP-attachment that extracts from a multimodal corpus features that help predict such attachments as either correct or not. This classifier is used to select among the different possible attachment points of a preposition the highest scoring one with respect to the classifier. Experiments showed that this method increases by 11 absolute points the correct PP-attachment rate. As expected the most relevant feature set is the lexical one, which is the most specific one. Conceptual features, although quite generic, obtain results close to lexical features. Visual features, limited in our case to spatial information, can improve greatly the accuracy of pp-attachment when used alone for some locative preposition, however they have no impact when mixed with more specific features.

We intend to extended this work in many directions. The first one is the definition of better visual features. We believe that more useful information can be extracted from the image to improve PP-attachment. We also consider defining a better correction strategy that will identify more possible governors to prepositions and, finally, introduce the new features directly in the parsing model.

Acknowledgments

This work has been carried out thanks to the support of French DGA in partnership with Aix-Marseille University as part of the "Club des partenaires Défense".

References

Eneko Agirre, Timothy Baldwin, and David Martinez. 2008. Improving parsing and pp attachment performance with sense information. In *ACL*. pages 317–325.

Enrique Henestroza Anguiano and Marie Candito. 2011. Parse correction with specialized models for difficult attachment types. In *Proceedings of the Conference on Empirical Methods in Natural Language Processing*. Association for Computational Linguistics, pages 1222–1233.

Giuseppe Attardi and Massimiliano Ciaramita. 2007. Tree revision learning for dependency parsing. In *HLT-NAACL*. pages 388–395.

Yonatan Belinkov, Tao Lei, Regina Barzilay, and Amir Globerson. 2014. Exploring compositional architectures and word vector representations for prepositional phrase attachment. *Transactions of the Association for Computational Linguistics* 2:561–572.

Gordon Christie, Ankit Laddha, Aishwarya Agrawal, Stanislaw Antol, Yash Goyal, Kevin Kochersberger, and Dhruv Batra. 2016. Resolving language and vision ambiguities together: Joint segmentation & prepositional attachment resolution in captioned scenes. *arXiv preprint arXiv:1604.02125* .

Pradeep Dasigi, Waleed Ammar, Chris Dyer, and Eduard Hovy. 2017. Ontology-aware token embeddings for prepositional phrase attachment. *arXiv preprint arXiv:1705.02925* .

Daniël de Kok, Jianqiang Ma, Corina Dima, and Erhard Hinrichs. 2017. Pp attachment: Where do we stand? *EACL 2017* page 311.

Benoit Favre, Dilek Hakkani-Tür, and Sebastien Cuendet. 2007. Icsiboost. `http://code.google.come/p/icsiboost`.

Keith Hall and Václav Novák. 2005. Corrective modeling for non-projective dependency parsing. In *Proceedings of the Ninth International Workshop on Parsing Technology*. Association for Computational Linguistics, pages 42–52.

Gerd Herzog and Peter Wazinski. 1994. Visual translator: Linking perceptions and natural language descriptions. *Artificial Intelligence Review* 8(2):175–187.

Mitchell P Marcus, Mary Ann Marcinkiewicz, and Beatrice Santorini. 1993. Building a large annotated corpus of english: The penn treebank. *Computational linguistics* 19(2):313–330.

Seyed Abolghasem Mirroshandel and Alexis Nasr. 2016. Integrating selectional constraints and subcategorization frames in a dependency parser. *Computational Linguistics* .

A. Nasr, F. Béchet, J.F. Rey, B. Favre, and J. Le Roux. 2011. Macaon: An nlp tool suite for processing word lattices. *Proceedings of the ACL 2011 System Demonstration* pages 86–91.

Joakim Nivre. 2003. An efficient algorithm for projective dependency parsing. In *Proceedings of the 8th International Workshop on Parsing Technologies (IWPT*. Citeseer.

Bryan A. Plummer, Liwei Wang, Chris M. Cervantes, Juan C. Caicedo, Julia Hockenmaier, and Svetlana Lazebnik. 2017. Flickr30k entities: Collecting region-to-phrase correspondences for richer image-to-sentence models. *International Journal of Computer Vision* 123(1):74–93.

Geetanjali Rakshit, Sagar Sontakke, Pushpak Bhattacharyya, and Gholamreza Haffari. 2016. Prepositional attachment disambiguation using bilingual parsing and alignments. *arXiv preprint arXiv:1603.08594* .

Oriol Vinyals, Alexander Toshev, Samy Bengio, and Dumitru Erhan. 2015. Show and tell: A neural image caption generator. In *Proceedings of the IEEE conference on computer vision and pattern recognition*. pages 3156–3164.

Peter Young, Alice Lai, Micah Hodosh, and Julia Hockenmaier. 2014. From image descriptions to visual denotations: New similarity metrics for semantic inference over event descriptions. *Transactions of the Association for Computational Linguistics* 2:67–78.

Exploiting Structure in Parsing to 1-Endpoint-Crossing Graphs

Robin Kurtz and **Marco Kuhlmann**
Department of Computer and Information Science
Linköping University, Sweden
robin.kurtz@liu.se and marco.kuhlmann@liu.se

Abstract

Deep dependency parsing can be cast as the search for maximum acyclic subgraphs in weighted digraphs. Because this search problem is intractable in the general case, we consider its restriction to the class of 1-endpoint-crossing (1ec) graphs, which has high coverage on standard data sets. Our main contribution is a characterization of 1ec graphs as a subclass of the graphs with pagenumber at most 3. Building on this we show how to extend an existing parsing algorithm for 1-endpoint-crossing trees to the full class. While the runtime complexity of the extended algorithm is polynomial in the length of the input sentence, it features a large constant, which poses a challenge for practical implementations.

1 Introduction

Motivated by applications in natural language understanding, recent work in dependency parsing has targeted 'deep' graphs, a term used to refer to representations that are not necessarily tree-shaped. Such graphs support intuitive analyses of argument sharing in control constructions, quantification, and semantic modification, among others. Data sets of deep dependency graphs are often derived from the derivations of expressive grammar formalisms; for an overview, see Kuhlmann and Oepen (2016).

Deep dependency parsing has been formalized as the search for maximum acyclic subgraphs in weighted digraphs (Schluter, 2014; Kuhlmann and Jonsson, 2015). Because this problem is known to be intractable in the general case (Guruswami et al., 2011), it is interesting to identify structural restrictions on the target graphs that can yield polynomial-time parsing algorithms without sacrificing too much of the empirical coverage.

Schluter (2015) and Kuhlmann and Jonsson (2015) propose to address deep dependency parsing under the restriction that the target structures should be *noncrossing*, a constraint related to projectivity as known from syntactic parsing. When the search space is restricted to the class of noncrossing graphs, maximum subgraph parsing is possible in time $O(n^3)$, where n is the length of the input sentence. Unfortunately, the restriction to noncrossing graphs excludes a large proportion of the linguistic data. It seems clear that deep dependency parsing, much more than syntactic parsing, needs algorithms that can handle graphs with crossing arcs.

An interesting weaker restriction than the noncrossing condition is the restriction to graphs which are *1-endpoint-crossing* (Pitler et al., 2013), a constraint originally formulated for tree-shaped graphs. The maximum 1-endpoint-crossing subtree of a weighted digraph can be found in time $O(n^4)$. In this paper we show how to generalize this result to non-trees. This is not straightforward, as the obvious modification of existing algorithm for trees turns out to be incomplete for general graphs. The key to a complete algorithm, and our main technical contribution, is a characterization of 1-endpoint-crossing graphs as a certain subset of the class of graphs with *pagenumber at most 3* (Section 3). The exact characterization refers to the restricted patterns in which arcs can cross each other. From this characterization we obtain an $O(n^5)$ algorithm for general graphs (Section 4). When a certain, rare type of crossing configurations is ruled out, the runtime complexity of the algorithm reduces to $O(n^4)$, the same as for trees.

While the runtime of both new algorithms is polynomial in the length of the input sentence, both feature large constants, which leads us to discuss challenges in extending our algorithm into a practical parser for deep dependency parsing (Section 5).

Proceedings of the 15th International Conference on Parsing Technologies, pages 78–87,
Pisa, Italy; September 20–22, 2017. ©2017 Association for Computational Linguistics

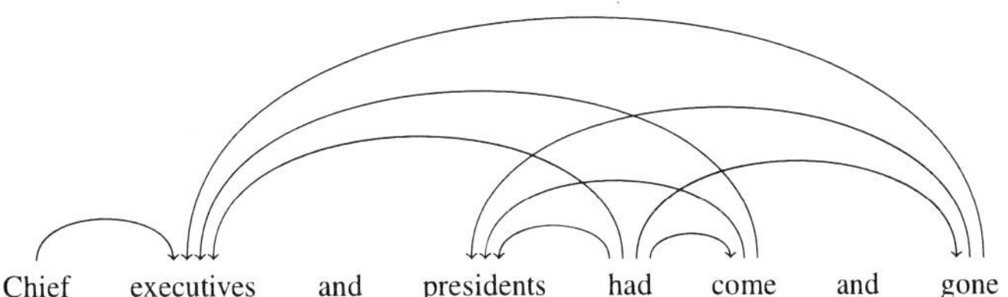

Figure 1: A sample dependency graph (Flickinger et al., 2016, CCD #20604004), drawn as an arc diagram. Note that each word is meant to represent one endpoint. (We leave some space between different arcs that share a common endpoint.) To save some space we draw arcs as semi-ellipses rather than semi-circles. The graph has pagenumber 3 and is 1ec.

2 Background

We start by giving some background on the classes of graphs that we study in this paper.

2.1 Graph Classes

A *dependency graph* for a natural language sentence x is an acyclic digraph whose vertices are in one-to-one correspondence with the words in x.[1] A sample dependency graph is shown in Figure 1. To draw a dependency graph, we place its vertices on an invisible line in the plane according to their left-to-right order, and draw each arc as a semi-circle in the half-plane bounded by that line. We refer to this type of drawing as an *arc diagram*. Given an arc diagram of a dependency graph, two arcs of the graph are said to *cross* if their corresponding semi-circles intersect in points other than a common endpoint.

A dependency graph is called *noncrossing* if its arc diagram does not feature crossing arcs. Noncrossing graphs have also been called 'planar' (Titov et al., 2009). We can generalize the noncrossing condition by allowing arcs to be drawn not only in the half-plane above the vertex line but also in that below it, or in any of some fixed number k of half-planes bounded by the vertex line. This type of graph drawing is known as a *book embedding* (Bernhart and Kainen, 1979). (We may picture the half-planes as the pages of a book, and the vertex line as the book spine.) The *pagenumber* of a graph is the smallest number k for which the graph has a crossing-free book embedding with k half-planes (pages). The graph in Figure 1 has pagenumber 3. Graphs whose pagenumber is at most k have also been called 'k-planar' (Gómez-Rodríguez and Nivre, 2010).

Our main interest in this paper is in the class of 1-endpoint-crossing graphs. A dependency graph is called *1-endpoint-crossing (1ec)* if for each of its arcs a, all arcs that cross a share a common endpoint (Pitler et al., 2013). The graph in Figure 1 is 1ec. The 1ec property was originally formulated for dependency trees, but the definition carries over to more general graphs without modifications.

2.2 Empirical Coverage

We assess the emprical coverage of 1ec graphs on a standard data set, the data used for the 2015 SemEval Task on Broad-Coverage Dependency Parsing (Flickinger et al., 2016). This data consists of token-aligned dependency graphs from four distinct linguistic traditions, dubbed DM, PAS, PSD, and CCD. For details about these target representations we refer to Oepen et al. (2016).

Table 1 gives the percentages of complete graphs (G) and individual arcs (A) that can be covered under the restriction to noncrossing graphs, graphs with bounded pagenumber (≤ 2), and 1ec graphs.[2] We see that the coverage of 1ec graphs clearly surpasses that of noncrossing graphs on all four representation types. Noncrossing graphs in fact seem to be a rather poor match for the data, especially on CCD, where it rules out more than half of the target graphs. With respect to pagenumber, even the low bound at ≤ 2 achieves very highest coverage, the highest among the three classes considered. The class 1ec is on average 2.11 percentage points behind in terms of coverage on complete graphs and 0.14 points on individual arcs.

---

[1] We restrict our attention to unlabelled dependency graphs.

[2] Arc coverage was calculated using a brute-force algorithm that removes the minimal number of arcs needed to make the remaining graph satisfy the relevant property.

class		DM	PAS	PSD	CCD
nc	G	69.29	59.85	65.04	49.53
	A	97.63	97.24	96.01	95.83
pn $\leq$ 2	G	99.46	99.48	97.64	98.33
	A	99.97	99.97	99.76	99.89
1ec	G	97.30	97.18	95.85	96.16
	A	99.83	99.85	99.60	99.75

Table 1: Coverage in terms of complete graphs (G) and individual arcs (A) for noncrossing graphs, graphs with pagenumber at most 2, and 1ec graphs.

2.3 Parsing Complexity

While high coverage is desirable, it often goes hand in hand with high parsing complexity. As already mentioned in the introduction, the maximum non-crossing subgraph can be found in time $O(n^3)$, where n is the length of the input sentence. The corresponding problem for the class of graphs with pagenumber at most 2 is NP-hard (Kuhlmann and Jonsson, 2015), which means that the high coverage of this class incurs a considerable price to pay. The relatively high coverage of 1ec graphs observed in Table 1 suggests that this class of graphs might strike a good balance between coverage and complexity.

3 The Structure of 1ec Graphs

In this section we derive the structural characterization of 1ec graphs that we will exploit in our parsing algorithm. Our point of departure is the result of Pitler et al. (2013, Theorem 1) that 1ec trees have pagenumber at most 2. This result does not carry over to general graphs; in fact we have already seen an empirical example of a 1ec graph with pagenumber 3 in Figure 1.

Lemma 1 *There are 1ec graphs with pagenumber 3.* □

Our first goal is to prove that pagenumber 3 is also the *maximal* pagenumber of 1ec graphs. To show this we will characterize 1ec graphs in terms of their *crossing graphs*.

3.1 Pagenumber of 1ec Graphs

The *crossing graph* of a dependency graph has a vertex corresponding to each arc, and an edge between two vertices if and only if the corresponding arcs cross. The crossing graphs of noncrossing dependency graphs consist of isolated vertices.

Crossing graphs are interesting because the pagenumber of a dependency graph equals the *chromatic number* of its crossing graph, the smallest number of colours needed to colour the vertices of the crossing graph in such a way that no two neighbouring vertices share the same colour. From a k-colouring of its crossing graph we obtain a crossing-free k-book embedding of the dependency graph by placing two arcs on the same page if and only if their corresponding vertices are coloured with the same colour. This correspondence has previously been studied by Gómez-Rodríguez and Nivre (2010) and Kuhlmann and Jonsson (2015), among others. The following lemma is due to Pitler et al. (2013, Lemma 2).

Lemma 2 *The crossing graphs of 1ec graphs do not contain triangles (cycles of length 3).* □

PROOF Suppose for the sake of contradiction that there exists a cycle $abca$. The arcs a and c must share an endpoint, as they both cross b. Because of this, they cannot cross, and therefore cannot be adjacent in the cycle. ∎

We use this lemma in the proof of the following:

Lemma 3 *The pagenumber of 1ec graphs is at most 3.* □

PROOF We show that the crossing graph of a 1ec graph is 3-colourable. To colour the crossing graph, we separately colour each of its components (also crossing graphs). We distinguish two cases:

1. The component does not contain a cycle, or contains cycles of length at most 4. By Lemma 2, the component does not contain a triangle, and therefore no odd cycle at all. We can therefore 2-colour the component by traversing the component using depth-first search and assigning to each vertex the opposite colour of its parent in the search tree.

2. The length of the shortest cycle in the component is at least 5. In the graph theory literature, our crossing graphs are better known as *circle graphs*, and the length of the shortest cycle in a graph is known as its *girth*. It has been shown that every circle graph with girth at least 5 is 3-colourable (Ageev, 1999).

Thus in each case, 3 colours suffice to colour the component, and hence the complete graph. ∎

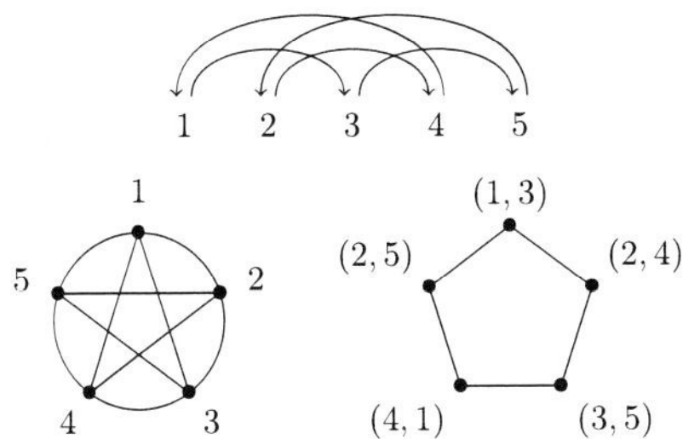

Figure 2: Counter-clockwise from top: dependency graph, chord diagram, crossing graph.

3.2 Isolation Property for Cog Belts

1ec graphs with pagenumber 3 (or subgraphs thereof) have a characteristic structure reminiscent of the teeth of a cogwheel; a minimal example is shown at the top of Figure 2. The proof of Lemma 3 also reveals that these graphs correspond to cycles of length 5 or more in the crossing graph. Because of this we will refer to these graphs as *cog belts*. Our aim for the remainder of this section is to show (in Lemma 6) that these structures are 'isolated', in the sense that no arcs other than the arcs in the cog belt can cross the cog belt. This property will be the key to the parsing algorithm in Section 4. To show it we study the relation between crossing graphs and *chord diagrams*.

The *chord diagram* of a dependency graph is obtained by placing the vertices of the graph on the boundary of a circle such that their clockwise order extends the left-to-right order in the original graph, and drawing each arc of the graph as a chord of the circle. An example is given in Figure 2. Note that the chord diagram representation does not contain information about the direction of the arcs of the dependency graph, and cannot be used to recover the exact linear positions of the vertices. Importantly though, we can still read off the crossing graph of a dependency graph from its chord diagram.

To prove the maximality property, we will reason about the chord diagram corresponding to a crossing graph. In general, this diagram is not uniquely determined. However, when we restrict ourselves to 'strict' chord diagrams in which there are exactly twice as many endpoints as there are chords, then there are certain crossing graphs that have a *unique* such chord diagram (up to symmetry).[3] In particular, this holds for cycles of length at least 5.

---

[3] These are exactly the graphs that are *prime* with respect to split decompositions; see Gabor et al. (1989).

We start by proving a lemma about another type of graphs with unique strict chord diagrams. A *domino* is a graph of the form ⊞.

Lemma 4 *The crossing graphs of 1ec graphs do not contain dominoes.* □

PROOF For the sake of contradiction, suppose that the crossing graph of a 1ec graph G contains a domino. The arcs that correspond to the vertices on this domino induce a subgraph of G. We reason about how the chord diagrams for this induced subgraph could look like. A domino has a unique 'strict' chord diagram (Gabor et al., 1989); this diagram looks as shown in the left half of Figure 3. However, this chord diagram cannot be the actual chord diagram of a 1ec dependency graph. For example, the chord b is crossed by chords a and d, but these chords do not share a common endpoint. We can try to 'repair' the chord diagram (without changing the underlying crossing graph) by merging some of the endpoints; in particular, we can merge the two endpoints a_2 and d_1 into one endpoint that we may refer to as ad, which removes one violation of the 1ec property at chord b. Eliminating as many violations as possible, we obtain the modified chord diagram in the right half of Figure 3. However, even in this diagram there are still some violations left: Apart from a and d, the chord b is also crossed by e, and this chord cannot be made to share an endpoint with a and d. We therefore conclude that the crossing graph of G does not contain a domino. ■

For our next lemma we need some terminology from geometry. A *polygram* is a non-convex regular polygon, drawn by connecting a given number of points placed at equal distance on the boundary of a circle. Polygrams can be denoted by its *Schläfli symbol* $\{p/q\}$, where p gives the number of corners, and q states that each corner should be connected to its neighbours q steps away. For example, $\{5/2\}$ denotes the pentagram in Figure 2.

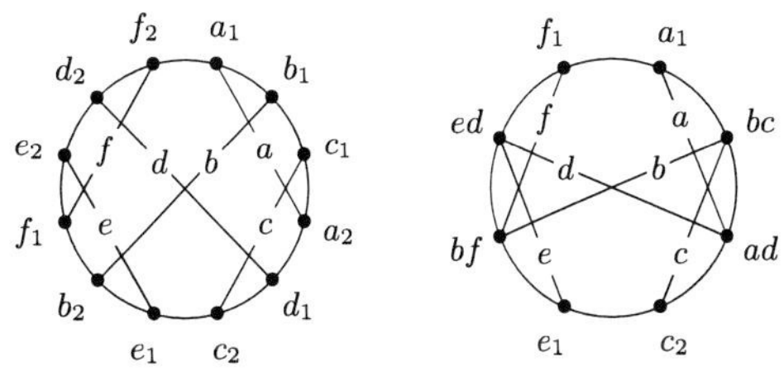

Figure 3: Proof of Lemma 4

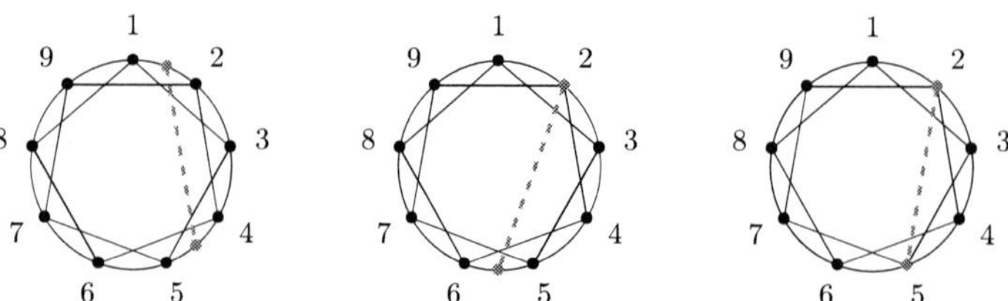

Figure 4: Proof of Lemma 6, illustrated using a cycle of length $m = 9$. The additional chord (red-dashed) violates the 1ec property: In the graph on the *left*, it creates additional endpoints for the chords 13, 29, 35, and 46; in the graph in the *middle*, it creates additional endpoints for the chords 46 and 57; in the graph on the *right*, the new chord is crossed by 13 and 46, which do not share an endpoint.

Lemma 5 *The chord diagram of the subgraph induced by a cycle of length $m \geq 5$ in a crossing graph of a 1ec graph is unique (up to symmetry) and forms a polygram $\{m/2\}$.* ☐

PROOF Similar to the proof of Lemma 4, we reason about how the chord diagrams for the subgraph induced by a cycle of length $m \geq 5$ in a crossing graph of a 1ec graph could look like. We illustrate our argument using concrete cycles, $abcdea$ ($m = 5$) and $abcdefa$ ($m = 6$). The strict chord diagrams for these examples look as follows.

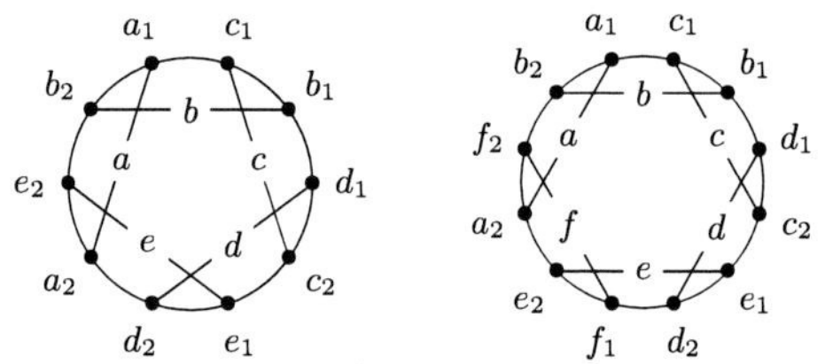

Again, these diagrams cannot be chord diagrams of 1ec dependency graphs; for example, the chord b is crossed by chord a and c, which do not have a common endpoint. The only way to repair the chord diagrams without changing the underlying crossing graph is to merge the two endpoints a_1 and c_1 into a common endpoint which we shall refer to as ac, and likewise for all the other chords. This yields the following (non-strict) chord diagrams:

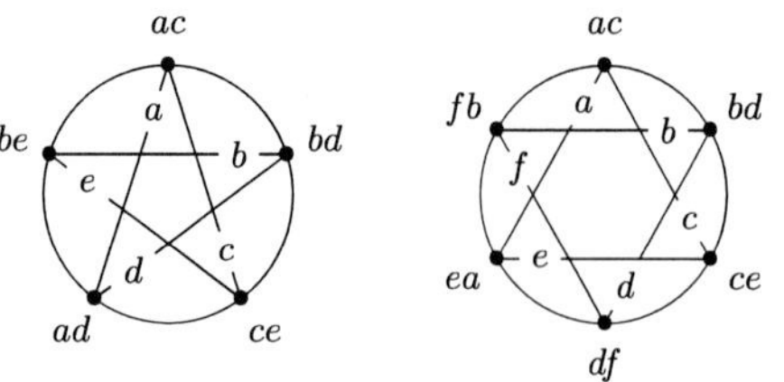

The left diagram is the pentagram $\{5/2\}$, the right diagram is the hexagram $\{6/2\}$ (6 corners, each of which is connected to the neighbour 2 steps away).

From these examples it is not hard to generalize to arbitrary values of m: If m is odd, then the chord diagram for the cycle forms a regular star polygon. If m is even, then the chord diagram forms a regular polygon compound consisting of two copies of a regular, convex $(m/2)$-gon. ∎

Pitler et al. (2013, Lemma 3) show that any odd cycle of length $m \geq 5$ in a crossing graph of a 1ec graph uses at most m vertices in the original graph. From Lemma 5 we get the stronger result that *any* cycle of length $m \geq 5$ uses *exactly* m vertices.

We are now ready to prove the isolation property:

Lemma 6 *Any cycle of length $m \geq 5$ in a crossing graph of a 1ec graph forms a connected component of that graph.* ☐

PROOF (SKETCH) The proof is by induction on m. We start by using the construction in the proof of Lemma 5 to obtain the polygram chord diagram for the cycle. We then suppose, for the sake of contradiction, that one of the vertices on the cycle has an incident edge that does not itself belong to the cycle, and reason about how to update the chord diagram. The new edge could either go to another on the cycle or to a new vertex. The second alternative would require us to add a new chord to the diagram. However, we can convince ourselves that any new chord will necessarily violate the 1ec property (see Figure 4). For the first alternative, we distinguish three cases: If $m = 5$, then adding a 'shortcut' edge to another vertex on the cycle will create a triangle, which is ruled out by Lemma 2. If $m = 6$, then adding a shortcut will create either a triangle or a domino, which is ruled out by Lemma 4. Finally, if $m \geq 7$, then adding a shortcut will create either a triangle, a domino, or a cycle of length $m \geq 5$, of which we may assume that it forms a connected component. ∎

4 Parsing Algorithm

In the previous section we have characterized 1ec graphs in terms of their crossing graphs. In this section we will exploit this characterization to show how to obtain a parsing algorithm for 1ec graphs. We follow Kuhlmann and Jonsson (2015) in casting dependency parsing as a maximum subgraph problem: Given an arc-weighted digraph G, our aim is to find a subset of arcs with maximum total weight such that the induced subgraph is 1ec. The weights of G should be learned from data.

4.1 Relaxed Deduction System for 1ec Trees

To obtain a parsing algorithm for 1ec graphs, an obvious idea is to take the corresponding algorithm for trees (Pitler et al., 2013) and 'relax' it by deleting all book-keeping that is used to enforce the tree constraint. We present the resulting algorithm as a *weighted deduction system* (Shieber et al., 1995; Nederhof, 2003). Such a system uses *inference rules* to derive information about sets of graphs; this information is represented by weighted formulas called *items*. Parsing amounts to finding the derivation of a *goal item* with maximum weight, starting from a set of *initial items*.

We assume that we are given an arc-weighted digraph $G = (V, A)$ with vertices $V = \{1, \ldots, n\}$. Items represent subgraphs of G corresponding to either *isolated intervals* $[i, j]$, where there are no arcs between vertices in the open interval (i, j) and vertices outside of $[i, j]$, or *isolated crossing regions* $[i, j] \cup \{x\}$, where there are i) no arcs between vertices in (i, j) and vertices outside of $[i, j] \cup \{x\}$, and ii) no arcs between the external vertex x and vertices in (i, j) that are crossed by arcs with both endpoints in (i, j). Isolated intervals are represented by items of the form $Int[i, j]$, and isolated crossing regions are represented by four different types of items that put a constraint on whether arcs from x into (i, j) may be crossed by arcs inside of $[i, j]$ with endpoints at the left border ($L[i, j, x]$), the right border ($R[i, j, x]$), both borders ($LR[i, j, x]$), or none of the two borders ($N[i, j, x]$). The initial items of the system correspond to one-vertex subgraphs and take the form $Int[i, i]$. The goal item is $Int[1, n]$, representing the complete graph that spans all vertices. Finally, the inference rules are shown in Figure 6. The weight of the item on the left-hand side of each rule is computed as the sum of weights of the items on the right-hand side and, if specified, the weight of a new arc.

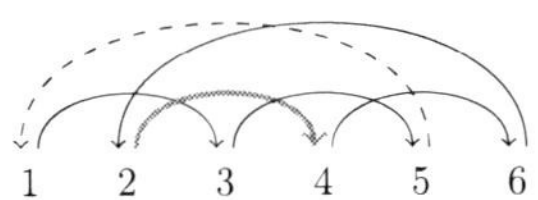

Figure 5: Non-completeness for general 1ec graphs. Splitting the item $LR[1, 5, 6]$ at $k = 3$ using rule (11) makes it impossible to retain the arc $2 \leftarrow 4$.

4.2 Non-Completeness for General Graphs

A deduction system is *correct* with respect to a class of graphs $\mathcal{G}$ if each of its derivations denotes (under an intended interpretation) a graph from $\mathcal{G}$ (*soundness*), and every graph from $\mathcal{G}$ has some derivation (*completeness*). While the algorithm of Pitler et al. (2013) is correct for the class of 1ec trees, it turns out that its relaxed version is *not* correct for the full class of 1ec graphs. More specifically, there are some 1ec graphs that do not have derivations in the relaxed system.

To illustrate the problem, we consider the cog belt in Figure 5 and reason backwards, reading inference rules as rules for *decomposing* a subgraph into smaller ones. The only way to decompose the example graph from an Int item is to instantiate rule (6) with $k = 5$. This removes the dashed arc $5 \rightarrow 1$, leaving the rest of the graph inside an LR item. Now to decompose the LR item we need to find a 'split vertex' $k \in (1, 5)$ for rule (11), creating items $L[1, k, 6]$ and $R[k, 5, 6]$. However, splitting the graph in this way makes it impossible to retain arcs that cover k – and inside the interval $(1, 5)$ *every* vertex is covered by some arc. This property prevents the decomposition of not only the graph in Figure 5, but more generally every cog belt.

4.3 Correctness for Graphs without Cog Belts

While the relaxed deduction system is not correct for general 1ec graphs, we can prove that it is correct for the class of all 1ec graphs that do not contain cog belts. The proof is straightforward but tedious, so here we content ourselves with sketching the structure and giving the most central intuitions.

Soundness To show that every derivation denotes a 1ec graph without cog belts, we use induction over the length of the derivation. The property obviously holds for the initial items. For the inductive case we need to check that the structural property is preserved by each rule. This is not hard to see with respect to the 1ec constraint, which is

"

(1) $Int[i,j] \leftarrow Int[i+1,j]$

(2) $Int[i,j] \leftarrow s[i,j] + Int[i,j]$

(3) $Int[i,j] \leftarrow s[i,k] + Int[i,k] + Int[k,j]$

(4) $Int[i,j] \leftarrow s[i,k] + R[i,k,l] + Int[k,l] + L[l,j,k]$

(5) $Int[i,j] \leftarrow s[i,k] + LR[i,k,l] + Int[k,l] + Int[l,j]$

(6) $Int[i,j] \leftarrow s[i,k] + LR[i,k,j] + Int[k,j]$

(7) $Int[i,j] \leftarrow s[i,k] + Int[i,l] + L[l,k,i] + N[k,j,l]$

(8) $Int[i,j] \leftarrow s[i,k] + R[i,l,k] + Int[l,k] + L[k,j,l]$

(9) $LR[i,j,x] \leftarrow R[i,j,x]$

(10) $LR[i,j,x] \leftarrow L[i,j,x]$

(11) $LR[i,j,x] \leftarrow L[i,k,x] + R[k,j,x]$

(12) $N[i,j,x] \leftarrow s[x,k] + N[i,k,x] + Int[k,j]$

(13) $N[i,j,x] \leftarrow Int[i,j]$

(14) $N[i,j,x] \leftarrow s[i,x] + N[i,j,x]$

(15) $N[i,j,x] \leftarrow s[j,x] + N[i,j,x]$

(16) $L[i,j,x] \leftarrow Int[i,j]$

(17) $L[i,j,x] \leftarrow s[x,k] + L[i,k,x] + Int[k,j]$

(18) $L[i,j,x] \leftarrow s[i,k] + L[i,k,x] + Int[k,j]$

(19) $L[i,j,x] \leftarrow s[x,k] + Int[i,k] + L[k,j,i]$

(20) $L[i,j,x] \leftarrow s[i,x] + L[i,j,x]$

(21) $L[i,j,x] \leftarrow s[j,x] + L[i,j,x]$

(22) $L[i,j,x] \leftarrow s[i,j] + L[i,j,x]$

(23) $R[i,j,x] \leftarrow Int[i,j]$

(24) $R[i,j,x] \leftarrow s[x,k] + Int[i,k] + R[k,j,x]$

(25) $R[i,j,x] \leftarrow s[j,k] + Int[i,k] + R[k,j,x]$

(26) $R[i,j,x] \leftarrow s[x,k] + R[i,k,j] + Int[k,j]$

(27) $R[i,j,x] \leftarrow s[i,x] + R[i,j,x]$

(28) $R[i,j,x] \leftarrow s[j,x] + R[i,j,x]$

(29) $R[i,j,x] \leftarrow s[i,j] + R[i,j,x]$

Figure 6: The rules of the 'relaxed' deduction system, following the basic rules of Pitler (2013). The scores for arcs $s[i,j]$ do not specify the arc's direction (we simply choose the arc with the higher weight). The indices may not overlap, giving rise to rule (6), the special case of rule (5) for $l = j$.

inherited from the tree-based system. Showing that the rule applications cannot result in cog belts is slightly more complicated. However, we can convince ourselves that the constraints implied by the item types and the constraints on the accessibility of vertices implied in the rules are sufficient to exclude the forbidden structures. In particular, a derivation cannot 'remember' the vertex that would be needed to close off a cog belt (see Figure 7).

Completeness To show that every 1ec graph without cog belts can be derived by the system, we use induction on the size of the graph, where size is measured as the total number of vertices and arcs. Graphs with size 1 (one vertex) are represented by the initial items. For the inductive case we need to check that every graph which satisfies the structural property is decomposable by some rule. We can use the same strategy as Pitler (2013), who classifies graphs into a number of templates and for each of those templates shows which rule can be applied to it. In particular we need to show that the subgraphs gained in each decomposition adhere to the intended interpretations, and that all arcs can be added. The important observation is that, if the graph does not contain a cog belt, then the information represented in each item is sufficient to build all arcs (see Figure 8).

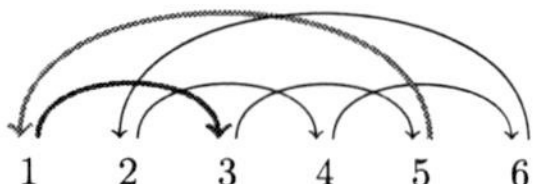

Figure 7: When attempting to derive this cog belt right-to-left we could instantiate rule (8) as $Int[1,6] \leftarrow s[1,3] + R[1,2,3] + Int[2,3] + L[3,6,2]$ which would add the blue arc. However, the right endpoint of the red arc (5) is no longer 'visible'.

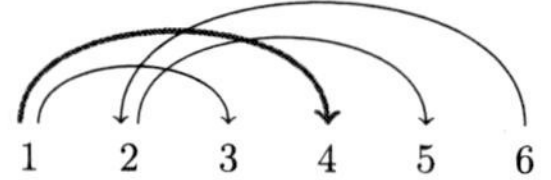

Figure 8: This dependency graph has a crossing graph with a cycle of length 4 and is therefore 'almost as hard' as a cog belt. It can be derived in the relaxed deduction system using rule (7): $Int[1,6] \leftarrow s[1,4] + Int[1,2] + L[2,4,1] + N[4,6,2]$

$$(30)\quad C[i,j,x,y] \leftarrow s[x,y] + s[i,j] + Int[i,y] + Int[y,j]$$

$$(31)\quad C[i,j,x,y] \leftarrow s[x,k] + Int[i,k] + C[k,j,i,y]$$

$$(32)\quad Int[i,j] \leftarrow s[i,k] + s[i,y] + s[l,j] + Int[i,l] + Int[l,k] + C[k,j,l,y]$$

Figure 9: Additional rules for cog belts.

4.4 Extension to the Full Class

We have just seen that the subgraphs which the relaxed deduction system fails to parse are exactly cog belts. We now show how to extend the system into a complete parser for the full class of 1ec graphs. The key idea is that because cog belts are isolated from the remainder of the graph in terms of crossing arcs as per Lemma 6, we can simply add new items and rules that build a cog belt on top of a set of isolated intervals.

The new items take the form $C[i,j,x,y]$ and represent partial cog belts on an interval $[i,j]$ with two additional vertices: one external vertex x (which always lies to the left of i) and one new internal vertex y, whose purpose is to 'remember' the vertex that will be needed to close the cog belt (cf. Figure 7). The new inference rules are given in Figure 9 and are set up to derive a cog belt right-to-left. Rule (30) starts the derivation, combining two isolated intervals and adding two arcs. Rule (31) extends the cog belt by one isolated interval, adding a new arc. Finally, rule (32) closes the cog belt by adding two final intervals and three new arcs. With this simple extension, the deduction system becomes sound and complete with respect to the full class of 1ec graphs.

Example derivation. To illustrate the workings of the new rules, we provide a derivation of a cog belt with length 6, which in Figure 5 we showed to be non-derivable in the relaxed system. We assume that we have already derived isolated interval items $Int[i,i+1]$ for all vertices $i < n$. We then instantiate rule (30) as

$$C[4,6,3,5] \leftarrow s[3,5] + s[4,6] \\ + Int[4,5] + Int[5,6]$$

and after that rule (31) as

$$C[3,6,2,5] \leftarrow s[2,4] + Int[3,4] + C[4,6,3,5]$$

To complete the derivation of the cog belt as a closed interval item we instantiate rule (32) as

$$Int[1,6] \leftarrow s[1,3] + s[1,5] + s[2,6] \\ + Int[1,2] + Int[2,3] + C[3,6,2,5]$$

The asymptotic runtime complexity of the extended algorithm is in $O(n^5)$, one order of magnitude higher than that of the tree-based algorithm. This is due to rules (31) and (32), each of which refers to five independent positions in the sentence.

5 Discussion

In this section we discuss our results and relate them to other published work.

5.1 Graph-Theoretical Results

The main technical contribution of this paper is a characterization of 1ec graphs as a subclass of graphs with pagenumber at most 3 via certain properties of their crossing graphs – in particular the absence of dominoes and the isolation of cycles of length at least five, which induce the substructures that we called cog belts (Section 3). The relations between the various graph classes discussed in this paper are visualized in Figure 10.

1ec graphs have previously been discussed primarily in the context of dependency parsing. The characterization in this paper was established using results from graph theory, in particular from the study of circle graphs (Ageev, 1999). Future work of this kind may help to identify new classes of interesting dependency graphs or new parsing algorithms.

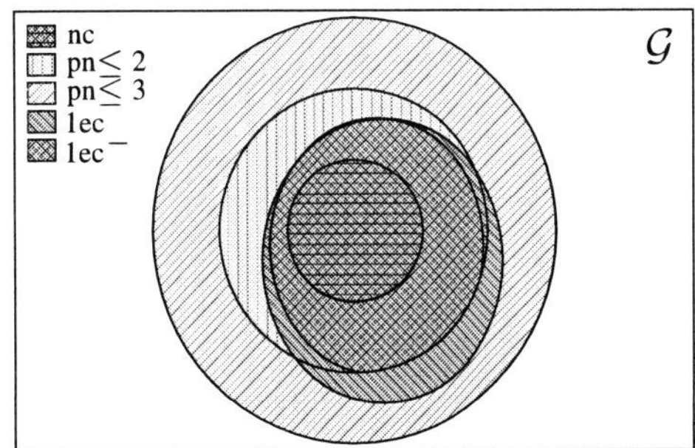

Figure 10: Relations between the classes of non-crossing graphs (nc), graphs with pagenumber at most k (pn $\leq$ 2, pn $\leq$ 3), 1ec graphs, and 1ec graphs without cog belts (1ec$^-$).

Two classes of graphs that appear to be very relevant for the study of 1ec graphs are *fan-planar graphs* (Kaufmann and Ueckerdt, 2014) and *outer-fan-planar graphs* (Bekos et al., 2014). Their defining property is essentially identical to the 1ec constraint; however, their vertices are not linearly ordered as in dependency graphs,

5.2 Parsing Algorithm

A second contribution of this paper is the extension of the parsing algorithm for 1ec trees (Pitler et al., 2013) to a quintic-time algorithm for the full class of 1ec graphs, and a quartic-time algorithm for the restricted class of 1ec graphs without cog belts. Closely related algorithms were recently proposed by Cao et al. (2017) and Kummerfeld and Klein (2017). The former use an approach similar to ours in Section 4.4 to parse what they call 'coupled staggered patterns' (our cog belts), albeit restricted to pagenumber 2; they report state-of-the-art results on the SemEval data. Kummerfeld and Klein (2017) apply 1ec graphs in the context of parsing to phrase structure representations with traces; their algorithm cannot parse what they call 'locked chains' (our cog belts), but has the benefit of enforcing acyclicity and uniqueness.

The proposed quintic-time algorithm may not be the most attractive one for practical parsing. We looked at the SemEval data from Section 2 and found that cog belts occur rarely, less than once per 2,000 sentences, and for only two of the representation types (PSD and CCD). A similar observation was made by Kummerfeld and Klein (2017) for the graphs they obtained from their treebank data.

In presenting our algorithms, our main focus was on theoretical properties (soundness and completeness). To support the implementation of a practical parser, the extended deduction system needs to be refined in several ways. For one thing, the system features a high degree of derivational ambiguity, which in particular can lead to the same arc being scored several times in a derivation. To avoid this, we would need to extend the items with information on whether an arc has already been set, very similar to the booleans used to control treeness in the original algorithm. For example, a modified version of rule (5) could look like this:

$$Int[i, j; F] \leftarrow s[i, k] + LR[i, k, l; F, b_{i,l}, b_{k,l}]$$
$$+ Int[k, l; F] + Int[l, j; b_{l,j}]$$

The LR item has three booleans, corresponding to the three arcs that could be present among the three sets of endpoints $\{i, k\}$, $\{i, l\}$, and $\{k, l\}$. The first boolean has to be F (false), as the arc between i and k is scored in the rule; the other two arcs may or may not be already present, so the values of the second and third boolean are free to choose. However, when the arc between k and l was set in the derivation of the LR item, it should not have been already set in the derivation of the $Int[k, l]$ item, which is why we need to set the boolean in this item to F.

The modified version of rule (5) is actually a *rule template* which in an actual parser implementation needs to be instantiated in all legal ways. This introduces a non-negligible constant factor into the runtime: assuming a minimal number of three boolean variables per rule and a fourth binary choice for the direction of the arc (which we have left underspecified), we would already get $32 \cdot 2^4 = 512$ actual rules. This ignores the additional bookkeeping that needs to be added in order to prevent cycles or enforce uniqueness of derivations, each of which would at least double the number of rules, and the increased complexity coming from labelled parsing.

The most promising parsing results so far on the SDP data have been achieved with a simple, quadratic-time parsing algorithm with very few constraints on the search space but a strong learning component (Martins and Almeida, 2014; Peng et al., 2017). A structurally restricted parsing algorithm such as the one described in this paper, even if its coverage is high, has the drawback that it is harder to combine with an expressive learning approach such as the recurrent neural networks used by Kiperwasser and Goldberg (2016).

6   Conclusion

We have shown how a new structural characterization of 1ec graphs in terms of their crossing graphs can be used to extend the parsing algorithm for 1ec trees to the full class of graphs. The class of 1ec graphs has a significantly higher coverage than the previously considered class of noncrossing graphs (Schluter, 2015; Kuhlmann and Jonsson, 2015) and may thus be a useful constraint on the search space for deep dependency parsing. However, to achieve state-of-the-art results the new parsing algorithm needs to be combined with a powerful machine learning component, a practical challenge that we leave to future work.

Acknowledgements

We thank the anonymous reviewers for their helpful comments. This work was supported by a Google Faculty Research Award to Marco Kuhlmann.

References

Alexander A. Ageev. 1999. Every circle graph of girth at least 5 is 3-colourable. *Discrete Mathematics* 195(1–3):229–233.

Michael A. Bekos, Sabine Cornelsen, Luca Grilli, Seok-Hee Hong, and Michael Kaufmann. 2014. On the recognition of fan-planar and maximal outer-fan-planar graphs. In *Graph Drawing*. Springer, volume 8871 of *Lecture Notes in Computer Science*, pages 198–209.

Frank Bernhart and Paul C. Kainen. 1979. The book thickness of a graph. *Journal of Combinatorial Theory, Series B* 27(3):320–331.

Junjie Cao, Sheng Huang, Weiwei Sun, and Xiaojun Wan. 2017. Parsing to 1-endpoint-crossing, pagenumber-2 graphs. In *Proceedings of the 55th Annual Meeting of the Association for Computational Linguistics (ACL)*. Vancouver, Canada, pages 2110–2120.

Dan Flickinger, Jan Hajič, Angelina Ivanova, Marco Kuhlmann, Yusuke Miyao, Stephan Oepen, and Daniel Zeman. 2016. SDP 2014 & 2015: Broad coverage semantic dependency parsing LDC2016T10. Web Download.

Csaba P. Gabor, Kenneth J. Supowit, and Wen-Lian Hsu. 1989. Recognizing circle graphs in polynomial time. *Journal of the Association for Computing Machinery* 36(3):435–473.

Carlos Gómez-Rodríguez and Joakim Nivre. 2010. A transition-based parser for 2-planar dependency structures. In *Proceedings of the 48th Annual Meeting of the Association for Computational Linguistics (ACL)*. Uppsala, Sweden, pages 1492–1501.

Venkatesan Guruswami, Johan Håstad, Rajsekar Manokaran, Prasad Raghavendra, and Moses Charikar. 2011. Beating the random ordering is hard: Every ordering CSP is approximation resistant. *SIAM Journal on Computing* 40(3):878–914.

Michael Kaufmann and Torsten Ueckerdt. 2014. The density of fan-planar graphs. *CoRR* abs/1403.6184.

Eliyahu Kiperwasser and Yoav Goldberg. 2016. Simple and accurate dependency parsing using bidirectional LSTM feature representations. *Transactions of the Association for Computational Linguistics* 4:313–327.

Marco Kuhlmann and Peter Jonsson. 2015. Parsing to noncrossing dependency graphs. *Transactions of the Association for Computational Linguistics* 3:559–570.

Marco Kuhlmann and Stephan Oepen. 2016. Towards a catalogue of linguistic graph banks. *Computational Linguistics* 42(4):819–827.

Jonathan K. Kummerfeld and Dan Klein. 2017. Parsing with traces: An $O(n^4)$ algorithm and a structural representation. *Transactions of the Association for Computational Linguistics* 5.

André F. T. Martins and Mariana S. C. Almeida. 2014. Priberam: A turbo semantic parser with second order features. In *Proceedings of the 8th International Workshop on Semantic Evaluation (SemEval 2014)*. Dublin, Republic of Ireland, pages 471–476.

Mark-Jan Nederhof. 2003. Weighted deductive parsing and Knuth's algorithm. *Computational Linguistics* 29(1):135–143.

Stephan Oepen, Marco Kuhlmann, Yusuke Miyao, Daniel Zeman, Silvie Cinková, Dan Flickinger, Jan Hajič, Angelina Ivanova, and Zdeňka Urešová. 2016. Towards comparability of linguistic graph banks for semantic parsing. In *Proceedings of the 10th International Conference on Language Resources and Evaluation (LREC)*. Portorož, Slovenia, pages 3991–3995.

Hao Peng, Sam Thomson, and Noah A. Smith. 2017. Deep multitask learning for semantic dependency parsing. In *Proceedings of the 55th Annual Meeting of the Association for Computational Linguistics (ACL)*. Vancouver, Canada, pages 2037–2048.

Emily Pitler. 2013. *Models for improved tractability and accuracy in dependency parsing*. Ph.D. thesis, University of Pennsylvania.

Emily Pitler, Sampath Kannan, and Mitchell Marcus. 2013. Finding optimal 1-endpoint-crossing trees. *Transactions of the Association for Computational Linguistics* 1:13–24.

Natalie Schluter. 2014. On maximum spanning DAG algorithms for semantic DAG parsing. In *Proceedings of the ACL 2014 Workshop on Semantic Parsing*. Baltimore, USA, pages 61–65.

Natalie Schluter. 2015. The complexity of finding the maximum spanning DAG and other restrictions for DAG parsing of natural language. In *Proceedings of the Fourth Joint Conference on Lexical and Computational Semantics*. Denver, CO, USA, pages 259–268.

Stuart M. Shieber, Yves Schabes, and Fernando Pereira. 1995. Principles and implementation of deductive parsing. *Journal of Logic Programming* 24(1–2):3–36.

Ivan Titov, James Henderson, Paola Merlo, and Gabriele Musillo. 2009. Online graph planarisation for synchronous parsing of semantic and syntactic dependencies. In *International Joint Conferences on Artificial Intelligence*. Pasadena, CA, USA, pages 1562–1567.

Effective Online Reordering with Arc-Eager Transitions

Ryosuke Kohita   **Hiroshi Noji**   **Yuji Matsumoto**
Graduate School of Information Science
Nara Institute of Science and Technology
8916-5 Takayama, Ikoma, Nara 630-0192, Japan
{kohita.ryosuke.kj9, noji, matsu}@is.naist.jp

Abstract

We present a new transition system with word reordering for unrestricted non-projective dependency parsing. Our system is based on decomposed arc-eager rather than arc-standard, which allows more flexible ambiguity resolution between a local projective and non-local crossing attachment. In our experiment on Universal Dependencies 2.0, we find our parser outperforms the ordinary swap-based parser particularly on languages with a large amount of non-projectivity.

1 Introduction

A dependency tree as illustrated in Figure 1 is called a *non-projective* tree, which contains discontinuous subtrees and is informally remarked with crossing arcs (arcs from $idea_4$ to $talking_8$ and from who_5 to to_9). Comparing to the class of projective trees, which has a weak equivalence to the context-free grammars (Gaifman, 1965), parsing non-projective trees is generally involved. This is particularly the case for *transition-based* dependency parsing; contrary to the graph-based approaches, in which a simple spanning-tree algorithm is capable of handling them (McDonald et al., 2005), due to the incremental nature, transition-based parsers need some extra mechanisms to find crossing arcs.

There are several attempts to handle crossing arcs in transition-based parsers. Among them online reordering with swap (Nivre, 2009) has a number of appealing properties, of which the most notable is that it inherits the standard architecture of the transition systems using a stack and buffer while covering all types of crossing arcs. This simplicity allows us to incorporate the ideas developed for the standard projective parsers, such

as neural network architectures (Chen and Manning, 2014; Dyer et al., 2015), and joint modeling with other phenomena (Hatori et al., 2011; Honnibal and Johnson, 2014), with a minimal effort. Such extensions with swap include a recent non-projective neural parser (Straka et al., 2015) and joint system with POS tagging (Bohnet and Nivre, 2012). Other approaches often employ additional data structures with non-trivial transitions (Covington, 2001; Choi and McCallum, 2013; Pitler and McDonald, 2015), which interfere with the transparency to the standard systems, or cannot handle all crossing arcs (Attardi, 2006).

Despite the popularity of the swap system, to our knowlege there is little work focusing on the swap mechanism, or the transition system itself, apart from the original proposal (Nivre, 2009; Nivre et al., 2009). In other words, we are still unsure whether the current swap mechanism is the best strategy for handling crossing arcs with word reordering.

In this work, we present a dependency parser with a new transition system that employs swap-based reordering but in a different manner from the existing one (Nivre, 2009) built on the arc-standard system. As we discuss (Section 2.2), in Nivre's transition system, choosing a correct swap transition is sometimes hard due to the parser's preference to local attachments. The proposed system (Section 3) alleviates this difficulty by allowing a swap transition for a token that is already linked on the stack. As we will see, it can be seen as an extension to the arc-eager system (Nivre, 2003) while we divide each attachment transition into two more primitive operations as in the divided formulation of Gómez-Rodríguez and Nivre (2013). The divided system is more flexible, and by operating swap on this we can deal with the issue of reordering at an appropriate step.

On this transition system we implement a pars-

88

Proceedings of the 15th International Conference on Parsing Technologies, pages 88–98,
Pisa, Italy; September 20–22, 2017. ©2017 Association for Computational Linguistics

ing model with the stack LSTMs (Dyer et al., 2015) (Section 4). We extensively examine the utility of new transition system (Section 5) with the recently released Universal Dependencies (UD) 2.0 dataset, which contains more than 60 treebanks with varying degree of non-projectivity, and find that our system is superior to the ordinary swap system particularly for languages with a larger amount of non-projectivity.

2 Background

We first introduce some notations and the concept of transition systems (Section 2.1), and then describe the existing swap-based transition system of Nivre (2009) (Section 2.2).

2.1 Transition System

We focus in this paper on a standard transition system operating on a triple called a *configuration* $c = (\sigma, \beta, A)$, where σ is a stack, β is a buffer, and A is a set of labeled arcs. See Nivre (2008) for the other variants and overview. In a configuration i-th token in a sentence is denoted by its index i while 0 denotes the special root token. Following the standard notations, by $\sigma|i$ and $j|\beta$, we mean i and j are the top-most tokens of the stack and buffer, respectively. We use $i \xrightarrow{l} j$ or (i, l, j) to denote an arc from i to j with label l.

Given a sentence of length n, the system begins parsing with the initial configuration $c_0 = ([0], [1, 2, 3, ...n], \phi)$ where only the root token is on the stack, all inputs are on the buffer, and the set of arcs is empty. Parsing finishes when it reaches a *terminal configuration*, in which any transitions cannot be performed, and the set of arcs A defines a labeled dependency tree. The system continues to make a transition decision at each step under the current configuration until it reaches a terminal configuration.

2.2 Arc-Standard Swap

Arc-standard swap system (ASS) (Nivre, 2009) is the most popular transition system for non-projective dependency parsing, which can handle arbitrary crossing arcs. ASS rows in Table 1 show the set of transitions, in which LA, RA, and SH are the transitions of the arc-standard system, which can only produce a projective tree by linking two adjacent tokens on the top of the stack. Swap (SW) is the key transition to support non-projectivity, which reorders the top two tokens on the stack by

moving the second top token back to the buffer. Reducing a reordered token by LA or RA means we create subtrees that are non-adjacent with each other, i.e., crossing arcs.

One potential issue in ASS is its tendency to prefer local attachments due to the mechanism of LA and RA, which at the same time reduce the dependent token. This is problematic in that because crossing arcs often involve a longer dependency arc, if two tokens on the stack are locally likely to be connected, choosing correct SW rather than LA and RA is quite difficult.

To see an example, let us consider the configuration in Figure 2 ($c = (\sigma|who|talking, to|\beta, A)$), which occurs when parsing the sentence in Figure 1. The correct action here is SW to create a crossing arc $talking_8 \xrightarrow{obl} who_5$. However, at this point LA is a more likely transition since $talking_8 \xrightarrow{obl} who_5$ is a typical arc in a relative clause. The problem is that since LA reduces $talking$, we will miss the arc $who_5 \xrightarrow{case} to_9$ if we choose LA rather than SW.

3 New System: Stay-Eager Swap

Now we describe our proposed transition system, which we call **Stay-Eager Swap** (SES). We first present the transitions and its advantage (Section 3.1), and then discuss oracles (Section 3.2) and some improvements (Section 3.3).

3.1 Transition System

SES rows in Table 1 show the set of transitions of the new system. To understand the mechanism, we first note that without SW, this system looks very much similar to the arc-eager transition system (Nivre, 2003). The main difference from the original one is in the attaching transitions, which we call STAY-LEFT (SL) and STAY-RIGHT (SR) and do not reduce a dependent token, but just establish an arc between two tokens on the stack top and buffer top. Specifically, this system is identical to the divided arc-eager transition system with the primitive operations in Gómez-Rodríguez and Nivre (2013); in the arc-eager system, LEFT-ARC first builds an arc and then reduces the top of the stack, i.e., it is a combination of SL $\rightarrow$ RD (reduce) in our system, while RIGHT-ARC builds an arc and shift the top token of the buffer, i.e., it can be seen as SR $\rightarrow$ SH.[1]

---

[1] To make this system without SW to fully mimic the original arc-eager system, we need a constraint to prohibit

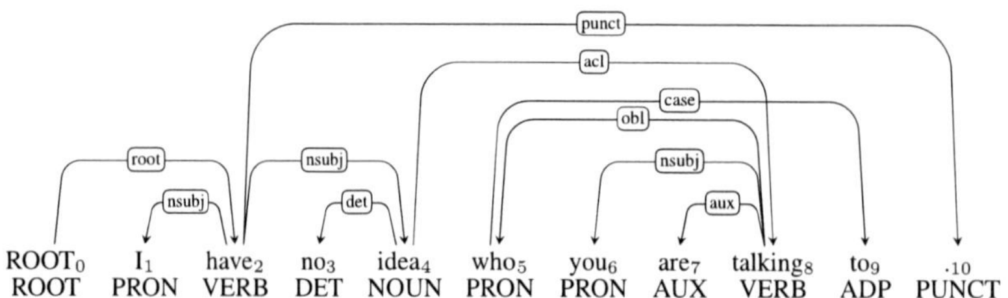

Figure 1: A non-projective sentence.

	Transition	Current configuration	$\Rightarrow$	Resulting configuration	Condition
ASS	LEFT-ARC$_l$ (LA)	$(\sigma\|i\|j,\ \beta,\ A)$	$\Rightarrow$	$(\sigma\|j,\ \beta,\ A \cup \{(j,l,i)\})$	$i \neq 0$
	RIGHT-ARC$_l$ (RA)	$(\sigma\|i\|j,\ \beta,\ A)$	$\Rightarrow$	$(\sigma\|i,\ \beta,\ A \cup \{(i,\cdot,j)\})$	
	SHIFT (SH)	$(\sigma,\ i\|\beta,\ A)$	$\Rightarrow$	$(\sigma\|i,\ \beta,\ A)$	
	SWAP (SW)	$(\sigma\|i\|j,\ \beta,\ A)$	$\Rightarrow$	$(\sigma\|j,\ i\|\beta,\ A)$	$0 < i < j$
SES	STAY-LEFT$_l$ (SL)	$(\sigma\|i,\ j\|\beta,\ A)$	$\Rightarrow$	$(\sigma\|i,\ j\|\beta,\ A \cup \{(j,l,i)\})$	$i \neq 0 \wedge (\cdot,\cdot,i) \notin A \wedge i \xrightarrow{*} j \notin A$
	STAY-RIGHT$_l$ (SR)	$(\sigma\|i,\ j\|\beta,\ A)$	$\Rightarrow$	$(\sigma\|i,\ j\|\beta,\ A \cup \{(i,l,j)\})$	$(\cdot,\cdot,j) \notin A \wedge j \xrightarrow{*} i \notin A$
	SHIFT (SH)	$(\sigma,\ i\|\beta,\ A)$	$\Rightarrow$	$(\sigma\|i,\ \beta,\ A)$	
	REDUCE (RD)	$(\sigma\|i,\ \beta,\ A)$	$\Rightarrow$	$(\sigma,\ \beta,\ A)$	$(\cdot,\cdot,i) \in A$
	SWAP (SW)	$(\sigma\|i,\ j\|\beta,\ A)$	$\Rightarrow$	$(\sigma,\ j\|i\|\beta,\ A)$	$0 < i < j$
AUX	UNSHIFT (UN)	$(\sigma\|i,\ [],\ A)$	$\Rightarrow$	$(\sigma,\ [i],\ A)$	$(\cdot,\cdot,i) \notin A$
	RIGHT-ROOT (RR)	$([0,i]\ [],\ A)$	$\Rightarrow$	$([0],\ [],\ A \cup \{(0,root,i)\})$	$(\cdot,\cdot,i) \notin A \wedge (0,root,i) \notin A$

Table 1: The set of transitions for arc-standard swap (ASS) and stay-eager swap (SES). $\cdot$ in conditions means an arbitrary value, e.g., $(\cdot,\cdot,i) \notin A$ means $\forall j.\forall h.(j,h,i) \notin A$ (i's head is unspecified). $i \xrightarrow{*} j \notin A$ means a path from i to j does not exist, which is needed to guarantee acyclicity.

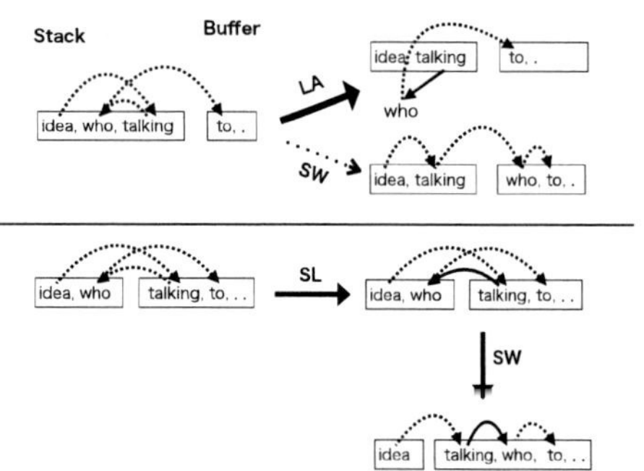

Figure 2: A configuration difficult for ASS (above), which fails when LA is selected (SW is correct). Our system avoides this difficulty by first attaching *who* to *talking* (SL) and then SW (below). Dotted arcs are correct arcs yet unattached.

We allow SW at an arbitrary point. This means we can insert SW just after SL and SR, by which we can alleviate the difficulty with an attachment vs. swap transitions discussed in Section 2.2. Fig-

ure 2 shows how our system can swap after resolving local projective attachments.

3.2 Static and Non-static Oracles

An oracle for a transition system is a function from a configuration to the action that leads to a given dependency tree. Before discussing in details, we first note that our system suffers from the spurious ambiguity as in the arc-eager system (Goldberg and Nivre, 2012), which means an oracle for some configurations is not unique.

Table 2 shows a specific oracle, which checks for each action in descending order whether the current configuration satisfies the condition, and select the first found one. [2] [3]

SL $\rightarrow$ SH and SR $\rightarrow$ RD, which cause a configuration never reached by the original one. For simplicity we do not impose such constraint. Rather, since our oracles prefer RD over SH by default it is not uncommon to explore such configurations during training.

[2]The priority of attaching transitions over SW is also helpful to avoid unnecessary SW transitions for nested non-projective structures. For example in Figure 1, if to_9 has a child node $x_{4.5}$ at the left to who_5 and SW is preferred than SL and SR, it causes an additional crossing between $talking_6 \rightarrow who_5$ and $to_9 \rightarrow x_{4.5}$. This is not the case for our oracle because $talking_6 \rightarrow who_5$ has been already attached and $isCross(i,j)$ ignores such attached arcs.

[3]The function $isCross(i,j)$ for SW could be defined like ASS style which reorders by projective order (Nivre, 2009). However their projective orders are different: for example in Figure 1, while to_9 comes up at sixth word for ASS, who_5 goes down at eighth word for SES. In this paper, we could not reach the detailed description and formal definition of projective order for SES, but they are the one of important

Transition	Configuration	Condition
STAY-LEFT$_l$	$(\sigma\|i,j\|\beta, A)$	$(j,l,i) \in A_g$
STAY-RIGHT$_l$	$(\sigma\|i,j\|\beta, A)$	$(i,l,j) \in A_g$
SWAP	$(\sigma\|i,j\|\beta, A)$	$isCross(i,j)$
REDUCE	$(\sigma\|i, \quad \beta, A)$	$(\cdot,\cdot,i) \in A \wedge \forall h.\forall j.((i,h,j) \in A_g \rightarrow (i,h,j) \in A)$
SHIFT	$(\sigma, \quad j\|\beta, A)$	$\forall i.\forall l.((j,l,i) \in A_g \wedge j < i) \rightarrow (j,l,i) \in A$

[1] $isCross(i,j)$ returns true if i and j are two endpoints of two crossing arcs yet unattached. Formally: $(\exists b.b \in \beta \wedge ((b,\cdot,i) \in A_g \wedge (b,\cdot,i) \notin A \vee (i,\cdot,b) \in A_g \wedge (i,\cdot,b) \notin A)) \wedge (\exists s.s \in \sigma \wedge ((s,\cdot,j) \in A_g \wedge (s,\cdot,j) \notin A \vee (j,\cdot,s) \in A_g \wedge (j,\cdot,s) \notin A))$.

Table 2: A static oracle for our transition system. A_g is the set of gold arcs. $\cdot$ means an arbitrary value.

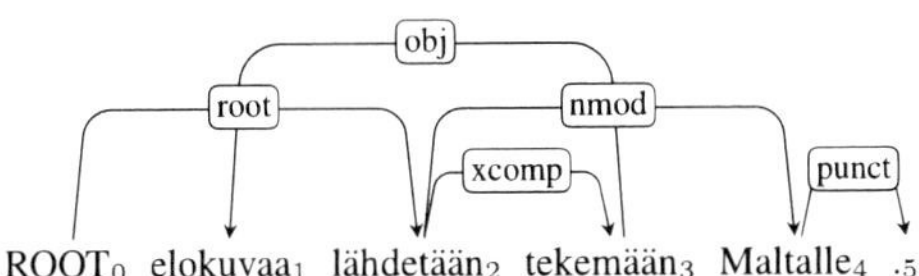

Figure 3: A non-projective sentence of Finnish.

t	Transition	Stack	Buffer	Added Arc
0		[0]	[1, 2, 3, 4, 5]	
1	SH	[0, 1]	[2, 3, 4, 5]	
2	SW	[0]	[2, 1, 3, 4, 5]	
3	SR	[0]	[2, 1, 3, 4, 5]	(0, root, 2)
4	SH	[0, 2]	[1, 3, 4, 5]	
5	SH	[0, 2, 1]	[3, 4, 5]	
6	SL	[0, 2, 1]	[3, 4, 5]	(3, obj, 1)
7	RD	[0, 2]	[3, 4, 5]	
8	SR	[0, 2]	[3, 4, 5]	(2, xcomp, 3)
9	SH	[0, 2, 3]	[4, 5]	
10	RD	[0, 2]	[4, 5]	
11	SR	[0, 2]	[4, 5]	(2, nmod, 4)
12	SH	[0, 2, 4]	[5]	
13	SR	[0, 2, 4]	[5]	(4, punct, 5)
14	RD	[0, 2]	[5]	
15	SH	[0, 2, 5]	[]	
16	RD	[0, 2]	[]	
17	RD	[0]	[]	

Table 3: Static oracle transitions by our system for the sentence in Figure 3.

This is a *static* oracle in that it is a deterministic function given a configuration. Table 3 shows the oracle transitions by this for the sentence in Figure 3. In addition to the static oracle, we also try a partially non-static oracle, which occasionally prefers SH over RD when both are applicable. Specifically, for this oracle when both conditions for SH and RD are satisfied we choose SH with some probability. This allows the parser to learn the transitions that postpone RD when possible, but stochastically, which we found effective in many languages in practice. This is a partially non-static oracle since it does not postpone the other transitions such as SL and SR. Designing

future works.

such oracle could also be possible; for example, in Figure 2, we can also build the gold tree by SW followed by SH and SR. We leave such fully non-static oracle as well as the dynamic oracle (Goldberg and Nivre, 2012) as a future work.

3.3 Auxiliary transitions

Our system employs the following two additional transitions (AUX in Table 1), which can be applied in restricted conditions.

UNSHIFT The arc-eager system is not guaranteed to output a single rooted tree, i.e., it may keep unconnected tree fragments in the stack while the buffer is empty (Nivre, 2008). Then, a parser becomes stack because no actions are permissible before reaching a terminal configuration, and our system suffers from the same issue. To escape from this, we employ the same hack as Nivre and Fernández-González (2014) and add a special transition UN, which pushes back the stack top node to the empty buffer. We only apply UN at decoding. It is deterministically chosen in the configuration $c = ([n], [], A \notin (\cdot,\cdot,n))$, so does not have any associated score.

RIGHT-ROOT This is our new transition to improve the root attachment accuracy for arc-eager. The arc-eager system attaches the sentence root to the special ROOT *eagerly* immediately after it collects all its left dependents, but this decision is sometimes hard for some types of garden-path. The purpose of RR is to postpone the decision of this root token until the terminal configuration, as in the arc-standard system.

To be concrete, during training, we allow the parser to select SH with some probability when the gold transition is SR$_{root}$. This eventually leads to a terminal configuration where the sentence root token not attached to ROOT remains on the stack. RR is used only for this configuration, also during decoding. Note that unlike UN, the parser ex-

91

plores this transition during training and learns the parameters associated with it. We hope by this the parser becomes capable of postponing the decision on the root token during decoding when it seems ambiguous locally. We use this transition only with the non-static oracle.

4 Parser Model

A model of a transition-based parser calculates the score of each transition at the current configuration. Our model is basically the stack-LSTM parser (Dyer et al., 2015)[4], which we slightly customize from the original architecture (Section 4.2). In this work we focus our attention on the incremental setting, in which the model is not able to access the full tokens in the buffer. With regard for transition-based parsers this is practically a more important scenario where the graph-based parser is not applicable.

4.1 Stack-LSTM parser

We first briefly describe the original model in Dyer et al. (2015) designed for the arc-standard system. For a configuration c_t at time t, the parser maintains the three vector representations, $\mathbf{s}_t$ that encodes the stack, $\mathbf{b}_t$ the buffer, and $\mathbf{a}_t$ the action history. Each of them is modeled with a stack LSTM, an LSTM that supports push and pop operations by keeping the representations of intermediate time steps. The stack LSTM for $\mathbf{s}_t$ is left-to-right while that for $\mathbf{b}_t$ is right-to-left. $\mathbf{a}_t$ encodes the entire action history from the initial action to the last action. Using these representations we encode the configuration into a single vector:

$$\mathbf{p}_t = \mathrm{ReLU}(\mathbf{W}[\mathbf{s}_t; \mathbf{b}_t; \mathbf{a}_t] + \mathbf{e}_p),$$

where $\mathbf{W}$ is the parameters. Here and the followings $\mathbf{e}_x$ denotes a bias vector.

Using this the probability for each valid transition z_t is obtained with restricted softmax:

$$p(z_t|\mathbf{p}_t) = \frac{\exp(\mathbf{g}_{z_t}^{\mathrm{T}}\mathbf{p}_t + q_{z_t})}{\sum_{z' \in \mathcal{A}(c_t)} \exp(\mathbf{g}_{z'}^{\mathrm{T}}\mathbf{p}_t + q_{z'})},$$

where $\mathbf{g}_z$ is the parameters and q_z is the bias term for action z. The set $\mathcal{A}(c_t)$ returns the set of valid transitions on c_t. After each transition we update

---

[4]Please refer Ballesteros et al. (2015), Ballesteros et al. (2016), Ballesteros et al. (2017) for the latest version which is sophisicated in some architectures (e.g. character information, dynamic oracle).

$\mathbf{s}_{t+1}$, $\mathbf{b}_{t+1}$, and $\mathbf{a}_{t+1}$ accordingly following the new configuration.

For the buffer, each element of the LSTM is a token representation, which Dyer et al. (2015) obtains from the word and POS embeddings. $\mathbf{b}_t$ is then the last output of the LSTM.

For the stack, each element of the LSTM is a compositional representation of a subtree, or a token if it is just a shifted one. The subtree representation of the stack element is updated in a recursive manner. In Dyer et al. (2015) when LA or RA builds an arc $h \xrightarrow{l} d$, the representation $\mathbf{h}$ for the subtree rooted at h is updated by:

$$\mathbf{h}' = \tanh(\mathbf{U}[\mathbf{h}; \mathbf{d}; \mathbf{l}] + \mathbf{e}_h), \qquad (1)$$

in which $\mathbf{d}$ is the representation for the subtree rooted at d, $\mathbf{l}$ is the label embeddings. $\mathbf{s}_t$ is then updated by popping the top two elements of the stack LSTM, $\mathbf{h}$ and $\mathbf{d}$, and pushing $\mathbf{h}'$.

4.2 Modifications

We modify the above basic architecture in the following three ways.

Configuration encoding This is a restriction that we impose on the model. While the original model exploits the entire sentence for the buffer representation $\mathbf{b}_t$ using the LSTM, this violates our assumption of incrementality, the main advantage of the transition-based parsers. We thus avoid to use $\mathbf{b}_t$ and instead use the representations of top three nodes on the buffer: $\mathbf{b1}_t$, $\mathbf{b2}_t$, and $\mathbf{b3}_t$. We also use the representations of the top three nodes (subtrees) on the stack, $\mathbf{s1}_t$, $\mathbf{s2}_t$, and $\mathbf{s3}_t$, which we found effective. The new encoding is:

$$\mathbf{o} = \mathbf{W}[\mathbf{s}_t; \mathbf{a}_t; \mathbf{s1}_t; \mathbf{s2}_t; \mathbf{s3}_t; \mathbf{b1}_t; \mathbf{b2}_t; \mathbf{b3}_t] + \mathbf{e}_p,$$
$$\mathbf{p}_t = \mathrm{ReLU}(\mathbf{o}).$$

Token representation Many languages in UD are annotated with XPOS, fine language specific tags, as well as FEATS, the morphological features. We utilize the embeddings of these features, initialized randomly. We also add character embeddings, which we obtain from character-level bidirectional LSTMs. Our token representation is:

$$\mathbf{x} = \mathrm{ReLU}(\mathbf{V}[\mathbf{w}; \mathbf{t}; \mathbf{tx}; \mathbf{f}; \mathbf{w}_{ch}] + \mathbf{e}_x),$$

where $\mathbf{w}$, $\mathbf{t}$, $\mathbf{tx}$, and $\mathbf{f}$ are word, POS, XPOS, and FEAT embeddings, respectively. $\mathbf{w}_{ch}$ is the output of linear mapping from the concatenation of the last hidden states of the forward and backward character-level LSTMs.

Composition This is the only modification needed to obtain the stack representation in our stay-eager transition system. The subtree representation in Dyer et al. (2015) is fully compositional in that **h** in Eq. 1 encodes the entire subtree with the recursive network. This is possible essentially because of the bottom-up nature of the arc-standard system. Unfortunately the same encoding is not straightforward in our system due to its arc-eager property, in which the right arcs are constructed top-down (Nivre, 2004). In this work, we give up the full compositionality of the original model, and simply mimic Eq. 1 with the following equation:

$$\mathbf{c}' = \tanh(\mathbf{U}[\mathbf{h}; \mathbf{d}; \mathbf{l}; \mathbf{c}] + \mathbf{e}_h). \qquad (2)$$

We update the node representation of both of the stack top and the buffer top. This means that apart from the original model we also update the dependent node with composition. In the equation, $\mathbf{c}'$ is the updated representation of the head or the dependent after SR or SL, which is originally $\mathbf{c}$. For example, after SL, since the stack top becomes dependent, its representation ($\mathbf{d}$) is updated to $\tanh(\mathbf{U}[\mathbf{h}; \mathbf{d}; \mathbf{r}; \mathbf{d}] + \mathbf{e}_h)$. Note that without $\mathbf{c}$ in Eq. 2, the representations of two updated nodes are identical. The role of $\mathbf{c}$ is thus to distinguish the two updates for $\mathbf{h}$ and $\mathbf{d}$.

5 Experiment

Data We use the 63 treebanks in 45 languages in Universal Dependencies 2.0 (Nivre et al., 2017), which are distributed with the training data in the recent shared task in CoNLL 2017 (Zeman et al., 2017).[5] Following the shared task, we focus on real world parsing and assume the raw input text. For all preprocessing (sentence segmantion, tokenization, and tagging), we use UDpipe 1.1 (Straka et al., 2015). We report the official F1 LAS used in the shared task.

Baseline To make a comparison between transition systems fair, we implement the arc-standard *lazy swap* (ASS) parser (Nivre et al., 2009) with almost the same settings as our stay-eager swap (SES) parser including our network architecture (Section 4.2).[6] We also report the scores of UD-

pipe 1.1, the baseline system in the shared task, although the results may not be directly comparable as they tune several settings including the oracle and learning rate etc. for each language.

Settings Our network sizes are: 100 dimensional word embeddings and LSTMs, 50 dimensional POS, XPOS, and FEATS embeddings, and 20 dimensional action and label embeddings, and 32 dimensional character embeddings and bi-LSTMs. We do not use any pre-trained embeddings. We use Adam (Kingma and Ba, 2014) for the optimizer, and set the learning decay of 0.08 and the dropout ratio in LSTMs of 0.33.

In addition to the greedy search, we also try beam search for learning and decoding (beam size is 8). Note that due to swap, each transition sequence may have a different number of actions. We alleviate this inconsistency by ranking with the average scores (Honnibal and Johnson, 2014).[7]

For non-static oracles, we set both probabilities to postpone RD and SR_{root} to 0.33, which works well for the development set.

Results The main results are shown in the left columns of Table 4. Comparing to ASS, our non-static SES achieves the higher LAS on average, regardless of search method. In more detail, it is on about half treebanks (27 for greedy and 28 for beam search) that the score improvements from ASS are more than 0.5 points. Also the static SES is not stronger, suggesting that non-static exploration during training is important for our system.

Focusing on the results on only non-projective sentences (right columns), the score improvements get larger: the average LAS difference between non-static SES and SAS is 1.54 points with greedy search, and 1.18 points with beam search.

To further inspect the parser behaviors on non-projective and projective sentences, we next compare the average LAS on a subset of treebanks, which we divide into four groups according to

---

[5]For small treebanks without the development set, we randomly divide the training data at 1:9 ratio for development and training.

[6] This baseline is competitive to or stronger than the original implementation of Dyer et al. (2015), which also

implements arc-standard swap (https://github.com/clab/lstm-parser). Example UAS on development sets (with gold tags) are: Arabic: 80.83 (Dyer et al.) vs. 82.01 (ours); English: 86.71 (Dyer et al.) vs. 85.28 (ours); and German: 82.87 (Dyers et al.) vs. 84.45 (ours). Both employ greedy search. Note that our system does not use the buffer LSTM.

[7] For learning, we find the following heuristics inspired by max-violation (Huang et al., 2012) works well. Our training is basically local with cross-entropy while for each sentence we calculate the max violation point by beam search and use only the prefix until that point. Although this is simpler than global structured learning (Andor et al., 2016), it provides some improvements with much faster training time.

<table>
<thead>
<tr><th rowspan="3">Language</th><th rowspan="3">Non-proj ratio</th><th colspan="4">All sentences</th><th colspan="4">Only non-projective sentences</th></tr>
<tr><th rowspan="2">ASS</th><th colspan="2">SES</th><th rowspan="2">UDpipe</th><th rowspan="2">ASS</th><th colspan="2">SES</th><th rowspan="2">UDpipe</th></tr>
<tr><th>static</th><th>non-static</th><th>static</th><th>non-static</th></tr>
</thead>
<tbody>
<tr><td>grc</td><td>64.40%</td><td>49.18 (51.28)</td><td>50.00 (53.04)</td><td>50.10 (53.85)</td><td>56.04</td><td>45.54 (47.54)</td><td>46.57 (49.89)</td><td>46.73 (50.72)</td><td>52.83</td></tr>
<tr><td>la</td><td>47.50%</td><td>37.78 (37.82)</td><td>38.32 (42.50)</td><td>41.22 (43.27)</td><td>43.77</td><td>32.64 (32.19)</td><td>32.76 (37.60)</td><td>35.51 (37.31)</td><td>38.22</td></tr>
<tr><td>grc_proiel</td><td>37.92%</td><td>60.67 (63.74)</td><td>60.92 (64.69)</td><td>60.66 (63.77)</td><td>65.22</td><td>54.57 (58.37)</td><td>56.15 (60.58)</td><td>56.61 (60.28)</td><td>60.77</td></tr>
<tr><td>la_ittb</td><td>35.87%</td><td>72.29 (75.20)</td><td>71.98 (75.01)</td><td>72.61 (75.64)</td><td>76.98</td><td>67.07 (71.10)</td><td>67.56 (70.56)</td><td>67.31 (72.03)</td><td>72.14</td></tr>
<tr><td>eu</td><td>31.80%</td><td>66.61 (67.67)</td><td>65.68 (67.66)</td><td>65.74 (68.96)</td><td>69.15</td><td>58.98 (60.01)</td><td>58.15 (60.86)</td><td>58.49 (62.21)</td><td>61.46</td></tr>
<tr><td>en_lines</td><td>29.54%</td><td>70.37 (72.16)</td><td>71.71 (72.59)</td><td>71.98 (73.02)</td><td>72.94</td><td>65.07 (66.96)</td><td>66.86 (67.30)</td><td>66.12 (67.69)</td><td>67.83</td></tr>
<tr><td>la_proiel</td><td>28.30%</td><td>50.56 (54.38)</td><td>53.71 (54.72)</td><td>53.87 (56.18)</td><td>57.54</td><td>45.80 (48.98)</td><td>48.52 (50.37)</td><td>48.98 (51.44)</td><td>53.22</td></tr>
<tr><td>nl_lassysmall</td><td>28.13%</td><td>76.48 (76.25)</td><td>77.35 (77.78)</td><td>77.63 (77.83)</td><td>78.15</td><td>71.76 (71.58)</td><td>73.90 (74.52)</td><td>75.36 (73.88)</td><td>74.12</td></tr>
<tr><td>pt</td><td>23.69%</td><td>77.12 (78.01)</td><td>74.89 (75.49)</td><td>75.07 (77.75)</td><td>82.11</td><td>71.06 (72.42)</td><td>70.01 (70.87)</td><td>69.54 (71.37)</td><td>77.04</td></tr>
<tr><td>de</td><td>23.23%</td><td>65.11 (66.94)</td><td>63.35 (66.64)</td><td>65.13 (66.83)</td><td>69.11</td><td>62.30 (64.51)</td><td>61.90 (64.53)</td><td>62.83 (64.99)</td><td>66.66</td></tr>
<tr><td>gl_treegal</td><td>23.00%</td><td>62.51 (63.78)</td><td>64.09 (63.66)</td><td>64.55 (64.48)</td><td>65.82</td><td>60.51 (62.51)</td><td>63.38 (62.28)</td><td>63.23 (62.94)</td><td>64.30</td></tr>
<tr><td>nl</td><td>22.92%</td><td>64.56 (65.69)</td><td>62.87 (66.86)</td><td>64.26 (67.99)</td><td>68.90</td><td>61.52 (63.79)</td><td>61.66 (67.03)</td><td>63.07 (66.33)</td><td>68.30</td></tr>
<tr><td>got</td><td>22.67%</td><td>54.07 (57.40)</td><td>55.46 (57.71)</td><td>56.66 (58.25)</td><td>59.81</td><td>47.04 (50.99)</td><td>48.73 (52.13)</td><td>49.44 (52.28)</td><td>53.45</td></tr>
<tr><td>hu</td><td>21.60%</td><td>61.64 (62.72)</td><td>60.61 (62.44)</td><td>61.94 (63.45)</td><td>64.30</td><td>56.79 (57.83)</td><td>56.18 (59.95)</td><td>57.22 (60.18)</td><td>60.05</td></tr>
<tr><td>cu</td><td>18.93%</td><td>58.50 (60.41)</td><td>61.17 (62.77)</td><td>60.66 (63.62)</td><td>62.76</td><td>51.25 (54.44)</td><td>53.23 (58.40)</td><td>54.44 (58.57)</td><td>56.21</td></tr>
<tr><td>ur</td><td>18.88%</td><td>75.91 (76.70)</td><td>75.46 (76.46)</td><td>75.85 (76.49)</td><td>76.69</td><td>69.50 (71.22)</td><td>69.61 (70.69)</td><td>70.06 (71.38)</td><td>71.45</td></tr>
<tr><td>sv_lines</td><td>18.38%</td><td>71.48 (72.77)</td><td>71.18 (72.58)</td><td>72.14 (73.95)</td><td>74.29</td><td>63.43 (65.56)</td><td>64.90 (65.77)</td><td>65.84 (67.05)</td><td>67.24</td></tr>
<tr><td>et</td><td>16.87%</td><td>56.02 (56.26)</td><td>56.33 (56.57)</td><td>56.10 (57.64)</td><td>58.79</td><td>48.12 (47.91)</td><td>47.88 (49.42)</td><td>49.42 (51.05)</td><td>52.32</td></tr>
<tr><td>da</td><td>16.46%</td><td>70.23 (72.03)</td><td>69.63 (70.24)</td><td>70.38 (72.31)</td><td>73.38</td><td>65.05 (67.83)</td><td>64.30 (66.07)</td><td>66.11 (69.15)</td><td>68.27</td></tr>
<tr><td>sl</td><td>15.99%</td><td>78.58 (79.85)</td><td>78.72 (79.49)</td><td>78.72 (79.95)</td><td>81.15</td><td>75.18 (75.59)</td><td>75.11 (76.73)</td><td>74.11 (78.28)</td><td>78.56</td></tr>
<tr><td>cs_cltt</td><td>15.76%</td><td>68.78 (68.66)</td><td>69.97 (70.06)</td><td>70.52 (71.30)</td><td>71.64</td><td>63.95 (64.15)</td><td>65.82 (66.12)</td><td>66.69 (65.85)</td><td>68.59</td></tr>
<tr><td>cs_cac</td><td>12.74%</td><td>79.92 (81.56)</td><td>80.10 (81.20)</td><td>79.42 (81.18)</td><td>82.46</td><td>74.47 (75.43)</td><td>75.16 (76.38)</td><td>74.52 (76.76)</td><td>77.34</td></tr>
<tr><td>hi</td><td>12.53%</td><td>85.29 (85.82)</td><td>84.22 (85.56)</td><td>84.38 (85.79)</td><td>86.77</td><td>82.05 (82.56)</td><td>81.06 (83.35)</td><td>81.98 (83.40)</td><td>83.54</td></tr>
<tr><td>sl_sst</td><td>12.18%</td><td>41.45 (42.67)</td><td>42.40 (44.15)</td><td>41.69 (44.40)</td><td>46.45</td><td>36.06 (37.91)</td><td>38.79 (41.10)</td><td>37.76 (40.71)</td><td>42.45</td></tr>
<tr><td>tr</td><td>12.10%</td><td>52.67 (51.56)</td><td>52.00 (52.54)</td><td>52.78 (52.49)</td><td>53.19</td><td>41.88 (41.97)</td><td>42.46 (43.23)</td><td>44.68 (41.59)</td><td>42.50</td></tr>
<tr><td>cs</td><td>11.98%</td><td>77.82 (80.43)</td><td>78.13 (79.62)</td><td>78.01 (80.36)</td><td>82.87</td><td>73.57 (77.03)</td><td>74.95 (77.10)</td><td>74.54 (77.69)</td><td>80.47</td></tr>
<tr><td>el</td><td>11.62%</td><td>76.89 (78.31)</td><td>76.67 (77.72)</td><td>77.73 (78.67)</td><td>79.26</td><td>76.56 (75.36)</td><td>76.02 (77.34)</td><td>75.66 (77.22)</td><td>77.52</td></tr>
<tr><td>ar</td><td>11.62%</td><td>63.79 (64.80)</td><td>64.97 (65.04)</td><td>64.27 (64.74)</td><td>65.30</td><td>55.58 (57.69)</td><td>57.65 (57.57)</td><td>56.82 (57.21)</td><td>58.24</td></tr>
<tr><td>kk</td><td>11.56%</td><td>21.83 (21.75)</td><td>18.43 (19.59)</td><td>20.08 (22.84)</td><td>24.51</td><td>15.65 (15.49)</td><td>11.85 (12.41)</td><td>12.86 (15.44)</td><td>16.46</td></tr>
<tr><td>fr</td><td>11.54%</td><td>78.05 (79.52)</td><td>77.70 (78.86)</td><td>77.97 (79.43)</td><td>80.75</td><td>75.14 (75.59)</td><td>72.99 (76.50)</td><td>74.52 (77.18)</td><td>78.03</td></tr>
<tr><td>ca</td><td>10.94%</td><td>82.94 (83.86)</td><td>83.28 (84.02)</td><td>83.40 (84.33)</td><td>85.39</td><td>78.01 (78.83)</td><td>78.35 (79.40)</td><td>78.97 (78.76)</td><td>80.07</td></tr>
<tr><td>ga</td><td>10.13%</td><td>58.58 (60.29)</td><td>60.50 (61.30)</td><td>61.34 (62.03)</td><td>61.52</td><td>56.14 (59.11)</td><td>58.89 (59.45)</td><td>59.89 (59.89)</td><td>60.34</td></tr>
<tr><td>es</td><td>10.09%</td><td>79.48 (80.42)</td><td>79.64 (80.81)</td><td>79.71 (80.49)</td><td>81.47</td><td>77.14 (78.49)</td><td>76.83 (78.69)</td><td>78.49 (78.33)</td><td>79.57</td></tr>
<tr><td>ro</td><td>9.74%</td><td>76.66 (78.25)</td><td>77.51 (78.34)</td><td>77.75 (78.92)</td><td>79.88</td><td>73.01 (74.78)</td><td>71.07 (74.48)</td><td>73.96 (74.17)</td><td>76.16</td></tr>
<tr><td>es_ancora</td><td>9.65%</td><td>81.43 (83.18)</td><td>81.99 (82.88)</td><td>81.72 (83.21)</td><td>83.78</td><td>75.74 (77.31)</td><td>76.56 (77.04)</td><td>75.22 (78.09)</td><td>77.37</td></tr>
<tr><td>ko</td><td>9.61%</td><td>73.70 (74.24)</td><td>72.11 (72.80)</td><td>72.33 (73.39)</td><td>59.09</td><td>65.50 (65.22)</td><td>63.02 (65.09)</td><td>63.02 (64.12)</td><td>47.56</td></tr>
<tr><td>ru</td><td>9.48%</td><td>71.08 (73.84)</td><td>72.49 (73.33)</td><td>72.17 (74.85)</td><td>74.03</td><td>58.79 (61.80)</td><td>62.84 (62.17)</td><td>62.84 (64.24)</td><td>63.31</td></tr>
<tr><td>ru_syntagrus</td><td>9.21%</td><td>83.89 (85.33)</td><td>84.26 (84.95)</td><td>84.17 (85.42)</td><td>86.76</td><td>78.42 (79.55)</td><td>78.97 (80.03)</td><td>79.16 (80.42)</td><td>82.24</td></tr>
<tr><td>no_nynorsk</td><td>9.20%</td><td>78.69 (79.52)</td><td>78.26 (78.78)</td><td>78.13 (79.56)</td><td>81.56</td><td>72.62 (74.25)</td><td>74.88 (73.71)</td><td>74.01 (75.90)</td><td>77.23</td></tr>
<tr><td>hr</td><td>9.17%</td><td>73.74 (76.08)</td><td>73.47 (75.63)</td><td>73.61 (75.41)</td><td>77.18</td><td>67.63 (70.20)</td><td>64.86 (71.32)</td><td>66.58 (70.73)</td><td>72.12</td></tr>
<tr><td>fr_sequoia</td><td>8.77%</td><td>77.22 (78.69)</td><td>77.09 (77.61)</td><td>78.19 (79.16)</td><td>79.98</td><td>73.91 (73.91)</td><td>74.58 (73.42)</td><td>73.29 (76.05)</td><td>76.35</td></tr>
<tr><td>uk</td><td>7.95%</td><td>57.85 (58.67)</td><td>58.97 (59.84)</td><td>59.80 (61.23)</td><td>60.76</td><td>50.63 (52.37)</td><td>52.42 (53.51)</td><td>52.10 (55.04)</td><td>54.55</td></tr>
<tr><td>no_bokmaal</td><td>7.63%</td><td>79.81 (80.69)</td><td>79.75 (80.37)</td><td>80.36 (81.31)</td><td>83.27</td><td>73.00 (73.28)</td><td>73.28 (74.01)</td><td>73.37 (75.40)</td><td>76.98</td></tr>
<tr><td>fa</td><td>7.17%</td><td>74.83 (77.89)</td><td>74.61 (77.42)</td><td>75.94 (77.87)</td><td>79.24</td><td>67.59 (73.42)</td><td>69.42 (72.61)</td><td>72.95 (74.64)</td><td>74.78</td></tr>
<tr><td>fi_ftb</td><td>7.02%</td><td>70.95 (73.15)</td><td>71.07 (72.03)</td><td>71.30 (72.75)</td><td>74.03</td><td>61.66 (66.13)</td><td>66.01 (67.56)</td><td>65.12 (68.01)</td><td>66.86</td></tr>
<tr><td>lv</td><td>6.64%</td><td>55.54 (57.10)</td><td>54.50 (56.76)</td><td>56.47 (57.35)</td><td>59.95</td><td>46.56 (47.83)</td><td>48.62 (49.25)</td><td>49.49 (50.20)</td><td>53.83</td></tr>
<tr><td>fi</td><td>6.24%</td><td>71.55 (72.37)</td><td>70.45 (72.62)</td><td>71.53 (72.18)</td><td>73.75</td><td>65.95 (67.94)</td><td>68.26 (68.74)</td><td>68.31 (67.56)</td><td>65.79</td></tr>
<tr><td>id</td><td>5.75%</td><td>71.48 (73.78)</td><td>72.17 (74.16)</td><td>72.49 (74.04)</td><td>74.61</td><td>62.20 (67.20)</td><td>64.43 (66.49)</td><td>65.50 (67.38)</td><td>66.13</td></tr>
<tr><td>it</td><td>4.98%</td><td>83.06 (84.68)</td><td>83.61 (84.30)</td><td>83.74 (84.92)</td><td>85.28</td><td>73.86 (77.20)</td><td>74.47 (76.29)</td><td>75.79 (75.08)</td><td>77.91</td></tr>
<tr><td>pt_br</td><td>4.90%</td><td>83.59 (84.39)</td><td>83.38 (83.92)</td><td>83.35 (84.04)</td><td>85.36</td><td>74.86 (76.47)</td><td>73.24 (75.25)</td><td>75.40 (75.35)</td><td>76.57</td></tr>
<tr><td>ug</td><td>4.78%</td><td>31.54 (34.02)</td><td>33.09 (33.04)</td><td>34.40 (34.57)</td><td>34.18</td><td>23.49 (25.44)</td><td>24.01 (23.23)</td><td>25.83 (27.13)</td><td>25.05</td></tr>
<tr><td>sk</td><td>4.34%</td><td>70.13 (70.76)</td><td>70.76 (70.99)</td><td>70.71 (70.69)</td><td>72.75</td><td>62.65 (64.85)</td><td>66.80 (64.59)</td><td>63.81 (68.35)</td><td>68.35</td></tr>
<tr><td>fr_partut</td><td>4.25%</td><td>75.86 (76.47)</td><td>76.81 (77.10)</td><td>77.43 (77.97)</td><td>77.38</td><td>70.48 (71.01)</td><td>71.01 (75.07)</td><td>69.60 (72.60)</td><td>70.13</td></tr>
<tr><td>en_partut</td><td>4.00%</td><td>71.00 (72.61)</td><td>71.04 (72.43)</td><td>71.78 (73.44)</td><td>73.64</td><td>65.95 (68.11)</td><td>66.52 (67.39)</td><td>66.95 (69.40)</td><td>68.97</td></tr>
<tr><td>en</td><td>3.71%</td><td>72.53 (73.56)</td><td>72.51 (73.81)</td><td>72.29 (73.90)</td><td>75.84</td><td>59.12 (61.13)</td><td>58.95 (63.04)</td><td>62.66 (61.95)</td><td>63.96</td></tr>
<tr><td>vi</td><td>3.25%</td><td>36.37 (36.37)</td><td>36.11 (37.00)</td><td>36.68 (37.47)</td><td>37.47</td><td>32.17 (31.98)</td><td>33.72 (33.14)</td><td>35.27 (31.98)</td><td>31.59</td></tr>
<tr><td>bg</td><td>2.87%</td><td>81.24 (82.02)</td><td>79.92 (81.32)</td><td>80.58 (81.79)</td><td>83.64</td><td>80.00 (79.67)</td><td>76.49 (80.67)</td><td>77.66 (78.66)</td><td>80.33</td></tr>
<tr><td>sv</td><td>2.30%</td><td>74.09 (74.67)</td><td>73.65 (74.29)</td><td>74.24 (75.35)</td><td>76.73</td><td>69.94 (66.34)</td><td>68.42 (69.53)</td><td>69.94 (69.67)</td><td>71.19</td></tr>
<tr><td>he</td><td>1.83%</td><td>55.02 (56.58)</td><td>54.91 (56.21)</td><td>56.33 (56.90)</td><td>57.23</td><td>55.34 (59.92)</td><td>52.29 (56.11)</td><td>61.07 (61.45)</td><td>61.45</td></tr>
<tr><td>zh</td><td>1.40%</td><td>53.55 (55.23)</td><td>51.65 (53.94)</td><td>51.93 (53.11)</td><td>57.40</td><td>42.11 (47.24)</td><td>42.88 (45.70)</td><td>45.96 (45.19)</td><td>50.58</td></tr>
<tr><td>pl</td><td>0.27%</td><td>76.80 (78.02)</td><td>77.70 (78.09)</td><td>77.26 (77.75)</td><td>78.78</td><td>66.67 (68.75)</td><td>81.25 (81.25)</td><td>83.33 (70.83)</td><td>66.67</td></tr>
<tr><td>gl</td><td>0.00%</td><td>76.16 (77.43)</td><td>77.24 (77.68)</td><td>77.04 (78.35)</td><td>77.31</td><td>0.00 (0.00)</td><td>0.00 (0.00)</td><td>0.00 (0.00)</td><td>0.00</td></tr>
<tr><td>ja</td><td>0.00%</td><td>71.47 (72.38)</td><td>63.91 (68.59)</td><td>66.96 (71.77)</td><td>72.21</td><td>0.00 (0.00)</td><td>0.00 (0.00)</td><td>0.00 (0.00)</td><td>0.00</td></tr>
<tr><td>Average.</td><td>13.76%</td><td>67.59 (68.93)</td><td>67.56 (68.88)</td><td>68.05 (69.55)</td><td>70.34</td><td>59.51 (61.18)</td><td>60.28 (61.98)</td><td>61.05 (62.36)</td><td>62.75</td></tr>
</tbody>
</table>

Table 4: LAS of all sentences and of only non-projective sentences ordered by the ratio of non-projective sentences in the test data. The scores in brackets are the results with beam search.

Sentence	Non-proj ratio	ASS	SES		UDpipe
			static	non-static	
All	HIGH	62.07 (63.79)	62.21 (64.34)	**62.96 (65.09)**	66.42
	MID	67.27 (68.30)	67.39 (68.35)	**67.64 (69.05)**	69.93
	LOW	73.23 (74.85)	73.25 (74.50)	**73.73 (75.11)**	75.19
	VERYLOW	67.49 (68.61)	67.09 (68.18)	**67.65 (68.80)**	69.68
Projective	HIGH	66.38 (67.91)	66.13 (67.92)	**66.85 (68.80)**	70.25
	MID	68.35 (69.27)	68.32 (69.14)	**68.59 (69.90)**	70.81
	LOW	74.17 (75.73)	74.09 (75.31)	**74.57 (75.87)**	76.06
	VERYLOW	67.91 (68.96)	67.46 (68.53)	**68.01 (69.14)**	70.07
Non-projective	HIGH	57.19 (59.20)	58.02 (60.61)	**58.60 (60.98)**	62.17
	MID	62.04 (63.27)	62.41 (63.99)	**63.02 (64.50)**	65.22
	LOW	66.21 (68.35)	67.28 (68.63)	**67.66 (69.47)**	68.75
	VERYLOW	59.74 (61.39)	60.77 (**62.40**)	**62.56** (62.13)	62.52

[1] HIGH (20%-) : grc, la, grc_proiel, la_ittb, eu, en_lines, la_proiel, nl_lassysmall, pt, de, gl_treegal, nl, got, and hu.

[2] MID (10%-20%) : cu, ur sv_lines, et, da, sl, cs_cltt, cs_cac, hi, sl_sst, tr, cs, el, ar, kk, fr, ca, ga, and es.

[3] LOW (5%-10%) : ro, es_ancora, ko, ru, ru_syntagrus, no_nynorsk, hr, fr_sequoia, uk, no_bokmaal, fa, fi_ftb, lv, fi, and id.

[4] VERYLOW (0%-5%) : it, pt_br, ug, sk, fr_rtut, en_partut, en, vi, bg, sv, he, zh, and pl.

[5] gl and ja are excluded when calculating the scores of "non-projective only" (bottom rows), as these treebanks only contain projective sentences in their test data.

Table 5: The average LAS on all, only projective, and only non-projective sentences on the grouped treebanks according to the ratio of non-projective sentences in the test set. The scores in brackets are the results with beam search.

the ratio of non-projective sentences (Table 5). When evaluating on all sentences (top rows), we can see the larger improvements by the non-static SES in HIGH, MID, and LOW groups (having non-negligible non-projectivity), which confirms the above results. Interestingly, for projective sentences only (mid rows) the scores of SES do not degrade comparing to ASS, or rather improves in all cases. This suggests our transition system also helps to recover the projective arcs.

6 Discussion

While the ordinary reordering-based transition system is built on the arc-standard system, we choose arc-eager as our basic architecture. One reason for this is that decomposing the arc-standard system is more involved than arc-eager; Gómez-Rodríguez and Nivre (2013) observe the RIGHT-ARC in arc-standard would be divided into four transitions including a nontrivial UN-SHIFT operation. Otherwise, we need two different reduce operations for each direction, which complicates the system and learning.

Though we have seen the empirical advantage, in terms of the reordering strategy our approach may not be optimal. Consider the sentence in Figure 4, which we borrow from Nivre et al. (2009). Our system needs more swap transitions than the Nivre et al.'s swap-lazy system for this sentence.

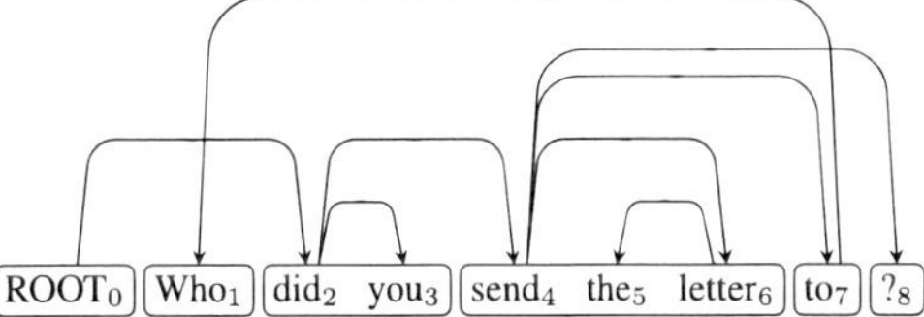

Figure 4: Another non-projective sentence.

In Nivre et al.'s system, swapping Who_1 and did_2 occurs after you_3 is reduced as a dependent of did_2. In our system, due to the right top-down nature of arc-eager, we need to build $ROOT_0 \rightarrow did_2$ before $did_2 \rightarrow you_3$. This means we also need an additional swap between Who_1 and you_3.

Past work shows that a smaller number of swap transitions improves accuracies (Björkelund and Nivre, 2015), and thus it is an important future work to revise our system to minimize the necessary swap transitions. Another direction might be to incorporate our idea to postpone swap transitions into the arc-standard system, possibly with the divided system as we did for arc-eager.

In our system each word is once attached, shifted, and reduced, so the total number of transitions is $3n$ plus the number of swap transitions. This is greater than Nivre et al.'s system, though we expect this additional cost is not substantial comparing to the other techniques, e.g., beam search with larger beam sizes.

7 Conclusion

We have shown for incremental non-projective parsing, explicitly separating the attachment and reduce transitions alleviates the difficulty of local decisions, and leads to higher parsing accuracies for both projective and crossing arcs. Non-projectivity is prevalent in multilingual parsing beyond the popular languages in the current NLP such as English and Chinese. Also incremental parsing is essential for many online applications, in particular the speech-oriented systems. In this paper, we proposed an alternative to the popular approach for incremental non-projective parsing. There are much rooms for improvements, and this is our first step of reconsidering the optimal mechanism to handle crossing arcs incrementally.

Acknowledgements

This work was supported by JST CREST Grant Number JPMJCR1513, Japan.

References

Daniel Andor, Chris Alberti, David Weiss, Aliaksei Severyn, Alessandro Presta, Kuzman Ganchev, Slav Petrov, and Michael Collins. 2016. Globally normalized transition-based neural networks. In *Proceedings of the 54th Annual Meeting of the Association for Computational Linguistics (Volume 1: Long Papers)*. Association for Computational Linguistics, Berlin, Germany, pages 2442–2452. http://www.aclweb.org/anthology/P16-1231.

Giuseppe Attardi. 2006. Experiments with a multilanguage non-projective dependency parser. In *Proceedings of the Tenth Conference on Computational Natural Language Learning (CoNLL-X)*. Association for Computational Linguistics, New York City, pages 166–170. http://www.aclweb.org/anthology/W/W06/W06-2922.

Miguel Ballesteros, Chris Dyer, Yoav Goldberg, and Noah A Smith. 2017. Greedy transition-based dependency parsing with stack lstms. *Computational Linguistics* .

Miguel Ballesteros, Chris Dyer, and Noah A. Smith. 2015. Improved transition-based parsing by modeling characters instead of words with lstms. In *Proceedings of the 2015 Conference on Empirical Methods in Natural Language Processing*. Association for Computational Linguistics, Lisbon, Portugal, pages 349–359. http://aclweb.org/anthology/D15-1041.

Miguel Ballesteros, Yoav Goldberg, Chris Dyer, and Noah A. Smith. 2016. Training with exploration improves a greedy stack lstm parser. In *Proceedings of the 2016 Conference on Empirical Methods in Natural Language Processing*. Association for Computational Linguistics, Austin, Texas, pages 2005–2010. https://aclweb.org/anthology/D16-1211.

Anders Björkelund and Joakim Nivre. 2015. Nondeterministic oracles for unrestricted non-projective transition-based dependency parsing. In *Proceedings of the 14th International Conference on Parsing Technologies*. Association for Computational Linguistics, Bilbao, Spain, pages 76–86. http://www.aclweb.org/anthology/W15-2210.

Bernd Bohnet and Joakim Nivre. 2012. A transition-based system for joint part-of-speech tagging and labeled non-projective dependency parsing. In *Proceedings of the 2012 Joint Conference on Empirical Methods in Natural Language Processing and Computational Natural Language Learning*. Association for Computational Linguistics, Jeju Island, Korea, pages 1455–1465. http://www.aclweb.org/anthology/D12-1133.

Danqi Chen and Christopher Manning. 2014. A fast and accurate dependency parser using neural networks. In *Proceedings of the 2014 Conference on Empirical Methods in Natural Language*

Processing (EMNLP). Association for Computational Linguistics, Doha, Qatar, pages 740–750. http://www.aclweb.org/anthology/D14-1082.

Jinho D. Choi and Andrew McCallum. 2013. Transition-based dependency parsing with selectional branching. In *Proceedings of the 51st Annual Meeting of the Association for Computational Linguistics (Volume 1: Long Papers)*. Association for Computational Linguistics, Sofia, Bulgaria, pages 1052–1062. http://www.aclweb.org/anthology/P13-1104.

Michael A. Covington. 2001. A fundamental algorithm for dependency parsing. In *In Proceedings of the 39th Annual ACM Southeast Conference*. pages 95–102.

Chris Dyer, Miguel Ballesteros, Wang Ling, Austin Matthews, and Noah A. Smith. 2015. Transition-based dependency parsing with stack long short-term memory. In *Proceedings of the 53rd Annual Meeting of the Association for Computational Linguistics and the 7th International Joint Conference on Natural Language Processing (Volume 1: Long Papers)*. Association for Computational Linguistics, Beijing, China, pages 334–343. http://www.aclweb.org/anthology/P15-1033.

Haim Gaifman. 1965. Dependency systems and phrase-structure systems. *Information and Control* 8(3):304 – 337. https://doi.org/http://dx.doi.org/10.1016/S0019-9958(65)90232-9.

Yoav Goldberg and Joakim Nivre. 2012. A dynamic oracle for arc-eager dependency parsing. In *Proceedings of COLING 2012*. The COLING 2012 Organizing Committee, Mumbai, India, pages 959–976. http://www.aclweb.org/anthology/C12-1059.

Carlos Gómez-Rodríguez and Joakim Nivre. 2013. Divisible transition systems and multiplanar dependency parsing. *Computational Linguistics* 39(4):799–845. http://www.aclweb.org/anthology/J/J13/J13-4002.pdf.

Jun Hatori, Takuya Matsuzaki, Yusuke Miyao, and Jun'ichi Tsujii. 2011. Incremental joint pos tagging and dependency parsing in chinese. In *Proceedings of 5th International Joint Conference on Natural Language Processing*. Asian Federation of Natural Language Processing, Chiang Mai, Thailand, pages 1216–1224. http://www.aclweb.org/anthology/I11-1136.

Matthew Honnibal and Mark Johnson. 2014. Joint incremental disfluency detection and dependency parsing. *Transactions of the Association for Computational Linguistics* 2:131–142. https://transacl.org/ojs/index.php/tacl/article/view/234.

Liang Huang, Suphan Fayong, and Yang Guo. 2012. Structured perceptron with inexact search.

In *Proceedings of the 2012 Conference of the North American Chapter of the Association for Computational Linguistics: Human Language Technologies*. Association for Computational Linguistics, Montréal, Canada, pages 142–151. http://www.aclweb.org/anthology/N12-1015.

Diederik Kingma and Jimmy Ba. 2014. Adam: A method for stochastic optimization. *arXiv preprint arXiv:1412.6980* .

Ryan McDonald, Fernando Pereira, Kiril Ribarov, and Jan Hajic. 2005. Non-projective dependency parsing using spanning tree algorithms. In *Proceedings of Human Language Technology Conference and Conference on Empirical Methods in Natural Language Processing*. Association for Computational Linguistics, Vancouver, British Columbia, Canada, pages 523–530. http://www.aclweb.org/anthology/H/H05/H05-1066.

Joakim Nivre. 2003. An efficient algorithm for projective dependency parsing. In *Proceedings of the 8th International Workshop on Parsing Technologies (IWPT)*. pages 149–160.

Joakim Nivre. 2004. Incrementality in deterministic dependency parsing. In Frank Keller, Stephen Clark, Matthew Crocker, and Mark Steedman, editors, *Proceedings of the ACL Workshop Incremental Parsing: Bringing Engineering and Cognition Together*. Association for Computational Linguistics, Barcelona, Spain, pages 50–57.

Joakim Nivre. 2008. Algorithms for deterministic incremental dependency parsing. *Computational Linguistics* 34(4):513–553. http://www.aclweb.org/anthology/J/J08/J08-4003.pdf.

Joakim Nivre. 2009. Non-projective dependency parsing in expected linear time. In *Proceedings of the Joint Conference of the 47th Annual Meeting of the ACL and the 4th International Joint Conference on Natural Language Processing of the AFNLP*. Association for Computational Linguistics, Suntec, Singapore, pages 351–359. http://www.aclweb.org/anthology/P/P09/P09-1040.

Joakim Nivre, Željko Agić, Lars Ahrenberg, Lene Antonsen, Maria Jesus Aranzabe, Masayuki Asahara, Luma Ateyah, Mohammed Attia, Aitziber Atutxa, Elena Badmaeva, Miguel Ballesteros, Esha Banerjee, Sebastian Bank, John Bauer, Kepa Bengoetxea, Riyaz Ahmad Bhat, Eckhard Bick, Cristina Bosco, Gosse Bouma, Sam Bowman, Aljoscha Burchardt, Marie Candito, Gauthier Caron, Gülşen Cebirolu Eryiit, Giuseppe G. A. Celano, Savas Cetin, Fabricio Chalub, Jinho Choi, Yongseok Cho, Silvie Cinková, Çar Çöltekin, Miriam Connor, Marie-Catherine de Marneffe, Valeria de Paiva, Arantza Diaz de Ilarraza, Kaja Dobrovoljc, Timothy Dozat, Kira Droganova, Marhaba Eli, Ali

Elkahky, Tomaž Erjavec, Richárd Farkas, Hector Fernandez Alcalde, Jennifer Foster, Cláudia Freitas, Katarína Gajdošová, Daniel Galbraith, Marcos Garcia, Filip Ginter, Iakes Goenaga, Koldo Gojenola, Memduh Gökrmak, Yoav Goldberg, Xavier Gómez Guinovart, Berta Gonzáles Saavedra, Matias Grioni, Normunds Grūzītis, Bruno Guillaume, Nizar Habash, Jan Hajič, Jan Hajič jr., Linh Hà M, Kim Harris, Dag Haug, Barbora Hladká, Jaroslava Hlaváčová, Petter Hohle, Radu Ion, Elena Irimia, Anders Johannsen, Fredrik Jørgensen, Hüner Kaşkara, Hiroshi Kanayama, Jenna Kanerva, Tolga Kayadelen, Václava Kettnerová, Jesse Kirchner, Natalia Kotsyba, Simon Krek, Sookyoung Kwak, Veronika Laippala, Lorenzo Lambertino, Tatiana Lando, Phng Lê Hng, Alessandro Lenci, Saran Lertpradit, Herman Leung, Cheuk Ying Li, Josie Li, Nikola Ljubešić, Olga Loginova, Olga Lyashevskaya, Teresa Lynn, Vivien Macketanz, Aibek Makazhanov, Michael Mandl, Christopher Manning, Ruli Manurung, Cătălina Mărănduc, David Mareček, Katrin Marheinecke, Héctor Martínez Alonso, André Martins, Jan Mašek, Yuji Matsumoto, Ryan McDonald, Gustavo Mendonça, Anna Missilä, Verginica Mititelu, Yusuke Miyao, Simonetta Montemagni, Amir More, Laura Moreno Romero, Shunsuke Mori, Bohdan Moskalevskyi, Kadri Muischnek, Nina Mustafina, Kaili Müürisep, Pinkey Nainwani, Anna Nedoluzhko, Lng Nguyn Th, Huyn Nguyn Th Minh, Vitaly Nikolaev, Rattima Nitisaroj, Hanna Nurmi, Stina Ojala, Petya Osenova, Lilja Øvrelid, Elena Pascual, Marco Passarotti, Cenel-Augusto Perez, Guy Perrier, Slav Petrov, Jussi Piitulainen, Emily Pitler, Barbara Plank, Martin Popel, Lauma Pretkalnia, Prokopis Prokopidis, Tiina Puolakainen, Sampo Pyysalo, Alexandre Rademaker, Livy Real, Siva Reddy, Georg Rehm, Larissa Rinaldi, Laura Rituma, Rudolf Rosa, Davide Rovati, Shadi Saleh, Manuela Sanguinetti, Baiba Saulīte, Yanin Sawanakunanon, Sebastian Schuster, Djamé Seddah, Wolfgang Seeker, Mojgan Seraji, Lena Shakurova, Mo Shen, Atsuko Shimada, Muh Shohibussirri, Natalia Silveira, Maria Simi, Radu Simionescu, Katalin Simkó, Mária Šimková, Kiril Simov, Aaron Smith, Antonio Stella, Jana Strnadová, Alane Suhr, Umut Sulubacak, Zsolt Szántó, Dima Taji, Takaaki Tanaka, Trond Trosterud, Anna Trukhina, Reut Tsarfaty, Francis Tyers, Sumire Uematsu, Zdeňka Urešová, Larraitz Uria, Hans Uszkoreit, Gertjan van Noord, Viktor Varga, Veronika Vincze, Jonathan North Washington, Zhuoran Yu, Zdeněk Žabokrtský, Daniel Zeman, and Hanzhi Zhu. 2017. Universal dependencies 2.0 CoNLL 2017 shared task development and test data. LINDAT/CLARIN digital library at the Institute of Formal and Applied Linguistics, Charles University. http://hdl.handle.net/11234/1-2184.

Joakim Nivre and Daniel Fernández-González. 2014. Arc-eager parsing with the tree constraint. *Computational linguistics* 40(2):259–267.

Joakim Nivre, Marco Kuhlmann, and Johan Hall. 2009. An improved oracle for dependency parsing with online reordering. In *Proceedings of the 11th International Conference on Parsing Technologies (IWPT'09)*. Association for Computational Linguistics, Paris, France, pages 73–76. http://www.aclweb.org/anthology/W09-3811.

Emily Pitler and Ryan McDonald. 2015. A linear-time transition system for crossing interval trees. In *Proceedings of the 2015 Conference of the North American Chapter of the Association for Computational Linguistics: Human Language Technologies*. Association for Computational Linguistics, Denver, Colorado, pages 662–671. http://www.aclweb.org/anthology/N15-1068.

Milan Straka, Jan Hajič, Jana Straková, and jr. Jan Hajič. 2015. Parsing universal dependency treebanks using neural networks and search-based oracle. In *14th International Workshop on Treebanks and Linguistic Theories (TLT 2015)*. IPIPAN, IPIPAN, Warszawa, Poland, pages 208–220.

Daniel Zeman, Martin Popel, Milan Straka, Jan Hajic, Joakim Nivre, Filip Ginter, Juhani Luotolahti, Sampo Pyysalo, Slav Petrov, Martin Potthast, Francis Tyers, Elena Badmaeva, Memduh Gokirmak, Anna Nedoluzhko, Silvie Cinkova, Jan Hajic jr., Jaroslava Hlavacova, Václava Kettnerová, Zdenka Uresova, Jenna Kanerva, Stina Ojala, Anna Missilä, Christopher D. Manning, Sebastian Schuster, Siva Reddy, Dima Taji, Nizar Habash, Herman Leung, Marie-Catherine de Marneffe, Manuela Sanguinetti, Maria Simi, Hiroshi Kanayama, Valeria dePaiva, Kira Droganova, Héctor Martínez Alonso, Çağr Çöltekin, Umut Sulubacak, Hans Uszkoreit, Vivien Macketanz, Aljoscha Burchardt, Kim Harris, Katrin Marheinecke, Georg Rehm, Tolga Kayadelen, Mohammed Attia, Ali Elkahky, Zhuoran Yu, Emily Pitler, Saran Lertpradit, Michael Mandl, Jesse Kirchner, Hector Fernandez Alcalde, Jana Strnadová, Esha Banerjee, Ruli Manurung, Antonio Stella, Atsuko Shimada, Sookyoung Kwak, Gustavo Mendonca, Tatiana Lando, Rattima Nitisaroj, and Josie Li. 2017. Conll 2017 shared task: Multilingual parsing from raw text to universal dependencies. In *Proceedings of the CoNLL 2017 Shared Task: Multilingual Parsing from Raw Text to Universal Dependencies*. Association for Computational Linguistics, Vancouver, Canada, pages 1–19. http://www.aclweb.org/anthology/K/K17/K17-3001.pdf.

Arc-Hybrid Non-Projective Dependency Parsing
with a Static-Dynamic Oracle

Miryam de Lhoneux   Sara Stymne   Joakim Nivre

Department of Linguistics and Philology
Uppsala University

Abstract

We extend the arc-hybrid transition system for dependency parsing with a SWAP transition that enables reordering of the words and construction of non-projective trees. Although this extension potentially breaks the arc-decomposability of the transition system, we show that the existing dynamic oracle can be modified and combined with a static oracle for the SWAP transition. Experiments on five languages with different degrees of non-projectivity show that the new system gives competitive accuracy and is significantly better than a system trained with a purely static oracle.

1 Introduction

Non-projective sentences are a notorious problem in dependency parsing. Traditional algorithms like those developed by Nivre (2003, 2004) for transition-based parsing only allow the construction of projective trees. These algorithms make use of a stack, a buffer and a set of arcs, and parsing consists of performing a sequence of transitions on these structures. Traditional algorithms have been extended in different ways to allow the construction of non-projective trees (Nivre and Nilsson, 2005; Attardi, 2006; Nivre, 2007; Gómez-Rodríguez and Nivre, 2010). One method proposed by Nivre (2009) is based on the idea of word reordering. This is achieved by adding a transition that swaps two items in the data structures used, enabling the construction of arbitrary non-projective trees while still only adding arcs between adjacent words (after possible reordering). This technique was previously used in the arc-standard transition system (Nivre, 2004). The first contribution of this paper is to show that it can also be combined with the arc-hybrid system

proposed by Kuhlmann et al. (2011).

Recent advances in dependency parsing have demonstrated the benefit of using dynamic oracles for training dependency parsers (Goldberg and Nivre, 2013). Traditionally, parsers were trained in a static way and were only exposed to configurations resulting from optimal transitions during training. Dynamic oracles define optimal transition sequences for any configuration in which the parser may be. The use of dynamic oracles enables training with exploration of errors, which mitigates the problem of error propagation at prediction time.

In order to define a dynamic oracle, we need to be able to compute the cost of any transition in any configuration, where cost is usually defined as minimum Hamming loss with respect to the best tree reachable from that configuration. Goldberg and Nivre (2013) showed that this computation is straightforward for transition systems that satisfy the property of *arc-decomposability*, meaning that a tree is reachable from a configuration if and only if every arc in the tree is reachable in itself. Based on this result, they defined dynamic oracles for the arc-eager (Nivre, 2003), arc-hybrid (Kuhlmann et al., 2011) and easy-first (Goldberg and Elhadad, 2010) systems.

Transition systems that allow non-projective trees are in general not arc-decomposable and therefore require different methods for constructing dynamic oracles (Gómez-Rodríguez and Fernández-González, 2015). The online reordering system of Nivre (2009) is furthermore based on the arc-standard system, which is not even arc-decomposable in itself (Goldberg and Nivre, 2013). The second contribution of this paper is to show that we can take advantage of the arc-decomposability of the arc-hybrid transition system and extend the existing dynamic oracle to deal with the added swap transition. The resulting or-

99

Proceedings of the 15th International Conference on Parsing Technologies, pages 99–104,
Pisa, Italy; September 20–22, 2017. ©2017 Association for Computational Linguistics

acle is static with respect to the new transition but remains dynamic for all other transitions. We show experimentally that this static-dynamic oracle gives a significant advantage over the alternative static oracle and results in competitive results for non-projective parsing.

2 An Extended Transition System

The arc-hybrid system has configurations of the form $c = (\Sigma, B, A)$, where

- Σ is a stack (represented as a list with the head to the right),

- B is a buffer (represented as a list with the head to the left),

- A is a set of dependency arcs (represented as (h, d) pairs).[1]

Given a sentence $W = w_1, \ldots, w_n$, the system is initialized to:

$$c_0 = ([\,], [1, \ldots, n, n{+}1], \{\,\})$$

where $n{+}1$ is a special root node, denoted r from now on. Terminal configurations have the form:

$$c = ([\,], [r], A)$$

and the parse tree is given by the arc set A.

The original arc-hybrid system from Kuhlmann et al. (2011) has three transitions:[2]

- LEFT$[(\sigma|s_0, b|\beta, A)] =$
  $(\sigma, b|\beta, A \cup \{(b, s_0)\})$

- RIGHT$[(\sigma|s_1|s_0, \beta, A)] =$
  $(\sigma|s_1, \beta, A \cup \{(s_1, s_0)\})$

- SHIFT$[(\sigma, b|\beta, A)] = (\sigma|b, \beta, A)$

There are preconditions such that SHIFT is legal only if $b \neq r$, RIGHT only if $|\Sigma| > 1$ and LEFT only if $|\Sigma| > 0$. In order to enforce that r has exactly one dependent, as required by some dependency grammar frameworks, we add a precondition such that LEFT is legal only if $|\Sigma| = 1$ or $b \neq r$.

In the extended system, we add a SWAP transition to be able to construct non-projective trees using online reordering:

- SWAP$[(\sigma|s_0, b|\beta, A)] = (\sigma, b|s_0|\beta, A)$

There is a precondition making SWAP legal only if $|\Sigma| > 0$, $|B| > 1$ and $s_0 < b$.[3]

The SWAP transition reorders nodes by moving the item on top of the stack (s_0) to the second position in the buffer, thus inverting the order of s_0 and b. The SHIFT and SWAP transitions together implement a simple sorting algorithm, which allows us to permute the order of nodes arbitrarily. As shown by (Nivre, 2009), this implies that we can construct any non-projective tree by reordering and adding arcs between adjacent nodes using LEFT and RIGHT.

As already observed, the main advantage of the arc-hybrid system over the arc-standard system is that it is arc-decomposable, which allows us to construct a simple and efficient dynamic oracle. The arc-eager system (Nivre, 2003) is also arc-decomposable but cannot be combined with SWAP because items on the stack in that system do not necessarily represent disjoint subtrees.

3 A Static-Dynamic Oracle

The dynamic oracle for arc-hybrid parsing defined by Goldberg and Nivre (2013) computes the cost of a transition by counting the number of gold arcs that are made unreachable by applying that transition. This presupposes that the system is arc-decomposable, a result that is proven in the same paper. Our construction of an oracle for arc-hybrid parsing with online ordering is based on the conjecture that we can retain arc-decomposition by only making SWAP transitions that are necessary to make non-projective arcs reachable and by enforcing all such transitions. Proving this conjecture is, however, outside the scope of this paper.

3.1 Auxiliary Functions and Notation

We assume that gold trees are preprocessed at training time to compute the following information for each input node i:

- PROJ(i) = the position of node i in the projective order.[4]

- RDEPS(i) = the set of reachable dependents of i, initially all dependents of i.

---

[1] For simplicity, we focus on unlabeled dependency trees in this paper. All results extend to the labeled case by adding a label parameter to the LEFT and RIGHT transitions as usual.

[2] Note that we use uppercase Σ and B to refer to the entire stack and buffer, respectively, while lowercase σ and β refer to relevant (possibly empty) sublists of Σ and B.

[3] The last condition is needed to guarantee termination.

[4] The projective order is a canonical (re)ordering of the words for which the tree is projective. It is obtained through an inorder traversal of the tree that respects the local order of a head and its dependents, as explained in Nivre (2009).

- LEFT:
$$\mathcal{C}(\text{LEFT}) = |\text{RDEPS}(s_0)| + [\![h(s_0) \neq b \text{ and } s_0 \in \text{RDEPS}(h(s_0))]\!]$$

  Updates: Set $\text{RDEPS}(s_0) = [\,]$ and remove s_0 from $\text{RDEPS}(h(s_0))$.

- RIGHT:
$$\mathcal{C}(\text{RIGHT}) = |\text{RDEPS}(s_0)| + [\![h(s_0) \neq s_1 \text{ and } s_0 \in \text{RDEPS}(h(s_0))]\!]$$

  Updates: Set $\text{RDEPS}(s_0) = [\,]$ and remove s_0 from $\text{RDEPS}(h(s_0))$.

- SHIFT:

  1. If there exists a node $i \in B_{-b}$ such that $b < i$ and $\text{PROJ}(b) > \text{PROJ}(i)$:
  $$\mathcal{C}(\text{SHIFT}) = 0$$

  2. Else:
  $$\mathcal{C}(\text{SHIFT}) = |\{d \in \text{RDEPS}(b) \mid d \in \Sigma\}| + [\![h(b) \in \Sigma_{-s_0} \text{ and } b \in \text{RDEPS}(h(b))]\!]$$

  Updates: Remove b from $\text{RDEPS}(h(b))$ if $h(b) \in \Sigma_{-s_0}$ and remove $d \in \Sigma$ from $\text{RDEPS}(b)$.

Figure 1: Transition costs and updates. Expressions of the form $[\![\Phi]\!]$ evaluate to 1 if Φ is true, 0 otherwise. We use s_0 and s_1 to refer to the top and second top item of the stack respectively and we use b to denote the first item of the buffer. Σ refers to the stack and Σ_{-s_0} to the stack excluding s_0 (if Σ is not empty). B refers to the buffer and B_{-b} to the buffer excluding b.

We use $h(i)$ to denote the head of a node i in the gold tree.

3.2 Static Oracle for SWAP

Our oracle is fully dynamic with respect to SHIFT, LEFT and RIGHT but basically static with respect to SWAP. This means that only optimal (zero cost) SWAP transitions are allowed during training and that we force the parser to apply the SWAP transition when needed.

Optimal: To prevent non-optimal SWAP transitions, we add a precondition so that SWAP is legal only if $\text{PROJ}(s_0) > \text{PROJ}(b)$.

Forced: To force necessary SWAP transitions, we bypass the oracle whenever $\text{PROJ}(s_0) > \text{PROJ}(b)$.[5]

3.3 Dynamic Oracle

Since we use a static oracle for SWAP transitions, these will always have zero cost. The dynamic oracle thus only needs to define costs for the remaining three transitions. To construct the oracle, we start from the old dynamic oracle for the projective

---

[5] This is equivalent to an *eager* static oracle for SWAP in the sense of Nivre et al. (2009).

system and extend it to account for the added flexibility introduced by SWAP. Figure 1 defines the transition costs as well as the necessary updates to RDEPS after applying a transition.

- LEFT: Adding the arc (b, s_0) and popping s_0 from the stack means that s_0 will not be able to acquire a head different from b nor any of its reachable dependents. In the old projective case, the loss was limited to a head in $s_0|\beta$ and dependents in $b|\beta$, but because s_0 can potentially be swapped back to the buffer, we instead define reachability explicitly through $\text{RDEPS}(s_0)$ (for dependents) and $\text{RDEPS}(h(s_0))$ (for the head) and update these accordingly after applying the transition.

- RIGHT: Adding the arc (s_1, s_0) and popping s_0 from the stack means that s_0 will not be able to acquire a head different from s_1 nor any of its reachable dependents. In the old projective case, the loss was limited to a head and dependents in $b|\beta$, but because s_0 can potentially be swapped back to the buffer, we again define reachability explicitly through $\text{RDEPS}(s_0)$ (for dependents)

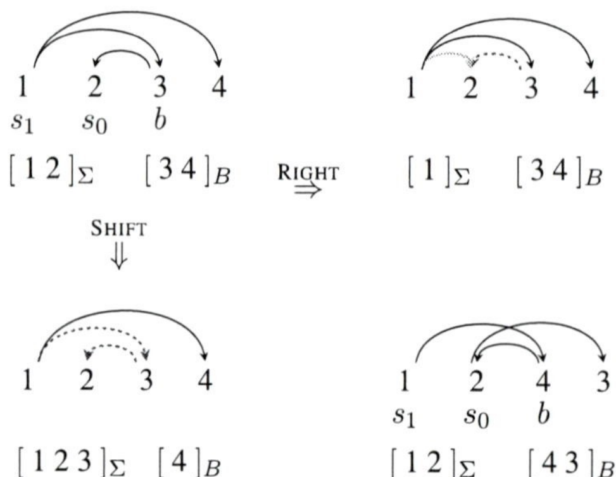

Figure 2: Top left: Configuration with all nodes in projective order and gold tree displayed above the nodes. Top right: Gold arc lost (the red dotted arc) when applying a RIGHT transition from the top left configuration. The arc added by the transition is in blue, it is not in the gold tree. Bottom left: Gold arcs lost (the red dotted arcs) when applying a SHIFT transition from the top left configuration. Bottom right: Configuration where b is higher in the projective order than a following node in the buffer.

and RDEPS$(h(s_0))$ (for the head) and update these accordingly after applying the transition.

- SHIFT: In the projective case, shifting b onto the stack means that b will not be able to acquire a head in Σ other than the top item s_0 nor any dependents in Σ. With the SWAP transition and a static oracle, we also have to consider the case where b can later be swapped back to the buffer, in which case SHIFT has zero cost. We therefore have two cases in Figure 1. In the first case, no updates are needed. In the second case, the updates are analogous to the old projective case.

To illustrate how the oracle works, let us look at some hypothetical configurations. First, we can have a situation as in the top left corner of Figure 2, where all nodes are in projective order given the gold tree displayed above the nodes. For simplicity, the nodes are named after their projective order.

Applying a RIGHT transition in this configuration makes it impossible for s_0 (2) to be attached to its head (3) and therefore makes us lose the arc $3 \rightarrow 2$, as shown in the top right corner. If we instead apply a SHIFT transition, we lose the arc between b (3) and its head (1) as well as the arc $3 \rightarrow 2$, as shown in the bottom left corner. By contrast, a LEFT transition has zero cost, because no arcs are lost so the best tree reachable in the orig-

inal configuration is still reachable after applying the LEFT transition.

Consider now a configuration, like the one in the bottom right corner of Figure 2, where the nodes are not in projective order. Here we can shift b (4) onto the stack without cost, because it will later be swapped back to the buffer to restore the projective order between 4 and 3. A RIGHT transition makes us lose the head and dependent of s_0 ($4 \rightarrow 2$ and $2 \rightarrow 3$). A LEFT transition makes us lose the dependent of s_0 ($2 \rightarrow 3$).

The combination of a dynamic oracle for LEFT, RIGHT and SHIFT with a static oracle for SWAP allows us to benefit from training with exploration in most situations and at the same time capture non-projective dependencies.

4 Experiments

We extend the parser we used in de Lhoneux et al. (2017), a greedy transition-based parser that predicts the dependency tree given the raw words of a sentence. That parser is itself an extension of the parser developed by Kiperwasser and Goldberg (2016). It relies on a BiLSTM to learn informative features of words in context and a feed-forward network for predicting the next parsing transition. It learns vector representations of the words as well as characters. Contrary to parsing tradition, it makes no use of part-of-speech tags. We released our system as UUparser 2.0, available at `https://github.com/UppsalaNLP/uuparser`.

We first compare our system, which uses our static-dynamic oracle, with the same system using a static oracle. This is to find out if we can benefit from error exploration using our partially dynamic oracle. We use the same set of hyperparameters as in that paper in all our experiments.

We additionally compare our method to a different approach to handling non-projectivity, pseudo-projective parsing, as performed in de Lhoneux et al. (2017). Pseudo-projective parsing was developed by Nivre and Nilsson (2005). In a pre-processing step, the training data is projectivised: some nodes get reattached to a close parent. Parsed data are then 'deprojectivised' in a post-processing step. In order for information about non-projectivity to be recoverable after parsing, when projectivising, arcs are renamed to encode information about the original parent of dependents which get re-attached. Note that hyperparameters were tweaked for the pseudo-projective system, possibly giving an unfair advantage.

Lastly, we compare to a *projective* baseline, using a dynamic oracle but no SWAP transition.[6] This is to find out the extent to which dealing with non-projectivity is important.

We selected a sample of 5 treebanks from the Universal Dependencies CoNLL 2017 shared task data (Nivre et al., 2017). We selected languages to have different frequencies of non-projectivity, both at the sentence level and at the level of individual arcs, ranging from a very high frequency (Ancient-Greek) to a low frequency (English), as well as some typological variety. Non-projective frequencies were taken from Straka et al. (2015) and are included in Table 1, which report our results on the development sets (best out of 20 epochs).

Comparing to the static baseline, we can verify that our static-dynamic oracle really preserves the benefits of training with error exploration, with improvements ranging from 0.5 to 3.5 points. (All differences here are statistically significant with p<0.01, except for Portuguese, where the difference is statistically significant with p<0.05 according to the McNemar test).

The new system achieves results largely on par with the pseudo-projective parser. Our method is better by a small margin for 3 out of 5 languages

Language	%NP	S-Dy	Static	PProj	Proj
A.Greek	9.8 / 63.2	**59.53**	56.04	59.22	46.98
Arabic	0.3 / 8.2	**77.08**	76.61	76.96	76.55
Basque	5.0 / 33.7	72.27	70.98	**74.16**	68.85
English	0.5 / 5.0	81.97	81.00	82.21	**82.37**
Portuguese	1.3 / 18.4	**87.34**	86.60	87.20	85.39

Table 1: LAS on dev sets with gold tokenization for our static-dynamic system (S-Dy), the static and projective baselines (Static, Proj) and the pseudo-projective system of de Lhoneux et al. (2017) (PProj). %NP = percentage of non-projective arcs/sentences.

and worse by a large margin for 1. Overall, these results are encouraging given that our method is simpler and more efficient to train, with no need for pre- or post-processing and no extension of the dependency label set.[7]

Comparing to the projective baseline, we see that strictly projective parsing can be slightly better than both online reordering and pseudo-projective parsing for a language with few non-projective arcs/sentences like English. For all other languages, we see small (Arabic) to big (Ancient Greek) improvements from dealing with non-projectivity in some way.

5   Conclusion

We have shown how the SWAP transition for on-line reordering can be integrated into the arc-hybrid transition system for dependency parsing in such a way that we still benefit from training with exploration using a static-dynamic oracle. In the future, we intend to test this further by evaluating our model on more languages with proper tuning of hyperparameters. We are also interested in the question of whether it is possible to define a fully dynamic oracle for our system and allow exploration for the SWAP transition too.

Acknowledgments

We thank Eli Kiperwasser who took part in the discussion where the main idea of this paper emerged. We acknowledge the computational resources provided by CSC in Helsinki and Sigma2 in Oslo through NeIC-NLPL (www.nlpl.eu).

---

[6]When training the projective baseline, we removed non-projective sentences from the training data.

[7]We made no systematic study of training time but observed that it took roughly half the time to train our parser compared to the pseudo-projective one.

References

Giuseppe Attardi. 2006. Experiments with a multilanguage non-projective dependency parser. In *Proceedings of the 10th Conference on Computational Natural Language Learning (CoNLL)*. pages 166–170.

Miryam de Lhoneux, Yan Shao, Ali Basirat, Eliyahu Kiperwasser, Sara Stymne, Yoav Goldberg, and Joakim Nivre. 2017. From raw text to universal dependencies - look, no tags! In *Proceedings of the CoNLL 2017 Shared Task: Multilingual Parsing from Raw Text to Universal Dependencies*. Association for Computational Linguistics, Vancouver, Canada, pages 207–217.

Yoav Goldberg and Michael Elhadad. 2010. An efficient algorithm for easy-first non-directional dependency parsing. In *Human Language Technologies: The 2010 Annual Conference of the North American Chapter of the Association for Computational Linguistics (NAACL HLT)*. pages 742–750.

Yoav Goldberg and Joakim Nivre. 2013. Training deterministic parsers with non-deterministic oracles. *Transactions of the Association for Computational Linguistics* 1:403–414.

Carlos Gómez-Rodríguez and Daniel Fernández-González. 2015. An efficient dynamic oracle for unrestricted non-projective parsing. In *ACL-15-SHORT*. pages 256–261.

Carlos Gómez-Rodríguez and Joakim Nivre. 2010. A transition-based parser for 2-planar dependency structures. In *Proceedings of the 48th Annual Meeting of the Association for Computational Linguistics (ACL)*. pages 1492–1501.

Eliyahu Kiperwasser and Yoav Goldberg. 2016. Simple and accurate dependency parsing using bidirectional LSTM feature representations. *Transactions of the Association for Computational Linguistics* 4:313–327.

Marco Kuhlmann, Carlos Gómez-Rodríguez, and Giorgio Satta. 2011. Dynamic programming algorithms for transition-based dependency parsers. In *Proceedings of the 49th Annual Meeting of the Association for Computational Linguistics (ACL)*. pages 673–682.

Joakim Nivre. 2003. An efficient algorithm for projective dependency parsing. In *Proceedings of the 8th International Workshop on Parsing Technologies (IWPT)*. pages 149–160.

Joakim Nivre. 2004. Incrementality in deterministic dependency parsing. In *Proceedings of the Workshop on Incremental Parsing: Bringing Engineering and Cognition Together (ACL)*. pages 50–57.

Joakim Nivre. 2007. Incremental non-projective dependency parsing. In *Proceedings of Human Language Technologies: The Annual Conference of the North American Chapter of the Association for Computational Linguistics (NAACL HLT)*. pages 396–403.

Joakim Nivre. 2009. Non-projective dependency parsing in expected linear time. In *Proceedings of the Joint Conference of the 47th Annual Meeting of the ACL and the 4th International Joint Conference on Natural Language Processing of the AFNLP (ACL-IJCNLP)*. pages 351–359.

Joakim Nivre, Željko Agić, Lars Ahrenberg, et al. 2017. Universal Dependencies 2.0. LINDAT/CLARIN digital library at the Institute of Formal and Applied Linguistics, Charles University, Prague. http://hdl.handle.net/11234/1-1983.

Joakim Nivre, Marco Kuhlmann, and Johan Hall. 2009. An improved oracle for dependency parsing with online reordering. In *Proceedings of the 11th International Conference on Parsing Technologies (IWPT'09)*. pages 73–76.

Joakim Nivre and Jens Nilsson. 2005. Pseudo-projective dependency parsing. In *Proceedings of the 43rd Annual Meeting of the Association for Computational Linguistics (ACL)*. pages 99–106.

Milan Straka, Jan Hajič, Jana Straková, and Jan Hajič jr. 2015. Parsing universal dependency treebanks using neural networks and search-based oracle. In *Proceedings of the 14th Workshop on Treebanks and Linguistic Theories (TLT)*.

Encoder-Decoder Shift-Reduce Syntactic Parsing

Jiangming Liu and **Yue Zhang**
Singapore University of Technology and Design,
8 Somapah Road, Singapore, 487372
`jmliunlp@gmail.com, yue_zhang@sutd.edu.sg`

Abstract

Encoder-decoder neural networks have been used for many NLP tasks, such as neural machine translation. They have also been applied to constituent parsing by using bracketed tree structures as a target language, translating input sentences into syntactic trees. A more commonly used method to linearize syntactic trees is the shift-reduce system, which uses a sequence of transition-actions to build trees. We empirically investigate the effectiveness of applying the encoder-decoder network to transition-based parsing. On standard benchmarks, our system gives comparable results to the stack LSTM parser for dependency parsing, and significantly better results compared to the aforementioned parser for constituent parsing, which uses bracketed tree formats.

1 Introduction

Neural networks have achieved the state-of-the-art for parsing under various grammar formalisms, including dependency grammar (Dozat and Manning, 2017), constituent grammar (Dyer et al., 2016) and CCG (Xu et al., 2016). For transition-based parsing, Chen and Manning (2014) employed a feed-forward neural network with cube activation functions for local action modeling, archiving better results compared to MaltParser (Nivre et al., 2007). Subsequent work extend this method by investigating more complex representations of configurations (Dyer et al., 2015; Ballesteros et al., 2015) and global training with beam search (Zhou et al., 2015; Andor et al., 2016).

Borrowing ideas from neural machine translation (NMT) (Bahdanau et al., 2015), a line of work utilizes a bidirectional RNN to **en-**code input sentences, using it for feature extraction, and observing improved performances for both transition-based (Kiperwasser and Goldberg, 2016; Dyer et al., 2016) and graph-based (Kiperwasser and Goldberg, 2016; Dozat and Manning, 2017) parsers. In particular, using such encoder structure, the graph-based parser of Dozat and Manning (2017) achieves the state-of-the-art results for dependency parsing.

The success of the encoder structure can be attributed to the use of multilayer bidirectional LSTMs to induce non-local representations of sentences. Without manual feature engineering, such architecture automatically extracts complex features for syntactic representation. For neural machine translation, such encoder structure has been connected to a corresponding LSTM **decoder**, giving the state-of-the-art for sequence-to-sequence learning. Compared to carefully designed feature representations, such as the parser of Chen and Manning (2014) and the stack-LSTM structure of Dyer et al. (2015), the encoder-decoder structure is conceptually simpler, and more general, which can be used across different grammar formalisms without redesigning the stack representation. Vinyals et al. (2015) applied the encoder-decoder structure to constituent parsing, generating the bracketed syntactic trees as the output token sequence without model combination. However, their model achieves relatively low accuracies.

The advantage of using a decoder LSTM is that it leverages a recurrent structure for capturing full sequence information in the output. Unlike greedy or CRF decoders (Durrett and Klein, 2015), which capture only local label dependencies, LSTM decoder models global label sequence relations. Vinyals et al. (2015) use bracketed syntactic trees as the output token sequence, which requires strong constraints to ensure that the output

Proceedings of the 15th International Conference on Parsing Technologies, pages 105–114,
Pisa, Italy; September 20–22, 2017. ©2017 Association for Computational Linguistics

strings correspond to valid dependency trees. On the other hand, a more commonly used sequential representation of syntactic structures is the transition-action sequences in shift reduce parsers. For both constituent (Sagae and Lavie, 2005; Zhang and Clark, 2009) and dependency (Yamada and Matsumoto, 2003; Nivre, 2003) parsing, output syntactic structures can be built using a sequence of inter-dependent shift-reduce actions, which convey incremental structural information.

Motivated by the above, we study the effectiveness of a highly simple encode-decoder structure for shift-reduce parsing. In particular, the encoder is used to represent the input sentence and the decoder is used to generate a sequence of transition actions for constructing the syntactic structure. We additionally use the attention over the input sequence (Vinyals et al., 2015), but with a slight modification, taking separate attentions to represent the stack and queue, respectively.

On standard PTB evaluation, our final model achieves 93.1% UAS for dependency parsing, which is comparable to the model of Dyer et al. (2015), and 90.5% on constituent parsing, which is 2.2% higher compared to Vinyals et al. (2015). We release our source code at `https://github.com/LeonCrashCode/Encoder-Decoder-Parser`.

2 Transition-based parsing

Transition-based parsers scan an input sentence from left to right, incrementally performing a sequence of transition actions to predict its parse tree. Partially-constructed outputs are maintained using a stack, and the next incoming words are ordered in a queue. The initial state consists of an empty stack and a queue containing the whole input sentence. At each step, a transition action is taken to consume the input and construct the output. The process repeats until the input queue is empty and the stack contains only one element, e.g. a *ROOT* for dependency parsing, and *S* for constituent parsing and CCG parsing.

In this paper, we investigate both dependency parsing and constituent parsing, which are shown in Figure 1(a) and (b), respectively. As can be seen in the figure, the two formalisms render syntactic structures from different perspectives. Correspondingly, the stack structures for transition-based dependency parsing and constituent parsing are different. For dependency parsing, the stack

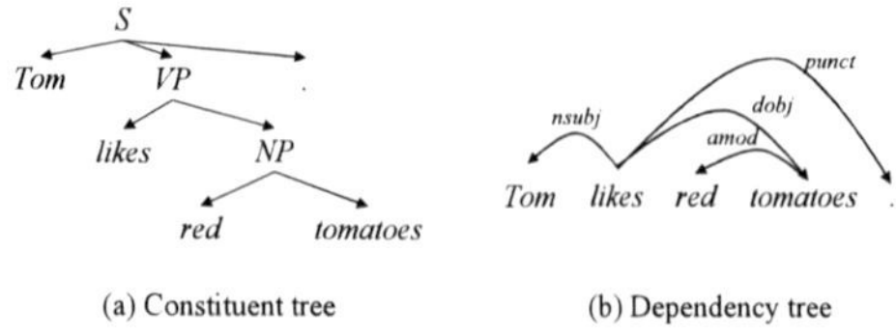

Figure 1: Constituent structure and dependency structure of the sentence "Tom likes red tomatoes."

contains words directly, while for constituent parsing, the stack contains constituent nodes, which cover spans of words in a sentence. In addition, the set of transition actions for building dependency and constituent structures are highly different, as shown by the examples in sections 2.1 and 2.2, respectively. Traditional approaches, such as the stack LSTM of Dyer et al. (2015, 2016), build different representations of the stack for dependency and constituent parsing. In contrast, our method is agnostic to the stack structure, using an encoder-decoder structure to "translate" input sentences to output sequences of shift-reduce actions. To this term, each grammar formalism is reminiscent of a unique foreign language.

2.1 Dependency parsing

We employ the arc-standard transition system (Nivre et al., 2007). Formally, a parsing state is denoted as a tuple (S, Q, L), where S is the stack $[..., s_2, s_1, s_0]$, Q is the queue containing coming words, and L is a set of dependency arcs that have been built. At each step, the parser chooses one of the following actions:

- SHIFT: pop the front word off the queue, and push it onto the stack.

- LEFT-ARC(l): add an arc with label l between the top two trees on the stack ($s_1 \leftarrow s_0$) and remove s_1 from the stack.

- RIGHT-ARC(l): add an arc with label l between the top two trees on the stack ($s_1 \rightarrow s_0$) and remove s_0 from the stack.

The arc-standard parser can be summarized as the deductive system in Figure 2a. For a sentence with size n, parsing stops after performing exactly $2n - 1$ actions. Given a sentence of Figure 1, the sequence of actions SHIFT, SHIFT, LEFT-ARC($nsubj$), SHIFT, SHIFT, LEFT-ARC($amod$), RIGHT-ARC($dobj$), SHIFT, RIGHT-ARC($punct$), can be used to construct its dependency tree.

| Initial State | (ϕ, Q, ϕ) |
| Final State | (s_0, ϕ, L) |

Induction Rules:

SHIFT $\dfrac{(S,q_0|Q,L)}{(S|q_0,Q,L)}$

LEFT-ARC(L) $\dfrac{(S|s_1|s_0,Q,L)}{(S|s_0,Q,L\cup s_1\leftarrow s_0)}$

RIGHT-ARC(L) $\dfrac{(S|s_1|s_0,Q,L)}{(S|s_1,Q,L\cup s_1\rightarrow s_0)}$

(a) Arc-standard dependency parsing.

| Initial State | $(\phi, Q, 0)$ |
| Final State | $(s_0, \phi, 0)$ |

Induction Rules:

SHIFT $\dfrac{(S,q_0|Q,n)}{(S|q_0,Q,n)}$

NT(X) $\dfrac{(S,Q,n)}{(S|e(x),Q,n+1)}$

REDUCE $\dfrac{(S|e(x)|s_j|...|s_0,Q,n)}{(S|e(x,s_j,...,s_0),Q,n-1)}$

(b) Top-down constituent parsing.

Figure 2: Deduction systems

2.2 Constituent parsing

We employ the top-down transition system of Dyer et al. (2016) for constituent parsing. Formally, a parsing state is denoted as a tuple (S, Q, n), where S is the stack $[..., s_2, s_1, s_0]$. Each element in S can be a open nonterminal[1], a completed constituent, or a terminal, Q is the queue, and n is the number of open nonterminals on the stack. At each step, the parser chooses one of the following actions:

- SHIFT: pop the front word off the queue, and push it onto the stack.

- NT(X): open a nonterminal with label X on top of the stack.

- REDUCE: repeatedly pop completed subtrees or terminal symbols from the stack until an open nonterminal is encountered, and then this open NT is popped and used as the label of a new constituent that has the popped subtrees as its children. This new completed

---

[1] An open nonterminal in top-down parsing is a nonterminal waiting to be completed

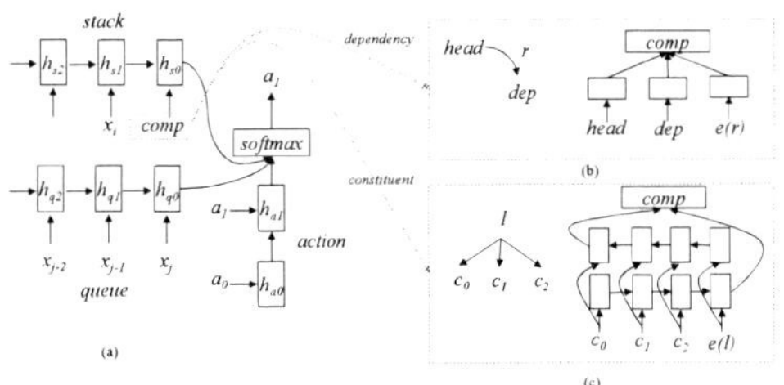

Figure 3: Structure of stack-LSTM with dependency and constituent composition, respectively.

constituent is pushed onto the stack as a single composite item.

The top-down parser can be summarized as the deductive system in Figure 2b. Given the sentence in Figure 1, the sequence of actions NT(S), SHIFT, NT(VP), SHIFT, NT(NP), SHIFT, SHIFT, RE-DUCE, REDUCE, SHIFT, REDUCE, can be used to construct its constituent tree.

2.3 Generalization

Both transition systems above can be treated as examples of a general sequence-to-sequence task. Formally, given a sentence $x_1, x_2, ..., x_n$ where x_i is the ith word in the sentence, the goal is to generate a corresponding sequence of actions $a_1, a_2, ..., a_m$, which correspond to a syntactic structure. Other shift-reduce parser systems, such as CCG (Zhang and Clark, 2011a), can be regarded as instantiation of this.

3 Baseline

We take two baseline neural parsers, namely the parser of Dyer et al. (2015, 2016) and the parser of Vinyals et al. (2015). The former is used to study the effect of our formalism-independent representation, while the latter is used to demonstrate the advantage of transition action sequences over bracketed tree structures for encoder-decoder parsing. We briefly describe the parsers of Dyer et al. (2015, 2016) in this section, and the structure of Vinyals et al. (2015) in Sections 4.1 and 4.2.

As shown in Figure 3(a), the parser of Dyer et al. (2015) consist of three main components: 1) a stack of partial outputs, implemented using a stack-LSTM, 2) the queue of incoming words using an LSTM and 3) a list of actions that has been taken so far encoded by an LSTM. The stack-LSTM is implemented left to right, the queue

LSTM is implemented right to left, and the action history LSTM in the first-to-last order. The last hidden states of each LSTM is concatenated and fed to a softmax layer to determine the next action given the current state:

$$p(act) = softmax(W[h_s; h_q; h_a] + b),$$

where h_s, h_q and h_a denote the last hidden states of the stack LSTM, the queue LSTM and the action history LSTM, respectively.

The stack-LSTM parser represents states on the stack by task-specific composition functions. We give the composition by using task-specific composition functions for dependency parsing (Dyer et al., 2015) and constituent parsing (Dyer et al., 2016) respectively below.

Dependency parsing The composition function models the dependency arc between a head and its dependent (i.e., $head \xrightarrow{r} dep$), when a RE-DUCE action is applied, as shown in Figure 3(b):

$$comp = tanh(W_{comp}[h_{s_{head}}; h_{s_{dep}}; e(r)] + b_{comp}),$$

where h_{s_h} is the value of the head, h_{s_d} is the value of the dependent and $e(r)$ is the arc relation embedding. After a LEFT-ARC(r) action is taken, h_{s_h} and h_{s_d} are removed from the stack-LSTM, and then $comp$ is push onto the stack-LSTM.

Constituent parsing The composition function models the constituent spanning their children (i.e., $(l\ (c_2)\ (c_1)\ (c_0))$), when a REDUCE action is applied, as shown in Figure 3(c):

$$comp = \text{BI-LSTM}_{comp}([h_{s_{c_2}}, h_{s_{c_1}}, h_{s_{c_0}}, e(l)]),$$

where $h_{s_{c_2}}$, $h_{s_{c_1}}$ and $h_{s_{c_0}}$ are the value of the children on stack, and $e(l)$ is the constituent label embedding. After a REDUCE action is taken, $h_{s_{c_2}}$, $h_{s_{c_1}}$ and $h_{s_{c_0}}$ are removed from the stack-LSTM, and then $comp$ is push onto the stack-LSTM.

It is worth noting that the stack contains overlapping information with the action history. This is because the content of the stack can be inferred when the action history is given. As a result, the stack structure of the parser by Dyer et al. (2015) can be regarded as redundant, serving to extract the same source of information as features from a different perspective, given the sequence of actions that have been applied. Our parser models only the action sequence, relying on the model to infer necessary information about the stack automatically.

4 Model

As shown in Figure 4, our model structure consists of two main components, namely *encoder* and *decoder*. The encoder is a bidirectional recurrent neural network, representing information of the input sentence; the decoder is a different recurrent neural network, used to output a sequence of transition actions. The encoder can be further divided into a stack and a queue, respectively, for transition-based parsing.

4.1 Encoder

We follow Dyer et al. (2015), representing each word using three different types of embeddings including pretrained word embedding, $\overline{e}_{w_i}$, which are not fine-tuned during training of the parser, randomly initialized embeddings e_{w_i}, which are fine-tuned, and randomly initialized part-of-speech embeddings e_{p_i}, which are fine-tuned. The three embeddings are concatenated, and then fed to nonlinear layer to derive the final word embedding:

$$x_i = f(W_{enc}[e_{p_i}; \overline{e}_{w_i}; e_{w_i}] + b_{enc}),$$

where W_{enc} and b_{enc} are model parameters, w_i and p_i denote the form of the POS of the ith input word, respectively, and f is a nonlinear function. In this paper, we use ReLu for f.

The encoder is based on bidirectional peephole connected LSTM (Greff et al., 2016), which takes sequence of the word embeddings x_i as input, and output the sequence of hidden state h_i. BI-LSTM is adopted in our models:

$$h_i = [h_{l_i}; h_{r_i}] = \text{BI-LSTM}(x_i).$$

The sequence of h_i is fed to the decoder.

4.2 Vanilla decoder

As shown in Figure 4(a), the decoder structure is similar to that of the decoder of neural machine translation. It applies an LSTM to generate sequences of actions:

$$s_j = g(W_{dec}[s_{j-1}; e_{a_{j-1}}; h_{att_j}] + b_{dec}),$$

where W_{dec} and b_{dec} are model parameters, a_{j-1} is previous action, $e_{a_{j-1}}$ is the embedding of a_{j-1}, s_{j-1} is the LSTM hidden state for a_{j-1}, and s_j

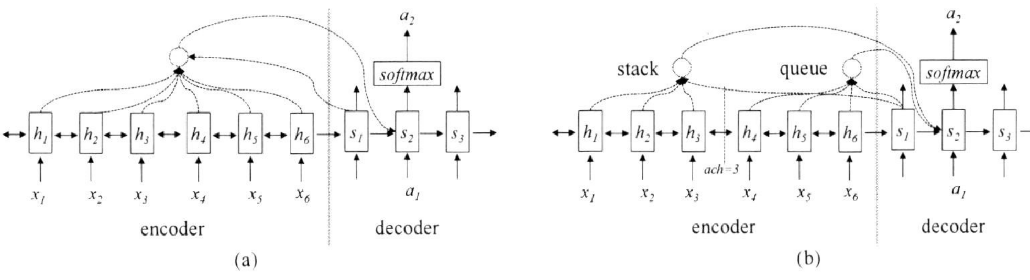

(a)   (b)

Figure 4: Encoder-decoder structure for parsing. (a) vanilla decoder; (b) Stack-queue decoder, where the stack and the queue are differentiated by ach, which is initialized to the beginning of the sentence ($ach = 0$), meaning the stack is empty and queue contains the whole sentence.

is the current LSTM state, from which a_j is predicted. h_{att_j} is the result of attention over the encoder states $h_1...h_n$ using the jth decoder state:

$$h_{att_j} = attention(1, n) = \sum_{i=1}^{n} \alpha_i h_i \qquad (1)$$

where

$$\alpha_i = \frac{exp(\beta_i)}{\sum_{k=1}^{n} exp(\beta_k)},$$

and the weight scores β are calculated by using the previous hidden state s_{j-1} and corresponding encoder hidden state h:

$$\beta_i = U^T tanh(W_{att} \cdot [h_i; s_{j-1}] + b_{att}).$$

s_j is used to predict the current action a_j:

$$p(a_j|s_j) = softmax(W_{out} * s_j + b_{out}).$$

Here $W_{att}, b_{att}, W_{out}, b_{out}$ are model parameters, g is a nonlinear activation function. We use the ReLU for g. For the encoder, the initial hidden states are randomly initialized model parameters; For the decoder, the initial LSTM state s_0 is the last the encoder hidden state $[h_{l_n}; h_{r_1}]$.

This vanilla encoder decoder structure is identical to the method of Vinyals et al. (2015). The only difference is that we use shift-reduce action as the output, while Vinyals et al. (2015) use bracketed string of constituent trees as the output.

4.3 Stack-Queue decoder

We extend the vanilla decoder, using two separate attention models over encoder hidden state to represent the stack and the queue, respectively, as shown in Figure 4(b). In particular, for a given state, the encoder is divided into two segments,

with the left segment (i.e. *stack segment*) containing words form x_1 to the word on top of the stack x_t, and the right segment (i.e. *queue segment*) containing words from the front of the queue x_{t+1} to x_n.

Attention is applied to the stack and the queue segments, respectively. In particular, the representation of the stack segment is:

$$h_{l_{att_j}} = attention(1, t) = \sum_{i=1}^{t} \alpha_i h_i,$$

and the representation of the queue segment is:

$$h_{r_{att_j}} = attention(t + 1, n) = \sum_{i=t+1}^{n} \alpha_i h_i,$$

where the function *attention* is the same with equation (1). Similar with the vanilla decoder, the hidden unit s_j is calculated using:

$$s_j = g(W_{dec}[s_{j-1}; e_{a_{j-1}}; h_{l_{att_j}}; h_{r_{att_j}}] + b_{dec}).$$

Where g is the same nonlinear function as in vanilla decoder.

4.4 Training

Our models are trained to minimize a cross-entropy loss objective with an l_2 regularization term, defined by

$$L(\theta) = -\sum_{i}\sum_{j} log\, p_{a_{ij}} + \frac{\lambda}{2}||\theta||^2,$$

where θ is the set of parameters, $p_{a_{ij}}$ is the probability of the jth action in the ith training example given by the model and λ is a regularization hyperparameter. $\lambda = 10^{-6}$. We use stochastic gradient descent with Adam (Kingma and Ba, 2015) to adjust the learning rate.

109

Parameter	Value
Encoder LSTM Layer	2
Decoder LSTM Layer	1
Word embedding dim	64
Fixed word embedding dim	100
POS tag embedding dim	6
Label embedding dim	20
Action embedding dim	40
encoder LSTM input dim	100
encoder LSTM hidden dim	200
decoder LSTM hidden dim	400
Attention hidden dim	50

Table 1: Hyper-parameters.

5 Experiments

5.1 Data

We use the standard WSJ sections in PTB (Marcus et al., 1993), where the sections 2-21 are taken for training data, section 22 for development data and section 23 for test for both dependency parsing and constituent parsing. For dependency parsing, the constituent trees are converted to Stanford dependencies (v3.3.0) using the Stanford parser[2]. We adopt the pretrained word embeddings generated on the AFP portion of English Gigaword.

5.2 Hyper-parameters

The hyper-parameter values are chosen according to the performance of the model on the development data for dependency parsing, and final values are shown in Table 1. For constituent parsing, we use the same hyper-parameters without further optimization.

5.3 Development experiments

Table 2 shows the development results on dependency parsing. To verify the effectiveness of attention, we build a baseline using average pooling instead (SQ decoder + average pooling). We additionally build a baseline (SQ decoder + treeLSTM) that is aware of stack structures, by using a tree-LSTM (Tai et al., 2015) to derive head node representations when dependency arcs are built. Attention on the stack sector are applied only on words on the stack, but not for their dependents. This representation is analogous to the stack representation of Dyer et al. (2015) and Watanabe and Sumita (2015).

Results show that the explicit construction of stack does not bring significant improvements

---

[2]https://nlp.stanford.edu/software/lex-parser.shtml

Model	UAS (%)
Dyer et al. (2015)	92.3
Vanilla decoder	88.5
SQ decoder + average pooling	91.9
SQ decoder + attention	92.4
SQ decoder + treeLSTM	92.4

Table 2: Dependency parsing dev results.

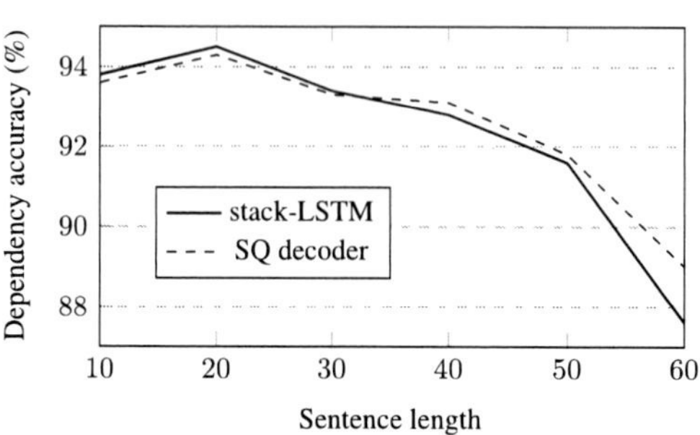

Figure 5: Accuracy against sentence length in bins of size 10, where 20 contains sentences with length [10, 20).

over our stack-agnostic attention model, which confirms our observation in Section 3 that the action history information is sufficient for inferring the stack structure. Our model achieved this goal to some extent. The SQ decoder with average pooling achieves a 3.4% UAS improvement, compared to the vanilla decoder (Section 4.2). The SQ decoder with attention achieves a further 0.5% UAS improvement, reaching comparable results to the stack-LSTM parser.

5.4 Comparison to stack-LSTM

We take a range of different perspectives to analyze the errors distribution of our parser, comparing them with stack-LSTM parser (Dyer et al., 2015). The parsers show different empirical performances over these measures.

Figure 5 shows the accuracy of the parsers relative to the sentence length. The parsers perform comparatively better in short sentences. The stack-LSTM parser performs better on relatively short sentences (≤ 30), while our parser performs better on longer sentences. The composition function is applied in the stack-LSTM parser to explicitly represent the partially-constructed trees, ensuring high precision of short sentences. On the other hand, errors are also fully represented and accumulated in long sentences. As the sentence grows longer, it is difficult to capture the stack structure.

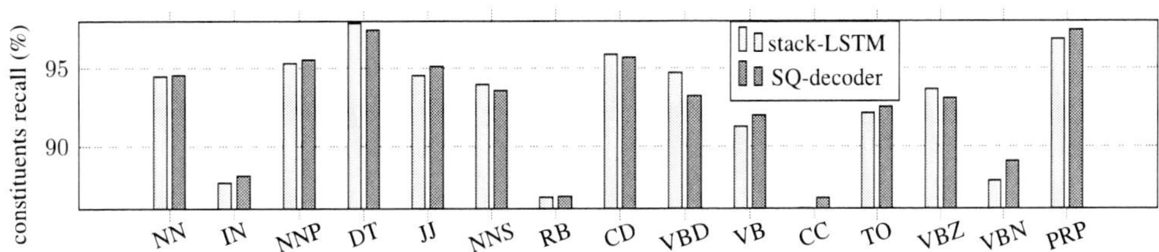

Figure 6: Accuracy against part-of-the-speech tags.

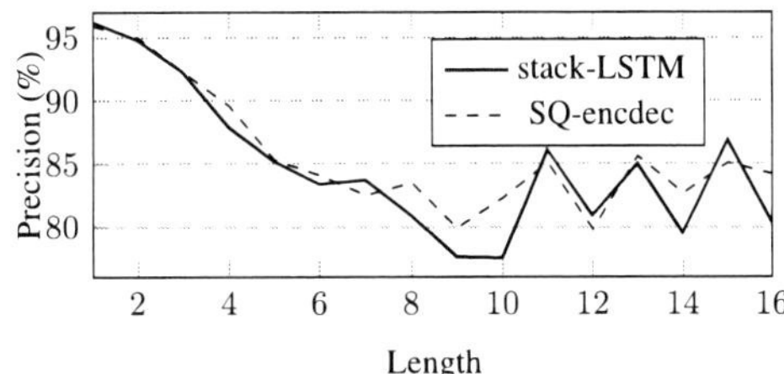

Figure 7: Arc precision against dependency length. The length is defined as the absolute difference between the indices of the head and modifier.

Model	UAS (%)	LAS (%)
Graph-based		
Kiperwasser and Goldberg (2016)	93.0	90.9
Dozat and Manning (2017)	95.7	94.1
Transition-based		
Chen and Manning (2014)	91.8	89.6
Dyer et al. (2015)	93.1	90.9
Kiperwasser and Goldberg (2016)†	93.9	91.9
Andor et al. (2016)	92.9	91.0
Andor et al. (2016)*	94.6	92.8
SQ decoder + attention	93.1	90.1

Table 3: Results for dependency parsing, where * use global training, † use dynamic oracle.

With stack-queue sensitive attention, SQ decoder implicitly represent the structures.

Figures 6 and 7 show comparison on various POS and dependency lengths, respectively. While the error distributions of the two parsers on the fine-grained metrics are slightly different, with our model being stronger on arcs that take relatively more steps to build, the main trends of the two models are consistent, which shows that our model can learn similar information compared to the parser of Dyer et al. (2015), without explicitly modeling stack information. This verifies the usefulness of the decoder on exploiting action history.

5.5 Contrast with Vinyals et al. (2015)

For constituent parsing, our models outperforms the parser of Vinyals et al. (2015) by differentiating stack and queue and generating transition actions instead. This shows the advantage of shift-reduce actions over bracketed syntactic trees as decoder outputs. Using the settings tuned on the dependency development data directly, our model achieves a F1-score of 90.5, which is comparable to the models of Zhu et al. (2013) and Socher et al. (2013). By using the rerankers of Choe and Charniak (2016) under the same settings, we obtain a 92.7 F1-score with fully-supervised reranking and a 93.4 F1-score with semi-supervised reranking.

5.6 Attention visualization

We visualize the attention values during parsing, as shown in Figure 8. The parser can implicitly extract the structure features by assigning different attention value to the elements on stack. In Figure 8(a), "Jones" on the top of stack and "industrials" on the front of queue dominates the prediction of SHIFT action. In Figure 8(b), "The" on the top of stack and "closed" on the front of queue contribute more to the prediction of LEFT-ARC, which constructs an left arc from "industrials" to "The" to complete dependency of the word "industrials". In Figure 8(c), "said" on the top of stack determines the prediction of NT(*SBAR*) for a clause. In Figure 8(d), "of" on the front of queue suggests to complete the noun phrase of "most". In Figure 8(e), "their major institutional" on top of the stack needs the word "investor" on the front of queue to complete a noun phrase.

Interestingly, these attention values capture information not only from nodes on the stack, but also their dependents, achieving similar effects as the manually defined features of Chen and Manning (2014) and Kiperwasser and Goldberg (2016). In addition, the range of features that our attention mechanism models is far beyond the manual feature templates, since words even on the

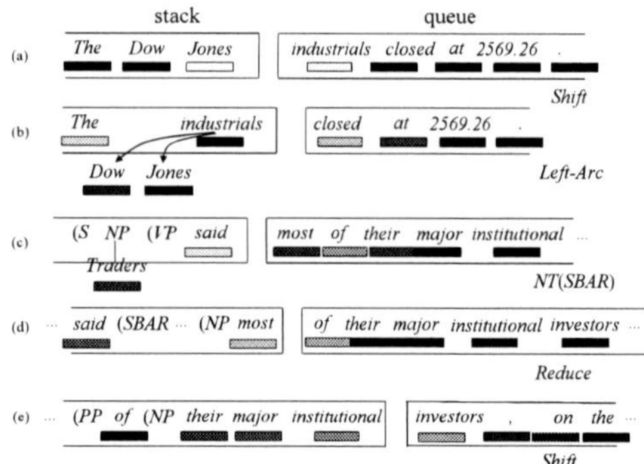

Figure 8: Output examples to visualize attention values. The grey scale indicates the value of the attention. (a) (b) are for dependency parsing, and (c) (d) (e) are for constituent parsing.

Model	F1 (%)
Vinyals et al. (2015)	88.3
Socher et al. (2013)	90.4
Zhu et al. (2013)	90.4
Shindo et al. (2012)	91.1
Dyer et al. (2016)	91.2
Liu and Zhang (2017b)	91.7
Liu and Zhang (2017a)	91.8
Choe and Charniak (2016) + rerank	92.4
Dyer et al. (2016) + rerank	93.3
Liu and Zhang (2017a) + rerank	93.6
SQ decoder + attention	90.5
SQ decoder + attention + rerank	92.7
SQ decoder + attention + semi-rerank	93.4

Table 4: Results for constituent parsing.

bottom of the stack can sometimes influence the decision, as shown in Figure 8(b). These are worth noting given that our model does not explicitly model the stack structure.

The decoder is used to model sequences of actions globally, and is less influenced by error propagation.

5.7 Final results

We compare the final results with previous related work under the fully-supervised setting (except for pretrained word embeddings), as shown in Table 3 for dependency parsing, and Table 4 for constituent parsing. For dependency parsing, our models achieve comparable UAS to the majority of parsers (Dyer et al., 2015; Kiperwasser and Goldberg, 2016; Andor et al., 2016).

6 Related work

LSTM encoder structures have been used in both transition-based and graph-based parsing. Among transition-based parsers, Kiperwasser and Goldberg (2016) use two-layer encoder to encode input sentence, extracting 11 different features from a given state in order to predict the next transition action, showing that the encoder structure lead to significant accuracy improvements over the baseline parser of Chen and Manning (2014). Among graph-based parsers, Dozat and Manning (2017) exploit 4-layer LSTM encoder over the input, using conceptually simple biaffine attention mechanism to model dependency arcs over the encoder, resulting in the stat-of-the-art accuracy in dependency parsing. Their success forms a strong motivation of our work.

Vinyals et al. (2015) can also be understood as building a language model over bracket constituent trees. A similar idea is proposed by Choe and Charniak (2016), who directly use LSTMs to model such output forms. The language model is used to rerank candidate trees from a baseline parser, and trained over large automatically parsing data using tri-training, achieving a current best results for constituent parsing. Our work is similar in that it can be regarded as a form of language model, over shift-reduce actions rather than bracketed syntactic trees. Hence, our model can potentially be used for under tri-training settings also.

There has also been a strand of work applying global optimization to neural network parsing. Zhou et al. (2015) and Andor et al. (2016) extend the parser of Zhang and Clark (2011b), using beam search and early update training. They set a max-likelihood training objective, using probability mass in the beam to approximate partition function of CRF training. Watanabe and Sumita (2015) study constituent parsing by using a large-margin objective, where the negative example is the expected score of all states in the beam for transition-based parsing. Xu et al. (2016) build CCG parsing models with a training objective of maximizing the expected F1 score of all items in the beam when parsing finishes, under a transition-based system. More relatedly, Wiseman and Rush (2016) use beam search and global max-margin training for the method of Vinyals et al. (2015). In contrast, we use a greedy local model; our method is orthogonal to these techniques.

7   Conclusion

We adopted a simple encoder-decoder neural network with slight modification for shift-reduce parsing, regarding the task as translating a sentence into a shift-reduce action sequence, achieving comparable results to the current state-of-the-art neural parsers under the same settings. One advantage of our model is that NMT techniques, such as scheduled sampling (Bengio et al., 2015), residual networks (He et al., 2016) and ensemble mechanisms (Luong et al., 2015), can be directly applied.

Acknowledgments

We thank the anonymous reviewers for their detailed and constructive comments. Yue Zhang is the corresponding author.

References

Daniel Andor, Chris Alberti, David Weiss, Aliaksei Severyn, Alessandro Presta, Kuzman Ganchev, Slav Petrov, and Michael Collins. 2016. Globally normalized transition-based neural networks. In *ACL*.

Dzmitry Bahdanau, Kyunghyun Cho, and Yoshua Bengio. 2015. Neural machine translation by jointly learning to align and translate. In *ICLR*.

Miguel Ballesteros, Chris Dyer, and Noah A. Smith. 2015. Improved transition-based parsing by modeling characters instead of words with lstms. In *EMNLP*.

Samy Bengio, Oriol Vinyals, Navdeep Jaitly, and Noam Shazeer. 2015. Scheduled sampling for sequence prediction with recurrent neural networks. In *Advances in Neural Information Processing Systems*. pages 1171–1179.

Danqi Chen and Christopher D. Manning. 2014. A fast and accurate de- pendency parser using neural networks. In *EMNLP*.

Do Kook Choe and Eugene Charniak. 2016. Parsing as language modeling. In *EMNLP*.

Timothy Dozat and Christopher D. Manning. 2017. Deep biaffine attention for neural dependency parsing. *ICLR* .

Greg Durrett and Dan Klein. 2015. Neural crf parsing. In *ACL*.

Chris Dyer, Miguel Ballesteros, Wang Ling, Austin Matthews, and Noah A. Smith. 2015. Transition-based dependency parsing with stack long short-term memory. In *ACL*.

Chris Dyer, Adhiguna Kuncoro, Miguel Ballesteros, and Noah A. Smith. 2016. Recurrent neural network grammars. In *NAACL*.

Klaus Greff, Rupesh K. Srivastava, Jan Koutník, Bas R. Steunebrink, and Jürgen Schmidhuber. 2016. Lstm: A search space odyssey. *IEEE transactions on neural networks and learning systems* .

Kaiming He, Xiangyu Zhang, Shaoqing Ren, and Jian Sun. 2016. Deep residual learning for image recognition. In *Proceedings of the IEEE Conference on Computer Vision and Pattern Recognition*. pages 770–778.

Diederik Kingma and Jimmy Ba. 2015. Adam: A method for stochastic optimization. In *ICLR*.

Eliyahu Kiperwasser and Yoav Goldberg. 2016. Simple and accurate dependency parsing using bidirectional lstm feature representations. *Transactions of the Association for Computational Linguistics* .

Jiangming Liu and Yue Zhang. 2017a. In-order transition-based constituent parsing. *arXiv preprint arXiv:1707.05000* .

Jiangming Liu and Yue Zhang. 2017b. Shift-Reduce Constituent Parsing with Neural Lookahead Features. *Transactions of the Association for Computational Linguistics* 5:45–58.

Thang Luong, Hieu Pham, and Christopher D. Manning. 2015. Effective approaches to attention-based neural machine translation. In *EMNLP*.

Mitchell P. Marcus, Beatrice Santorini, and Mary Ann Marcinkiewicz. 1993. Building a Large Annotated Corpus of English: The Penn Treebank. *Computational Linguistics* 19(2):313–330.

Joakim Nivre. 2003. An efficient algorithm for projective dependency parsing. In *IWPT*. Citeseer.

Joakim Nivre, Johan Hall, Jens Nilsson, Atanas Chanev, Gülsen Eryigit, Sandra Kübler, Svetoslav Marinov, and Erwin Marsi. 2007. Maltparser: A language-independent system for data-driven dependency parsing. *Natural Language Engineering* 13(02):95–135.

Kenji Sagae and Alon Lavie. 2005. A classifier-based parser with linear run-time complexity. In *IWPT*. Association for Computational Linguistics, pages 125–132.

Hiroyuki Shindo, Yusuke Miyao, Akinori Fujino, and Masaaki Nagata. 2012. Bayesian symbol-refined tree substitution grammars for syntactic parsing. In *ACL*. Association for Computational Linguistics, pages 440–448.

Richard Socher, John Bauer, Christopher D. Manning, and Andrew Y. Ng. 2013. Parsing with compositional vector grammars. In *ACL*. pages 455–465.

Kai Sheng Tai, Richard Socher, and Christopher D. Manning. 2015. Improved semantic representations from tree-structured long short-term memory networks. In *ACL*.

Oriol Vinyals, Łukasz Kaiser, Terry Koo, Slav Petrov, Ilya Sutskever, and Geoffrey Hinton. 2015. Grammar as a foreign language. In *ICLR*.

Taro Watanabe and Eiichiro Sumita. 2015. Transition-based neural constituent parsing. In *ACL*. pages 1169–1179.

Sam Wiseman and Alexander M. Rush. 2016. Sequence-to-sequence learning as beam-search optimization. In *EMNLP*.

Wenduan Xu, Michael Auli, and Stephen Clark. 2016. Expected f-measure training for shift-reduce parsing with recurrent neural networks. In *NAACL*. pages 210–220.

Hiroyasu Yamada and Yuji Matsumoto. 2003. Statistical dependency analysis with support vector machines. In *IWPT*. volume 3, pages 195–206.

Yue Zhang and Stephen Clark. 2009. Transition-based parsing of the chinese treebank using a global discriminative model. In *IWPT*. Association for Computational Linguistics, pages 162–171.

Yue Zhang and Stephen Clark. 2011a. Shift-reduce ccg parsing. In *ACL*. Association for Computational Linguistics, pages 683–692.

Yue Zhang and Stephen Clark. 2011b. Syntactic processing using the generalized perceptron and beam search. *Computational linguistics* 37(1):105–151.

Hao Zhou, Yue Zhang, Shujian Huang, and Jiajun Chen. 2015. A neural probabilistic structured-prediction model for transition-based dependency parsing. In *ACL*. pages 1213–1222.

Muhua Zhu, Yue Zhang, Wenliang Chen, Min Zhang, and Jingbo Zhu. 2013. Fast and accurate shift-reduce constituent parsing. In *ACL*. pages 434–443.

Arc-Standard Spinal Parsing with Stack-LSTMs

Miguel Ballesteros
IBM T.J Watson Research Center
Yorktown Heights, NY 10598. U.S.
miguel.ballesteros@ibm.com

Xavier Carreras
Naver Labs Europe
Meylan, France
xavier.carreras@naverlabs.com

Abstract

We present a neural transition-based parser for spinal trees, a dependency representation of constituent trees. The parser uses Stack-LSTMs that compose constituent nodes with dependency-based derivations. In experiments, we show that this model adapts to different styles of dependency relations, but this choice has little effect for predicting constituent structure, suggesting that LSTMs induce useful states by themselves.

1 Introduction

There is a clear trend in neural transition systems for parsing sentences into dependency trees (Titov and Henderson, 2007; Chen and Manning, 2014; Dyer et al., 2015; Andor et al., 2016) and constituent trees (Henderson, 2004; Vinyals et al., 2014; Watanabe and Sumita, 2015; Dyer et al., 2016; Cross and Huang, 2016b). These transition systems use a relatively simple set of operations to parse in linear time, and rely on the ability of neural networks to infer and propagate hidden structure through the derivation. This contrasts with state-of-the-art factored linear models, which explicitly use of higher-order information to capture non-local phenomena in a derivation.

In this paper, we present a transition system for parsing sentences into spinal trees, a type of syntactic tree that explicitly represents together dependency and constituency structure. This representation is inherent in head-driven models (Collins, 1997) and was used by Carreras et al. (2008) with a higher-order factored model. We extend the Stack-LSTMs by Dyer et al. (2015) from dependency to spinal parsing, by augmenting the composition operations to include constituent information in the form of spines. To parse sen-tences, we use the extension by Cross and Huang (2016a) of the arc-standard system for dependency parsing (Nivre, 2004). This parsing system generalizes shift-reduce methods (Henderson, 2003; Sagae and Lavie, 2005; Zhu et al., 2013; Watanabe and Sumita, 2015) to be sensitive to constituent heads, as opposed to, for example, parse a constituent from left to right.

In experiments on the Penn Treebank, we look at how sensitive our method is to different styles of dependency relations, and show that spinal models based on leftmost or rightmost heads are as good or better than models using linguistic dependency relations such as Stanford Dependencies (De Marneffe et al., 2006) or those by Yamada and Matsumoto (2003). This suggests that Stack-LSTMs figure out effective ways of modeling non-local phenomena within constituents. We also show that turning a dependency Stack-LSTM into spinal results in some improvements.

2 Spinal Trees

In a spinal tree each token is associated with a spine. The spine of a token is a (possibly empty) vertical sequence of non-terminal nodes for which the token is the head word. A spinal dependency is a binary directed relation from a node of the head spine to a dependent spine. In this paper we consider projective spinal trees. Figure 1 shows a constituency tree from the Penn Treebank together with two spinal trees that use alternative head identities: the spinal tree in 1b uses Stanford Dependencies (De Marneffe et al., 2006), while the spinal tree in 1c takes the leftmost word of any constituent as the head. It is direct to map a constituency tree with head annotations to a spinal tree, and to map a spinal tree to a constituency or a dependency tree.

Proceedings of the 15th International Conference on Parsing Technologies, pages 115–121,
Pisa, Italy; September 20–22, 2017. ©2017 Association for Computational Linguistics

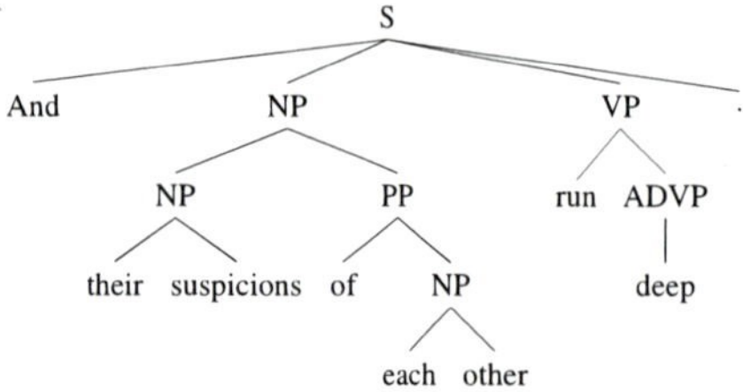

(a) A constituency tree from the Penn Treebank.

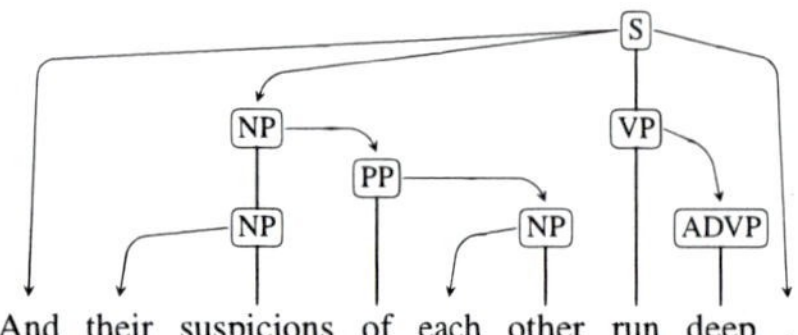

And their suspicions of each other run deep .

(b) The spinal tree of (1a) using Stanford Dependency heads.

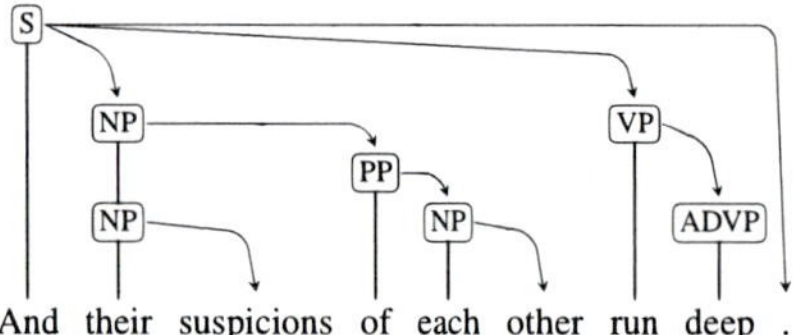

And their suspicions of each other run deep .

(c) The spinal tree of (1a) using leftmost heads.

Figure 1: A constituency tree and two spinal trees.

3 Arc-Standard Spinal Parsing

We use the transition system by Cross and Huang (2016a), which extends the arc-standard system by Nivre (2004) for constituency parsing in a head-driven way, i.e. spinal parsing. We describe it here for completeness. The parsing state is a tuple $\langle \beta, \sigma, \delta \rangle$, where β is a buffer of input tokens to be processed; σ is a stack of tokens with partial spines; and δ is a set of *spinal* dependencies. The operations are the following:

- shift : $\langle i{:}\beta, \sigma, \delta \rangle \rightarrow \langle \beta, \sigma{:}i, \delta \rangle$

  Shifts the first token of the buffer i onto the stack, i becomes a base spine consisting of a single token.

- node (n) : $\langle \beta, \sigma{:}s, \delta \rangle \rightarrow \langle \beta, \sigma{:}s{+}n, \delta \rangle$

  Adds a non-terminal node n onto the top element of the stack s, which becomes $s{+}n$. At this point, the node n can receive left and right children (by the operations below) until the node is closed (by adding a node above, or by reducing the spine with an arc operation with this spine as dependent). By this

single operation, the arc-standard system is extended to spinal parsing.

- left-arc :
  $\langle \beta, \sigma{:}t{:}s{+}n, \delta \rangle \rightarrow \langle \beta, \sigma{:}s{+}n, \delta{\cup}(n, t) \rangle$

  The stack must have two elements, the top one is a spine $s{+}n$, where n is the top node of that spine, and the second element t can be a token or a spine. The operation adds a spinal from the node n to t, and t is reduced from the stack. The dependent t becomes the leftmost child of the constituent n.

- right-arc :
  $\langle \beta, \sigma{:}s{+}n{:}t, \delta \rangle \rightarrow \langle \beta, \sigma{:}s{+}n, \delta{\cup}(n, t) \rangle$

  This operation is symmetric to left-arc, it adds a spinal dependency from the top node n of the second spine in the stack to the top element t, which is reduced from the stack and becomes the rightmost child of n.

At a high level, the system builds a spinal tree headed at token i by:

1. Shifting the i-th token to the top of the stack. By induction, the left children of i are in the stack and are complete.
2. Adding a constituency node n to i's spine.
3. Adding left children to n in head-outwards order with left-arc, which are removed from the stack.
4. Adding right children to n in head-outwards order with right-arc, which are built recursively.
5. Repeating steps 2-4 for as many nodes in the spine of i.

Transition	Buffer β	Stack σ	New Arc in δ
	[And, their, …]	[]	
shift	[their, suspicions, …]	[And]	
shift	[suspicions, of, …]	[And, their]	
shift	[of, each, …]	[… , their, susp.]	
node (NP)	[of, each, …]	[… , their, susp.+NP^1_3]	
left-arc	[of, each, …]	[And, susp.+NP^1_3]	(NP^1_3,their)
node (NP)	[of, each, …]	[And, susp.+NP^1_3+NP^2_3]	
shift	[each, other, …]	[… , susp.+NP^1_3+NP^2_3, of]	
node (PP)	[each, other, …]	[… , susp.+NP^1_3+NP^2_3, of+PP^1_4]	
shift	[other, run, …]	[… , of+PP^1_4, each]	
shift	[run, deep, …]	[… , each, other]	
node (NP)	[run, deep, …]	[… , each, other+NP^1_6]	
left-arc	[run, deep, …]	[… , of+PP^1_4, other+NP^1_6]	(NP^1_6, each)
right-arc	[run, deep, …]	[… , susp.+NP^1_3+NP^2_3, of+PP^1_4]	(PP^1_4, NP^1_6)
right-arc	[run, deep, …]	[And, susp.+NP^1_3+NP^2_3]	(NP^2_3, PP^1_4)
…			

Figure 2: Initial steps of the arc-standard derivation for the spinal tree in Figure 1b, until the tree headed at "suspicions" is fully built. Spinal nodes are noted n^j_i, where n is the non-terminal, i is the position of the head token, and j is the node level in the spine.

Figure 2 shows an example of a derivation. The process is initialized with all sentence tokens in the buffer, an empty stack, and an empty set of dependencies. Termination is always attainable and occurs when the buffer is empty and there is a single element in the stack, namely the spine of the full sentence head. This transition system is correct and sound with respect to the class of projective spinal trees, in the same way as the arc-standard system is for projective dependency trees (Nivre, 2008). A derivation has $2n + m$ steps, where n is the sentence length and m is the number of constituents in the derivation.

We note that the system naturally handles constituents of arbitrary arity. In particular, unary productions add one node in the spine without any children. In practice we put a hard bound on the number of consecutive unary productions in a spine[1], to ensure that in the early training steps the model does not generate unreasonably long spines. We also note there is a certain degree of non-determinism: left and right arcs (steps 3 and 4) can be mixed as long as the children of a node are added in head-outwards order. At training time, our *oracle derivations* impose the order above (first left arcs, then right arcs), but the parsing system runs freely. Finally, the system can be easily extended with dependency labels, but we do not use them.

4   Spinal Stack-LSTMs

Dyer et al. (2015) presented an arc-standard parser that uses Stack-LSTMs, an extension of LSTMs (Hochreiter and Schmidhuber, 1997) for transition-based systems that maintains an embedding for each element in the stack.[2]. Our model is based on the same architecture, with the addition of the node (n) action. The state of our algorithm presented in Section 3 is represented by the contents of the STACK, the BUFFER and a list with the history of actions with Stack-LSTMs. This state representation is then used to predict the next action to take.

Composition: when the parser predicts a left-arc() or right-arc(), we compose the vector representation of the head and dependent elements; this is equivalent to what it is presented by Dyer et al. (2015). The

---

[1] Set to 10 in our experiments

[2] We refer interested readers to (Dyer et al., 2015; Ballesteros et al., 2017).

representation is obtained recursively as follows:

$$\mathbf{c} = \tanh\left(\mathbf{U}[\mathbf{h}; \mathbf{d}] + \mathbf{e}\right).$$

where $\mathbf{U}$ is a learned parameter matrix, $\mathbf{h}$ represents the head spine and $\mathbf{d}$ represents the dependent spine (or token, if the dependent is just a single token) ; $\mathbf{e}$ is a bias term.

Similarly, when the parser predicts a node (n) action, we compose the embedding of the non-terminal symbol that is added ($\mathbf{n}$) with the representation of the element at the top of the stack ($\mathbf{s}$), that might represent a spine or a single terminal symbol. The representation is obtained recursively as follows:

$$\mathbf{c} = \tanh\left(\mathbf{W}[\mathbf{s}; \mathbf{n}] + \mathbf{b}\right). \tag{1}$$

where $\mathbf{W}$ is a learned parameter matrix, $\mathbf{s}$ represents the token in the stack (and its partial spine, if non-terminals have been added to it) and $\mathbf{n}$ represents the non-terminal symbol that we are adding to $\mathbf{s}$; $\mathbf{b}$ is a bias term.

As shown by Kuncoro et al. (2017) composition is an essential component in this kind of parsing models.

5   Related Work

Collins (1997) first proposed head-driven derivations for constituent parsing, which is the key idea for spinal parsing, and later Carreras et al. (2008) came up with a higher-order graph-based parser for this representation. Transition systems for spinal parsing are not new. Ballesteros and Carreras (2015) presented an arc-eager system that labels dependencies with constituent nodes, and builds the spinal tree in post-processing. Hayashi et al. (2016) and Hayashi and Nagata (2016) presented a bottom-up arc-standard system that assigns a full spine with the shift operation, while ours builds spines incrementally and does not depend on a fixed set of full spines. Our method is different from shift-reduce constituent parsers (Henderson, 2003; Sagae and Lavie, 2005; Zhu et al., 2013; Watanabe and Sumita, 2015) in that it is head-driven. Cross and Huang (2016a) extended the arc-standard system to constituency parsing, which in fact corresponds to spinal parsing. The main difference from that work relies on the neural model: they use sequential BiLSTMs, while we use Stack-LSTMs and composition functions. Finally, dependency parsers have been extended to

	LR	LP	F1	UAS $_{(SD)}$
Leftmost heads	91.18	90.93	91.05	-
Leftmost h., no n-comp	90.20	90.76	90.48	-
Rightmost heads	91.03	91.20	91.11	-
Rightmost h., no n-comp	90.64	91.24	90.04	-
SD heads	90.75	91.11	90.93	93.49
SD heads, no n-comp	90.38	90.58	90.48	93.16
SD heads, dummy spines	-	-	-	93.30
YM heads	90.82	90.84	90.83	-

Table 1: Development results for spinal models, in terms of labeled precision (LP), recall (LR) and F1 for constituents, and unlabeled attachment score (UAS) against Stanford dependencies. Spinal models are trained using different head annotations (see text). Models labeled with *"no n-comp"* do not use node compositions. The model labeled with *"dummy spines"* corresponds to a standard dependency model.

constituency parsing by encoding the additional structure in the dependency labels, in different ways (Hall et al., 2007; Hall and Nivre, 2008; Fernández-González and Martins, 2015).

6 Experiments

We experiment with stack-LSTM spinal models trained with different types of head rules. Our goal is to check how the head identities, which define the derivation sequence, interact with the ability of Stack-LSTMs to propagate latent information beyond the local scope of each action. We use the Penn Treebank (Marcus et al., 1993) with standard splits.[3]

We start training four spinal models, varying the head rules that define the spinal derivations:[4]

- Leftmost heads as in Figure 1c.
- Rightmost heads.
- Stanford Dependencies (SD) (De Marneffe et al., 2006), as in Figure 1b.
- Yamada and Matsumoto heads (YM) (Yamada and Matsumoto, 2003).

Table 1 presents constituency and dependency metrics on the development set. The model using rightmost heads works the best at 91.11 F1, followed by the one using leftmost heads. It is worth to note that the two models using structural head

---

identities (right or left) work better than those using linguistic ones. This suggests that the Stack-LSTM model already finds useful head-child relations in a constituent by parsing from the left (or right) even if there are non-local interactions. In this case, head rules are not useful.

The same Table 1 shows two ablation studies. First, we turn off the composition of constituent nodes into the latent derivations (Eq 1). The ablated models, tagged with *"no n-comp"*, perform from 0.5 to 1 points F1 worse, showing the benefit of adding constituent structure. Then, we check if constituent structure is any useful for dependency parsing metrics. To this end, we emulate a dependency parser using a spinal model by taking standard Stanford dependency trees and adding a dummy constituent for every head with all its children. This model, tagged "SD heads, dummy spines", is slightly outperformed by the "SD heads" model using true spines, even though the margin is small.

Tables 2 and 3 present results on the test, for constituent and dependency parsing respectively. As shown in Table 2 our model is competitive compared to the best parsers; the generative parsers by Choe and Charniak (2016b), Dyer et al. (2016) and Kuncoro et al. (2017) are better than the rest, but compared to the rest our parser is at the same level or better. The most similar system is by Ballesteros and Carreras (2015) and our parser significantly improves the performance. Considering dependency parsing, our model is worse than the ones that train with exploration as Kiperwasser and Goldberg (2016) and Ballesteros et al. (2016), but it slightly improves the parser by Dyer et al. (2015) with static training. The systems that calculate dependencies by transforming phrase-structures with conversion rules and that use generative training are ahead compared to the rest.

7 Conclusions

We have presented a neural model based on Stack-LSTMs for spinal parsing, using a simple extension of arc-standard transition parsing that adds constituent nodes to the dependency derivation. Our experiments suggest that Stack-LSTMs can figure out useful internal structure within constituents, and that the parser might work better *without* providing linguistically-derived head words. Overall, our spinal neural method is sim-

	LR	LP	F1
Spinal (leftmost)	90.30	90.54	90.42
Spinal (rightmost)	90.23	90.77	90.50
Ballesteros and Carreras (2015)	88.7	89.2	89.0
Vinyals et al. (2014) (PTB-Only)			88.3
Cross and Huang (2016a)			89.9
Choe and Charniak (2016a) (PTB-Only)			91.2
Choe and Charniak (2016a) (Semi-sup)			93.8
Dyer et al. (2016) (Discr.)			91.2
Dyer et al. (2016) (Gen.)			93.3
Kuncoro et al. (2017) (Gen.)			93.5
Liu and Zhang (2017)	91.3	92.1	91.7

Table 2: Constituency results on the PTB test set.

	UAS test
Spinal, PTB spines + SD (TB-greedy)	93.15
Spinal, dummy spines + SD (TB-greedy)	93.10
Dyer et al. (2015) (TB-greedy)	93.1
Cross and Huang (2016a)	93.4
Ballesteros et al. (2016) (TB-dynamic)	93.6
Kiperwasser and Goldberg (2016) (TB-dynamic)	93.9
Andor et al. (2016) (TB-Beam)	94.6
Kuncoro et al. (2016) (Graph-Ensemble)	94.5
Choe and Charniak (2016a)* (Semi-sup)	95.9
Kuncoro et al. (2017)* (Generative)	95.8

Table 3: Stanford Dependency results (UAS) on
PTB test set. Parsers marked with * calculate dependencies by transforming phrase-structures with
conversion rules.

ple, efficient, and very accurate, and might prove
useful to model constituent trees with dependency
relations.

References

Daniel Andor, Chris Alberti, David Weiss, Aliaksei Severyn, Alessandro Presta, Kuzman Ganchev,
Slav Petrov, and Michael Collins. 2016. Globally normalized transition-based neural networks.
In *Proceedings of the 54th Annual Meeting of the
Association for Computational Linguistics (Volume
1: Long Papers)*. Association for Computational
Linguistics, Berlin, Germany, pages 2442–2452.
http://www.aclweb.org/anthology/P16-1231.

Miguel Ballesteros and Xavier Carreras. 2015.
Transition-based spinal parsing. In *Proceedings
of the Nineteenth Conference on Computational Natural Language Learning*. Association
for Computational Linguistics, pages 289–299.
https://doi.org/10.18653/v1/K15-1029.

Miguel Ballesteros, Chris Dyer, Yoav Goldberg, and
Noah Smith. 2017. Greedy transition-based dependency parsing with stack lstms. *Computational Linguistics* 43(2).

Miguel Ballesteros, Yoav Goldberg, Chris Dyer, and
Noah A. Smith. 2016. Training with exploration improves a greedy stack lstm parser. In *Proceedings of
the 2016 Conference on Empirical Methods in Natural Language Processing*. Association for Computational Linguistics, Austin, Texas, pages 2005–2010.
https://aclweb.org/anthology/D16-1211.

Xavier Carreras, Michael Collins, and Terry Koo. 2008.
*CoNLL 2008: Proceedings of the Twelfth Confer-
ence on Computational Natural Language Learning*, Coling 2008 Organizing Committee, chapter
TAG, Dynamic Programming, and the Perceptron
for Efficient, Feature-Rich Parsing, pages 9–16.
http://aclweb.org/anthology/W08-2102.

Danqi Chen and Christopher Manning. 2014. A
fast and accurate dependency parser using neural
networks. In *Proceedings of the 2014 Conference on Empirical Methods in Natural Language
Processing (EMNLP)*. Association for Computational Linguistics, Doha, Qatar, pages 740–750.
http://www.aclweb.org/anthology/D14-1082.

Do Kook Choe and Eugene Charniak. 2016a. Parsing as language modeling. In *Proceedings of the
2016 Conference on Empirical Methods in Natural Language Processing*. Association for Computational Linguistics, Austin, Texas, pages 2331–2336.
https://aclweb.org/anthology/D16-1257.

Kook Do Choe and Eugene Charniak. 2016b. Parsing as language modeling. In *Proceedings
of the 2016 Conference on Empirical Methods in Natural Language Processing*. Association
for Computational Linguistics, pages 2331–2336.
http://aclweb.org/anthology/D16-1257.

Michael Collins. 1997. Three generative, lexicalised
models for statistical parsing. In *Proceedings of
the 35th Annual Meeting of the Association for
Computational Linguistics*. Association for Computational Linguistics, Madrid, Spain, pages 16–23.
https://doi.org/10.3115/976909.979620.

James Cross and Liang Huang. 2016a. Incremental parsing with minimal features using bidirectional lstm. In *Proceedings of the 54th Annual Meeting of the Association for Computational
Linguistics (Volume 2: Short Papers)*. Association for Computational Linguistics, pages 32–37.
https://doi.org/10.18653/v1/P16-2006.

James Cross and Liang Huang. 2016b. Span-based
constituency parsing with a structure-label system
and provably optimal dynamic oracles. In *Proceedings of the 2016 Conference on Empirical
Methods in Natural Language Processing*. Association for Computational Linguistics, pages 1–11.
http://aclweb.org/anthology/D16-1001.

Marie-Catherine De Marneffe, Bill MacCartney,
Christopher D Manning, et al. 2006. Generating typed dependency parses from phrase structure
parses. In *Proceedings of LREC*. Genoa, volume 6,
pages 449–454.

Chris Dyer, Miguel Ballesteros, Wang Ling, Austin Matthews, and Noah A. Smith. 2015. Transition-based dependency parsing with stack long short-term memory. In *Proceedings of the 53rd Annual Meeting of the Association for Computational Linguistics and the 7th International Joint Conference on Natural Language Processing (Volume 1: Long Papers)*. Association for Computational Linguistics, Beijing, China, pages 334–343. http://www.aclweb.org/anthology/P15-1033.

Chris Dyer, Adhiguna Kuncoro, Miguel Ballesteros, and Noah A. Smith. 2016. Recurrent neural network grammars. In *Proceedings of the 2016 Conference of the North American Chapter of the Association for Computational Linguistics: Human Language Technologies*. Association for Computational Linguistics, San Diego, California, pages 199–209. http://www.aclweb.org/anthology/N16-1024.

Daniel Fernández-González and T. André F. Martins. 2015. Parsing as reduction. In *Proceedings of the 53rd Annual Meeting of the Association for Computational Linguistics and the 7th International Joint Conference on Natural Language Processing (Volume 1: Long Papers)*. Association for Computational Linguistics, pages 1523–1533. https://doi.org/10.3115/v1/P15-1147.

Johan Hall and Joakim Nivre. 2008. *Proceedings of the Workshop on Parsing German*, Association for Computational Linguistics, chapter A Dependency-Driven Parser for German Dependency and Constituency Representations, pages 47–54. http://aclweb.org/anthology/W08-1007.

Johan Hall, Joakim Nivre, and Jens Nilsson. 2007. *Proceedings of the 16th Nordic Conference of Computational Linguistics (NODALIDA 2007)*, University of Tartu, Estonia, chapter A Hybrid Constituency-Dependency Parser for Swedish, pages 284–287. http://aclweb.org/anthology/W07-2444.

Katsuhiko Hayashi and Masaaki Nagata. 2016. Empty element recovery by spinal parser operations. In *Proceedings of the 54th Annual Meeting of the Association for Computational Linguistics (Volume 2: Short Papers)*. Association for Computational Linguistics, pages 95–100. https://doi.org/10.18653/v1/P16-2016.

Katsuhiko Hayashi, Jun Suzuki, and Masaaki Nagata. 2016. Shift-reduce spinal tag parsing with dynamic programming. *Transactions of the Japanese Society for Artificial Intelligence* 31(2).

James Henderson. 2003. Inducing history representations for broad coverage statistical parsing. In *Proceedings of the 2003 Conference of the North American Chapter of the Association for Computational Linguistics on Human Language Technology - Volume 1*. Association for Computational Linguistics, Stroudsburg, PA, USA, pages 24–31.

James Henderson. 2004. Discriminative training of a neural network statistical parser. In *Proceedings of the 42nd Meeting of the Association for Computational Linguistics (ACL'04), Main Volume*. Barcelona, Spain, pages 95–102. https://doi.org/10.3115/1218955.1218968.

Sepp Hochreiter and Jürgen Schmidhuber. 1997. Long short-term memory. *Neural Computation* 9(8):1735–1780.

Eliyahu Kiperwasser and Yoav Goldberg. 2016. Simple and accurate dependency parsing using bidirectional lstm feature representations. *Transactions of the Association for Computational Linguistics* 4:313–327. https://transacl.org/ojs/index.php/tacl/article/view/885.

Adhiguna Kuncoro, Miguel Ballesteros, Lingpeng Kong, Chris Dyer, Graham Neubig, and Noah A. Smith. 2017. What do recurrent neural network grammars learn about syntax? In *Proceedings of the 15th Conference of the European Chapter of the Association for Computational Linguistics: Volume 1, Long Papers*. Association for Computational Linguistics, Valencia, Spain, pages 1249–1258. http://www.aclweb.org/anthology/E17-1117.

Adhiguna Kuncoro, Miguel Ballesteros, Lingpeng Kong, Chris Dyer, and Noah A. Smith. 2016. Distilling an ensemble of greedy dependency parsers into one mst parser. In *Proceedings of the 2016 Conference on Empirical Methods in Natural Language Processing*. Association for Computational Linguistics, Austin, Texas, pages 1744–1753. https://aclweb.org/anthology/D16-1180.

Jiangming Liu and Yue Zhang. 2017. Shift-reduce constituent parsing with neural lookahead features. *Transactions of the Association of Computational Linguistics* 5:45–58. http://aclanthology.coli.uni-saarland.de/pdf/Q/Q17/Q17-1004.pdf.

Mitchell P. Marcus, Beatrice Santorini, and Mary A. Marcinkiewicz. 1993. Building a Large Annotated Corpus of English: The Penn Treebank. *Computational Linguistics* 19(2):313–330.

Joakim Nivre. 2004. Incrementality in deterministic dependency parsing. In Frank Keller, Stephen Clark, Matthew Crocker, and Mark Steedman, editors, *Proceedings of the ACL Workshop Incremental Parsing: Bringing Engineering and Cognition Together*. Association for Computational Linguistics, Barcelona, Spain, pages 50–57.

Joakim Nivre. 2008. Algorithms for deterministic incremental dependency parsing. *Computational Linguistics* 34(4):513–553.

Kenji Sagae and Alon Lavie. 2005. A classifier-based parser with linear run-time complexity. In *Proceedings of the Ninth International Workshop on Parsing Technology*. Association for Computational Linguistics, Vancouver, British Columbia, pages 125–132.

http://www.aclweb.org/anthology/W/W05/W05-1513.

Ivan Titov and James Henderson. 2007. A latent variable model for generative dependency parsing. In *Proceedings of the Tenth International Conference on Parsing Technologies*. Association for Computational Linguistics, Prague, Czech Republic, pages 144–155. http://www.aclweb.org/anthology/W/W07/W07-2218.

Oriol Vinyals, Lukasz Kaiser, Terry Koo, Slav Petrov, Ilya Sutskever, and Geoffrey E. Hinton. 2014. Grammar as a foreign language. *CoRR* abs/1412.7449. http://arxiv.org/abs/1412.7449.

Taro Watanabe and Eiichiro Sumita. 2015. Transition-based neural constituent parsing. In *Proceedings of the 53rd Annual Meeting of the Association for Computational Linguistics and the 7th International Joint Conference on Natural Language Processing (Volume 1: Long Papers)*. Association for Computational Linguistics, Beijing, China, pages 1169–1179. http://www.aclweb.org/anthology/P15-1113.

Hiroyasu Yamada and Yuji Matsumoto. 2003. Statistical dependency analysis with support vector machines. In *Proceedings of IWPT*. volume 3, pages 195–206.

Muhua Zhu, Yue Zhang, Wenliang Chen, Min Zhang, and Jingbo Zhu. 2013. Fast and accurate shift-reduce constituent parsing. In *Proceedings of the 51st Annual Meeting of the Association for Computational Linguistics (Volume 1: Long Papers)*. Association for Computational Linguistics, Sofia, Bulgaria, pages 434–443. http://www.aclweb.org/anthology/P13-1043.

Coarse-To-Fine Parsing for Expressive Grammar Formalisms

Christoph Teichmann and **Alexander Koller**
Saarland University, Saarbrücken
`{cteichmann|koller}@coli.uni-saarland.de`

Jonas Groschwitz
Macquarie University, Sydney
`jonas.groschwitz@students.mq.edu.au`

Abstract

We generalize coarse-to-fine parsing to grammar formalisms that are more expressive than PCFGs and/or describe languages of trees or graphs. We evaluate our algorithm on PCFG, PTAG, and graph parsing. While we achieve the expected performance gains on PCFGs, coarse-to-fine does not help for PTAG and can even slow down parsing for graphs. We discuss the implications of this finding.

1 Introduction

Coarse-to-fine (CTF) parsing (Charniak et al., 2006) is one of the most effective pruning techniques for PCFG parsing. Its basic idea is to simplify a grammar by systematically merging nonterminals together. One then parses the input with the simple grammar, and uses statistics calculated from the resulting parse chart to constrain parsing with the original grammar. This can speed up parsing by an order of magnitude at no loss in accuracy (Charniak et al., 2006; Petrov and Klein, 2007).

We present an algorithm for CTF parsing for grammar formalisms that are more expressive than PCFGs – to our knowledge, for the first time. More precisely, we extend CTF parsing to Interpreted Regular Tree Grammars (IRTGs, Koller and Kuhlmann (2011)), a very general grammar formalism which captures PCFGs, tree-adjoining grammars (TAGs, Joshi and Schabes (1997)), hyperedge replacement graph grammars (HRGs, Chiang et al. (2013)), and many others. Our direct application of CTF to expressive grammar formalism contrasts with related work (van Cranenburgh, 2012; Zhang and Krieger, 2011) which limits entries for the parse chart of the expressive formalism using the parse chart of a PCFG approximation.

We then evaluate our generalized CTF algorithm on a number of grammar formalisms. On PCFGs, we obtain the expected speedups. However, we observe no speedups for TAG parsing compared to unpruned parsing, and HRG parsing on abstract meaning representations (Banarescu et al., 2013) is even slowed down by CTF. We discuss these findings and show how the efficacy of CTF parsing relies on specific properties of PCFG grammars derived from treebanks. Because these properties do not depend on the specifics of our formalism, they would generalize to formalism specific implementations of CTF for TAG or HRG.

2 Interpreted Regular Tree Grammars

Interpreted Regular Tree Grammars (IRTGs, Koller and Kuhlmann (2011)) generalize a wide range of grammar formalisms, including (probabilistic) context-free grammars (PCFGs), tree-adjoining grammars (Joshi and Schabes, 1997; Koller and Kuhlmann, 2012), hyperedge replacement grammars (Chiang et al., 2013; Groschwitz et al., 2015), as well as synchronous and transducer versions of these formalisms. They achieve this by distinguishing carefully between the generation of grammatical derivation trees and the way in which these derivation trees are interpreted as values of some algebra.

Formally, a (monolingual) IRTG $\mathcal{G} = (G, h, \mathcal{A})$ consists of a weighted regular tree grammar (RTG, (Comon et al., 2007)) G over some signature Σ of node labels, an algebra $\mathcal{A}$ over some signature Δ into which the derivation trees are interpreted, and a tree homomorphism $h : T_\Sigma \to T_\Delta$ that maps derivation trees into terms over the algebra. The RTG G generates a language $L(G) \subseteq T_\Sigma$ of *derivation trees*. Based on these, the language of the IRTG, $L(\mathcal{G}) = \{[\![h(t)]\!]_\mathcal{A} \mid t \in L(G)\}$, is obtained by mapping each derivation tree $t \in L(\mathcal{G})$

Proceedings of the 15th International Conference on Parsing Technologies, pages 122–127,
Pisa, Italy; September 20–22, 2017. ©2017 Association for Computational Linguistics

into a term $h(t)$ over the algebra, and then evaluating this term in the algebra.

Fig. 1 shows a simple IRTG. The RTG G is shown on the left; it derives, among others, the derivation tree $t = r_1(r_4, r_2(r_6, r_5)) \in L(G)$. The tree homomorphism shown on the right maps this to the term $h(t) = *(\text{john}, *(\text{loves}, \text{mary}))$. By evaluating this term over a string algebra $\mathcal{A}$ which interprets the symbol $*$ as string concatenation, we obtain "John loves Mary" $\in L(\mathcal{G})$. For simplicity we will identify rules of G with their labels, i.e. we simply write r_1 for the first rule in Fig. 1.

IRTGs can capture different grammar formalisms by varying the algebra into which derivation trees are interpreted. For instance, TAG requires a string algebra with a string wrapping operation (Koller and Kuhlmann, 2012). It is also possible to extend the IRTG formalism in order to allow for multiple homomorphisms and algebras, which is useful for mapping between inputs and outputs and can be used e.g. in semantic parsing (Koller, 2015).

Grammars from different formalisms also tend to vary in the complexity of the homomorphism h. For instance, all binary rules of a PCFG in CNF map to simple concatenation (cf. r_1, r_2 in Fig. 1). By contrast, IRTG encodings of TAG grammars can use h to associate entire elementary trees with a single rule.

Parsing for IRTGs proceeds in three steps. First, given an input object $w \in \mathcal{A}$, we compute a *decomposition grammar* D_w which generates all terms over $\mathcal{A}$ that evaluate to w. Then we compute the *inverse homomorphism (invhom)* of D_w, i.e. an RTG I_w with $L(I_w) = \{t \in T_\Sigma \mid h(t) \in L(D_w)\}$. This RTG thus describes all derivation trees that are interpreted to w. Finally, we intersect I_w with G - the RTG from $\mathcal{G}$, obtaining an RTG M – the *parse chart* – which compactly describes the grammatically correct derivation trees. Similar to intersection constructions for e.g. finite state automata, the nonterminals of M are pairs AJ of nonterminals A of G and J of I_w and M has rules of the form $A_0 J_0 \to r(A_1 J_1, \ldots, A_n J_n)$.

When the rules of G are assigned weights, as in Fig. 1, we can use the Viterbi algorithm to extract the highest-weight derivation tree from M. We can also compute inside and outside weights $\text{in}(AJ)$ and $\text{out}(AJ)$ for every nonterminal in M as usual.

$$
\begin{array}{ll|l}
\text{S} \to r_1(\text{NP}, \text{VP}) & [1] & h(r_1) = *(x_1, x_2) \\
\text{VP} \to r_2(\text{VP}, \text{NP}) & [0.5] & h(r_2) = *(x_1, x_2) \\
\text{VP} \to r_3(\text{VP}, \text{NP}) & [0.1] & h(r_3) = *(\text{to}, *(x_1, x_2)) \\
\text{NP} \to r_4 & [0.5] & h(r_4) = \text{john} \\
\text{NP} \to r_5 & [0.5] & h(r_5) = \text{mary} \\
\text{VP} \to r_6 & [0.4] & h(r_6) = \text{loves}
\end{array}
$$

Figure 1: An example IRTG.

3 Coarse-to-fine parsing for IRTGs

Coarse-to-fine parsing for PCFGs. In PCFG parsing, CTF parsing is an established pruning technique for computing the best parse tree of a sentence w given a PCFG G_F. We assume a *fine-to-coarse map* C, which maps the nonterminal symbols of G_F into a set of coarse-grained nonterminal symbols, potentially making two nonterminals of G_F the same. By merging rules of G_F that now have the same nonterminals on the left and right hand side, we obtain a smaller PCFG G_C (the *coarse* grammar). For instance, if we have $C(\text{S}) = C(\text{NP}) = C(\text{VP}) = \text{HP}$, then the rules S $\to$ NP VP and VP $\to$ VP NP are both mapped to the same rule, HP $\to$ HP HP. The fine-to-coarse mapping may have multiple *levels*, providing increasingly coarse-grained grammars.

CTF parsing then proceeds by parsing w with respect to G_C and computing the inside and outside probabilities of all edges in the (coarse) parse chart. Edges whose probabilities are too low are pruned away. The others are refined into edges for a parse chart with respect to G_F. Thus if an edge $\text{HP}[2-7] \to \text{HP}[2-3] \; \text{HP}[3-7]$ in the coarse chart (describing a split of the substring from 2 to 7 at position 3) is sufficiently likely, it will be refined into both $\text{S}[2-7] \to \text{NP}[2-3] \; \text{VP}[3-7]$ and $\text{VP}[2-7] \to \text{VP}[2-3] \; \text{NP}[3-7]$. The Viterbi parse tree of this fine chart will then be a parse tree of w with respect to G_F.

Coarsification for IRTGs. We generalize this procedure to IRTGs. In doing this, we need to pay special attention to the fact that the rules of an IRTG may differ not only in their nonterminal symbols, but also in their homomorphic interpretations. As mentioned above, this is prevalent in expressive grammar formalisms, such as TAG.

We define two rules $A_0 \to r_1(A_1, \ldots, A_n)$ and $B_0 \to r_2(B_1, \ldots, B_n)$ of an IRTG to be *equivalent* with respect to a fine-to-coarse map C iff $C(A_i) = C(B_i)$ for all i and $h(r_1) = h(r_2)$, i.e. both rules are interpreted in the same way by the input homomorphism. Using the mapping C from above, we find that r_1 and r_2 in Fig. 1 are equivalent to each other, but not to r_3.

We can then partition the rules of a fine-grained IRTG $\mathcal{G}_F$ into their equivalence classes, and build a *coarse-grained* IRTG $\mathcal{G}_C$ over the same algebra with one rule for each equivalence class. Let $R = \{r_1, \ldots, r_k\}$ be an equivalence class containing the fine-grained rule $A_0 \rightarrow r_1(A_1, \ldots, A_n)$. Then $\mathcal{G}_C$ will contain the rule $H_0 \rightarrow R(H_1, \ldots, H_n)$, where $H_i = C(A_i)$ for all i, and $h_C(R) = h_F(r_1)$. The choice of r_1 among the elements of R does not matter, because equivalent rules have the same homomorphic image and map to the same coarse-grained nonterminals. In this paper, we will simply let the weight of the coarse rule be the sum of the weights of the fine rules in order to set the inside score of an item in a coarse chart to approximately the sum of the weights of the finer items it represents; if suitable data is available, these weights could also be re-estimated from a treebank (Charniak et al., 2006; Petrov and Klein, 2007). In the example, we obtain $HP \rightarrow R_1(HP, HP)$ and $HP \rightarrow R_2(HP, HP)$ with $R_1 = \{r_1, r_2\}$ and $R_2 = \{r_3\}$. This construction generalizes easily to multiple CTF levels.

Coarse-to-fine parsing with IRTGs. Given this precomputation, we can now perform coarse-to-fine parsing. Given an input object w, we first compute a complete parse chart M_C using the coarse-grained IRTG $\mathcal{G}_C$, e.g. using one of the parsing algorithms of Groschwitz et al. (2016). The entries e of this chart are rules $H_0 J_0 \rightarrow R(H_1 J_1, \ldots, H_n J_n)$, such that $H_0 \rightarrow R(H_1, \ldots, H_n)$ is a rule of $\mathcal{G}_C$ and the invhom grammar I_w contains a rule $J_0 \rightarrow r(J_1, \ldots, J_n)$ for one, and thus all, $r \in R$.

We compute $\mathsf{in}(AJ)$ and $\mathsf{out}(AJ)$ for every nonterminal AJ of M_C, and use them to calculate a score

$$s(e) = \mathsf{out}(H_0 J_0) \cdot w(R) \cdot \mathsf{in}(H_1 J_1) \cdot \ldots \cdot \mathsf{in}(H_n J_n)$$

for each chart entry e, where $w(R)$ is the rule weight in $\mathcal{G}_C$. We let $Z = \mathsf{in}(HJ)$ be the total inside weight of the start nonterminal of M_C, which combines the start nonterminal H of $\mathcal{G}_C$ and the start nonterminal J of I_w.

Then we refine the coarse-grained chart M_C into a fine-grained chart M_F. If $s(e) < \theta \cdot Z$ for some fixed threshold θ, we discard e. Otherwise, we add an entry $A_0 J_0 \rightarrow r(A_1 J_1, \ldots, A_n J_n)$ to M_F for each rule $A_0 \rightarrow r(A_1, \ldots, A_1)$ in the fine-grained IRTG $\mathcal{G}_F$ with $r \in R$.

If we have k coarse-to-fine levels ($k - 1 = $ coarsest, $0 = $ finest), we repeat this refinement step $k - 1$ times to obtain a chart for the original IRTG and then find the best derivation using Viterbi decoding.

4 Evaluation

Using this algorithm, we can do CTF parsing for all grammar formalisms that can be encoded as IRTGs. We evaluate it on PCFG, TAG, and graph parsing, using the efficient algorithms of Groschwitz et al. (2016) to compute the coarsest charts. These algorithms are lazy and try to avoid computing rules of the inverse homomorphism grammar which cannot participate in a derivation. This means that the number of rules in the inverse automaton differs depending on the grammar with which we are parsing. The evaluation grammars and fine-to-coarse mappings are available as supplementary material for this paper, and our coarse-to-fine parser is implemented as part of the Alto Toolkit.[1]

PCFG evaluation. First, we reproduce the known result that CTF parsing speeds up PCFG parsing. We read off a PCFG from the parse trees of the WSJ portion of the Penn Treebank (Sections 02–21), using the gold POS tags as terminal symbols; binarize it with the "inside" binarization strategy of Klein and Manning (2003); and convert it to an IRTG. This yields an IRTG grammar with 23817 rules and 8202 nonterminals, of which 8131 were created during binarization. We then parsed the sentences in Section 23 of up to 40 words, both without pruning and with the CTF parser (longer sentences were infeasible with the unpruned parser). For CTF we used the four-level fine-to-coarse mapping from Charniak et al. (2006) and a threshold of $\theta = 10^{-5}$. We also apply the fine-to-coarse mapping to the nonterminals introduced during binarization. If the nonterminal 'NP' is mapped to 'HP' for the level k, then a nonterminal 'NP$\rangle\rangle$NP' – which is created during binarization to represent a sequence of two 'NP' children, signified with the $\rangle\rangle$ notation – would correspond to a nonterminal 'HP$\rangle\rangle$HP' on the level

---

[1] Alto is available at `https://bitbucket.org/tclup/alto` and the grammars and fine-to-coarse mappings used are available at `https://bitbucket.org/tclup/alto/downloads/coarse_to_fine_experiments_grammars_and_mappings.zip`

Approach	f-score	time	invhom	sat
PCFG				
Unpruned	73.7	1230	2190	0.22
CTF	73.9	58	2260	–
TAG				
Unpruned	70.9	11258	159203	0.03
CTF:10^{-5}	51.8	11178	159203	–
CTF:10^{-9}	68.5	11198	159203	–

Table 1: Results for PCFG and TAG parsing, with mean runtime (in ms), invhom rules used in the chart, and saturation per sentence.

Approach	best %	time	invhom	sat
Unpruned	100.0	622	9042	0.04
Self	100.0	640	–	–
– Level 1	–	629	8963	0.04
– Level 0	–	7	12	0.03
Unsplit	95.8	751	–	–
– Level 1	–	739	9930	0.05
– Level 0	–	9	13	0.04
Unroot	96.0	3279	–	–
– Level 1	–	3245	35476	0.12
– Level 0	–	31	13	0.03
Both	88.8	3926	–	–
– Level 2	–	3887	34353	0.13
– Level 1	–	36	15	0.05
– Level 0	–	1	9	0.04

Table 2: Results for HRG parsing, with mean percent best found, runtime (in ms), invhom rules used in the chart, and saturation per graph.

k. The results are shown in Table 1 (top): For IRTG encodings of treebank PCFGs, we obtain a 20x speedup at no loss in f-score.

TAG evaluation. To assess the efficacy of CTF parsing on more expressive grammar formalism, we first evaluated it on the probabilistic TAG grammar induced from WSJ Section 00 by Chen and Vijay-Shanker (2004), binarized with the "inside" strategy and converted to an IRTG. To avoid data sparsity issues, we also evaluated the grammar on Section 00, thus f-scores should be read with care. We used a variant of the four-level fine-to-coarse mapping from Charniak et al. (2006), which always preserves the distinction between nonterminals at the root of initial trees and those at the root of auxiliary trees.[2] We tried the threshold values $\theta = 10^{-5}$ and $\theta = 10^{-9}$. The results are shown in Table 1 (bottom). Unexpectedly, while CTF pruning with these thresholds already reduces the f-score, the parsing time barely improves.

HRG evaluation. We also evaluated CTF on parsing Abstract Meaning Representation (AMR) graphs with hyperedge replacement grammars (HRGs, Chiang et al. (2013)). We use the HRG grammar of Groschwitz et al. (2015), which was induced from the "Little Prince" AMR corpus (Banarescu et al., 2013) and converted to an IRTG. This grammar describes how a graph can be constructed from atomic parts. It uses complex nonterminal symbols such as $N_0\{0,\underline{1},2\}$, indicating that the nonterminal should derive a subgraph with three sources 0, 1, and 2 (these describe nodes at which further edges can be added during the derivation), and the 1-source should be the AMR's "root" node. The symbol before the curly brack-

ets can be one of N_0 or N_1, to allow the grammar to make finer distinctions beyond the source information. In total, the grammar has 39 nonterminals and 13681 rules.

We tried a number of fine-to-coarse mappings in parsing Groschwitz et al.'s corpus. The "Unsplit" mapping removes the distinction between N_0 and N_1, so the above nonterminal coarsifies to $N\{0,\underline{1},2\}$. "Unroot" removes the marking of the root source, i.e. coarsifies to $N_0\{0,1,2\}$. "Both" applies the two in sequence, i.e. coarsifies to $N\{0,1,2\}$. As a sanity check, we also looked at a "Self" mapping, which "coarsifies" every nonterminal to itself. We used an aggressive pruning threshold of $\theta = 10^{-2}$.

The results are shown in Table 2. Because we do not have access to gold standard derivation trees in this dataset, we report the percentage of sentences on which a CTF parser produced the same Viterbi derivation tree as the unpruned parser ("best %"). We find that the Unsplit and Unroot mappings produce high-quality parses. However, in striking contrast to the PCFG case, all nontrivial mappings make the parser slower than the unpruned one – in the case of Unroot and Both, dramatically so.

5 Discussion

The fact that we find no speed improvements for TAG parsing and observe slowdowns for HRG parsing when we use CTF is a surprising negative result. To understand it, we first note that it is a result about CTF parsing in general and not

---

[2] For full details on the mappings used throughout the paper see the supplementary data.

about our implementation: We do obtain the expected performance gains on PCFGs, and the Self mapping yields comparable HRG performance to the unpruned parser. IRTGs allow us to use the same infrastructure for CTF parsing with TAGs and HRGs which we used for CTF parsing with PCFGs. There are systematic structural differences between the PCFG, PTAG, and HRG grammars which explain the differences in the usefulness of CTF.

One difference is the number of nonterminals from which a substructure can be derived. In treebank-induced PCFGs, most substrings of sufficient length can be derived from almost every phrasal nonterminal (Klein and Manning, 2001). This is reflected in a measure called *saturation*, which we formalize as the number of chart nonterminals (A_0, J_0) that occur in the edges of the chart, divided for comparability by the total number of nonterminals A in $\mathcal{G}_C$ and the number of invhom nonterminals J used in the chart. We only compute this measure for nonterminals A_0 that were present in the grammar before binarization. For the unpruned PCFG parser, we obtain a mean saturation of 0.22, confirming Klein and Manning's findings. By contrast, mean saturation is 0.04 for the unpruned HRG parser and 0.03 for the unpruned TAG parser. Thus, the TAG and HRG grammars are more restrictive than the PCFG. The TAG grammar only derives each substring from a few nonterminals as each lexical anchor determines the root of its elementary tree; in the HRG, the annotation for the nonterminals encodes what sources are available for a merge operation. This leaves little room for CTF to increase parsing speed.

A second difference between the HRG and PCFG grammars is that only a small fraction of all of a graph's subgraphs can be derived from *any* nonterminal with the HRG grammar in the first place. This would be comparable to a setting for PCFG parsing for which most spans are ungrammatical. This is quantified by the "invhom" column in Table 2, which shows the mean number of rules of the invhom grammar that are enumerated during parsing; for HRGs, each of these describes how to split a subgraph into parts. The "Unroot" and "Both" mappings delete source information, which substantially increases the number of subgraph combinations the parser explores. PCFGs tend not to rule out many subspans, which

is not a problem as the growth of subspans is only quadratic in the length of any sentence being parsed. For HRG parsing the number of possible subgraphs grows with a larger exponent, which depends on the grammar, and this means that parsing is only feasible as long as many small subgraphs can be identified as ungrammatical and many larger subgraphs are never considered. When ruling out substructures is a key element of efficient parsing, then pruning techniques other than CTF are needed for speed-ups, because the coarser grammars will generally be more permissive and therefore increase parsing times. This also makes it clear that the slowdown under CTF parsing is not a result of the particular implementation, as the number of substructures that need to be considered will be a bottleneck for any parser.

6   Conclusion

In this paper, we have defined an algorithm for coarse-to-fine parsing with IRTG grammars and, for the first time, applied CTF parsing to grammar formalisms that are more expressive than PCFGs. However, we have not observed the expected efficiency gains for such grammars, as fewer rules are equivalent and nonterminals are more informative, at least in the grammars used in our evaluation. Indeed, treebank PCFGs are especially well-suited to CTF parsing because they have many rules which only concatenate strings without introducing any terminal symbols and their nonterminals can derive almost arbitrary substrings. Neither is true for the TAG or HRG grammars we used.

Our results offer guidance on grammar requirements for successful use of CTF parsing and provide a general algorithm that will work when they are met. In the future, it would be interesting to extend CTF parsing to work in the absence of these requirements, e.g. by broadening the notion of rule equivalence, or by giving feedback from the fine level to the coarser levels in a priority search.

Acknowledgements   We thank the anonymous reviewers for their comments. We are grateful to Johannes Gontrum for some early implementation work and to Mark Johnson for discussions about the paper. This work was supported by the DFG grant KO 2916/2-1. Jonas Groschwitz was supported by a Macquarie University Research Excellence Scholarship.

References

Laura Banarescu, Claire Bonial, Shu Cai, Madalina Georgescu, Kira Griffitt, Ulf Hermjakob, Kevin Knight, Philipp Koehn, Martha Palmer, and Nathan Schneider. 2013. Abstract Meaning Representation for sembanking. In *Proceedings of the 7th Linguistic Annotation Workshop and Interoperability with Discourse*. http://www.aclweb.org/anthology/W13-2322.

Eugene Charniak, Mark Johnson, Micha Elsner, Joseph Austerweil, David Ellis, Isaac Haxton, Catherine Hill, R. Shrivaths, Jeremy Moore, Michael Pozar, and Theresa Vu. 2006. Multi-level coarse-to-fine PCFG parsing. In *Proceedings of the Human Language Technology Conference of the North American Chapter of the ACL*. http://www.aclweb.org/anthology/N06-1022.pdf.

John Chen and K. Vijay-Shanker. 2004. Automatic extraction of TAGs from the Penn Treebank. In *New developments in parsing technology*, Springer, pages 73–89.

David Chiang, Jacob Andreas, Daniel Bauer, Karl Moritz Hermann, Bevan Jones, and Kevin Knight. 2013. Parsing graphs with hyperedge replacement grammars. In *Proceedings of the 51st Annual Meeting of the Association for Computational Linguistics*. https://www.aclweb.org/anthology/P/P13/P13-1091.pdf.

Hubert Comon, Max Dauchet, Rémi Gilleron, Florent Jacquemard, Denis Lugiez, Sophie Tison, Marc Tommasi, and Christof Löding. 2007. *Tree Automata techniques and applications*. published online - http://tata.gforge.inria.fr/. http://tata.gforge.inria.fr/.

Jonas Groschwitz, Alexander Koller, and Mark Johnson. 2016. Efficient techniques for parsing with tree automata. In *Proceedings of the 54th Annual Meeting of the Association for Computational Linguistics*. http://aclweb.org/anthology/P16-1192.

Jonas Groschwitz, Alexander Koller, and Christoph Teichmann. 2015. Graph parsing with S-graph Grammars. In *Proceedings of the 53rd Annual Meeting of the Association for Computational Linguistics and the 7th International Joint Conference on Natural Language Processing*. http://www.aclweb.org/anthology/P15-1143.

Aravind K. Joshi and Yves Schabes. 1997. Tree-Adjoining Grammars. In G. Rozenberg and A. Salomaa, editors, *Handbook of Formal Languages*, Springer-Verlag, volume 3.

Dan Klein and Christopher D. Manning. 2001. Parsing with treebank grammars: Empirical bounds, theoretical models, and the structure of the Penn Treebank. In *Proceedings of 39th Annual Meeting of the Association for Computational Linguistics*. http://aclweb.org/anthology/P/P01/P01-1044.pdf.

Dan Klein and Christopher D. Manning. 2003. A* parsing: fast exact viterbi parse selection. In *Proceedings of the 2003 Conference of the North American Chapter of the Association for Computational Linguistics on Human Language Technology*. https://doi.org/10.3115/1073445.1073461.

Alexander Koller. 2015. Semantic construction with graph grammars. In *Proceedings of the 11th International Conference on Computational Semantics*. pages 228–238. http://anthology.aclweb.org/W/W15/W15-0127.pdf.

Alexander Koller and Marco Kuhlmann. 2011. A generalized view on parsing and translation. In *Proceedings of the 12th International Conference on Parsing Technologies*. http://www.aclweb.org/anthology/W11-2902.

Alexander Koller and Marco Kuhlmann. 2012. Decomposing TAG algorithms using simple algebraizations. In *Proceedings of the 11th International Workshop on Tree Adjoining Grammars and Related Formalisms (TAG+11)*. http://aclweb.org/anthology/W/W12/W12-4616.pdf.

Slav Petrov and Dan Klein. 2007. Improved inference for unlexicalized parsing. In *Human Language Technologies 2007: The Conference of the North American Chapter of the Association for Computational Linguistics*. http://www.aclweb.org/anthology/N/N07/N07-1051.

Andreas van Cranenburgh. 2012. Efficient parsing with linear context-free rewriting systems. In *Proceedings of the 13th Conference of the European Chapter of the Association for Computational Linguistics*. http://aclweb.org/anthology/E12-1047.

Yi Zhang and Hans-Ulrich Krieger. 2011. Large-scale corpus-driven pcfg approximation of an hpsg. In *Proceedings of the 12th International Conference on Parsing Technologies*. http://www.aclweb.org/anthology/W11-2923.

Evaluating LSTM models for grammatical function labelling

Bich-Ngoc Do[◇] and **Ines Rehbein**[♣]

Leibniz ScienceCampus

Universität Heidelberg[◇] / Institut für Deutsche Sprache Mannheim[♣]

`{do|rehbein}@cl.uni-heidelberg.de`

Abstract

To improve grammatical function labelling for German, we augment the labelling component of a neural dependency parser with a decision history. We present different ways to encode the history, using different LSTM architectures, and show that our models yield significant improvements, resulting in a LAS for German that is close to the best result from the SPMRL 2014 shared task (without the reranker).

1 Introduction

For languages with a non-configurational word order and rich(er) morphology, such as German, grammatical function (GF) labels are essential for interpreting the meaning of a sentence. *Case syncretism* in the German case paradigm makes GF labelling a challenging task. See (1) for an example where the nouns in the sentence are ambiguous between different cases, which makes it hard for a statistical parser to recover the correct reading.

(1) Telefonkarten   bleibt   nichts   erspart.
     phone cards$_{Nom/Acc/Dat}$ remains nothing$_{Nom/Acc}$ spared.
     "Phone cards are subjected to all kinds of abuse."

We approach the problem of GF labelling as a subtask of dependency parsing, where we first generate unlabelled trees and, in the second step, try to find the correct labels. This pipeline architechture gives us more flexibility, allowing us to use the labeller in combination with our parser, but also to apply it to the unlabelled output of other parsing systems without the need to change or retraining the parsers.

The approach also makes it straightforward to test different architectures for GF labelling. We are especially interested in the influence of different input structures representing different (surface versus structural) orders of the input. In particular, we compare models where we present the unlabelled tree in linear order with a model where we encode the parser output as a tree. We show that all models are able to learn GFs with a similar overall LAS, but the model where the tree is encoded in a breadth-first order outperforms all other models on labelling core argument GFs.

2 Related Work

Grammatical function labelling is commonly integrated into syntactic parsing. Few studies have adressed the issue as a separate classification task. While most of them assign grammatical functions on top of constituency trees (Blaheta and Charniak, 2000; Jijkoun and de Rijke, 2004; Chrupała and van Genabith, 2006; Klenner, 2007; Seeker et al., 2010), less work has tried to predict GF labels for unlabelled dependency trees. One of them is McDonald et al. (2006) who first generate the unlabelled trees using a graph-based parser, and then model the assignment of dependency labels as a sequence labelling task.

Another approach has been proposed by Zhang et al. (2017) who present a simple, yet efficient and accurate parsing model that generates unlabelled trees by identifying the most probable head for each token in the input. Then, in a post-processing step, they assign labels to each head-dependent pair, using a two-layer rectifier network.

Dependency Parsing as Head Selection Our labelling model is an extension of the parsing model of Zhang et al. (2017). We use our own implementation of the head-selection parser and focus on the grammatical function labelling part. The parser uses a bidirectional LSTM to extract a dense, positional representation a_i of the word w_i at position i in a sentence:

Proceedings of the 15th International Conference on Parsing Technologies, pages 128–133,
Pisa, Italy; September 20–22, 2017. ©2017 Association for Computational Linguistics

$$h_i^F = \text{LSTM}^F(x_i, h_{i-1}^F) \qquad (1)$$

$$h_i^B = \text{LSTM}^B(x_i, h_{i+1}^B) \qquad (2)$$

$$a_i = [h_i^F; h_i^B] \qquad (3)$$

x_i is the input at position i, which is the concatenation of the word embeddings and the tag embeddings of word w_i. An artificial root token w_0 is added at the beginning of each sentence.

The unlabelled tree is then built by selecting the most probable head for each word. The score of word w_j being the head of word w_i is computed by a single hidden layer neural network on their representations a_j and a_i.

An additional classifier with two rectified hidden layers is used to predict dependency labels, and is trained separately from the unlabeled parsing component, in a pipeline architecture. The classifier predictions are based on the representations of the head and the dependent, b_j and b_i, which are the concatenation of the input and the bidirectional LSTM-based representations:

$$b_i = [x_i; a_i] \qquad (4)$$

Despite its simplicity and the lack of global optimisation, Zhang et al. (2017) report competitive results for English, Czech, and German.

3 Labeling Dependencies with History

Although the labelling approach in Zhang et al. (2017) is simple and efficient, looking at head and dependent only when assigning the labels comes with some disadvantages. First, some labels are easier to predict when we also take context into account, e.g. the parent and grandparent nodes or the siblings of the head or dependent.

Consider, for example, the following sentence: *Is this the future of chamber music?* and its syntactic structure (figure 1). If we only consider the nodes *this* and *future*, there is a chance that the edge between them is labelled as *det* (determiner). However, if we also look at the local context, we know that node *the* to the left of *future* is more likely to be the determiner, and thus *this* should be assigned a different label.

Second, when looking at the parser output, we notice some errors that are well-known from other local parsing models, such as the assignment of duplicate subjects for the same predicate. To address this issue, we propose an extended labelling

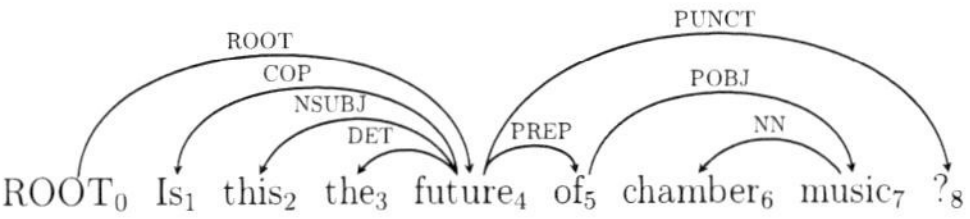

Figure 1: The dependency tree of the sentence *Is this the future of chamber music?*

model that incorporates a decision history. To that end, we design different LSTM architectures for the labelling task and compare their performance on German, Czech and English.

Label prediction as a sequence labelling task
Presenting the input to the labeller in sequential surface order does not seem very intuitive when we want to assign labels to a tree. This approach, however, was adapted by McDonald et al. (2006). In their work, they consider all dependents $x_{j1}, ..., x_{jM}$ of a head x_i and label those edges $(i, j1), ..., (i, jM)$ in a sequence.

We argue, however, that it is not enough to know the labels of the siblings, but that we also need to consider nodes at different levels in the tree. Therefore, when predicting the label for the current node, we consider all label decisions in the history, and feed them to a bidirectional LSTM. Given a sequence of nodes $S = (w_1, ..., w_N)$ and their corresponding head $(h_1, ..., h_N)$, at each recurrent step, we input the learned representation of the head and the dependent:

$$h_i^{F(\text{lbl})} = \text{LSTM}_{\text{lbl}}^F(b_i, b_{h_i}, h_{i-1}^{F(\text{lbl})}) \qquad (5)$$

$$h_i^{B(\text{lbl})} = \text{LSTM}_{\text{lbl}}^B(b_i, b_{h_i}, h_{i+1}^{B(\text{lbl})}) \qquad (6)$$

After that, the concatenated hidden states $[h_i^{F(lbl)}; h_i^{B(lbl)}]$ are projected to a softmax layer to predict the label.

When presenting a tree as a sequence, we experiment with two different input orders:

- **BiLSTM(L)**: Tree nodes are ordered according to their surface order in the sentence (linear order; figure 2).

- **BiLSTM(B)**: Tree nodes are ordered according to a breadth-first traversal (BFS) of the tree, starting from the root node. Here, siblings are closer to each other in the history.

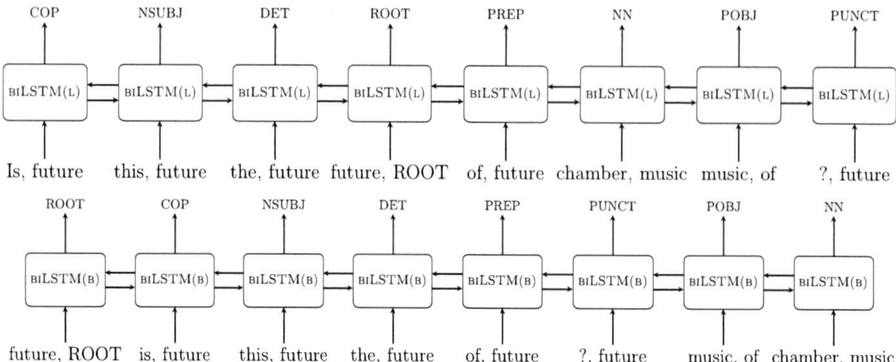

Figure 2: The processing order of the sentence in figure 1 a) in the BiLSTM(L) model (top) and b) in the BiLSTM(B) model (bottom).

Top-down tree LSTM Intuitively, it seems more natural to present the input as a tree structure when trying to predict the dependency labels. We do that by adopting the top-down tree LSTM model (Zhang et al., 2016) that processes nodes linked through dependency paths in a top-down manner. To make it comparable to the previous LSTM models, we only use *one LSTM* instead of four, and do not stack LSTMs. The hidden state is computed as follow:

$$h_i^{(lbl)} = \text{treeLSTM}(b_i, h_{i-1}) \qquad (7)$$

After that, we proceed as we did for the **BILSTM** models (see above). Note that the processing order i is also the BFS order. We call this model **TREELSTM** (figure 3).

4 Experiments

Our interest is focussed on German, but to put our work in context, we follow Zhang et al. (2017) and report results also for English, which has a configurational word order, and for Czech, which has a free word order, rich morphology, and less ambiguity in the case paradigm than German.

For English, we use the Penn Treebank (PTB) (Marcus et al., 1993) with standard training/dev/test splits. The POS tags are assigned using the Stanford POS tagger (Toutanova et al., 2003) with ten-way jackknifing, and constituency trees are converted to Stanford basic dependencies (De Marneffe et al., 2006). The German and Czech data come from the CoNLL-X shared task (Buchholz and Marsi, 2006) and our data split follows Zhang et al. (2017). As the CoNLL-X testsets are rather small ($\sim$ 360 sentences), we also

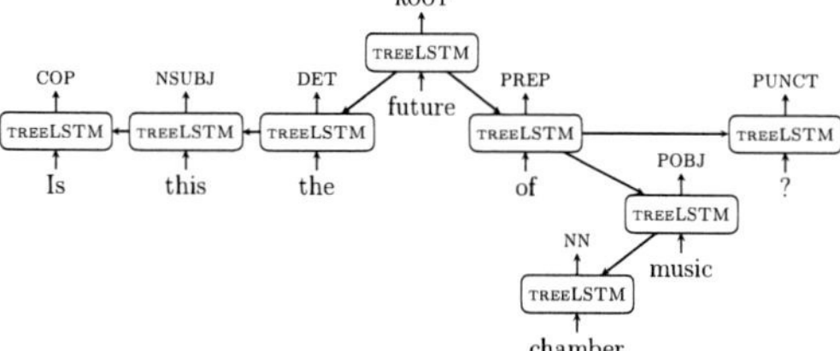

Figure 3: The processing order of the sentence in figure 1 in the TREELSTM model.

train and test on the much larger German SPMRL 2014 shared task data (Seddah et al., 2014) (5,000 test sentences). For the SPMRL data we use the predicted POS tags provided by the shared task organisers.

4.1 Setup

We test different labelling models on top of the unlabelled trees produced by our re-implementation of the *parsing as head selection* model (§2).

We first train the unlabelled parsing models for the three languages. Unless stated otherwise, all parameters are set according to Zhang et al. (2017), and tag embedding size was set to 40 for all languages. Please note that we do *not* use pre-trained embeddings in our experiments.

In the next step, we train four different labelling models: the labeller of Zhang et al. (2017) that uses a rectifier neural network with two hidden layers (**baseline**), two bidirectional LSTM models (**BILSTM(L)** and **BILSTM(B)**), and one tree LSTM model (**TREELSTM**) (§3).

The hidden layer dimension in all LSTM models was set to 200. The models were trained for 10 epochs, and were optimized using Adam

Model	en	cs	de_{CoNLL}	de_{SPMRL}
UAS	93.35	89.70	93.09	91.29
Baseline	91.58	83.42	90.22	88.15
BiLSTM(L)	**91.92***	**84.08***	90.87*	88.73*
BiLSTM(B)	91.91*	83.80	**90.97***	**88.74***
TREELSTM	**91.92***	83.82	90.89*	**88.74***
DENSE	91.90	81.72	89.60	-

Table 1: Results for different labellers applied to the unlabelled parser output. The first row reports UAS for the input to the labellers. The last row (DENSE) shows the results from Zhang et al. (2017). (*) indicates that the difference between the model and the baseline is statistically significant ($p < .001$).

(Kingma and Ba, 2015) with default parameters (initial learning rate 0.001, first momentum coefficient 0.9, second momentum coefficient 0.999). We used L2 regularization with a coefficient of 10^{-3} and max-norm regularization with an upper bound of 5.0. The dropout (Srivastava et al., 2014) rate was set to 0.05 for the input connections, and 0.5 for the rest.

4.2 Results

Table 1 shows the unlabelled attachment score (UAS) for the unlabelled trees and the labelled attachment scores (LAS) for the different labellers (excluding punctuation). All history-based labelling models perform significantly better than the local baseline model,[1] but for English the improvements are smaller (0.3%) than for the non-configurational languages ($\sim$0.7%).

While we tried to reimplement the model of Zhang et al. (2017) following the details in the paper, our reimplemented model yields higher scores for German, compared to the results in the paper. The scores for English are slightly lower since, in contrast to Zhang et al. (2017), we do not use pre-trained embeddings. When using our history-based labellers, we get similar results for English (91.9%) and higher results for both Czech (84.1% vs. 81.7%) and German (91.0% vs. 89.6%) on the same data *without* using pre-trained embeddings or post-processing.

On the SPMRL 2014 shared task data, our results are only 0.3% lower than the ones of the winning system (Björkelund et al., 2014) *without* reranker (*blended*).[2] To further illustrate the ef-

de_{SPMRL}	SB	OA	DA	PD
	# 6,638	# 3,184	# 568	# 1,045
baseline	90.3	83.6	64.7	77.1
BiLSTM(L)	91.4	85.3	67.7	80.0
BiLSTM(B)	**91.9**	**85.4**	**69.3**	**80.5**
treeLSTM	91.2	85.1	68.6	79.8
de_{SPMRL}	AG	PG	OC	OG
	# 2,241	# 388	# 3,652	# 21
baseline	91.3	80.0	90.1	0
BiLSTM(L)	91.3	81.6	90.5	16.0
BiLSTM(B)	**91.5**	**82.4**	**90.7**	**37.0**
treeLSTM	91.4	81.4	90.2	27.6

Table 2: LAS for core argument functions (German SPMRL data), and frequency (#) of GF in the testset (SB: subj, OA: acc.obj, DA: dat.obj, PD: pred, AG: gen.attribute, PG: phrasal genitive, OC: clausal obj, OG: gen.obj).

fectiveness of our models, we also ran our labeller on the *unlabelled output* of the SPMRL 2014 winning system and on *unlabelled gold* trees. On the output of the *blended* system LAS slightly improves from 88.62% to 88.76% (TREELSTM).[3] When applied to *unlabelled gold* trees, the distance between our models and the baseline becomes larger and the best of our history-based models (BiLSTM(B), 97.38%) outperforms the original labeller of Zhang et al. (2017) (96.15%) by more than 1%.

We would like to emphasize that our history-based LSTM labeller is practically simple and computationally inexpensive (as compared to global training or inference), so our model manages to preserve simplicity while significantly improving labelling performance.

4.3 Discussion

Most strikingly, all three models seem to perform roughly the same, and the TREELSTM model fails to outperform the other two models. However, in comparison to the BiLSTM models, the TREELSTM model has a smaller number of parameters, and the history only flows in one direction. The tree model also has a shorter history chain since nodes are linked by paths from the root (figure 3), which might explain why it does not yield better results than the linear LSTM models.

The overall results suggest that the order in which the nodes are presented in the history does not have any impact on the labelling results. However, when looking at results for individual core argument functions (subject, direct object, etc.), a

---

[1] For significance testing, we use Bikel's Randomized Parsing Evaluation Comparator (`http://www.cis.upenn.edu/~dbikel/software.html`).

[2] The shared task winner is a complex ensemble system that generates a tree by *blending* the output of three parsers (Mate, Turbo, BestFirst; see (Björkelund et al., 2014)).

[3] Following Björkelund et al. (2014), here we include punctuation in the evaluation.

	GF	**en**	**cs**	**de**$_{SPMRL}$
dep-length	sb	3.1	3.4	3.9
	dobj	2.5	*2.4	4.2
	iobj	1.7	-	4.7
left-head ratio	sb	4.6	32.5	34.2
	dobj	97.4	*77.5	37.2
	iobj	100.0	-	27.5

Table 3: Avg. dependency length and ratio of left arcs vs. all (left + right) arc dependencies for args. (* in the Czech data, *Obj* subsumes all types of objects, not only direct objects)

more pronounced pattern emerges (table 2).[4] Here we see the benefit of encoding the siblings close to each other in the history: For all core argument functions, the BILSTM(B) model outperforms the other models.

To find out why the history-based models work better for Czech and German than for English, we compared the average dependency length as well as the variability in head direction (how often e.g. the head of a subject is positioned to the left, in relation to the total number of subjects). Table 3 suggests that the success of the history-based models is not due to a better handling of long dependencies but that they are better in dealing with the uncertainty in head direction (also see Gulordava and Merlo (2016)).

5   Conclusions

We have shown that GF labelling, which is of crucial importance for languages like German, can be improved by combining LSTM models with a decision history. All our models outperform the original labeller of Zhang et al. (2017) and give results in the same range as the best system from the SPMRL-2014 shared task (without the reranker), but with a much simpler model. Our results show that the history is especially important for languages that show more word order variation. Here, presenting the input in a structured BFS order not only significantly outperforms the baseline, but also yields improvements over the other LSTM models on core grammatical functions.

Acknowledgments

We would like to thank Minh Le for his help with data pre-processing. This research has been conducted within the Leibniz Science Campus "Em-

---

pirical Linguistics and Computational Modeling", funded by the Leibniz Association under grant no. SAS-2015-IDS-LWC and by the Ministry of Science, Research, and Art (MWK) of the state of Baden-Württemberg.

References

Anders Björkelund, Özlem Çetinoğlu, Agnieszka Faleńska, Richárd Farkas, Thomas Müller, Wolfgang Seeker, and Zsolt Szántó. 2014. Introducing the IMS-Wroclaw-Szeged-CIS entry at the SPMRL 2014 Shared Task: Reranking and Morphosyntax meet Unlabeled Data. In *Proceedings of the First Joint Workshop on Statistical Parsing of Morphologically Rich Languages and Syntactic Analysis of Non-Canonical Languages*. Dublin City University, Dublin, Ireland, pages 97–102. http://www.aclweb.org/anthology/W14-6110.

Don Blaheta and Eugene Charniak. 2000. Assigning function tags to parsed text. In *Proceedings of the 1st North American Chapter of the Association for Computational Linguistics Conference*. NAACL '00, pages 234–240.

Sabine Buchholz and Erwin Marsi. 2006. CoNLL-X shared task on multilingual dependency parsing. In *Proceedings of the Tenth Conference on Computational Natural Language Learning*. Association for Computational Linguistics, Stroudsburg, PA, USA, CoNLL-X '06, pages 149–164.

Grzegorz Chrupała and Josef van Genabith. 2006. Using machine-learning to assign function labels to parser output for Spanish. In *Proceedings of the COLING/ACL on Main Conference Poster Sessions*. COLING-ACL '06, pages 136–143.

Marie-Catherine De Marneffe, Bill MacCartney, and Christopher D. Manning. 2006. Generating typed dependency parses from phrase structure parses. In *The fifth international conference on Language Resources and Evaluation*. LREC'06, pages 449–454.

Kristina Gulordava and Paola Merlo. 2016. Multilingual dependency parsing evaluation: a large-scale analysis of word order properties using artificial data. *TACL* 4:343–356.

Valentin Jijkoun and Maarten de Rijke. 2004. Enriching the output of a parser using memory-based learning. In *Proceedings of the 42nd Annual Meeting of the Association for Computational Linguistics*. pages 311–318.

Diederik Kingma and Jimmy Ba. 2015. Adam: A method for stochastic optimization. In *The International Conference on Learning Representations*. San Diego.

Manfred Klenner. 2007. Shallow dependency labeling. In *Proceedings of the 45th Annual Meeting of the

---

[4]We evaluate GFs on the German SPMRL data which are sufficiently large with 5,000 test sentences. The CoNLL datasets, in comparison, only include ~360 test sentences.

ACL on Interactive Poster and Demonstration Sessions. ACL '07, pages 201–204.

Mitchell P. Marcus, Mary Ann Marcinkiewicz, and Beatrice Santorini. 1993. Building a large annotated corpus of English: the Penn treebank. *Computational Linguistics* 19(2):313–330.

Ryan McDonald, Kevin Lerman, and Fernando Pereira. 2006. Multilingual dependency analysis with a two-stage discriminative parser. In *Proceedings of the 10th Conference on Computational Natural Language Learning*. CoNLL-X '06, pages 206–210.

Djamé Seddah, Sandra Kübler, and Reut Tsarfaty. 2014. Introducing the SPMRL 2014 shared task on parsing morphologically-rich languages. In *Proceedings of the First Joint Workshop on Statistical Parsing of Morphologically Rich Languages and Syntactic Analysis of Non-Canonical Languages*. Dublin City University, Dublin, Ireland, pages 103–109. http://www.aclweb.org/anthology/W14-6111.

Wolfgang Seeker, Ines Rehbein, Jonas Kuhn, and Josef van Genabith. 2010. Hard constraints for grammatical function labelling. In *Proceedings of the 48th Annual Meeting of the Association for Computational Linguistics*. ACL '10, pages 1087–1097.

Nitish Srivastava, Geoffrey Hinton, Alex Krizhevsky, Ilya Sutskever, and Ruslan Salakhutdinov. 2014. Dropout: A simple way to prevent neural networks from overfitting. *Journal of Machine Learning Research* 15:1929–1958. http://jmlr.org/papers/v15/srivastava14a.html.

Kristina Toutanova, Dan Klein, Christopher D. Manning, and Yoram Singer. 2003. Feature-rich part-of-speech tagging with a cyclic dependency network. In *Proceedings of the 2003 Conference of the North American Chapter of the Association for Computational Linguistics on Human Language Technology*. NAACL '03, pages 173–180.

Xingxing Zhang, Jianpeng Cheng, and Mirella Lapata. 2017. Dependency parsing as head selection. In *Proceedings of the 15th Conference of the European Chapter of the Association for Computational Linguistics*. EACL'17, pages 665–676.

Xingxing Zhang, Liang Lu, and Mirella Lapata. 2016. Top-down tree long short-term memory networks. In *Proceedings of the 2016 Conference of the North American Chapter of the Association for Computational Linguistics: Human Language Technologies*. Association for Computational Linguistics, San Diego, California, pages 310–320. http://www.aclweb.org/anthology/N16-1035.

Author Index

Ballesteros, Miguel, 115
Bechet, Frederic, 72
Bhat, Irshad, 61
Bhat, Riyaz A., 61
Bohnet, Bernd, 11

Carreras, Xavier, 32, 115
Çetinoğlu, Özlem, 18

de Lhoneux, Miryam, 99
Delecraz, Sebastien, 72
Do, Bich-Ngoc, 128
Don, J. Buddhika K. Pathirage, 50

Falenska, Agnieszka, 18
Favre, Benoit, 72

Groschwitz, Jonas, 122

Hayashi, Katsuhiko, 56
Hayashibe, Yuta, 1

Kawahara, Daisuke, 1
Kohita, Ryosuke, 88
Koller, Alexander, 122
Kuhlmann, Marco, 78
Kurohashi, Sadao, 1
Kurtz, Robin, 78

Lee, John, 44, 50
Leung, Herman, 44
Li, Keying, 44
Liu, Jiangming, 105

Madhyastha, Pranava Swaroop, 32
Martínez Alonso, Héctor, 25
Matsumoto, Yuji, 88
Morita, Hajime, 1

Nagata, Masaaki, 56
Nasr, Alexis, 72
Nivre, Joakim, 99
Noji, Hiroshi, 88

Quattoni, Ariadna, 32

Rehbein, Ines, 128

Sagot, Benoît, 25
Søgaard, Anders, 67
Sharma, Dipti, 61
Stymne, Sara, 99

Tanaka, Takaaki, 56
Teichmann, Christoph, 122

Yu, Juntao, 11

Zhang, Yue, 105